Praise for *Exploring Capitalist Fiction*

"Although his prior books establish Dr. Younkins as a scholarly and prolific philosopher of liberty, *Exploring Capitalist Fiction* focuses not on the philosophy of business but on the complex lives of fictional men who implement it. Its twenty-five plot summaries illustrate, unsurprisingly, that businessmen are neither more nor less moral or confused than the rest of us, from the crony-capitalist railroaders in Norris's *The Octopus*, Cahan's wealthy but unhappy David Levinsky, and Lewis's terrified conformist Babbitt to more heroic, less conflicted figures like Hawley's Cash McCall, Kesey's Stamper family, and King Vidor's Steve Dangos. Dr. Younkins occasionally offers a valuable philosophical or economic insight, but the book is principally a welcome, fascinating, even-handed study of business and capitalism in literature." —**John Egger**, professor emeritus of Economics, Towson University

"*Exploring Capitalist Fiction* is one of those books I have needed for a long time, but just didn't know it. In this volume, Younkins assembles a remarkable collection of insights about how business is portrayed in literature and film. Perhaps the most remarkable feature of the book is Younkins's ability to balance historical viewpoints with contemporary and whimsical perspectives with serious ones, across both film and print. And he does so while striking a balance between supportive and critical outlooks on business and capitalism that I would not have thought possible. This is an excellent book." —**Marshall Schminke**, BB&T professor of Business Ethics, University of Central Florida

"Perhaps no subject has been so much discussed in literature and film, yet so underanalyzed and examined as business. This volume is a virtual pioneer in remedying this situation. Drawing from novels, plays, and films, and ranging over a variety of attitudes towards business, Younkins selects works of depth and importance for anyone interested in exploring the treatment of business in fiction and thereby coming to appreciate its cultural and moral significance. Especially refreshing is Younkins's selection process which avoids the temptation to concentrate on contemporary works. Instead we see selections from a number of different eras with attention paid to lesser known works as well as some obvious favorites. I have little doubt that this book will become a standard reference work for those interested in the treatment of business through creative fiction." —**Douglas Den Uyl**, vice president of educational programs, Liberty Fund

"Why do critics of laissez faire capitalism have all the good folk songs? All the good novels (well, most of them)? Ditto for poems, plays, stories. Why is virtually all of literature, music, and art almost a wholly owned subsidiary of those who oppose economic freedom? Probably, because they work harder at it than we do. It is all the more important, then that those of us who treasure the free marketplace and private property rights get into this 'industry' as well. Now along comes a very important contribution in this regard: Ed Younkins's new book: *Exploring Capitalist Fiction: Business Through Literature and Film*. He unerringly explores, contemplates, and analyzes twenty-five important books and movies that deal with business. I cannot possibly overestimate the importance of this initiative in promoting liberty and the free society. I have been a fan of Ed's for many years now. I greatly admire his previous works, and this one fully lives up to his previous contributions. I am delighted to recommend this book, highly, to all those with an interest in both literature and freedom. A note to English majors: read this book! It will give you a perspective on literature you are unlikely, in the extreme, to have ever seen before. It will be a real thrill to see these books and movies not from the eyes of your typical leftish literature professor, but from the vantage point of someone who celebrates liberty." —**Walter Block**, Harold E. Wirth Scholar Endowed Chair and professor of Economics, Loyola University, New Orleans

"Most people today spend at least a third of their weekday lives in the business world. Some view that world as a second family. Younkins's superb summaries and analyses of twenty-five works of capitalist fiction create the feel of what it's like to work in the modern institution known as business. In all of these fictional cases there are many complex personal, ethical, and psychological interactions: government vs. business, employer vs. employee, supplier vs. client, and, of course, fellow entrepreneur/employee vs. fellow entrepreneur/employee. Ethical issues are the star. Indeed, the book could easily be used as a text in business ethics courses." —**Jerry Kirkpatrick**, professor emeritus of International Business and Marketing, California State Polytechnic University

"The struggle for liberty must consist of more than an intellectual appeal. As Ayn Rand demonstrated in her novels, the establishment of a free society will succeed only if people have an emotional investment in such an outcome. It is art that creates and supports the level of personal involvement required to motivate and sustain people in the face of unrelenting and unforgiving opposition. In his book *Exploring Capitalist Fiction: Business Through Literature and Film*, Edward Younkins recognizes the power of art as a force both for and against the ideals necessary for a world in which we can exist fully as human beings. Tapping into a wide range of source material, Younkins explores the role of fiction in sustaining or retarding the course the Founders set for our nation. Providing clear yet succinct summaries of a variety of works—including *The Great Gatsby*, *Death of a Salesman*, *Atlas Shrugged*, and the film *Wall Street*—Younkins succeeds in explaining and analyzing these twenty-five diverse works in the context of his book's themes. Readers of *Exploring Capitalist Fiction* will enjoy these bite-sized introductions to unfamiliar works as well as explorations of fiction they have already enjoyed. With luck, Younkins's efforts here will spark more interest in expanding the arguments for freedom beyond dry academic journals to include art that moves us, involves us, and provides us emotional fuel in the face of the greatest task of our lives." —**Russell Madden**, author of *Death is Easy*

"Ed Younkins's newest book will be indispensable to anyone either teaching or studying the portrayal of business in American fiction, plays, and films over the past century and a quarter. His admirably evenhanded summaries of twenty-five important works in this tradition, and his exhaustive lists of other titles not discussed at length, will be useful also to the general reader who simply wants to discover more about how commercial enterprise has been depicted in novels, plays, and movies over the past hundred years or so." —**Jeff Riggenbach**, author of *In Praise of Decadence and Why American History Is Not What They Say: An Introduction to Revisionism*

"This work includes essays on an amazingly wide range of American novels, plays, and films from the past two centuries, all containing business and economic themes and content. Younkins's insightful reading of many of the major texts that explore issues of business and capitalism is a welcome addition to interdisciplinary studies. It can easily serve as a guideline for a course in either a college of business or a college of liberal arts." —**Mimi R. Gladstein**, professor of English and Theatre Arts, University of Texas at El Paso

"Once more Ed Younkins has come up with an insightful discussion of an important topic. Professor Younkins writes in a way that is intelligible to the general audience while retaining the rigor of thought expected of an academic. *Exploring Capitalist Fiction* is fun to read and will change the way you look at a film, read a book, or watch a play." —**Gary Wolfram**, William Simon professor of Economics and Public Policy, Hillsdale College

Exploring Capitalist Fiction

Business through Literature and Film

Edward W. Younkins

LEXINGTON BOOKS
Lanham • Boulder • New York • Toronto • Plymouth, UK

PS
374
.B87
Y68
2014

Published by Lexington Books
An imprint of The Rowman & Littlefield Publishing Group, Inc.
4501 Forbes Boulevard, Suite 200, Lanham, Maryland 20706
www.rowman.com

16 Carlisle Street, London W1D 3BT, United Kingdom

Copyright © 2014 by Lexington Books
First paperback edition 2014

All rights reserved. No part of this book may be reproduced in any form or by any
electronic or mechanical means, including information storage and retrieval systems,
without written permission from the publisher, except by a reviewer who may quote
passages in a review.

British Library Cataloguing in Publication Information Available

Library of Congress Cataloging-in-Publication Data
The hardback edition of this book was previously cataloged by the Library of Congress as follows:

Younkins, Edward W. (Edward Wayne), 1948-
Exploring capitalist fiction : business through literature and film / Edward W. Younkins.
pages cm
Includes bibliographical references and index.
1. American fiction--20th century--History and criticism. 2. Business in literature. 3. Capitalism in
literature. 4. Business in motion pictures. I. Title.
PS374.B87Y68 2014
813'.5093553--dc23
2013027020

ISBN: 978-0-7391-8426-4 (cloth : alk. paper)
ISBN: 978-1-4985-0072-2 (pbk. : alk. paper)
ISBN: 978-0-7391-8428-8 (electronic)

∞™ The paper used in this publication meets the minimum requirements of American
National Standard for Information Sciences Permanence of Paper for Printed Library
Materials, ANSI/NISO Z39.48-1992.

Printed in the United States of America

37.40

3-15

This book is dedicated to my parents, Russell and Anna Younkins, whose example has encouraged me to read and to appreciate both fiction and the world of business.

Contents

Preface

The origins of this book go back to the spring of 1992 when I began teaching a course called Business through Literature in Wheeling Jesuit University's MBA program. *Exploring Capitalist Fiction: Business through Literature and Film* is heavily based on my lectures and notes on the novels, plays, and films used in the popular course over the years and on what I have learned from my students in class discussions and in their papers.

The underpinning premise of this book and of my course is that fiction, including novels, plays, and films, can be a powerful force to educate students and employees in ways that lectures, textbooks, articles, case studies, and other traditional teaching approaches cannot. Works of fiction can address a range of issues and topics, provide detailed real-life descriptions of the organizational contexts in which workers find themselves, and tell interesting, engaging, and memorable stories that are richer and more likely to stay with the reader or viewer longer than lectures and other teaching approaches. Imaginative literature can enrich business teaching materials and provide an excellent supplement to the theories, concepts, and issues that students experience in their business courses. Reading novels and plays and watching films are excellent ways to develop critical thinking, to learn about character, and to instill moral values. It is likely that people who read business novels and plays and watch movies about business will continue to search for more of them as sources of entertainment, inspiration, and education.

The idea to write this book originated a few years ago when one of Wheeling Jesuit University's MBA graduates, who had taken and enjoyed the Business through Literature course, proposed that I write a book based on the novels, plays, and films covered in that course. I agreed as I concluded that the subject matter was important and bookworthy and that the book would be fun for me to write and for others to read. I went on to select twenty-five works to include in the book out of the more than eighty different ones that had been used in my course over the years. I have endeavored to select the ones that have been the most influential, are the most relevant, and are the most interesting. In a few instances, I have chosen works that I believe to be undervalued treasures.

After an introduction, the book consists of twenty-five chapters, each one discussing and analyzing a particular business novel, play, or film. The works are presented chronologically based on the year of their debut. These chapters are followed by a conclusion that examines the nature and uses of the fictions of business and that supply a historical retrospective of many of the works within this classification. Three appendices follow:

1. a list of business novels and plays
2. a list of business films
3. an essay disclosing the findings of a survey conducted by my Koch Research Fellows, Jomana Krupinski and Kaitlyn Pytlak, and myself.

This article summarizes the findings of a survey that asked business professors and literature professors to rank what they believe to be the best business novels and plays.

Work on this book was assisted by the Charles Koch Foundation and the BB&T Charitable Foundation. The Koch Foundation funded my research assistants who helped with proofreading the book and with the book's appendices. I am grateful to them for their fine and diligent work. The BB&T Foundation provided a gift in 2006 that resulted in the founding of Wheeling Jesuit University's Institute for the Study of Capitalism and Morality which is dedicated to an examination of all aspects of capitalism and to an in-depth examination of a free society. As is the case with my other books, I am indebted most of all to Carla Cash, Administrative Assistant in WJU's Institute for the Study of Capitalism and Morality, for her most capable and conscientious work in bringing this book to print.

—Edward W. Younkins, Wheeling Jesuit University

Introduction

The Fictions of Capitalism

Imaginative literature contributes to the freedom and individual development of both authors and readers. Fiction unleashes the imaginative and creative powers of the author and stimulates the inventive, evaluative, and decision-making capabilities of readers. Fiction presents possibilities that go beyond current reality and invites the examination of options to any particular state of affairs. Novels, plays, and films can be useful in relating ideas found in the fictional world to the real world and to what is found in articles, textbooks, and so on. Over time, imaginative literature has been an energizing force in social and cultural development and to the advancement and shaping of civilization. The power of fiction transcends history and location as works from various times and places can be sources of pleasure and education at future times and in a variety of locations.

Many works of fiction have moral purposes. Novels, plays, and films can help people to develop greater awareness of the complexity of moral and ethical situations. They present a wide range of characters with diverse beliefs, desires, and behaviors. They enable the reader or viewer to see what various characters are dealing with. People who read or view normative fiction are likely to be better prepared to recognize and attend to moral dilemmas in their own lives. Literary authors and filmmakers frequently present life-altering events that involve fundamental normative questions and decisions. One benefit of such works is to activate the process of self-examination. They act as catalysts prompting a person to step back to gain a better perspective on the important things in life such as being moral and virtuous. When moral dilemmas are posed the moral imagination is activated. Imagination can be considered to be a way to illuminate facts.

Many fictional works address the business world. This is appropriate because the real everyday business world is filled with great stories involving heroism, genius, comedy, stupidity, backstabbing, romance, tragedy, farce, moral and immoral behavior, interpersonal problems, and so on. All of these can be ingredients of successful imaginative literature. It follows that studying business fiction can provide understanding to business people and students regarding real life situations. Fiction can also stimulate people's imagination, judgment, and entrepreneurial vision. Each person's life has a narrative structure and fiction can help in creating one's own story.

Business and all of the varied activities and relationships that take place in that realm may be viewed as a story that embodies values and meaning. Business stories, especially those that deal with ethical dilemmas, have the power to stick with readers (or viewers) and to inspire them to delve deeper into issues. Fiction immerses people in the contextualized experiences of others and stimulates their personal reflection. The context of specific situations must be established in order for the reader or viewer to gain knowledge and wisdom. Imaginative literature can help people make sense of the business world.

Fiction tends to focus on the interaction of characters thus enabling the reader or viewer to become involved in the situation at hand. This prompts people to empathize with a wide range of character and personality types. In addition, a person can identify what character types and personalities respond favorably and unfavorably to different management styles. People can readily relate to the experiences of characters in particular situations who experience conflict, challenges, opportunities, threats, and so on. By studying what various characters do, people can investigate their own values and discern how they would act in the situations portrayed in fictional works. Fiction has the potential to bring about personal change. For example, imaginative literature can help to teach people how to maintain their individuality and personal integrity while conforming to a corporation's culture.

The use of works of imaginative literature to portray and explain the behavior of individuals in business is arguably a method that is richer and more realistic than what is presented in journal articles, textbooks, and even cases. Literature and films allow the asking of more complex questions than case studies do. Business cases can be complex, but not to the same extent as multifaceted novels, plays, and films. People can learn as much, if not more, about the nature and culture of business and effective management as from lectures, books, case studies, and so on.

Fiction provides a powerful teaching tool to sensitize business students without business experience and to educate and train managers in real businesses. Studying business literature and films can prepare students for future situations that they have not encountered before when they enter the workplace. Many works of imaginative fiction present ethical dilemmas that young professionals may potentially encounter at some point in their careers. Literary works and movies can play a significant role both in college classrooms and in management development programs. Not only is business fiction interactive, it portrays a more complete and more human picture of the business world than what is communicated through traditional teaching materials. Fiction brings values to life and is also useful in bridging the gap between theory and practice.

Novels, plays, and films all have their own features that make them attractive for use in college courses and in management and professional development training programs. Novels are interactive, foster reader involvement, and are able to provide depth and breadth of detailed information. Plays are shorter, are able to cover a similar number of issues as do novels and films, and portray dynamic scenarios focused on the interaction of characters. Commercial movies capture the spirit of their times, provide visual platforms, take less time and less effort to watch compared to what is required to read a novel or play, and are engaging and interesting because of high production standards, huge budgets, and good acting. It is likely that people with distinct personalities and learning styles are differentially attracted to theses teaching tools. Much can be learned by observing, analyzing, and understanding business, business people, business culture, and business situations as depicted in novels, plays, and films. Narratives can be a fundamental mode of understanding the business world and the actions people take in that world.

I began teaching a course called Business through Literature in Wheeling Jesuit University's MBA program during the 1991–1992 academic year. Over the years more than eighty different novels, plays, and films have been used in this popular course. I have been extremely impressed with the quality and willingness to work of the graduate business students who have taken this course. They have enthusiastically responded to the novels, plays, and films covered in this class. The business and ethical insights made in their papers and discussions have been outstanding. I am hopeful that people who have taken this course will continue to seek out business novels, plays, and films for inspiration, entertainment, and education. A few years ago one of our MBA graduates, who had taken the Business through Literature course, suggested that I write a book based on analyses of the works treated therein. I agreed that the topic was one worthy of being addressed in book form.

Selectivity must be employed when choosing from such a great number and variety of works. An investigation such as the one undertaken in *Exploring Capitalist Fiction: Business through Literature and Film* is necessarily judicious and interpretive by virtue of what is included, what is omitted, and by the method of presentation of what is included therein. I have attempted to include those that have had substantial influence, are the most relevant, and are the most interesting. In several cases, I have selected works that I believe to be underappreciated gems. The summary analyses of twenty-five novels, plays, and films are presented chronologically based on the year of their first appearance. I encourage people to read the novels and plays in full, to watch the films, and to explore on their own the imaginative literature of the business world.

The overall literary and cinematic treatment accorded capitalism, business, and businessmen has been unkind, hostile, and unflattering over the years. The commercial world has received bad press at the hands of many novelists, playwrights, and filmmakers. Fortunately, there are also a number of sympathetic business portraits that depict commerce in a more favorable, even heroic, image. Viable capitalist heroes have appeared in a number of works that emphasize the virtues, positive traits, and accomplishments of businessmen. Some feature brilliant, thoughtful, and dauntless business leaders and employees. The works selected for inclusion in this volume include those that support my own pro-capitalist and pro-business free-market perspective, those that are in strong opposition to that view, and those that partially support it. In large part, this book is the outgrowth of my teaching notes for my Business through Literature course and of what I have learned from my students.

What follows now is a preview of each of the twenty-five works discussed in depth and in detail in the chapters of this book. The chapters represent self-contained treatments of the novel, play, or film at hand. The chapters do not have to be read in progressive order to be of use and/or of interest to the reader. Reading the brief summaries may point a given reader to a chapter on a particular work. In turn, after reading that chapter, the reader may decide to read the work in full.

The first work discussed in the book is William Dean Howells's realistic 1885 novel, *The Rise of Silas Lapham*, which is concerned with the complexities of moral actions in a conditional, socially interdependent world. In the world of nineteenth-century Boston, a newly rich industrialist, Silas Lapham, and his family try to enter the city's society of old money. Silas is a mineral paint tycoon who rose from the backwoods of Vermont to marry, to serve in the Civil War, and to run a successful mineral paint business. He is a simple, uncultured, and practical man with a sense of morality. Despite this, his wife blames him for what she perceives as his mistreatment of a former partner in his business. Viewing the old partner as a victim, she encourages Silas to make amends. This, along with some other events, causes Lapham to spin headlong toward financial ruin. At the end of the story, Lapham finds peace and continues to manufacture a small line of paints.

In *Looking Backward* (1888) Edward Bellamy describes a new egalitarian social order that he argues is possible to have in the future. The protagonist, Julian West, is a young aristocratic Bostonian who falls into a deep sleep while under a hypnotic trance in 1887 to deal with his insomnia. In a trance for 113 years, he wakes up in the year 2000 and finds a progressive utopian society in which equality has been attained. America has evolved into a cooperative society and private capital has been eliminated—the government owns all of the capital. Industry has been nationalized and there is no need for money because credit cards are issued to citizens who all receive the same exact amount of credit. This is in stark contrast to 1887 Boston where wealth is unevenly distributed. In the year 2000 people are motivated differently and they work for pride. There have been dramatic changes in the human condition as public caring and public service are abundant in the future that West encounters. War, poverty, and hunger have been eliminated. People retire at age forty-five according to a representative of the future. The novel is replete with discussions between West and this representative of the future regarding the new world and how it compares and contrasts with the old one. Life under one great trust does not allow for differentiation and there is the problem of incentives to be productive. Nationalism does not seem to be a sufficient motivator. The novel does not explain who actually produces the goods in this command economy that emphasizes the distinction between production and distribution. This socialist novel led to a social reform movement toward the end of the nineteenth century.

Frank Norris's sweeping, epic novel, *The Octopus* (1901), is based on an actual occurrence and specific struggle in California between wheat farmers and the powerful railroad toward the end of the nineteenth century. By this time, the corporation in the form of a trust had permitted businesses to grow to gigantic proportions involving the predatory consequences of monopoly. The railroad company owns the land that its tracks run through and tenant wheat ranchers farm it. The ranchers believe that they have an agreement to purchase the land at nominal prices in the near future. The railroad company not only drastically raises the price per acre; it also adopts the policy of charging high freight prices to ship wheat. The ranchers resort to bribery in order to elect their own representatives on the state's railroad commission. The plan fails and a bloody battle occurs between the farmers and agents of the powerful, anti-social entity. Through a complex chronicle of events, the novel illustrates that there are greater forces than the human element. An underlying premise is that the individual is unimportant; that natural laws propel the inexorable expansion of the power of the railroad and directs the production and distribution of wheat. *The Octopus* demonstrates the impersonality, power, and pervasiveness of market forces. It also shows wheat as the incarnation of natural, dynamic, and orderly determinism. Nature is indifferent to men and evil is short-lived. Natural laws lead to social benefits even though particular individuals may suffer. The novel thus leaves open the question of personal responsibility and agency.

The Financier (1912) is the first of Theodore Dreiser's trilogy dealing with American businessman and financial superman, Frank Cowperwood. Dreiser illustrates that the financier is who makes the modern world and is a member of a new breed of ruthless supermen. Cowperwood is modeled on the life of Frank Yerkes, a late nineteenth-century streetcar magnate. In *The Financier* Dreiser shows that he has mastered the details of finance. Cowperwood is an amoral force who embodies the traits of real-life financial titans and who turns aside every obstacle. The author captures the spirit and energy of the 1870s. The novel's strongly Darwinian tone explains the need for social inequality fostered by capitalism. Individuals such as Cowperwood are shown to be compelled to seek profit, power, women, and success. The protagonist is shown to engage in legally questionable acts and spends over a year in prison for using the city's money for personal gain in partnership with the city treasurer. The fall of this brilliant, ambitious, and unrepentant man of force is not permanent when he restores his fortune through his financial dealings during the panic of 1873. Cowperwood is a shrewd opportunist who exploits the deficiencies and shortcomings of others.

Abraham Cahan's *The Rise of David Levinsky* (1917) is a great example of business fiction, immigrant fiction, and social history. It tells the story of an impoverished boy in Russia who comes to America and, over a thirty-year period, becomes the owner of a leading ready-made cloak and suit factory. The story is told in the form of a fictional autobiography. The novel tells the story of the process of adaptation to American life on the East Side of New York City by a Russian Jewish immigrant. It is a tale of the emptiness and loneliness of financial success. David is a millionaire but he is not a happy man. Unlike many business novels, the author of *The Rise of David Levinsky* pays great attention to the details of running a business.

Sinclair Lewis's *Babbitt* (1922) was the first American book to receive a Nobel Prize. Babbitt is a complacent, somewhat prosperous, middle-class real estate agent in the Midwest who conforms to what he sees as the business ideals of success. He lives in the middle-size town of Zenith where many people exhibit the sameness of thought, vocabulary, dress, morals, and so on. The first section of the novel is devoted to Babbitt's typical workday. Much of the book consists of a compilation of sociological observations on various aspects of American life including work, family, culture, religion, etc. This satire or parody serves as an adverse reaction to perversions of the business *ethos* and spirit in American life. Babbitt, a strict conformist, realizes and admits that his life is not fulfilling. Feeling trapped, living for values that others view to be respectable, he wants to break away but he is afraid of being ostracized. The pathetic but sympathetic, slightly corrupt social climber experiences a psychological crisis and attempts to rebel. He decides to no longer participate in his many social groups such as the Boosters, church, real estate association, and so on. The disoriented businessman experiments with nonconformity by throwing in with liberal politicians and unions, having an affair, and running around with a Bohemian party crowd. His rebellion is destructive to his life and it too has its restrictions. His desperate attempt to escape proves to be futile. In his life he has gone from conformity to rebellion and back to conventionality.

Another 1922 business novel is Garet Garrett's *The Driver*. The action takes place during an economic crisis in America during the 1890s. The narrator of the novel takes a position with a railroad where he meets stock speculator and entrepreneur, Henry Galt, who buys large amounts of the corporation's stock. When the railroad goes bankrupt, Galt takes over as leader and rebuilds and reengineers the company. He goes on to become a powerful railroad magnate who is plotted against by his competition and the United States government.

F. Scott Fitzgerald's *The Great Gatsby* (1925) centers on a character with enormous hopes and dreams. The ambitious self-made man is sensitive to the promise of American life in the 1920s. In this novel, the author provides a critique of the American dream of business success. It tells the story of excess, pleasure, folly, emptiness, and moral decay among the wealthy. Gatsby is a strong-minded, striving, and organized man who wants to recapture his past with Daisy Buchanan, who lives a life of privilege having married the wealthy but immoral Tom Buchanan. Gatsby's ambition is to rekindle his romance with Daisy. He strives to attain wealth and power because he equates Daisy with them. Gatsby hastens the earning of his fortune via dubious and illegal means in the underworld. Despite this, Gatsby is perceived as the embodiment of the American Dream. He ultimately fails his quest to regain Daisy.

The 1944 film, *An American Romance*, is director King Vidor's tribute to hard work, family, and the American Dream. This rags-to-riches movie tells the story of a man, Steve Dangos, who comes to America from Europe at the beginning of the twentieth century. The Czech immigrant starts out as a laborer in the iron mines of Minnesota. He works his way up from miner to employment in the steel mills of Ohio and to automobile manufacturing where he becomes a successful industrialist. He uses his knowledge of steel to build a safer, full-frame car. This fully-developed immigrant story includes stunning documentary style sequences depicting the production of steel, cars, and planes that are built for World War II. Dangos marries a school teacher, takes risks to succeed, values education, and has a tremendous work ethic. His wife encourages him to excel in his career. His sons are all named after American presidents and he loses one of them in World War I. The film portrays America as the land of unlimited possibilities.

Arthur Miller's 1949 play, *Death of a Salesman*, tells the story of Willy Loman, a man who worshipped success and popularity and who achieves neither of them. He was a failure as a salesman and he was not loved by his friends and family. Willy is a man living in a delusional world as a shield against reality. He wanted to "succeed" by being well-liked and personally attractive as opposed to becoming successful through skill and hard work.

Willy did not know himself and he had all the wrong dreams. He did not like being a salesman and he was not good at it. However, he liked to work with his hands doing carpentry work and he was good at it. Unfortunately, this was not his chosen career path.

John P. Marquand's *Point of No Return* (1949) offers a portrait of a businessman's frenzied parade to nowhere. It tells the story of banker Charles Gray's long career devoted to climbing up the company ladder. Gray is a man who wants to free himself from a life that seems to be stereotypical and preordained. He is part of dominating social and business systems and he knows that there is nothing he can do about it. Deterministic philosophy underpins this novel in which the protagonist is not permitted to choose for himself. The novel tells how different events in people's lives make them who they are. Gray is a man seeking a promotion who is in competition with a flashy rival for it. The reader gets the story of Charles's life via flashbacks. A large part of the book is devoted to his youth, family life, and first romance in the small traditional New England town of Clyde, Massachusetts. The novel supplies detailed pictures of the life and times of caste-like New England and New York during the 1920s, 1930s, and 1940s. Now in his mid-forties, Charles is back from war and working at a small traditional bank in New York City. The upper middle-class banker went to Dartmouth, rather than Harvard, where most of his colleagues attended. In the end the honest and dependable Gray gets the promotion but he feels little pleasure in it. There has always been some kind of contrived order to his life.

Economist Henry Hazlitt's novel, *Time Will Run Back* (1951), is set in the year 2100, one hundred and fifty years since the victory of socialism over capitalism and the establishment of Wonworld. A new reluctant "dictator" has grown up on an isolated island. Noticing something wrong with the socialist policies run by the government in Moscow, he and a trusted friend rethink the economic basis of the system. Their Socratic-style discussions address topics such as pricing calculations, production, money, exchange, ownership, markets, entrepreneurship, and so on. They attempt to discover and correct the problems of socialism and to implement new policies. To do this they embark on a series of reforms that dismantle central planning and replace it with a market system. The novel does a fine job of describing how the socialist world works and how the transition to that world had taken place. It also provides a great lesson on how a market economy works and its advantages over a socialist economy. After an assassination attempt and a battle, the protagonists create a new country called Freeworld. The moral of the story is that a great idea such as capitalism cannot be permanently lost or kept in check because reason is capable of rediscovering the truth about the nature of man and the world.

Executive Suite (1952), by former businessman Cameron Hawley, is a business story about how business operates and what talents are required to run a successful business. The story opens with a crisis when the president, Avery Bullard, dies suddenly and unexpectedly from a brain hemorrhage. Bullard had not groomed or named a successor. The novel then proceeds to demonstrate the implications and consequences of negligence in developing a succession plan. Five vice-presidents compete for the position and engage in a lot of office politics. The novel illustrates the tactics and strategies used by people in their attempts to move up the corporate ladder. Bullard had been a one-man show and had kept the others in their respective management silos. The workaholic Bullard had valued the welfare of his corporation much more than he had valued his personal life. He was a hard-driving, single-minded entrepreneur of the old school. At the end of the novel there is jostling for power between cost-conscious corporate controller, Loren Shaw, and production manager, Don Walling. Shaw is the financial officer who watches costs and Walling runs the factory. Walling wants to attain financial success by producing quality products. He wants to give consumers better furniture and workers more satisfying jobs. In the end, the controlling shareholders choose Walling over Shaw. After Walling is elected he appoints Shaw as his executive vice-president.

In Cameron Hawley's *Cash McCall* (1955) the hero is a misunderstood tycoon and financier who is viewed by many as an unscrupulous robber baron who takes over companies, lays-off employees, and sells the firms for large profits. He often finds ways to achieving synergy with the operations of the companies. Cash McCall is actually a shrewd, productive, and efficient businessman who rebuilds acquired companies, operates them more effectively and efficiently than their incumbent management, has high standards of personal and human ethics, and creates wealth without guilt. *Cash McCall* portrays business as an honorable activity in a benevolent, life-affirming universe. Business is a noble pursuit that is ethically based on win-win agreements. Both Hawley's *Cash McCall* and *Executive Suite* have been made into fine motion pictures.

Sloan Wilson's *The Man in the Gray Flannel Suit* (1956) is about how a World War II veteran and member of the greatest generation handles the corporate rat race. Tom Rath, after experiencing great horror in the war, struggles to find the right job and to keep a happy family life. Rath suffers from PTSD and has a number of inner conflicts. He wants the best for his wife and kids and finds a better job at UBC Television Corporation. Our sympathetic hero finds little substance in his work there, discovers that he is living a fragmented life, and eventually recognizes the costs of business success. Rath observes the single-minded devotion to work of his boss and mentor, Mr. Hopkins. Work comes first for Hopkins who has attained great business success but who has a travesty of a family life. Unwilling to have a corporation dominate his life, Tom turns down a promotion and settles for a lesser position that is not all-consuming. Unlike the typical "organization man" who strives for corporate status and power, he prefers to work at a lower level and to be a family man. Rath decides to be a nine to five man, thereby finding time for his family and for what he considers to be the more important things in life. He decides not to be a face in the corporate crowd.

Ayn Rand's prophetic masterpiece, *Atlas Shrugged* (1957), takes place at a time when government is seeking ever more control and where the men of industry are mysteriously disappearing. The United States is the only nation that has not become a People's State. This novel depicts the businessman's role as heroic and the business hero as a persistent independent thinker. It also presents an integrated conceptual and moral case for freedom and against collectivism. *Atlas Shrugged* tells the story of the last stages of conflict between productive businessmen and looter politicians and bureaucratic rent-seeking businessmen who use government edicts to gain favorable treatment for their companies. The theme of the novel is the role of the mind in human existence. It illustrates this theme by showing what the world would be like if the rationally purposeful creators stopped producing by going on strike.

Sometimes a Great Notion (1964) is Ken Kesey's epic story of an Oregon logging family celebrating individualism and the power of the human spirit to conquer nature and to overcome man-made obstacles. The hardworking Stampers are heroic businessmen who are anti-union, anti-socialist, and unamenable to anyone who tries to tell them what to do. The strong, independent members of the family confront problems head-on and fight for what they believe in. Their logging business is not a union shop. When union loggers go on strike the large lumber companies can only meet their own contracts by buying from small non-union companies like the Stampers's business. Hank Stamper, along with his father, Henry, and brother, Lee, overcome obstacles with grit and determination in order to deliver the lumber that has been ordered from them. They battle against a local union and their community and suffer the tragedy that accompanies their quest. Toughness permeates the entire novel and is found in Hank, the weather, the river, the loggers' work, and so on. The besieged family members work, fight, and struggle together and ultimately meet the goal. *Sometimes a Great Notion* embodies the themes of independence, individualism, family, and self-reliance.

The observer-protagonist of Wilfrid Sheed's novel, *Office Politics* (1966), is a newly-hired number four editor at the liberal magazine, *The Outsider*. The new editor had left a well-paid position at CBS for the prospective satisfaction of accomplishing something that fulfills him and that he can believe in. Sensitivities are high in the shabby office which is controlled by a charismatic chief editor who rules with an iron hand. He edits with a piercing and perceptive editorial pen leading the contributing editors to believe and to feel that their work is edited too severely. The staff of misfits and oddballs backstab, conspire, connive, and are not loyal to the magazine or to one another. When the chief editor suffers a heart attack, a power struggle among the editors ensues as they vie for control. When he returns to work, he overwhelms the staff with his charismatic personality and mastery of office politics thereby restoring order.

In Stanley Elkin's *The Franchiser* (1976) Ben Flesh attempts to imitate or to become other people in the mid-1970s when he attempts to homogenize America by establishing a variety of franchise stores all across the nation. Ben was willed the prime interest rate that existed at the time of his benefactor's death. He subsequently uses the money obtained at low cost to purchase various franchises. His goal is to democratically help individuals to obtain the things that they need and/or want. Flesh strives for his own goals through small franchise operations that come under the umbrella of a large corporation. This man of franchise enthusiastically wants to eradicate regional differences and to be the person who made America look like America.

In his play, *Glengarry Glen Ross*, David Mamet provides a two-day snapshot of the lives of four pathetic real estate salesmen and their inexperienced office manager in a shabby real estate office in Chicago in the 1980s. Selling real estate is a hard way of making a living in this bleak world. These salesmen misrepresent, tell stories, and connive in order to make deals. The premium leads are reserved for closers only. The salesmen are sly and convincing when talking to clients. Ultimately, the office is broken into and the premium leads are stolen by one (or more) of the salesmen who did not have access to the superior leads. This play is an insightful study of human interactions among desperate and despairing cutthroat salesmen who despise their cruel, hostile, and heartless boss. The men depicted in this play are part of a dying breed.

The 1987 film *Wall Street* presents the story of Bud Fox, an ambitious young stockbrocker who is desperate to succeed. Bud is from a working class family and his values clash with those of his father, Carl, who works hard at an airline where he is also a union leader. Bud gets involved with Gordon Gekko, an exploitative, rich corporate raider, who gives Bud money and asks to get insider information for him. Fox becomes wealthy because of the huge commissions he garners from the charismatic Gekko's trading activities. Gekko has taken Bud under his wing and has given him a taste of wealth, power, and high living. Bud is on the road to becoming a major player as he continues to spy and to gain insider information for Gekko. The junior stockbroker realizes that Gekko has gone too far when he sees Gekko trying to take over and liquidate the airlines where Bud's father is employed. Bud takes part in a scheme to make Gekko lose a great deal of money. When Bud is eventually charged with insider trading he sets a trap for Gekko and both of them go to prison.

The 1988 movie *Tucker: The Man and His Dream* tells the story of a man caught in the middle of an imperfectly competitive market for automobiles and the power of a federal government that has been captured by the "Big Three" automakers. Preston Tucker is a real-life contrarian who fought the power that controlled the automobile market in the late 1940s. Tucker wanted to design and manufacture a revolutionary, safe, and innovative new car called the Tucker Torpedo. It had a rear-mounted engine, seatbelts, pop-out windshield, disc brakes, fuel injection, padded dash, push-button controls, and more. This partially fictionalized but mostly true story tells of the destruction of Tucker's dream at the hands of his competitors who needed the power of the federal government in order to stop Tucker. The "Big Three" wanted to crush Tucker and had connections with a powerful senator from Detroit. The SEC investigated Tucker's business practices and charged him with making false promises. He was taken to court for fraud with the accusation that he would not deliver on his promise to produce fifty cars by a certain date. Although he was found not guilty, his business had been ruined. The exuberant and visionary maverick to this day serves as a symbol of the American entrepreneurial can-do spirit.

David Lodge's *Nice Work* (1988) is set in mid-1980s, Thatcherite Great Britain. It takes place in a city modeled after Birmingham. An Industry Year government program assigns a feminist literature professor specializing in the nineteenth-century industrial novel to shadow the managing director of a local factory. She has no practical experience of industry and has never set foot in a factory. In turn, the managing director has no time for university people and their theories. The goal of this exchange program is to promote mutual understanding between "town and gown." Each of the participants is intelligent, narrow-minded, and opinionated. One is a hard-working, practical, industrial type while the other values the collegiate lifestyle. *Nice Work* is a story of how polar opposites can evolve and find common ground and respect for the other's worldview and lifestyle. In the end he has learned to appreciate women's studies, deconstructionism, and postmodernism and she has learned a great deal about the workings of English industry. He develops his philosophical and literary side and she comes to understand the problems and issues found in the business world. They continue on in their respective careers but their worlds are no longer so insular.

In Jerry Sterner's 1989 play, *Other People's Money*, a Wall Street corporate raider attempts to acquire a nearly one hundred-year-old New England wire and cable company. The play is a great primer on the nature, operations, and nomenclature of takeovers. The paternal CEO of the family-owned New England Wire and Cable cares about his employees and community. He is a kind man who has not kept up with the times. He should have upgraded the facilities. The outmoded but debt-free company desperately needed to be reengineered. The corporate raider buys up companies that have undervalued stock. He talks of the mismanagement of the investors' money. He wants to maximize shareholders' wealth by paying them money for their stock that they can invest more profitably elsewhere. They can invest in more viable businesses. The play demonstrates that corporate takeovers are not always made by greedy people who enrich themselves at the expense of everyone else. If the factory closes then some people will be out of work and will need to be flexible and to adapt. The passionate and idealistic CEO needed to realize that he does not own the company but simply manages it for the stockholders. The fight for principles on both sides of a corporate takeover is masterfully presented in impassioned speeches by the two protagonists at a stockholders' meeting. The takeover decision is left up to the shareholders who vote in a proxy fight.

The 2010 film *Wall Street: Money Never Sleeps* is a sequel to the 1987 film *Wall Street*. It is set in New York and revolves around the 2008 financial crisis. Gordon Gekko is released from prison after serving time for insider trading. He wants to reconcile with his daughter, Winnie, who is in love with Jake Moore, an employee of Keller Zabel Investments (KZI). Rumors are spreading about KZI and its problems with sub-prime debt. KZI collapses and is not offered a bailout. Jake seeks to understand the reasons for KZI's collapse and enlists the help of Gekko who, in turn, wants Jake to help him reconcile with his daughter. They discover that Bretton James and his firm, Churchill Schwartz, were behind the rumors and were illegally betting to destroy KZI. Jake obtains a position with Churchill Swartz after causing that company to lose one hundred and twenty million dollars. Bretton James says that he would invest in the fusion energy project that Jake has been promoting. James changes his mind and, instead, goes into fossil fuel and solar panels. The angry Jake then obtains and disseminates information that causes the arrest of James.

After the presentation of detailed chapters on the twenty-five novels, plays, and films outlined above, a concluding chapter will discuss the nature and uses of business fiction and will provide a historical survey of many of the works within this genre. Three appendices are included at the end of the book:

1. a list of business novels and plays
2. a list of business films
3. an article describing the findings of a survey conducted by my Koch research associates, Jomana Krupinski and Kaitlyn Pytlak, and myself.

The survey asked business professors and literature professors to rank what they consider to be the best business novels and plays.

Chapter One

The Rise of Silas Lapham

A Story of Self-Identity, Self-Respect, and Morality

William Dean Howells's *The Rise of Silas Lapham* (1885) was the first important realistic novel to focus on an American businessman. The author intended his highly regarded novel to provide moral education to the readers. Early in the novel Howells presents an essential business-related moral dilemma that has repercussions throughout the entire story. The main story depicts a man's moral rise while his prosperity is declining.

Silas Lapham is a man from a humble background who has become rich through hard work. The story is set in a time period when many old fortunes were diminishing and when the newly rich were frequently wealthier than the old rich. Silas is a *nouveaux riche*, post-civil war millionaire, who, along with his family, attempts to become part of Boston society. He was determined to place his wife and his daughters among that city's aristocracy. The novel's secondary but interrelated plot chronicles his family's awkward attempts to gain acceptance into cultured society.

The book begins with reporter Bartley Hubbard interviewing Silas for an article on the businessmen of Boston. The self-assured Lapham is being profiled in this feature article and dictates his biography to the newspaper interviewer. When the upper class Hubbard returns home he ridicules Lapham for his crudeness, lack of breeding, and simple upbringing. Hubbard's wife asks him not to make fun of the uncultured and inarticulate Lapham in the piece he is writing. Through this interview the reader learns a great deal about Lapham's past.

Silas had been a poor child with a solid Christian background. He was raised on a family farm in rural northern Vermont near the Canadian border. His mother taught him the virtues of the Old Testament and Poor Richard's

Almanac. In 1835 Silas's father, Nehemiah, discovered a mineral paint deposit. Nehemiah experimented with the paint and thought it had the potential to be profitable but unfortunately, at that time, people could not afford to paint their houses.

Silas traveled to the West as a young man but returned to Vermont. He first worked in a sawmill and then as a stableman at a hotel. After his parents died, Silas moved to Lumberville where he drove a stage, bought and managed the stage line, and met and married the village schoolteacher, Persis. Silas married his ideal woman. Throughout the novel, he displays respect and high regard for all the women in his life—his mother, his wife, and later his intelligent daughter, Penelope, and his beautiful daughter, Irene. He was proud of them all.

Lapham rented a tavern stand. In 1855, Persis urged him to paint the tavern he rented in order to improve its appearance. As a result, he investigated the paint mine on his father's farm, mixed up some paint, and tried it. He had the ore analyzed and found it that it was quite valuable. When he had it tested he found that it contained seventy-five percent peroxide of iron making it capable of withstanding fire, water, and acid. The demand for flame resistant paint had soared after many passengers had been killed in boat fires in the West. Silas returned to Lumberville after he received the test results, sold out everything that he had, put it all into his naturally-superior, weather-resistant paint, and become a prosperous paint manufacturer. Silas named his brand of paint after his wife. After all, it was she who prompted him to develop the paint. He became the proud owner of a paint company called "The Works."

Silas was confident that his wife could handle any situation. She encouraged, helped, and guided him in his various endeavors. Persis also acts as Silas's moral conscience throughout most of the novel. Her opinions carry great weight with him. His actions are greatly influenced by what he believes will please his wife. The value of her contributions and her moral assessments diminishes as the story progresses.

When Silas left to fight in the Civil War, she managed the paint business for him. During the war, he fights gallantly, is wounded at Gettysburg, and is promoted to the rank of full colonel. Silas's friend, Jim Millen, died saving his life in the war. Millen took a bullet that was intended for Lapham. As a result, Silas felt an obligation to Millen's wife (Molly) and daughter (Zerilla). Later in the novel, we see Silas risk his reputation by supporting the dubious, alcoholic widow and daughter of the man who saved his life in combat. Rumor regarding Silas and the two women led Persis to misread Silas's relationship with Zerilla, his typist.

Silas's business suffered during the war. When he returned from the Civil War in 1865, he found a changed business world characterized by rapidly changing dynamic markets, large firms, international trade, and strong competition. After the Civil War there were more interconnections with suppliers and customers because of railroads, steamships, canals, etc., and distant and local events were affecting one another. He wanted to expand his business, but was reluctant to take in a partner—he wanted to keep the business to himself. Persis convinces him to acquire a partner with capital to expand and to secure the company from failure. Against his own better judgment, Silas takes on Milton K. Rogers as a partner because he thought his wife always knew what was best.

Silas saw Rogers as unknowledgeable about the paint business and as never having added value to the firm. His intuition was that Rogers would seriously harm the business if he remained with the company. After benefiting from the use of his partner's capital, Silas gave Rogers the chance of either buying Silas out or selling out to Silas. Rogers was unable to buy Silas out so Silas bought out Rogers, paying him more then he originally invested. After Rogers left the business, Lapham became a millionaire during the post-Civil War period.

Persis believes that her husband used Rogers's capital to get rich and accuses him of unloading Rogers just before the price of paint soared. She thinks that Silas mistreated Rogers and never lets him forget that she is disappointed regarding his treatment of his former partner. She never truly forgives him for being unfair in crowding Rogers out of the business. Persis believes that her husband had stolen the future profits that Rogers's investments had made possible. Throughout the novel she endeavors to make Silas see his "moral failure" and to pay back Rogers in some way. Persis thinks that Silas ruined Rogers's life through this transaction.

In no way is it self-evident that Lapham had been unfair to Rogers—at most we could argue for an ambivalent interpretation with respect to his behavior. The business prospered but the partnership did not succeed. Rogers had an option and received a good deal more than he had invested. Lapham contends that he did nothing wrong in buying Rogers out just before the business took off. He says that it was a prudent business decision. Silas thought that Rogers was a hindrance and that he had paid a fair price. Persis tried to make Silas feel guilty but it is uncertain as to whether or not there was any moral wrong to feel guilty about.

Lapham relocates his paint manufacturing company to Boston while maintaining the mining portion of the business on the family farm near Lumberville. Once his business is a success, the Laphams buy a house in Nankeen Square in the South End and their daughters, Penelope and Irene, attend public school. Penelope, the eldest daughter, was smart and witty, plain in appearance, liked to read and attend church lectures, and had no interest in high society. The beautiful Irene was three years younger, loved to shop, also (at first) had no interest in society, and was not as smart or as witty as her sister. As the story progresses the Laphams become social climbers.

Irene and her mother vacation on the St. Lawrence where they meet Anna Corey and her two daughters. Anna becomes ill and Persis cares for her until the doctor arrives. Anna's son, Tom, joins his family on vacation and appears to be captivated by Irene. On her return home, Persis tells Silas that she was impressed with the aristocratic Corey family. The chance meeting with the Coreys leads to a reevaluation of the Lapham's lifestyle, and Persis becomes conscious of the difference between her family and members of Boston's upper class society. The barely educated, uncultured Silas has no personal interest in culture and society but loves his wife and daughters, wants them to be happy, and encourages them to approach society.

The Coreys are a prestigious, traditional, old money family who initially associates with the Laphams because of Persis's kindness to Anna on the Canadian trip. Anna's husband, Bromfield, is a snob who does not work and who has never worked a day in his life. He had inherited wealth from his father, Giles Corey, a merchant who imported goods from India to New England. Anna had never been in the Lapham's undesirable part of town. She is afraid that her son might marry one of the Lapham girls. Both Bromfield and Anna do not hold high opinions with respect to commercial people. The Coreys's fortune had dwindled and the Laphams were actually in much better financial standing than the Coreys. Rather than enter the business world, Bromfield sells a house and cuts back on some of his family's social activities.

Although the Lapham girls were uneasy in society, Persis and Silas thought that their daughters needed to be introduced to society and that it would be best for them to move from their old house in South End and to build a new house in the Back Bay area on the sophisticated and exclusive Beacon Street. They decided to build a mansion on the water side of Beacon Street. To Persis and Silas, this new house represented Penelope and Irene's futures in upper class society. They thought that moving to an elite neighborhood would place the family in the center of society. They did not realize that it would take more than money to break social barriers. For example, the resentful Mrs. Corey remarked that Back Bay is being very common these days.

Silas's old partner, the unscrupulous Rogers, shows up and asks for help. Silas lends money to Rogers and accepts as collateral land (i.e., a deed to mill property out West) and questionable securities that he believes to be worthless. Rogers indeed has pledged worthless land and watered stock as collateral. Overlooking the risks, Lapham makes this and additional loans to Rogers throughout the rest of the story. It is unclear if Silas makes these loans out of a true sense of guilt and wrongdoing, or to gain approval from his wife. Although Silas listened to his wife to lend Rogers money, it is not evident that down deep he believed that he had done anything wrong.

Persis views the income earned after Rogers had been "forced out" to be a result of Rogers's capital investment. She believes that money was taken from him, and she attributes all of Rogers's subsequent financial failures as due to her husband's actions. Persis thinks that Silas lends money to Rogers as an attempt to ease his guilty conscience due to his forcing Rogers out. As a result, she begins to forgive Silas and to view him as a moral person again. Over the years, she has scolded her husband for his inability to share his paint company with anyone.

On the other hand, Silas consistently maintains that his buyout of Rogers was a business transaction in which he acted justly. He explains that Rogers did not contribute to the business and was not a benefit to it. It may be that he got involved with Rogers a second time because he wanted to please his wife, who attempts to serve as his moral conscience throughout the novel.

The Coreys and the Laphams continue to get involved socially. Both Irene and Penelope are attracted to Tom Corey. Because the Coreys were running low on money, Tom did not want to continue drawing upon his father's wealth and, therefore, told his father that he is going to ask Silas for a job. Tom's parents thought that his desire to work for Lapham might be because he was attracted to Irene. The Coreys thought that it wrong for Tom to be interested in the uninteresting, dull, and socially-inept Irene. Anna does not want Tom to work for Lapham or to marry one of his daughters. She perceives Irene as vapid and Penelope as introverted.

Silas, who does not waste time and is devoted to hard work, criticizes Tom Corey for not working. However, the uneducated Silas is impressed with Tom's knowledge of several languages. Tom had traveled extensively abroad and was fluent in several languages. Tom believes in the paint business and asks Silas about his entering the business. Tom wants to enter a profession that he can be passionate about. He wants to do something with his life.

Tom asks Lapham if he would permit him to invest in the paint company and to open branches outside the United States, starting with Mexico. There were emerging opportunities to export mineral paint to Spain, France, Germany, Italy, and other countries. Silas does not want a partner but he agrees to take Tom on as an employee. The young Corey agrees to work for Silas and says the fact that he had gone to college won't hurt him. Silas was flattered when the young man from one of Boston's leading families asks him for a job.

Tom had offered to work for Silas on a commission only basis. He told Lapham that, given his knowledge of foreign languages, he would be able to promote the paint products in a number of different countries. Silas gives Tom a few months to learn the business, lets him do office work and translate foreign correspondence, and appoints him to be head of foreign paint sales.

The newly rich Silas spent money on charities and church but not on social activities. He did not learn to spend his wealth in the manner that accepted families of society did. His language is not acceptable and he is somewhat boastful and obnoxious. Silas flaunts his wealth and he is unfamiliar with social conventions. Lacking manners, culture, and the social graces, he is shunned socially and deemed to be socially inadequate. For much of the story he did not understand that his own prosperity and crudeness could be inconsistent with culture, education, and so on. Despite his deficiencies, Silas comes off in the novel as generally smart, likeable, powerful, and just.

The Coreys invite the Laphams to attend a dinner party at their tastefully decorated house. Penelope decided not to attend to event because she felt uneasy around Anna Corey and because she thought her father might boast too much. In fact, Silas, who was fearful of making social errors, drinks too much wine and talks too much. As the evening wore on he became louder and more boastful.

Silas attempted to apologize to Tom at work the next day. Tom brushed the apology aside and said that Silas's intoxication was the fault of Tom's family, who knew that Silas did not drink. After the dinner party incident, Lapham realizes that his pride and ambition had overreached himself. At the dinner he was challenged to understand that his habits, demeanor, education, and manners were inadequate. After the dinner party, Silas becomes honest with his genuine self-identity and self-interest. He sets aside the notion of social propriety for himself in favor of his honest and self-reliant personal pursuits of his own objective values. Of course, he continues to support his daughters in their own efforts to join the social elite.

Tom Corey expresses his love for Penelope rather than for Irene. No one had suspected that Penelope was the sister that he was in love with. Tom desired a smart and witty woman with depth and a good personality. Penelope also had feelings for Tom but she feared that Irene would be devastated if she and Tom began a romantic relationship. Penelope was pleasantly surprised when she learned about Tom's love for her, but she is hesitant and does not want to betray Irene who loved Tom first.

Penelope informs her parents about Tom. They speak about the situation to Reverend Sewell who observes that Penelope and Tom would be doing no wrong. He explains that keeping Penelope and Tom apart would only bring unhappiness for all concerned. Sewell's analysis was based on what he termed the "economy of pain" which stated that pain should be limited to the fewest number of individuals possible. Sewell says that Penelope and Tom should pursue their love. In that case, only one person would be hurt. On the other hand, if Penelope gives Tom up, then all individuals involved would be hurt. As expected, Irene takes the news hard, but she tells Penelope that what happened was not Penelope's fault. After learning of the situation Irene departs to live for a while in the Laphams's Vermont home. Penelope initially refuses Tom's proposal of marriage. This decision reflects the mistaken ideal of self-sacrifice.

All the while, Rogers has repeatedly been coming to Lapham to borrow more money to invest in his speculative, unsuccessful, and sometimes scandalous dealings. Silas continues to rely on Persis's sentimental and mistaken judgments and lends Rogers more and more money.

Silas's paint business begins to deteriorate as the economy slumped, competition increased, and his paint sales dropped. He encountered a keen competitor with respect to paint production from a West Virginia firm that could produce paint less expensively because the company owned natural gas wells which brought down its fuel costs. The West Virginia firm has natural advantages that Silas cannot compete with. The discovery of natural gas by the West Virginia company alters the relative cost structure between the two companies.

Lapham has also been supporting the family of Jim Millen who had saved Silas's life during the Civil War. He gives money to the wife, Molly, and hires the daughter, Zerilla, to work as a typist in his office. Persis advises Silas's not to give the Millens any more assistance because she believed that Silas had already done enough to meet his obligation to them. This is opposite of the opinion she had with regard to Silas's debt to Rogers.

The cost of the home Silas is building has skyrocketed to more than $100,000. Silas considers filing for bankruptcy or selling the house in order to escape financial ruin. The young Corey offers Silas money, but Silas declines and decides to sell his house instead.

Silas receives an offer to buy the lavish new house that he is building. He goes to see the house one more time, makes a fire in the chimney, and decides not to take the offer. He fails to completely extinguish the fire, which ultimately destroys the house. At first Persis is afraid that Silas will be charged with insurance fraud, but that would not be the case because the insurance policy had expired a week earlier.

Lapham has loaned money to Rogers and has accepted as collateral a number of mills in the West that he knows to be of very low value. Needing money, it appears that Silas will have to sell out to a railroad company at a very low price because of his inability to negotiate with the company. The property on which his mills are located is served by a spur line of a railroad company that wants to purchase the property at a bargain price. The owner of the railroad realizes that the company can decrease the property's value to whatever price it desires to pay by restricting services to the land in question. The railroad company wants to buy the mills and the mills are dependent on the railroad.

Rogers brings to Silas dishonest men who want to buy the land for unsuspecting clients from England. Rogers shows up with an offer from some Englishmen who desire to buy the mills for a great deal of money. Lapham assumes that the people with whom Rogers is dealing do not realize the worthlessness of the land. Lapham has to decide whether to sell the land to these supposedly unaware people, or to refuse to sell, thereby saving the other party from losing money due to Rogers's scheme.

In fact, the Englishmen are Rogers's accomplices who were to be paid out of Rogers's share of the purchase money. These individuals are agents for a philanthropic charitable group in England that wants to establish a utopian community on the mill property. These agents know that the mill property is worthless—they simply want to garner high commissions for their work.

Silas did not want to be a part of the swindle of Rogers's prospective buyers. He goes to these Englishmen to expose Rogers, but they said they are already aware of the land's value. They tell Silas that the loss will be borne by wealthy men in England for whom they are working. They assure Silas that their principals are aware of the potential risks and that they are ready to assume them. For a short period, Lapham is ambivalent and undecided about doing business with the agents of the British philanthropic society. If he would sell to the agents, both they and Rogers would make money and his paint business would survive. The loser would be the English gentlemen from the utopian charitable group. Silas realizes that he would be cheating them.

Silas makes the just and moral choice by refusing to sell the Western mill property to the agents of the charitable organization. When Lapham decides that it is wrong for him to sell to these men, Rogers offers an alternative. He suggests that Lapham sell to him and he would then, in turn, sell to the agents. His presumption is that such a tactic would absolve Silas of any personal moral responsibility. Of course, Silas declines to accept Rogers's offer. Silas makes these moral judgments himself without the guidance of his wife. He decides not to sell thus accelerating his impending bankruptcy. He ends up accepting a low offer from the railroad. The morally righteous Lapham was unwilling to stoop to deceit to save his paint business. As a free moral agent, Lapham controls the probability of his own bankruptcy.

Facing bankruptcy, Lapham attempts to forge a merger with his West Virginia competitor. In order to go forward with the merger he needs to obtain capital from another investor. Shortly after Silas refuses to sell to the English agents, a potential New York investor offers the needed substantial new capital in order to join Lapham's firm. Facing another opportunity to act honestly and justly, Silas resists the chance to misrepresent his failing company to this interested investor. He completely and objectively discloses all of the relevant financial details of his company and makes it known that he intends to use the investor's cash to effect a merger with his West Virginia company thereby avoiding bankruptcy. The potential investor withdraws his offer as a result.

Lapham files for bankruptcy and turns his Boston home, business, and other assets over to his creditors. After liquidating his assets, he leaves Boston as an honest man who has self-respect, self-esteem, and self-knowledge. Silas and his family return to his homestead in Vermont where he continues to manufacture his Persis line of paint but on a smaller scale.

Silas arranges for Tom Corey to obtain a position with the West Virginia paint company where he becomes part owner. The young Corey goes to Vermont to ask Penelope to marry him before he leaves for South America to be a salesman for the West Virginia company. Penelope ultimately decides to marry Tom.

Although the younger Laphams do join the social elite, back in Vermont, Silas and Persis no longer are concerned with culture and social etiquette. They have happily returned to a peaceful and quiet country life where social position does not matter. Silas is not broken. He knows that he is an honest, moral, and independent man who had made something of himself through hard work. He is honest, both with others and with himself, and possesses underlying dignity and decency. He knows that his business and personal decisions had been made based on justice and fairness rather than on emotion and sentiment.

Chapter Two

Taking a Look at Edward Bellamy's
Looking Backward

Edward Bellamy's popular novel, *Looking Backward: 2000–1887*, is frequently cited as one of the most influential books in America between the 1880s and the 1930s. This novel of social reform was published in 1888, a time when Americans were frightened by working class violence and disgusted by the conspicuous consumption of the privileged minority. Bitter strikes occurred as labor unions were just beginning to appear and large trusts dominated the nation's economy. The author thus employs projections of the year 2000 to put 1887 society under scrutiny. Bellamy presents Americans with portraits of a desirable future and of their present day. He defined his perfect society as the antithesis of his current society. *Looking Backward* embodies his suspicion of free markets and his admiration for centralized planning and deliberate design.

Looking Backward is a promotional argument and an attempt to informally educate the American public through the medium of the romantic novel. From this perspective, it is like Ayn Rand's monumental *Atlas Shrugged* (1957)—both present blueprints for the future and have been potential sources for social change. *Looking Backward* launched a national political movement based on a system of scientific and systematic socialism as readers of his day embraced Bellamy's novel. By the early 1890s, there were 165 Bellamy Clubs. In *Looking Backward* Bellamy called his ideology nationalism, and never used the term socialism. This ideology viewed the nation as collectively activated in the pursuit of sustenance and survival. As a philosophy of collective control of the nation's economy, its goal was to nationalize the functions of production and distribution. To this day, many American intellectuals have been attracted to such a system of economic paternalism.

Julian West, a thirty-year-old privileged aristocrat in 1887 Boston is the main character and narrator of *Looking Backward*. Having been born into an upper class family, he thought himself to be superior to the working masses and believed that he deserved his privileged life. West is the third generation of his family to have a great deal of money. He is set to marry Edith Bartlett when a house he is having built is completed. Strikes had delayed the completion of West's house and he, therefore, simply viewed labor conditions as an annoyance due to the setbacks in its construction. He looked at strikes with anger and disdain. West was unconcerned about the great divide between the rich and poor and the gaps between social classes.

On May 30, 1887, Decoration Day, Julian attends ceremonies celebrating and remembering Civil War veterans with Edith Bartlett and her family. He suffers from a sleeping disorder, and upon returning home, he retires to his soundproof and fireproof underground sleeping chamber. In the secluded vaulted bedroom, Dr. Pillsbury, a trained mesmerist, puts Julian into a deep trancelike sleep. Only Dr. Pillsbury and Julian's servant, Sawyer, knew how to wake him. That night the house burns down and Julian is assumed to have died in the fire along with Sawyer. Edith also thought that Julian had perished. Even she did not know about the sleeping disorder, the hypnosis, and the sleeping chamber. The basement vault is not discovered and West is left undisturbed to sleep for 113 years with his organs and functions in a state of suspended animation.

In the year 2000, Dr. Leete, a retired physician, discovers the vault and Julian's ageless and uncorrupted body (he has not aged a day) when he is excavating for a new laboratory. The excavation reveals the hidden cellar and West's perfectly preserved body. When Julian awakens he meets Dr. and Mrs. Leete and their daughter, Edith, and he finds himself in very unfamiliar territory—the twentieth century is vastly different from the nineteenth. Throughout the rest of the novel West questions Leete about the changes that had occurred. As a spokesman for the twentieth century and for Bellamy's ideas on social reform, Dr. Leete systematically and rationally answers Julian's questions and responds to his concerns. In turn, West serves as a spokesman for Bellamy's nineteenth-century audience. It is through West's eyes that the reader views the contrasts between the old order and the new utopia.

Leete explains that the year 2000's collaborative utopian society is a logical outcome of the nineteenth century's rapid industrialization. The new society is a natural evolution of the economy that resulted from the advances of large-scale production. In the year 2000, there is a system of publicly-owned capital with the government controlling the nation's total production and distributing the national output equally among all of the citizens. The nineteenth century's system of monopolistic capitalism had somehow evolved and merged into government. Large companies had formed monopolies that eventually became nationalized. Bellamy's book is glaringly short on details as to how all this took place.

Businesses had merged into huge combinations and these, in turn, evolved into the placement of all capital in the hands of the government. Leete explains that, during the early years of the twentieth century, monopolies grew ever larger until the state took over the monopolies, including the means of production, to become one gargantuan state trust. He states that the existence of capitalistic monopolies was a necessary transitional stage that preceded a society of a totally nationalized economy. Bellamy thus viewed industrialization and giant conglomerates as potential benefactors, rather than as enemies, of mankind.

Leete tells Julian that market consolidation of industry was due to economies of scale and technological and industrial progression. Together, these produced material abundance that met society's needs. He notes that the scarcity problem had been solved by means of the rational organization of production. Bellamy's message is that society could be changed peacefully through evolution, education, and persuasion. It would thus be by the will of the people that all the means of production and distribution could gradually be consolidated under government control.

At first, West defends the nineteenth century but eventually becomes persuaded that twentieth-century utopia is superior. He concludes that the changes in society are not due to changes in human nature but, rather, from the economic equalization of all members of society. The equal distribution of property leads to what Bellamy sees as a vastly morally improved society without money and without private enterprises. In this society, people work for pride rather than for money. In addition, the patriotic desire to serve the government and the common good has replaced the profit motive. Whereas the nineteenth century emphasized individualism and private business, the twentieth century now emphasizes cooperation and the contribution by all to the common good and the general improvement of society. Bellamy based his good society on a system of cooperative equality. Assuming the natural goodness of man, he contends that, given the right system, rational people would respond with cooperation.

During the late nineteenth century, intellectuals began to contend that society, rather than the individual, is the fundamental fact of human existence. Bellamy, as one of these intellectuals, created his "perfect" society by removing social status and making everyone economically equal. These thinkers unfortunately ignore the fact that people, by nature, are individuals. Each person exists, perceives, experiences, thinks, and acts in and through his own body, and therefore from unique points in time and space. Each person is born an individual with respect to his mind and body. Each one has inborn differences based on his brain structure and physical endowments. Each person has peculiar aptitudes, which can be recognized, developed, and used. Each person has his own mental faculty, distinctive set of drives, ways of thinking, and the like. Because each person is distinctive, people differ in their preferred ways of pursuing their happiness. Although the individual is metaphysically primary (and communities are secondary and derivative) communities are important because an individual needs to belong to these in order to reach his potential for happiness. A person's moral maturation requires a life with others, and each individual is responsible for voluntarily choosing, creating, and entering relationships that enable him to flourish. A community or a society is simply the association of persons for cooperative action—it is not some concrete thing distinct from its members.

Looking Backward condemns nineteenth-century industrial society as brutal and primitive compared to the egalitarian and peaceful society of the year 2000. Bellamy damns a competitive economic system as unjust, degrading, wasteful, and vicious. His novel is intended to illustrate that, without private property, there would no longer be social issues such as shortages, social class divisions, joblessness, poor working conditions and long hours, child labor, strikes, poverty, hunger, crime, and war. In his ideal society there is no competition, no duplication of producers and distributors, no waste due to overproduction, no idle capital or labor, no political parties, and no cyclical crises. In his vision of the United States in the year 2000, there exists total equality of income, universal public education, social welfare and healthcare systems from cradle to grave and universal employment in an industrial army. Bellamy envisioned his society in 2000 as perfect, and thus no additional social engineering was needed.

Over the 113 year period that Julian slept, the workforce transformed into an industrial army of patriotic citizens. Every able-bodied person owed his country a term of service to make certain that there was a general abundance of life's necessities. Although considered to be equal to men, women served in a separate auxiliary force in the industrial army where they performed tasks best suited for their physical capabilities. Everyone is paid the same amount and people are persuaded to serve in whatever capacity their talents and skills are best suited. Because everyone is expected to work to his fullest potential (even without monetary incentives) every person receives an equal share of the wealth. Everyone gets the same compensation because everyone tries their hardest at their respective jobs.

People are encouraged to stay in school until, at age twenty-one, they became enlistees in the industrial army. Everyone has the opportunity to receive a college-level education and is free to choose a career after serving as a common laborer for the first three years. At age twenty-four people are given tests and asked questions to determine their abilities and job preferences. Although most people select their occupations after three years of common service, others attend professional schools to become physicians, teachers, etc. A final career choice must be made during the person's thirtieth year. In *Looking Backward* work is seen as a disagreeable, painful, and necessary duty to be performed until retirement at age forty-five when one begins to really enjoy life. October 15th is muster day when the twenty-four-year-olds enter the industrial army and the forty-five-year-olds depart from it.

Leete explains that, because incomes are equal, incentives take the form of adjustments to hours of labor and working conditions and in the form of public recognition. These adjustments serve to make a job more or less attractive. One idea is to make the hours of labor vary in different trades according to their difficulty. This, of course, results in differential hourly wage rates.

Dr. Leete tells Julian that workers are motivated by honor, distinction, national pride, devotion to the common good, and pride in the job itself. A worker can receive advancement as a reward based on his efforts to achieve the common good. There is a complex system of workers' rankings and rewards in the form of medals of distinction, ribbons, and badges. Every industry has emblems, badges, and ribbons. There exist numerous gradations and minor promotions meant to convey gratitude and esteem to the workers according to the service rendered to the community. There are also punishments for those who do not want to work. Those refusing to work find themselves in solitary confinement in prison with only a bread and water diet. Handicapped individuals are assigned tasks that they are capable of performing. Those too handicapped or too ill to work make up an invalid corps and receive the same amount of credit as everyone else. Because "salaries" are equal, people vie for honor and status rather than for wealth.

One's rank in the industrial army is the only path to honor and prestige except for those in the arts and the professions who are eligible for a few perquisites and minor privileges. Red ribbons make up the highest honors for those employed as artists, authors, engineers, inventors, physicians, teachers, and so on. The reward systems in the arts and professions are more complex than the system for other jobs. For example, an author is permitted to reduce his regular work hours by any earned royalties. All books and newspapers are published by the government. There is no censorship and the state is obligated to publish any work as long as the author pays for the first printing.

According to Dr. Leete, credit cards are given to all citizens enabling them to acquire goods and services necessary for a comfortable life. Each citizen is provided with an annual allotment of goods and services. Each time that a purchase is made a cardboard credit card is punched according to the "prices" assigned by government bureaucrats. Money is used only as a unit of account. These credit cards function in a very similar manner as today's debit cards. Identical amounts are deposited by the U.S. Treasury into every cardholder's account. Different people consume different combinations of goods and services. Government administrators set "prices," and individuals make these purchases using their cards. When excess demand or supply occurs, prices or production levels are adjusted. When funds are needed for investment purposes, government officials remove the required amount from the pool to be distributed among the citizens.

Each credit card includes an amount sufficient to live comfortably in society. Any unused credit is returned to the government. In addition, individuals could will personal possessions freely to their descendants, but because most needs are met by the government the majority of these possessions revert to the state. The government uses such excesses to make improvements that are shared by all.

The credit cards can only be used at government-owned distribution centers with each center carrying the same products. Edith Leete takes Julian to see one of these centers where sample rooms display the various commodities. She explains that orders can be sent by a small pneumatic tube to a central warehouse with goods being shipped to people's houses across town via a system of larger pneumatic tubes. The "prices" are symbols that expedite government accounting. The nonexistence of competition permits government bureaucrats to set "prices" any way they want to.

All the world's great nations have copied the American system of nationalism (actually command socialism) with universally honored credit cards. There are no wars or other international conflicts. International trade is accomplished by accounting procedures with balances being settled every few years by an international trade council. There is free trade and free emigration as people have the freedom to select and change their nationality. In addition, each person speaks a native language and a universal language.

Leete explains that crime is nearly nonexistent because everyone receives the same credit and, therefore, there is no need to steal and there is virtually no need for prisons. There are no crimes involving monetary gains because there is no money. No people are involved in financial operations. Crime faded away among the educated except for the mentally ill who were treated in hospitals. There exists no military, few police, few prisons, no Internal Revenue Service, no charity, no government debt, no political parties, no banks, no strikes, no jury system, no attorneys (legal decisions are made by judges appointed by the president), and no churches, denominations, sects, or clergy. However, individuals are permitted to broadcast their religious views in sermons delivered over a type of radio or telephone system.

Without greed there is no government corruption. A small group of bureaucrats ran the entire economy. The sole function of the government administration is to direct the nation's industries. Higher bureaucratic positions are filled by, and elected by, individuals who have retired from the industrial army and are past forty-five years of age. The job of the government is to provide economic abundance and a social welfare system. Democracy exists with voting at various levels. A president serves for a term of five years.

The government provides public kitchens with central public and private dining rooms. This system does not allow for the individuality of food, but does permit social interaction and eliminates the need for the individual to prepare meals. Housework is mechanical and washing is done in public laundries. Electric power has replaced fossil fuels, thus eliminating the pollution of coal furnaces. Healthcare is socialized. Medical care is provided by the state with doctors selected individually but paid by the government. Music is piped into rooms via a type of cable radio system in which a person can select programs "on-demand" and can control the volume.

The message of *Looking Backward* is that everyone shares equally because all people alive at a particular time have received the aggregated technological accomplishments of preceding generations of men, and every person alive at a certain time has a right to an equal share of what has been accumulated. It is argued that a program of equalization would eliminate social ills, bring about the feeling of solidarity, and transform the nation into a brotherhood of man. Income equality is based on common humanity because civilization is people's common inheritance and, therefore, all individuals are entitled to an equal share of the country's income.

The above idea reminds me of, and is analogous to, Harvard philosopher John Rawls's idea that there is no good reason to allow the distribution of wealth and income to be determined by the possession of natural endowments or by social and historical factors. Rawls contends that individuals do not deserve the genetic or other assets they are born with. He explains that, from a moral perspective, the level of effort people are willing to put forth is, to a great extent, influenced by their natural endowments. Consequently, those who are more productive due to their greater natural abilities have no moral right to greater rewards, because the abilities and motivations that make up their work cannot be morally considered to be their own. He considers the distribution of natural talents as a common asset and argues that people should share in the fruits of this distribution. Rawls also maintains that individuals who are not fortunate enough to have wealthy parents do not merit worse starting points and, consequently, worse life prospects than those who were so fortunate. He contends that society should equalize the prospects of the least well off by taxing the undeserved inherited gains of children of rich persons, and using the tax proceeds to aid the least well off.

Julian falls in love with Edith Leete and discovers that she is the great granddaughter of his former fiancée, Edith Bartlett. Julian hears a sermon by Mr. Barton on the evils of the nineteenth century and the immeasurable advances that have been made since then. He becomes depressed because he realizes that he was once part of that inhumane and barbaric system. He has changed and now realizes how bad the nineteenth century was.

Toward the end of the novel Julian has a nightmare in which he is back in 1887 Boston. As he wanders around town, he sees misery, waste, filth, and the gap between the many struggling poor and the privileged few. In his dream, he tries to explain to his friends (including Edith Bartlett) the horrendous nature of the nineteenth century and the joys of twentieth-century society. They become furious with him and will not listen. When he awakens, he finds that he is still in the year 2000.

Bellamy claimed that all people voluntarily conformed to the new society of equality based on solidarity and camaraderie. He maintained that everyone is perfectly satisfied with an arrangement of the equal distribution of property. Based on an understanding of human nature, it is improbable, unrealistic, and absurd that people living in a capitalist system would surrender to this new arrangement that eliminates money, the profit motive, social status, individualism, and materialism. No details are provided regarding how this change occurred. What made people no longer care about money, wealth, and property? Bellamy simply said that it was the equal distribution of property that led to tremendous moral improvement and to the elimination of crime and wickedness. He optimistically had faith in the power of reason to control men's actions. He presented this situation as an accomplished fact that occurred early during the twentieth century. This certainly goes against what we know about human nature. Crimes are committed no matter what system is in effect.

What about the problem of incentives and motivation in a socialist economy? This is a great difficulty for *Looking Backward* and for Bellamy. How and why will people do things without incentives? Bellamy has a hard time explaining why people work hard when their material circumstances will not be affected. His system of prizes, deprivations, and love of country is certainly not adequate or persuasive. People are motivated differently and some are not motivated at all. Bellamy puts a great deal of faith in centralized government and very little in individual initiative. He ignores man's nature to work for the betterment of himself and his family. Markets create incentives to search for opportunities that a person's singular knowledge provides to him. Knowledge and opportunities are constantly changing, highly local, and individuated. A person's actions are motivated from within. Individuals may seek to attain their goals and values, to better the conditions of their lives, to accomplish something outstanding, and so on. Capitalism offers freedom and a variety of goods and services. Socialism, on the other hand, stifles incentives, discourages originality, fosters political corruption, eliminates the diversification and differentiation of goods and services and encourages people to act in the same ways.

There are also problems in *Looking Backward* with respect to deciding what to produce and how to allocate what is produced. Bellamy emphasizes the distinction between production and distribution. However, he has bureaucrats make both production and allocation decisions rather than relying on market responses as would be done under a capitalist system. There are just too many details in complexities to be grasped by utopian planners who are much more concerned with wholes than with particulars.

According to Austrian economist Ludwig von Mises, it is impossible to have rational central planning under socialism. Without market-based prices, decision-making by central planners would be irrational and arbitrary. Because of the elimination of market-based prices, a centralized planned economy would be unable to allocate resources rationally. Socialism is inherently unworkable, destroys individual motivation, and suppresses the means of economic calculation. Monetary calculation is a tool of action. It is prices, articulated through the common denominator of money, that makes economic calculation possible.

Socialism destroys the incentives of profits and losses, private ownership of property, and the benefits of competition. Without market prices to convey information to decision-makers, there would be no competition and no profit-or-loss system. Competitively determined market prices permit individuals to assess the relative values of scarce means in competing applications. Market prices are used to discover relative values of alternative uses of goods and services. The social function of the price system is to promote the use of knowledge in society by making calculations possible. Calculation is necessary for a person to determine the best allocation of his scarce resources. Rational economic calculation depends on the shorthand signals of market prices to make decisions regarding the alternative uses of scarce resources.

Looking Backward is the story of an overweening state that supplies too much. However, ironically, we never see anyone actually working, striving, pursuing, or producing anything. The novel portrays a world in which it is permissible to obtain things from a government agency but not from an individual producer or seller. Such buying and selling is thought to be antisocial. Bellamy likes the notion of conscious design, appreciates the need to organize and administer production, and calls for public ownership and management of the means of production, an industrial army, equal income, and a welfare system. He apparently condemns the market system because it does not result from deliberate design. He does not understand that something can be useful, and even be superior, even if it is not the result of the articulated rationality of central planners. If Bellamy were alive today and could see our socioeconomic conditions, he would still think he was correct and would argue that his utopia has been postponed but that it will still one day be a reality.

Chapter Three

Frank Norris's *The Octopus*

An Epic of Wheat and Railroads

The Octopus (1901) is Frank Norris's first volume in a projected trilogy of wheat that would examine many facets of the world through the movement of wheat from seed to consumption. Norris believed that a series of thematically linked novels was an excellent way of illustrating a vast philosophical and social theme. To do this, he decided to treat the subject of wheat under the three stages of production, transportation, and consumption. *The Octopus*, the first book in the planned but uncompleted trilogy, illustrates the struggles between nature, the man-made machine (the railroad), corporations, ranches, and individual human beings. The second book, *The Pit* (1902), focuses on speculation in the Chicago marketplace, and the never-written third volume, *The Wolf*, was to describe how wheat was consumed by the hungry masses in famine-stricken Europe. Unfortunately, Norris died suddenly in 1902 at the age of thirty-two. Fortunately, *The Octopus* is complete in itself.

Norris's goal was to write a particularized regional novel (i.e., *The Octopus*) that would also have national significance and that would additionally declare the unity of all life. In *The Octopus* he presents his view of a specific time and place in American history. The story reflects the California experience of economics from the Civil War until 1900, a period when the West was a new open land of promise. This masterful novel is about wheat ranchers and the railroad with the West and California as a background. At one level it is a story of conflict between one huge enterprise, the railroad, and another large one, the collective ranchers. At another level, it portrays and alternates between a philosophy of free will and morality, and one of optimistic determinism.

The Octopus is a masterpiece of structure with interweaving plots and an integrated series of dramas. It is a novel of the commonplace and concrete that is also intended to reveal great truths. This multiple story involves the lives of many secondary characters who emanate from virtually the entire spectrum of the social order and who reflect many varieties of good and evil. Full of local color, this multifarious novel is filled with vivid, distinctive characterizations and descriptions. Each well-drawn character is tested much as characters are in the ancient Greek tragedies. This work of American naturalism and brutal realism clearly portrays the harsh realities of life. The tragic incidents in the novel portray Norris's power of graphic description. The author was a magnificent exponent of realism and his novel included no heroes.

The story is based on the true-life struggle between the ranchers and the railroad which culminated in 1880 in an armed battle called the Mussel-Slough Affair (or Massacre). The land had earlier been offered to the farmers at a low future price by the railroad in the hopes that they would settle the land and improve it. After years of cultivating the land, the farmers offered to purchase the land from the railroad at the agreed-upon price, but the railroad had decided to significantly raise the price that it was asking. The government practice at that time was to award railroad companies large tracts of public land adjoining their lines as a stimulus to railroad construction. The alternate parcels had been sold to the wheat growers who then leased the railroad's vacant adjacent parcels with the option to buy them later. The ranchers worked hard and made improvements thereby increasing the value of the land. The dispute ended with an armed conflict between the agents of the Southern Pacific Railroad and the wheat farmers of Tulare County in May of 1880. All of the incidents in *The Octopus* lead up to the tragic and deadly confrontation between the settlers and the railroad agents of what Norris called the Pacific and Southwest Railroad. He chose not to use the real name—the Southern Pacific Railroad.

Norris studied hard to write *The Octopus*. Toward this purpose he went to California where he lived on a ranch. In preparation for writing the novel, he studied library materials and consulted the files of the *San Francisco Chronicle* for information on the Mussel-Slough Affair. In addition to frequenting libraries and newspaper offices, he interviewed and wrote letters to ranchers, railroad officials, and politicians and compiled notebooks filled with newspaper clippings and other information.

It is interesting that the major conflict in *The Octopus* is between upper-middle class ranch owners and upper-class railroad executives. Norris includes only a few tenant farmers and railroad workers. For the most part, the ranchers can be viewed as private capitalists who have large investments in land and equipment and who compete with the railroad's corporate capitalists for the riches of the land.

The deal regarding the purchase price of the land was made between the ranchers and the railroad prior to the story detailed in the novel. The first chapter begins with Presley traversing the countryside around the town of Bonneville in the San Joaquin Valley on his bicycle. Presley is a thirty-year-old poet who graduated with honors from an Eastern college and who went to live on the Los Muertos ranch owned by the prosperous and powerful Magnus Derrick, called the "Governor," to improve his health after a bout with tuberculosis and to write a vaguely conceived grand romantic epic poem on the spirit of the West. He desires to be a literary force. Presley provides the novel with the point of view of an outsider with a refined and educated perceptiveness. For the most part, he is an observer of the turmoil and disputes between the farmers and the railroad. He is present at every crisis and sees characters on both sides of the disputes. His point of view is not necessarily Norris's point of view—he does not speak for the author. Given Presley's background, he has a limited and biased perspective on the railroad for much of the story. Despite this, he is the novel's most prominent character.

While searching for a plot for his epic poem, Presley cycles across the countryside to neighboring ranches encountering and introducing other characters including Hooven, Harran, Dyke, Annixter, and Vanamee. The first, Hoover, is a tenant farmer on the Los Muertos ranch. He is of German origin and speaks with a thick accent. He is upset because Magnus Derrick had just told him that he was planning to farm all of Los Muertos by himself. Hoover is disturbed because the ranch hands would be let go and he does not want to lose his job. He petitions the Derricks to remain upon the ranch as Magnus's tenant.

Turning on to Derrick's land, Presley encounters Harran, Magnus Derrick's youngest son. He is a friend to Presley and is responsible for managing the day-to-day operations at Los Muertos ranch. Harran is an honest and hard-working man. Presley's bicycle ride was next stopped by Dyke, a close friend of his. Dyke is a railroad engineer and a widower who provided for his mother and little daughter. He tells Presley that he has been fired by the P. and S.W. and that he has been blacklisted from work on the other railroads. He had been a non-member of the union brotherhood who had worked during a strike. Dyke explains that all of the railroads are controlled by the P. and S.W. He goes on to explain that he has decided to go into hop farming. Dyke has saved some money and will lease a field and plant a crop.

After having a meal at a restaurant, Presley reaches his good friend Annixter's ranch house where he is reading in a hammock. He too had heard of Hooven's troubles and of Dyke's misfortune. Annixter is college-educated, holds a degree in civil engineering, and loves to read and to learn. He is the proprietor of Quien Sabe ranch. Annixter is an angry, argumentative, gruff, abrasive, and brilliant man who was bad at social relationships, especially with women. He is a maverick, cynic, and strong woman-hater. His only significant relationship with a woman had ended badly.

Presley next meets up with Vanamee, a strange, mystical, spiritual shepherd who had been away from the San Joaquin Valley for a number of years. Eighteen years ago he had been in love with a girl, Angéle Varian, who he would meet at night at the garden of the Old Mansion. She lived on a nearby seed ranch. One night Vannamee found her raped and beaten, Angéle died nine months later while giving birth to the daughter of her attacker. The baby was taken by her parents. For years the college-educated Vanamee wandered through deserts. One day he returned to San Joaquin and was met by Fr. Sarria of the Mission. Vanamee sought "the answer" and attempts to bring back Angéle with his mental conjuring. He has the ability to summon Fr. Sarria, Presley, and others with his supernatural power. The solitary Vanamee and Fr. Sarria connect the modern San Joaquin Valley with the romance of the Spanish past.

Chapter 1 ends with Presley witnessing a railroad engine ploughing its way through a flock of Vanamee's sheep which had somehow gotten through the barbed-wire fence and wandered upon the track:

> The pathos of it was beyond expression. It was a slaughter, a massacre of innocents. The iron monster had charged full into the midst, merciless, inexorable. To the right and left, all the width of the right of way, the little bodies had been flung; backs were snapped against the fence posts; brains knocked out. Caught in the barbs of the wire, wedged in, the bodies hung suspended. Under foot it was terrible. The black blood, winking in the starlight, seeped down into the clinkers between the ties with a prolonged sucking murmur . . . and abruptly Presley saw again, in his imagination, the galloping monster, the terror of steel and steam, with its single eye, cyclopean, red, shooting from horizon to horizon; but saw it now as a symbol of a vast power, huge, terrible, flinging the echo of its thunder over all the reaches of the valley, leaving blood and destruction in its path; the leviathan, with tentacles of steel clutching into the soil, the soulless Force, the iron-heated Power, the monster, the Colossus, the Octopus. (50–51)

The symbolic use of a locomotive cutting through a herd of sheep supplies emotional weight to the force that is the railroad company. Not only does the locomotive engine symbolize an unassailable malevolent and omnipotent monster driven by greed and conception, it also represents the destruction of the old order.

The following day Magnus Derrick returns to his ranch from San Francisco. A mining prospector in his younger days, Magnus is the proud and successful patriarchal leader of Los Muertos ranch. As a man of character, he represents the old-school integrity of previous generations. Referred to by others as "Governor," Magnus is the epitome of the new farmers. Annie

Payne Derrick is Magnus's wife and the mother of Lyman and Harran. A well-educated, one-time teacher of literature, she had unquestioningly followed Magnus's political and mining endeavors as well as his early ventures in ranching. But now the new order of unbounded profit-oriented ranches makes her feel uneasy. The ranchers are, for the most part, capitalists who have large sums invested in machinery and equipment (such as ploughs, seed drills, and harvesters) and who employ hundreds of workers. She witnesses Magnus and his fellow ranch-owners becoming reckless, would-be profiteers, who think in terms of the large fortune that they may earn. Magnus and his comrades are relying heavily on the current year's crop and have made huge investments in equipment and irrigation ditches.

Magnus is angered when he spots ploughs that he has purchased on a flatbed car at the train station. He is told by railroad agent, S. Behrman that regulations stipulate that they must ship all the way to San Francisco and then back to Guadalajara before he can take possession of them. It was a rule that all freighters had to travel to the terminal point and then be shipped back to its destination. Behrman explains that the railroads must be permitted to earn a fair return on their investment. The load can't stop at Bonneville, where it is consigned, but has to go up to San Francisco first at a rate of forty cents per ton and then be reshipped from San Francisco back to Bonneville at fifty-one cents per ton, the short-haul rate. Behrman tells the Derricks that he cannot change the freight regulations.

S. Behrman can be considered to be the villain in *The Octopus*. He has his hands in many businesses. He is a real estate agent, a banker who deals in mortgages, a grain speculator, a political boss, and a representative of the P. and S.W. Railroad. He performs the dirty politics for the railroad in that region. Behrman argues that freight rates are determined by economic laws when, in fact, they are determined by Behrman and the other railroad executives. His desire is to destroy the farmers, thus making his villainy something distinct from economic forces.

Harran spots Dyke who has decided to go into hops farming. Harran remarks that hops prices have been increasing but he also warns Dyke to investigate the freight rates on hops. He tells Dyke to be sure to have a clear understanding with the railroad about the rate. Dyke will later risk his life savings in hops growing when he is unofficially "promised" a freight rate of two cents per pound on his hops.

S. Behrman attributed the slaughter of the sheep by the locomotive to a hole in Annixter's fence. He visits Annixter and orders him to mend his fence. The angry Annixter tells him to "go to the devil." This occurs at the same time when the woman-hating Annixter notices that Hilma Tree is attractive. He has observed her flirting with Delaney, the worker on Annixter's ranch who was responsible for fixing the fence a week ago. The incensed Annixter fires him.

Magnus has several of the local wheat growers over to his house that evening to discuss the impending grading of the lands and the possibility of railroad rate increases. Neither Derrick, Annixter, Osterman, nor Broderson actually own all of land that they work. This is because when the P. and S.W. Railroad first came through it was given a bonus for the construction. The federal government had granted to the company the alternate sections of land on either side of the line of route for a distance of twenty miles. The growers were given rights to the other parcels. The farmers had purchased these parcels and farmed both them and, with permission, the railroad's adjacent parcels with the "understanding" that, after they were graded, the railroad would sell the land to them for about $2.50 per acre. In the beginning, deeds had not yet been issued to the railroad for their sections but the railroad stated that the land would be graded for value and offered for sale as soon as the land was legally its property.

Given this understanding, for eight years the ranchers improved the land, dug irrigation ditches, built houses, and so on. Now, after two dry years, they are about to reap a bonanza harvest. Genslinger, newspaper editor of the local paper called the *Mercury*, is sympathetic to the P. and S.W. and commented that he does not believe that the railroad would let the land go for such a low figure. He explains that both the farmers' improvements and the presence of the railroad have added value and that they should, therefore, share in the increase in the value of the land.

Annixter retorts that the railroad had agreed to sell at $2.50 per acre in the circulars and pamphlets that they disseminated. He and the other ranchers thought that they had iron-clad contracts. They pulled out the old circulars and pamphlets and noticed a number of ambiguous statements. For example, one section read: "The lands are not uniform in price, but are offered at various figures from $2.50 upward per acre. . . . Most is for rates at $2.50 and $5.00." They did not find provisions such as this to be very reassuring. It appears that the circulars and pamphlets were framed as to deceive the settlers.

Magnus Derrick had just lost a grain-rate case against the railroad. He had also heard rumors that rates for the hauling of grain are to be increased. Harran notes that S. Behrman had manipulated the entire affair but that it was Shelgrim, president of the railroad, who was behind him and who had the courts, the railroad commissioners, and the men in the senate, in his pocket. The ranchers always lose their cases.

Osterman suggests that the game to play is to buy commissioners. He thus proposes a scheme of bribery. The ethical Magnus does not want to be involved in dirty politics. He is staunch in his refusal to bribe politicians to get members sympathetic to the ranchers seated on the railroad commission. Annixter, Osterman, Broderson, and Harran Derrick disagree with Magnus and raise sufficient money to bribe the appropriate politicians. A politician is bought and he appoints a commissioner for another district (the third) who would be favorable to the ranchers of the second district. At that point the ranchers concentrate all of their efforts in putting their man in their own district (the second).

Later, Annixter becomes incensed when he reads an article in the *Mercury* claiming that the railroad will not accept $2.50 per acre. Calling to mind the explicit terms of the agreement, he dismisses the matter from his mind. He comes across milkmaid Hilma Tree, the nineteen-year-old daughter of a couple who lives on Annixter's ranch. Meaning no disrespect, he attempts to kiss her, but only manages to frighten her. Later that day, he apologizes but she does not accept his apology, says that she does not like him at all, and runs away from him.

Annixter next goes to see Ruggles, the clerk at the railroad office, to inquire about buying his land. Ruggles gives him the run-around stating that he has an indefinite option on the land, and that the railroad is not yet ready to sell, and that the price has not yet been set. Shortly thereafter, Dyke visits the railroad office and is quoted a rate of two cents a pound to ship his hops in car-load lots. A bit later, Annixter spots Dyke meeting with Behrman to mortgage his house in order to have enough money to buy the hops farm that he hopes will make his fortune. Returning home, Annixter encounters Hilma Tree who admits that she does not dislike him. She just disliked what he had tried to do.

Annixter decides to throw a party to celebrate the completion of his gigantic barn. While there, he and Hilma take a walk and dance together. At the barn dance, the fired Delaney shows up drunk and carrying a pistol. A gun is fired and Annixter clutches Hilma to protect her. Annixter and Delaney duel and Delaney is driven away. Annixter observes that Hilma is concerned about him and it is clear that they care for one another. At the ball that night a messenger arrives with letters for each of the ranchers informing them that the prices for the parcels of land will range between twenty-two dollars and thirty dollars per acre. The price for land on Magnus Derrick's ranch was fixed at twenty-seven dollars per acre.

Osterman, who has a flair for political intrigue, shouts that "organization" was needed to fight the railroad. The outraged ranchers decide to form their own group called "The League" to prevent the railroad from stealing their land and to elect railroad commissioners that are for the farmers. The enraged ranchers demand that their natural leader, the honest Magnus Derrick, join them. His wife wants him to stay out of the League's blackmail scheme. Against his better judgment, he reluctantly agrees to support them and to lead them. When he accepts the leadership of this defensive league he has tacitly committed himself to the League's fraudulent tactics. The League is devoted to fighting the case in the courts and to promoting the election of a friendly majority on the Board of Commissions who would attain a favorable revision of freight rates on wheat. The Governor does hold out for a long period against bribery and the buying of delegates but he eventually yields. Placed in a moral dilemma, Magnus compromises with his conscience and engages in corrupt practices.

Lyman Derrick, the Governor's younger son, lives in San Francisco and is involved in politics. He has aspirations of becoming governor of the state. He gets elected to the railroad commission with the help of his father and the wheat growers. They resorted to bribery to get him elected so that he can represent the interests of the league of wheat growers. The members of the League are excited because Lyman is negotiating with the railroad regarding new shipping rates. Both Lyman and another commissioner, Darrell, were pledged to an average ten per cent cut of the grain rates throughout the entire state. Lyman's father, Magnus, says that he wants fairness to the farmers in the form of lower shipping rates. When asked to suppose that a future commission might raise the rates, the Governor betrays a lapse in his character when he answers, "By then it will be too late. We will, all of us, have made our fortunes by then"(298).

In San Francisco, Lyman Derrick introduces his father, brother, and Presley to a wealthy manufacturer and shipbuilder, Cedarquist, who had owned now-closed Atlas Iron Works. He has a number of other profitable interests. He spoke of the realities of free trade and economic laws and contrasted these with art which he considered to be frivolous and superficial. Cedarquist tells Magnus that trusts exploit people and that wheat should be sent to China, rather than to Europe. He goes on to explain that trusts exploit the people because the indifferent people allow it. Toward the end of the get-together, Magnus hears a man reading a newspaper report of the judge's decision in the case of the League versus the railroad. The ruling is that the title to the lands in question belongs to the P. and S.W. that the ranchers have no title, and that their possession is wrongful. This decision implies that, because the land was the property of the railroad, it had the right to ask its lessees to pay whatever it considered to be appropriate.

Unable to contain his love for Hilma, Annixter meets with her and professes his love for her. She mentions marriage and he says that he is not the marrying kind. The deeply offended and horrified Hilma runs away when she realizes that Annixter is not looking for a wife, but rather for a mistress. She and her parents leave the ranch and move to San Francisco. Later Annixter realizes that he wants to marry her and he vows to find her.

Dyke's plight worsens when the railroad more than doubles its rate to ship hops. He discovers at the railroad office that the rates have increased from two cents per pound to five cents per pound. This angers Dyke because his profits on his bumper crop will be wiped out. In addition, he realizes that S. Behrman will also be able to foreclose on his property. He asks Behrman what his rule is and Behrman says "All-the-traffic-will-bear" (350). Dyke, the ill-fated hop farmer, has never drank much in his life but he soon frequents the saloon of Caraher, a revolutionary who promulgates tirades against capitalism and for anarchy. Dyke soon becomes an alcoholic who is strongly influenced by Caraher, an anarchist saloon-keeper who has become a passionate hater of monied power after his wife's death by the hands of Pinkerton strikebreakers. After a while, Dyke goes missing.

The rough, self-centered, intolerant Annixter attempts to fight off his love for Hilma, but he realizes his great love for her in the presence of the sprouting new wheat. At this moment he begins to transform from a ruthless, angry man to a humane and kind one. He decides to find Hilma and to persuade her to marry him. His moment of insight, revelation, growth, and conversion occurs in the presence of the just-emerging wheat, a symbolic and spiritual catalyst affirming the teleological beneficence of the universe. Annixter is to become a more thoughtful and generous man. The wheat is portrayed as the living manifestation of an evolutionary force as Annixter recognizes his love for Hilma as the wheat thrusts through the ground in the dawn light.

Presley transforms from artist to radical. After being inspired by a French painting he had seen in Cedarquist's art gallery and by seeing how the railroad was destroying the ranchers, Presley writes a poem called "The Toilers" about the exploitation of workers. He sends the poem to a San Francisco newspaper which publishes it, and it ultimately gets reprinted across the country and gains national success and attention, especially among the radicals who hailed Presley as a revolutionary new voice. Presley, a friend of the ranchers, has abandoned his plan of writing a vaguely-conceived grand romantic epic in order to portray the current plight of the oppressed farmers. He has come to view the important social issue of the day as organized wealth against the people. No longer an over-refined poet, Presley is becoming a man with a spirit of revolt and unrest. Abandoning the positive and forward-looking worldview that he was going to praise in his planned "Song of the West," his poem, "The Toilers," is a work of socialist propaganda that reflects his newly found vision of a somewhat deterministic world of conflicting forces.

The mystic and ascetic prophet, Vanamee, possesses a strange power to summon other people. He attempts to bring Angéle back with his mental appeals and, in a sense, she returns in the form of her daughter who was born at the same instant that Angéle died. The notion of life out of death is preserved by the arrival of the dead Angéle's daughter the night of the advent of the season's first wheat. During the same night that Annixter has a spiritual realization, Vanamee has a physical one. Angéle's daughter appears simultaneously with the emergence of the new wheat. While standing on the edge of a wheat field, Vanamee is overcome with mysticism and his life is reshaped. Not only can Vanamee now cope with his suffering, he has also regained the ability to find happiness. Vanamee has found his answer in the daughter of the lost Angéle.

Annixter locates Hilma in San Francisco and persuades her to become his bride. While on the train that they are taking back to the valley from San Francisco, an armed bandit dynamites and robs the train. The beaten and ruined former railroad employee and hops farmer, Dyke, is recognized to be the robber. Dyke had killed two men in the process of hijacking the train and stealing five thousand dollars in gold coins. As a result, a five-hundred dollar reward is placed on his head and a posse is formed to track him down.

The reticent Lyman Derrick meets with the wheat grower's committee (i.e., the League) to report the provisions of the proposed plan of the Railroad Commission. He says that the commission has made great advances and that the promised ten percent cut in shipping rates has been enacted. Unfortunately for the ranchers of San Joaquin Valley, the cuts are averaged across the state. Huge cuts come in areas of the state that do not even harvest wheat. There is no rate cut where the ranchers reside. He explains that the rates technically comply with the pledges of the commissioners. The ranchers are angry and feel cheated when Lyman announces that none of the reductions in shipping rates apply to them.

The farmers turn on Lyman and correctly accuse him of selling out to the railroad. The farmers had employed bribery to get him elected but he supported the railroad instead. The ranchers had resorted to bribery only to be sold out by the man whose election they bought. Instead, Lyman betrays his trust to the ranchers for railroad money. Genslinger, the local newspaper editor, later confirms that Lyman has secretly worked for the railroad for two years and that he took the ranchers' money with no intention of helping them. In fact, Lyman was the particular man that the railroad corporation wanted to be commissioner. Lyman is disowned by his father, Magnus.

The newspaper man, Genslinger, blackmails Magnus for ten thousand dollars about the deal with Lyman, who has told Genslinger about the bribery scheme. Also, the commissioners have given signed affidavits revealing Magnus Derrick's crime to the editor of the *Mercury*. Magnus pays him the money to keep him from printing the story in his paper.

Pursued by a posse of men hired by the railroad (including Delaney), Dyke arrives at Annixter's ranch. After he leaves Annixter's ranch, he steals a detached locomotive and is chased by the posse. He abandons the engine and attempts to escape to the shelter of the hills. Trapped by the posse, he tries to kill the despised S. Behrman but the gun misfires. Dyke is captured and he is sentenced to serve life behind bars in prison. The first of the rebels can fight the railroad no longer.

The railroad has hired U.S. Marshalls to threaten the ranchers to either pay the asked price for the land or to leave their farms. The P. and S.W. has been selling ranch lands to its own dummy buyers and has been bringing and wining lawsuits to evict the ranchers. The ranchers are up in the hills hunting jackrabbits and having a barbecue. The rabbit drive and the festivities are interrupted when they receive word that railroad employees, accompanied by the U.S. Marshall and his deputies, are on their way to the ranchers to remove them from their property and to put in new tenants to live there. They receive word that Annixter's farm has been taken over and all six hundred members of the League are asked to go there. Most back out and only a few ranchers head toward the farm to try to stop the takeover. The armed agents of the railroad and the ranchers face off at the irrigation ditch. Neither side wants to do battle. Unfortunately, there is a slight chance movement resulting in the brushing of, and spooking of, a horse and both sides fire. A gun battle ensues between the railroad employees and the farmers and many people die, including central figures of the story such as Harran, Derrick, Osterman, Broderson, Annixter, Hooven, and Delaney. The finally-happy Annixter leaves behind his widow, the lovely Hilma Tree. In addition, Hooven's family will have a hard time surviving and will have to take to the streets. Little people are crushed in the hopeless struggle against a great force such as the railroad.

All of the actions of the story have led up to this tragic, deadly, and distressing conflict between the ranchers and the railroad agents at the irrigation ditch. The sympathetic, but inept and doomed ranchers had formed the League in order to defend (as well as exploit) their lands. They had decided to use the weapons of their enemy, the railroad corporation, such as fraud and violence. The question remains whether or not it is legitimate (i.e., just) to use such tactics against a rights-violator such as the railroad. It can be logically argued that force can be properly used in retaliation against those who initiate its use.

Members of the League along with many others meet at the Opera House to discuss what had transpired. After several speeches by members of the League, Presley jumps to the stage and unleashes a diatribe against the evil railroad.

> They own us, these task-masters of ours; they own our homes, they own our legislatures. We cannot escape from them. There is no redress. We are told we can defeat them by the ballot box. They own the ballot box. We are told that we must look to the courts for redress; they own the courts. We know them for what they are—ruffians in politics, ruffians in finance, ruffians in law, ruffians in trade, bribers, swindlers, and tricksters. No outrage too great to daunt them, no petty larceny too small to shame them; despoiling a government treasury of a million dollars, yet picking the pockets of a farmhand of a loaf of bread. "They swindle a nation of a hundred million and call it Financing; they levy a blackmail and call it Commerce; they corrupt a legislature and call it Politics; they bribe a judge and call it Law; they hire blacklegs to carry out their plans and call it Organization; they prostitute the honor of a State and call it Competition." (551)

Magnus Derrick arrives to address the crowd gathered at the Bonneville Opera House. As he begins to speak he is cut off by the shout of a man calling him a briber. People begin passing around copies of the newspaper, the *Mercury*, containing a detailed account of Magnus Derrick's role in the fraudulent election of two commissioners. After agreeing not to print the story for ten thousand dollars, Genslinger prints the information about the bribes. Under pressure from the crowd, Magnus admits to bribing the delegates. His reputation has been ruined. His son, Harran, had died and his other son, Lyman, was worse than dead. The scorned Magnus will later have his property taken over by S. Behrman who evicts all of the ranchers who had survived the gunfight. At one point, Behrman hires Magnus to work for him. By the end of the story, Annie Payne Derrick is taking care of her defeated, half-insane, penniless husband while she teaches literature at a seminary. She had warned her now-broken husband to keep out of the blackmail scheme, but the loyal woman still stands by him in the end.

Presley, distressed and tormented by the deaths of his friends, Dyke's imprisonment, and Magnus's fall, throws a bomb through the dining room window of S. Behrman's home. The room is wrecked but by a miracle, S. Behrman emerges unscathed. After this incident, Presley viewed himself as a failure. His attempt to write a great epic, his efforts to help people, and even his attempt to destroy his enemy, had all been ineffective. He is confused by the events and the results of these events.

Presley journeys to San Francisco to confront Shelgrim, the president of the railroad, and discovers that he is not an evil man. In fact, Presley finds the president of the P. and S.W. Railroad to be a compassionate person. When a manager recommends firing an alcoholic employee to Shelgrim, he decides to nearly double the man's salary instead. The cultured Shelgrim has read Presley's poem, "The Toilers," and he has viewed the French painting that inspired it. The sentimental art critic and railroad president says that he prefers the picture to the poem. He observes that the picture is by a master and thus leaves nothing more to be said. He tells Presley that he might as well have said nothing. Shelgrim would rather listen to what the great French painter has to say, than to what Presley has to say about what the painter has already said. Not only does Shelgrim have intelligent opinions about painting and poetry, he also holds a modest philosophy with respect to an individual's place in the grand scheme of things. In this matter he lectures Presley on the forces of determinism and other factors beyond the control of any one person.

Shelgrim's naturalistic view is that human beings are not to blame for the tragedy of other people. Rather, conditions or forces (such as supply and demand) are to blame. The fatalistic Shelgrim contends that the natural order of things is what is responsible. He explains that, although powerful individuals such as Behrman and himself are blamed for the exploitation and poverty of others, they are not really in control but are merely pawns in the game. His perspective is that the wheat will grow and the trains will move, no matter what happens to individual people. He tells Presley that the suffering of the wheat farmers is out of his control and that it is not his choice. Whether or not they suffer is irrelevant. In either case, the wheat will grow, the trains will move the wheat, and the wheat will be consumed.

Shelgrim seems to retreat behind impersonal forces, conditions, and the laws of supply and demand. He says to Presley:

> Try to believe this—to begin with—*that Railroads build themselves*. Where there is a demand sooner or later there will be a supply. Mr. Derrick, does he grow his wheat? The Wheat grows itself. What does he count for? Does he supply the force? What do I count for? Do I build the Railroad? You are dealing with forces, young man when you speak of Wheat and the Railroads, not with men. There is the Wheat, the supply. It must be carried to feed the People. There is the demand. The Wheat is one force, the Railroad, another, and there is the law that governs them—supply and demand. Men have only little to do in the whole business. Complications may arise, conditions that bear hard on the individual—crush him maybe—*but the Wheat will be carried to feed the people* as inevitably as it will grow. If you want to fasten the blame of the affair at Los Muertos on any one person, you will make a mistake. Blame conditions, not men. (576)

This new idea puzzles Presley. He thinks to himself:

> Was no one then to blame for the horror at the irrigating ditch? Forces, conditions, laws of supply and demand—were these then the enemies, after all? Not enemies; there was no malevolence in Nature. Colossal indifference only, a vast trend toward appointed goals. Nature was, then, a gigantic engine, a vast cyclopean power, huge, terrible, a leviathan with a heart of steel, knowing no compunction, no forgiveness, no tolerance; crushing out the human atom standing in its way, with nirvanic calm, the agony of destruction sending never a jar, never the faintest tremour through all that prodigious mechanism of wheels and cogs. (576–77)

Presley does not appear to be totally satisfied with Shelgrim's explanation of cause and effect. Although Shelgrim says to blame conditions rather than men, he has made decisions to cut wages and employees and has resorted to corruption, bribery, extortion, contract breaking, tampering with laws, conspiracy, and so on. Isn't it true a person can freely choose to take actions that bring about results? Presley seems to be caught between the idea of forces compelling behavior and the notion of freedom of the will. On one hand, he sees the railroad, as well as the wheat, as gigantic, impersonally propelled forces. On the other hand, he sees people who freely make decisions that affect forces and other people. Nature can be creative or destructive depending on men's ability to comprehend and adjust their actions to nature's unchangeable laws. In a way, *The Octopus* is a story about a conflict between the natural law and individuals who try to manipulate or obstruct it for their own purposes. All entities, including man, are determined by universal natural laws to exist and to act in a given definite and fixed manner. It follows that men are not free in the sense of being able to do anything whatsoever. This may help to explain the paradox that Presley is encountering.

Mrs. Hooven and her two daughters, Minna and Hilda, had gone to San Francisco after the death of the German farmer, Hooven. When Minna returns to the lodging house, after a day's unsuccessful efforts to find employment, she was told that her mother and Hilda had been arrested and are gone. The landlady had lost the note that was to be given to Minna. For many days Minna searched frantically for them and for employment. Facing starvation, the once sweet and caring girl is driven to prostitution by her poverty. One afternoon, Presley comes face to face with Minna. She tells him that she had become separated from her mother and her sister. He asks how she was doing and she cried, "Oh, I've gone to hell. It was either that or starvation" (588).

The shaken Presley is sick with the dread of all that has happened. Thinking of himself only with loathing, he dresses to keep his engagement to dine with Cedarquists. Mrs. Cedarquist informs him that they are to dine with the Gerards. Mr. Gerard is one of the vice-presidents of the railroad that Presley despises. Presley is perplexed as he shares a most lavish feast with some of the richest people in society. Presley finds no enjoyment in the occasion as his thoughts keep going back to Los Muertos and the irrigating ditch at Hooven's where many of his friends had perished.

At this point of the novel, the author juxtaposes scenes of the opulent dinner in the home of a vice-president of the P. and S.W. Railroad with scenes of Hooven's widow and daughter stalking and starving on the streets of the city. Mrs. Gerard, the wife of the railroad vice-president, displays her disinterest in the plight of the local farmers. Instead, inspired by Presley's poem, she decides to found a relief organization that will send wheat to India. It is ironic that her philanthropy comes at the expense of the local starving and suffering wheat farmers. At the moment the banquet ends Mrs. Hooven is pronounced dead. She dies from starvation and fatigue with her little daughter, Hilda, lying by her side. While she had struggled through her last evening, Presley had been dining with two of San Francisco's wealthiest families.

The Los Muertos ranch, under its new owner, S. Behrman, had never experienced a more successful growing season—it was a "bonanza." He had recently made a deal with an Indian Famine Relief Committee that the wealthy women of San Francisco had organized for an entire shipload of wheat to be sent to the starving people of India. Behrman has chartered the "Swanhilda" to deliver the wheat.

Presley decides to go to India for his health and makes his rounds to say goodbye to his friends. He sees Magnus and his wife, Annixter's widow Hilma, and Mrs. Dyke and Sidney. While talking with Hilma his heart goes out to her. He says that he wants to be her friend and does not want to see her life wasted. She says that she hopes he will still be that when, and if, he returns.

As Presley reaches the highest crest of the hills by Broderson's Creek he looks out over the gigantic sweep of the San Joaquin and there comes to him a strong and true sense of the significance of the enigma of growth. For one moment he seems to brush the explanation of existence arriving at a cosmological conclusion.

> Vanamee had said that there was no death. But for one second Presley could go one step further. Men were naught, death was naught, life was naught; FORCE only existed—FORCE that brought men into the world, FORCE that crowded them out of it to make way for succeeding generations, FORCE that made the wheat grow, FORCE that governed it from the soil to give place to the succeeding crop. It was the mystery of creation, the stupendous miracle of re-creation; the vast rhythm of the seasons, measured, alternative, the sun and the stars keeping time as the eternal supply of reproduction swung in it tremendous cadences like the colossal pendulum of an almighty machine—primordial energy flung out from the hand of the Lord God himself, immortal, calm, infinitely strong. (634)

As Presley stands looking down upon the great valley, he becomes aware of a figure of a man approaching in the distance. The man is Vanamee, happy because his dead Angéle had returned to him in the form of her daughter. They talk for hours, and the "prophet" Vanamee reveals to Presley the truth he has learned from nature.

> Death and grief are little things. . . . They are transient. Life must be before death, and joy before grief. Else there are no such things as death or grief. . . . There is only life and the suppression of life that we, foolishly, say is death. "Suppression," I say, not extinction. Life never departs. Life simply *is*. For certain seasons, it is hidden in the dark, but is that death, extinction, annihilation? I take it, thank God, that it is not. Does the grain of what hidden for certain seasons in the dark, die? The grain we think is dead *resumes again*; but how? So are life. Death is only real for all the detritus of the world, for all the sorrow, for all the injustice, for all the grief. Presley, the good never dies; evil dies, cruelty, oppression, selfishness, greed—these die; but nobility, but love, but sacrifice, but generosity, but truth, . . . these live forever, these are eternal. . . . What is it that remains after all is over, after the dead are buried and the hearts are broken? Look at it all from the vast height of humanity—"the greatest good to the greatest numbers." What remains? Men perish, men are corrupted, hearts are sent asunder, but what remains untouched, unassailable, undefiled? Try to find that, not only in this, but in every crisis of the world's

> life, and you will find, if your view is large enough, that it is *not* evil, but good,
> that in the end remains. . . . We should probably never meet again . . . but if
> these are the last words I ever speak to you, listen to them, and remember
> them, because I know I speak the truth. Evil is short-lived. Never judge of the
> whole round of life by the mere segment you can see. The whole is, in the end,
> perfect. (635–36)

The sentence, "Evil is short-lived" implies that there is a greater purpose for everything. The cycle will continue, no matter what, toward the greater good. Vanamee suggests that there is a natural dynamism when he presents nature as a living, conscious, benign force. His idea of a spiritual connection with nature suggests that there is an orderly determinism. Vanamee points Presley toward a "larger view" in which nature is not indifferent, but is, instead, beneficent and a manifestation of divine design. From this perspective, the war between the ranchers and the railroad was simply a stage in the progress toward the "good." Vanamee explains that if one views the disaster from the vast height of nature, then it is not evil, but rather it is good. His perspective is one of "cosmic optimism." Although individual men can be temporarily defeated by political and economic forces, natural immutable forces—as symbolized by the wheat—will ultimately bring about the greatest good for the greatest number. People get fed by the wheat despite social and personal evils such as unjust freight rates, corrupt politicians, and broken promises.

S. Behrman goes to the Swanhilda to inspect his cargo of wheat. Peering into the hold of the ship he gets his foot entangled in a coil of rope and falls headfirst in the wheat vat. In a horrific scene, Behrman suffocates to death under an avalanche of wheat after tripping and falling into the open hatch. The would-be "Master of the Wheat" is smothered by the wheat that he so desperately desired.

While waiting to depart for India on the Swanhilda, Presley goes to Cedarquist's office to say good-bye. They discuss how Lyman Derrick has entered the new politics with a vengeance and how he is the Republican nominee for governor of California. Cedarquist informs Presley that his new venture, organizing a line of clipper ships for Pacific and Oriental trade, is prospering.

While on the ship the terrible drama through which Presley had lived rises again in his memory. He saw it all and now the drama was over. The fight between the ranchers and the railroad had come to its dreadful close. The railroad has prevailed. He wonders if there is no hope and if the good is destined to be overthrown and evil to prevail.

Then suddenly Vanamee's words came back to his mind. What was the larger view, what contributed the greatest good to the greatest numbers? What was the full round of the circle whose segment only he beheld? In the end, the ultimate, final end of all, what was left? Yes, good issued from the crisis, untouched, unassailable, undefiled . . .

> Falseness dies; injustice and oppression in the end of everything fade and vanish away. Greed, cruelty, selfishness, and inhumanity are short-lived; the individual suffers, but the race goes on. . . . The larger view always and through all shame, all wickedness, discovers the Truth that will, in the end, prevail, and all things, surely, inevitably, restlessly work together for good. (651–52)

Throughout the novel, Presley has evolved toward his ultimate perception of Truth. He has developed a moral perspective on a cosmic or universal level. Presley, like Annixter and Vanamee, has undergone a transformation in his beliefs and values stemming from an understanding of the process of growth. Presley has come to recognize the insignificance of the individual in comparison to the colossal and benevolent forces of nature. He now concludes that all things inevitably work together for the good. Presley's moral development has gone through various stages. He begins the story as an aspiring, and pretending to be, literary force. Presley next becomes a social activist. Finally, in the end, he accepts Vanamee's insights as an unambiguous and true cosmological vision.

Earlier in the novel, Presley had viewed nature as an amoral force, but at the story's end he sees it as a dominant and triumphant good. Translating the supernatural into the natural, the wheat serves as a symbol and manifestation of divine force, energy, and destiny. This spiritual connection with nature bespeaks of an orderly determinism. Throughout the story, Presley discovers the spirituality of the universe. He learns that the wheat and its processes embody an immanent God and a moral order of things.

Presley's pantheistic revelation enables him to cope with the existence of violent and evil forces in the world. There is no ontological hierarchy for the pantheist. For him, the transcendent world does not exist. For example, Spinoza, the archetype pantheist philosopher, proclaims there is no world except the existing one. He maintains that all things in the universe are modifications of the same divine substance and are determined by universal natural laws to exist and to act in a given definite and fixed manner. Man is modification (or mode) of the unique, infinite substance that is God or Nature. Every single mode is caused by God's infinite power that necessarily creates the whole of nature. Human beings are bound by the same natural laws as are all other segments of the universe. According to Spinoza, primacy of self-interest is a basic law of human nature. He says that human beings share a common drive for self-preservation and seek to maintain the power of their being.

Spinoza says that there is no freedom if we understand freedom to be the power of performing an action without cause or reason. Everything, including man, is bound by laws of nature and other natural constraints. Man functions as an individual relative to other entities, and, at the same time, he is part of the universe. How can freedom exist in a pantheistic "deterministic" universe? According to Spinoza's definition of freedom, a thing is said to be free which exists by the mere necessity of its own nature and is determined in its actions by itself alone. Real freedom thus means acting according to the necessary nature of man. If morality, ethics, and virtue are possible, then there must be a mode in which determinism is combined with freedom. It is in a person's interest to be moral and virtuous. Virtue involves the development of one's individuality. The attainment of virtue is a legitimate end because it is an action congruent with the notion of a man striving to persist in his own being.

Spinoza concludes that people live in a universe determined by a type of relative necessity in the circumstances and not one of absolute necessity. Man's necessary nature (i.e., to persist in his own being) is not absolutely necessary. Instead, it is possible, contingent, and voluntarily acquired depending upon an effective person's chosen activities. Freedom means the existence of options and the ability to make value judgments and decisions. To behave virtuously is to act, live, and preserve one's being in accordance with reason and on the basis of what is in our own interest and what is useful to us. To be free is to be guided by the law of one's own nature which is never inconsistent with the law of another's nature. We are free when the causes of our action are internal to us and we are unfree when those causes are external to us. Spinoza teaches that the role of the state must be deduced from the common nature of man. He thus sees the real purpose of the state as freedom—what we would call the protection of individual's natural rights.

Such a pantheistic perspective can explain Presley's acceptance of the dichotomy of optimistic determinism on the cosmic level and free will on the personal level. The ranchers, railroad executives, and politicians all have free will and have the ability to make moral or immoral decisions. Men can act for good or for evil. This view can be coupled with Vanamee's declaration that evil is short-lived and that, in the end, the good is inevitable and the whole is perfect.

At the end of the book Vanamee and Presley view God as a divine utilitarian immanent in a process that provides the greatest good for the greatest number. Evil is a transient and minor factor within the larger cosmic progression toward the good. This worldview of evolutionary theism or evolutionary naturalism attempts to explain the paradoxical emergence of good out of evil.

The idea of force appears repeatedly in *The Octopus*. For example, toward the end of the novel, Presley comes to believe that there is a universal force inherent in the life processes of both human and nonhuman existence. This notion of force is found in the writings of Herbert Spencer, the most important figure in the philosophy of evolution in the mid-to-late nineteenth century. Spencer's theory of progress was based on a combination of physics and biology. Arguing from the law of the conservation of energy, Spencer maintained that the basic constituent of the universe was force. For him, evolution was the universal process of change caused by the persistence and omnipresence of force. He offered a comprehensive worldview uniting everything in nature under the ideas of force and evolution. His philosophical system was to apply to every aspect of reality, living or non-living. His model was a fully deterministic and mechanical one. Spencer was not relig-ious, but many of his readers saw the opportunity to identify force with divine energy that is immanent in nature and in the benevolent laws and process of nature.

Spencer explained that force operates in all of the various aspects of reality resulting in a steady and necessary progress. His evolutionary synthe-sis held that progress was from the simple, undifferentiated, and homogenous toward greater distinctiveness, individuality, heterogeneity, and complexity. This occurs in all areas and levels of reality. Underpinning many of Spen-cer's ideas is the belief in persistence of force.

Spencer went on to explain that persistence of force is a principle of nature that cannot be produced artificially by the state. It follows that the best government is the one that interferes least in the lives of its citizens. Spencer is against government interference in the lives of persons. State interference with natural evolutionary processes is immoral and dangerous. In the natural evolutionary process the individual is integrated by adaptation in accordance with the functions he is required to execute. Spencer's optimal development path for society is one where people's conduct is regulated primarily by competitive market forces and by ethical principles. For Spencer, the evolu-tionary process is progressive in a moral sense. This progress is conditional. Moral sentiments are subject to evolutionary progress if suitable conditions are sustained. He says that only when the individual is free to live under the law of equal freedom can social and moral evolution reach its highest level. Spencer explains that a free society of mutual noninterference among its members is necessary in order to develop the moral sentiments.

I do not know whether or not the author, Frank Norris, studied the writ-ings of Spinoza and/or Spencer, but it is evident that many ideas and prem-ises found in *The Octopus* can be observed in their works and in the writings of their popularizers. Norris combines some of their ideas with the doctrine of utilitarianism to develop a worldview of evolutionary theism as espoused by his characters, Vanamee and Presley.

Much of *The Octopus* identifies the corporation as a monster in the form of a railroad that destroys the farmers, their homes, and their free lives. Within this framework, the corporation is viewed as evil. This view, called corporate capitalism, describes a marketplace characterized by the dominance of hierarchical, bureaucratic corporations. Corporate capitalism has been criticized for the power corporations have over government policy and individuals. In *The Octopus* the railroad corporation is disparaged for violating verbal contracts, bribing government officials, unjustly discharging employees, blacklisting faithful employees, blackmailing individuals, and exploiting a variety of parties.

Having observed the above, the novel also illustrates the moral culpability of individual railroad executives and other employees, farmers, and politicians. All of these individuals have free will and many of them decide to engage in what today we would call "crony capitalism." Under crony capitalism, government bestows a variety of principles that would be unattainable in a free market. In a mixed economy "success" in business depends on close relationships between individuals in business and government officials.

It is the entry of the state into the business realm that leads to favoritism and unfair advantages. When a failed or faltering business is rescued by a government bailout, it is no longer a business. Likewise, when a businessman obtains his results outside the market framework by receiving special privileges granted by the government, he forfeits his status as a businessman. Sometimes businesses lobby government for special privileges such as bailouts, subsidies, price supports, resource privileges, grants of monopoly, trade protection, loan guarantees, and so on. *The Octopus* provides many examples of crony capitalism in operation.

A close reading of *The Octopus* teaches that a proper government should have no economic favors to convey. It follows that the proper role of government is only to protect man's natural rights through the use of force, but only in response, and only against those who initiate its use. By permitting and protecting free market transactions, free-market capitalism allows commerce to develop. In order to provide the maximum self-determination for each person, the state should be limited to maintaining justice, police, and defense, and to protecting life, liberty, and property. There is a huge difference between the free market, which is based on freedom and competition and crony capitalism, which is based on privilege. A moral business would succeed or fail on its own without any government assistance. A moral businessman profits only if he satisfies the needs of people by offering better products or services or at a lower price than do others.

Chapter Four

The Financier

Theodore Dreiser's Portrait of a Darwinian Businessman

The Financier (1912) is the first book in Theodore Dreiser's "trilogy of desire" novels that also includes *The Titan* (1914) and the unfinished *The Stoic*, begun in the 1920s and published in 1945. This "trilogy of desire" is centered around financial capitalism and the life and traits of Frank Algernon Cowperwood, Dreiser's semi-fictional financier of the Civil War and post-Civil War eras. *The Financier* can be viewed as a celebration of Nietzsche's superman.

The world of finance had captured Dreiser's imagination. As a result, he decided to examine the financial world and to detail the state of business in the nineteenth century. Dreiser chose financier Charles Tyson Yerkes as the prototype financier for his novel. The life of the fictional Frank Cowperwood closely parallels Yerkes's personal history and the political and economic conditions in which he flourished. Uncompromising in its realism, *The Financier* chronicles Cowperwood's rise to success, downfall, and return to wealth and power. The novel both details a series of dubious financial deals and pays tribute to the historical development of financial capitalism. The novel follows the protagonist as he sells soap as a lad, works as a bookkeeper at a grain commission house, establishes a brokerage business, marries an older woman, begins acquiring a great fortune by financing a city streetcar system, makes money while involved with corrupt politicians, finds a younger mistress, uses subtle innovative but illegal maneuvers to enhance his wealth, is caught and made a scapegoat because of his questionable transactions, serves time in prison, and reemerges to regain his fortune.

The Financier is a departure from previous business novels which tended to be moralistic and polemical. Unlike the novels of William Dean Howells,

Frank Norris, Robert Herrick, Upton Sinclair, and others, Dreiser's goal is to paint an ethically neutral portrait of Frank Cowperwood. The author presents the amoral characteristics and actions that permit Cowperwood to thrive in the business world without making any explicit moral evaluations or comments on his business practices. Dreiser reports what occurs and allows the reader to formulate his own conclusions.

Frank Cowperwood was born in Philadelphia in 1837. The novel begins when Frank is ten years old. He was the oldest of three brothers and a sister and had a loving family. His father, Henry Worthington Cowperwood, was a banker who taught young Frank about the world of finance. Henry was a reliable, respectable, and respected banker who began as a teller and ultimately advanced to be bank president. His career was based on traditional virtues rather than on shrewdness and power. The conservative and patient Henry steadily moved up within the bank for which he worked. Over the years, Frank judges his father to be weak and unimaginative and he disapproves of his conservative banking practices. Frank's mother was a gentle, quiet, meek, and religious woman who cared greatly for her family.

As a boy, Frank was consumed by the question of how life was organized. Two incidents helped him to answer this question. The first involved a fight that he had with a gang leader in his neighborhood. He learned the value of pragmatism when he used the silver ring on his hand to deliver a crushing blow to the bully McGlathey's jaw. The second occasion was when he observed a lobster and a squid together in a large fish display tank. He observed the unequal encounter between the two. The squid had no weapon and no way of killing the lobster. However, the lobster had both protection and a weapon. The outcome of the battle was inevitable as the lobster would consistently snip off small pieces of the squid with its claws. The lobster devoured the squid bit by bit, gradually and relentlessly destroying the weaker opponent. This symbolic passage at the beginning of the novel showed young Frank that the strong survive over the weak.

The animal imagery of the fish tank parable taught Frank that the powerful feeds on its prey and that the only operative law in the universe is the law of nature, or better yet, the law of the jungle. Frank reasoned that human society is an extension of the jungle and that men lived on other men. As a Social Darwinist, he saw life as essentially a battle between the strong and the weak. He knows to always be the lobster and to never be the squid.

Frank was a clever and industrious boy who exhibited an early aptitude for business. He conducted his first business transaction at age thirteen when he used his pocket money to buy seven cases of Castille Soap at an auction for thirty-two dollars and quickly sold it to a local grocer for sixty-two dollars. In order to participate in the transaction, he relied on his father's respected position as a reference. Frank went on to diversify his business ventures as a young man. He sold subscriptions to a boy's paper, sold a new type of ice skate, and organized the boys in his neighborhood into a group so that they could buy their summer straw hats at reduced prices. He was viewed as skillful, energetic, and defiant, and as having common sense and a passion for finance and economics. Frank was also indifferent to anything that did not immediately benefit him.

Frank attended Central High School and his classmates considered him to be a born leader. He was unimpressed with the curriculum of Philadelphia's public schools and quit school at age seventeen to work on the sugar docks in Philadelphia as an assistant weigher for his uncle, Seneca Davis. Seneca was the brother of Frank's mother and had been a sugar cane planter and rancher in Cuba. Uncle Seneca took a liking to Frank and was instrumental in advancing Frank into the world of business.

Seneca helped Frank to gain a clerk/bookkeeper position with Waterman and Company, a grain and commissions business. Working without pay for the first year, Frank worked hard and became the company's most efficient and attentive clerk and head bookkeeper. At the end of the year, he was rewarded with a Christmas bonus of five hundred dollars and was offered a position that paid thirty dollars per week. It was clear that Frank had the natural ability to interpret financial information. While at Waterman and Company, Cowperwood had observed and mastered the routine transactions of commodities traders.

At age eighteen, Frank took a position with Tighe and Company, bankers and brokers, to work as a floor man. He learned from Edward Tighe that Pennsylvanians never pay for anything that they can issue bonds for instead. He also learned that such bonds are rarely paid on time but that when they were paid, the money would first go to the treasurer's friends and people with political clout.

Cowperwood was an excellent worker for Tighe and Company and, as a result, the company bought him a seat on the exchange. Frank saw himself as being simply an agent or tool that was being used by the company. He reasoned that a real man was not a tool but one who used tools to create and to lead. He vowed to never again be a tool for others.

When Tighe asked Frank to be a partner, he turned the offer down because he wanted to develop his own note brokerage business. His Uncle Seneca had died, leaving him an inheritance of fifteen thousand dollars which he used to establish his own brokerage house at No. 64 South Third Street at twenty-one years of age. Frank was the sole employee of Cowperwood and Company but he thought that the name would give the appearance of being an established firm.

While working for Tighe and Company Frank had met Alfred and Lillian Semple. Mr. Semple was a shoe store owner and a client of Tighe and Company. Cowperwood is attracted to Mrs. Semple, who is five years his senior. Although he was not eager for her money, he was falling in love with

Lillian, who stood to inherit a good deal of money. After Alfred Semple dies unexpectedly, Frank pursues the beautiful older woman and, at age twenty-one, he marries her. Cowperwood was a young man of intelligence and force who was attracted to and marries an older and more experienced woman. They had a son and a daughter.

Cowperwood thought only about business and himself, and dismissed anything unrelated to his business and whatever did not immediately profit him. He was unconcerned with issues such as the Civil War, slavery, secession, North versus South, and so on. He lusts after money, power, and the love of women and he associates power with beauty. The morally aloof Cowperwood is an anti-intellectual doer with great rational powers who is committed to the aggressive pursuit of wealth and power by any means necessary. He begins to amass an immense business empire even before he begins investing illegally in street railway securities. At age twenty-two, he had bought his first legitimate interest in a street railway in Philadelphia. Cowperwood had understood early that city streetcar lines needed to be merged into a united urban transit system. He found ways to acquire controlling shares of Philadelphia's streetcar system essential to the post-Civil War boom.

Knowing that money was power, Cowperwood surrounded himself with wealthy and influential people. He trusted no one except his father. As he grew rich, Frank began to appreciate the finer things of life and decorated his house with fine paintings, rare pieces of art, sculptures, tapestries, etc. As Cowperwood becomes wealthy, he and Lillian progressively move up the social ladder.

Pennsylvania had a system where state and city officials along with bankers and brokers, could easily make money for themselves. No interest was paid to the state or city when state and city funds were deposited into banks or brokerage houses. As a result, the money could be invested as bankers, brokers, and government officials could use the money at no cost. Philadelphia's elite could use their positions of power to obtain interest-free loans from state and city tax funds, invest the money in safe but profitable investments, and return the principal to the city treasury after appropriating the earnings. This arrangement resulted in bankers pocketing interest, politicians receiving kickbacks, and brokers garnering commissions.

Frank wanted to be part of the above scheme. In July of 1861 he took steps toward his entrance into this racket when he made money on government bonds used to finance the Civil War. At age twenty-seven, Cowperwood met with Edward Butler, a contractor, and expressed interest in bidding for five million dollars of state issued bonds. He only actually wanted to invest in one million dollars of bonds, but he wanted to gain the prestige of having made a larger bid. Butler decided to help the confident and aggressive Cowperwood who did well in this transaction. In post-Civil War Philadelphia, businessmen were limited because of the scarcity of investment capital and Cowperwood was about to find ways to gain the investment capital that he needed by using state and city funds along with local politicians.

Not only did Cowperwood meet Butler through his brokerage business, he also met and became involved with George Stener (city treasurer), Mark Simpson (state senator), Henry Moldenhauer (coal dealer and investor), and Edward Strobik (president of the Philadelphia city council). These men with political standing saw Frank as a person who could invest public funds for them at considerable interest rates. The pragmatic and shrewd Cowperwood was able to further his own plans to control the streetcar lines by earning a commission and more by investing the politician's loans at higher interest rates than the rates that he had guaranteed to them.

Cowperwood schemed with Butler to acquire a larger share of the streetcar system. The two families became close and frequently entertained one another. Frank became attracted to the daughter of the man instrumental to the rise of his success. Aileen Butler was young, beautiful, energetic, and outspoken, and the daughter of his business partner. An illicit love affair began and the two would meet at a home that Cowperwood maintained for their clandestine affair, keeping it secret from her father.

Lillian had become less attractive and exciting to Frank who viewed her as passive and as not being very intelligent. Dreiser describes the couple as being "temperamentally incompatible." Frank tires of Lillian, who ages quickly and loses her beauty and her hold on him. He grew unhappy with his marriage as he saw his wife to be inferior to the young and beautiful Aileen in so many ways. He found that he and Aileen were bound by a passion for one another and by a common lust for money and possessions. Aileen Butler is described as having a "definite force personality." She possesses animal strength and beauty. The two fall in love when he is twenty-nine and she is nineteen.

Cowperwood puts to his own use and extends the corrupt practices of city government officials. He assumes that wide arrays of illegal trading practices are "legitimate" if the trader's subtlety permits him to avoid being caught and prosecuted. With a sense of entitlement, Frank finds ways to get around legal restrictions in order to use city monies for personal use. He learns to "embezzle" funds with impunity to buy streetcar stock using leverage. He begins to use Philadelphia's stock in railroads as collateral against large loans that he could use the proceeds of in order to advance his own financial empire.

Cowperwood's dealings with Butler, Mollenhauer, and Simpson had led him into many working illegal arrangements with city treasurer George Stener. Stener enlisted Frank's involvement in many shady transactions. The two found that they could manipulate public funds and make them both huge profits. They found that money that was deposited in one place could constructively be used in other places concurrently to make money for themselves. Such manipulation gave them the effective purchasing power of multiples of the original amounts deposited.

Cowperwood's shady deals included pyramid schemes and kiting. He would pay off each loan as it came due with other borrowed funds. Frank had Stener rubber stamp loans and they shared the earnings of the invested funds. Cowperwood had learned early in life that a man could best serve his own self-interest by appealing to the self-interest of others.

On October 7, 1871, disaster hits far away from Philadelphia when the Great Chicago Fire burns the commercial district to the ground, causing an immediate and widespread panic in the business world. Banks and insurance companies needed cash and the stock market crashed as the prices of stocks and bonds plummeted. Many insurance companies closed their doors causing losses to manufacturers and wholesalers. Banks called in their loans and investors in Cowperwood's brokerage house clamored to remove money from their funds. With the drop in the market, he could not recover the money that he illegally acquired from Stener. Frank is unable to produce, and needed his friends to bail him out as he had failed to keep sufficient money on reserve or make alternate plans in the event of such an occurrence.

Finding out that Stener was out of town and unable to be reached, Cowperwood turned to Mr. Butler for help by explaining his dire situation and unscrupulous dealings. Unfortunately for Frank, Butler had discovered his affair with Aileen and he refused to help him. Butler had received a letter from one of Aileen's schoolmates exposing the affair. Butler had also hired a private investigator who confronted the couple. Butler felt betrayed, both as an outraged parent and as one of Cowperwood's earliest supporters. The enraged father was determined to use all of his political clout against Frank. Despite this, the confident and arrogant Cowperwood thought that he was still in control and that he could get out of the situation. He thought that he was infallible.

When Stener returns, he finds out that his dubious dealings have been brought to light, and the political elite forbid him to help Cowperwood. When Stener refuses to help him, Cowperwood talks Stener's assistant into signing off on a loan without his boss's permission. This is found out and Frank is ultimately tried in court.

The politically powerful Butler wanted Cowperwood to be exposed and destroyed, so he influenced the political coalition to make Frank the scapegoat. Butler, Mollenhauer, Simpson, and others were in a similar predicament because they had also taken loans from the city for their personal gain. They needed someone to blame and to cover up their own indiscretions. They had Stener's secretary manufacture letters that implicated both Cowperwood and Stener while removing any wrongdoing by themselves.

Cowperwood and Stener were betrayed by the political machine and made scapegoats by others who did similar things but did not get caught.

Both are accused and tried for embezzlement and larceny. They are found guilty and Frank is sentenced to serve four years and three months in prison. Although he was tried and convicted, Cowperwood refused to turn state's evidence against Butler, Simpson, and Mollenhauer. Frank's devastated father, Henry, resigns from his position at his bank. Throughout the novel, Frank attempts to shield his mother from anything unpleasant, but he can't protect her from the shame of his imprisonment.

Cowperwood appealed and was released for two months while the appeal process was going on. During this time he appointed an individual to act on his financial behalf and to retain his seat on the exchange. Frank felt no remorse and was matter of fact about the whole situation—he just happened to get caught. Most people realized that he was not exceptional with respect to his corruption. Even those who convict him are essentially in accord with his Darwinian view of life.

Cowperwood lost his appeal and began serving his sentence. He went to prison and made the best of it. Frank would get to meet occasionally with Aileen. He was a model prisoner who made friends with the guards. The warden took a liking to him and gave him many privileges. It was apparent that Cowperwood had the ability to become whatever people needed him to be without changing his true identity. He had the ability to mask his true nature and interests.

Cowperwood is pardoned and released after thirteen months of imprisonment upon petition to the governor by various financiers and brokers. The timing of his release could be attributed to the death of Edward Butler, who could no longer appeal Frank's release. Butler had relished in having played a key part in Cowperwood's ruination. After he is pardoned, he divorces Lillian, marries Aileen, and starts over. Cowperwood is not broken or ashamed by his imprisonment which he assumes was merely a matter of bad luck. He is unshaken by his prison term and launches his career anew.

Frank resumed his duties with Wingate and Company and six months after his release he has a seat on the stock exchange representing that company. He had been released in time for the crash of Jay Cooke and Company on September 18, 1873. The banking house of Jay Cooke closes down and a panic ensues. Frank sells high and buys low, thus becoming rich again. He and his brother, under the appearance of Wingate and Company, sold and then bought back at significantly lower prices. He makes a fortune by selling short. By exploiting the great panic of 1873, Frank recovers his fortune and triumphs over his rivals who had attempted to ruin him. At the end of the novel, Frank and Aileen move to Chicago where he opens Frank A. Cowperwood, a grain business. After recouping his fortune, he and his wife leave Philadelphia to begin a new life and to pursue new adventures in Chicago.

Dreiser's naturalistic novel again employs animal imagery at the end of the novel as it did at the outset when young Frank identified with the lobster.

In a symbolic passage at the novel's conclusion, the author identifies Cowperwood with the Black Grouper, a subtle marine animal equipped with remarkable powers of deception. Representative of the practical and productive powers of nature, the chameleon-like Black Grouper changed colors to avoid danger and to attack its enemies. Like the grouper, Cowperwood could change himself to play whatever role was needed to attain what he desired. The charming, intelligent, ruthless, clever, cunning, and greedy Cowperwood was able to continually change his appearance, performance, and angle of attack in his efforts to amass a fortune.

Imagery from animal life is employed to illustrate that the rapacious, Machiavellian superman's primary kinship is with nature rather than with society. Cowperwood is a firm believer in the "survival of the fittest." His credo is "I satisfy myself." The supremely confident financier is crafty, totally amoral, and driven without limits with respect to his desire for wealth. For Frank, sex is a matter of availability and animal desire, and both his sexual activities and art collecting are related to his hunger for possessions and power. His pursuit of beauty in both women and art are calculated endeavors aimed at satisfying his desires. Dreiser's novel convincingly portrays a commercial predator who grows rich in the market by destroying his adversaries.

Cowperwood understood that success in human affairs is based on force, foresight, quickness of wit, coolness under stress, and, of course, subtlety. He assumes a façade of regularity in both his business and personal affairs in order not to arouse suspicion. While destroying his opponents, Frank is able to maintain the appearance of normality.

The single-minded Cowperwood disapproved of emotional individuals and believed that sentimentality and success were incompatible. He repudiated religious principles and considered organized religion and social conventions to be manifestations of sentimentality. For Frank, these were the refuge of the weak. Even as a boy, he was a religious skeptic, found the Bible to be implausible, and had disdain for anyone who accepted any form of spiritual authority. He had no morals to preach and he did not follow popular trends or tastes. Our financial wizard knew that conventional morality was not a factor in the money game. Cowperwood was convinced that morality is irrelevant to one's thriving in the financial arena. He had no scruples, regarded conventional morality as a costly delusion, and had contempt for anyone who believed there was such a thing as morality, and who evaluated the actions of people according to so-called ethical standards.

Unlike previous authors working within the genre of the business novel, Theodore Dreiser does not attack or praise his character's assumptions, strategies, tactics, and actions. The events in *The Financier* are dramatized and the characters are carefully described. Everything is reported to the reader in a journalistic manner. Dreiser presents the reader with information and does not tell him what to think or to feel. The reader is given evidence and it is up to him to make a reasoned judgment. *The Financier* also differs from most conventional novels in that its amoral and aggressive main character rises, falls, is completely unrepentant, and rises again. Most stories end with the fall of such a character.

Chapter Five

Abraham Cahan's
The Rise of David Levinsky

During the first decade of the twentieth century, Abraham Cahan enjoyed enormous success and great influence in New York City's Jewish Community. Cahan, who came to America in 1892, helped to construct the cultural pattern of the city's Jewish Community. As an instructor to both the masses and intellectuals, he was the main reconciling force between Jewish immigrants and the other residents of the city. He served as literary guide bringing imaginative literature to the general American public.

In the early 1890s, novelist William Dean Howells read one of Cahan's short stories, was impressed with his writing, encouraged him, and helped launch Cahan's career as a novelist. The result was Cahan's first novel, *Yekl: A Tale of the New York Ghetto* in 1895, for which Howells wrote a very favorable review. Cahan became, for forty years and until his death, the highly respected editor of the influential *Jewish Daily Forward*.

In 1913, Cahan received a request from *McClure's* magazine to write a series of articles describing the success of East European immigrants in the United States garment trade. The series of articles published was called "The Autobiography of a Jew" and became the basis for the novel, *The Rise of David Levinsky*, which appeared in 1917. It can be considered to be one of the best novels of American business and of immigrant fiction. Cahan's genre piece is a masterful study of American business culture and of Jewish character.

During the late 1800s, Jews occupied a prominent position in the ready-made clothing industry in New York. By 1880, East European Jewish entrepreneurs controlled the New York clothing industry. There was massive immigration of Russian Jews to America between 1882 and the start of World War I. They faced the problem of transitioning from their traditional world of ghetto and *shetl* to the new world of city life, industrial labor, and the free society. Adjustment and assimilation did not come easily. Clothing manufacturing was the most lucrative and prominent industry in the ghetto of New York's Lower East Side during this period. It was in these sweatshops that a great many new Jewish immigrants were employed. *The Rise of David Levinsky* vividly depicts the lives and struggles of these estranged workers and peddlers. By 1900, Russian Jewish tailors will have driven out most of the German Jewish firms.

Cahan cast his story of Jewish business success in America as a first-person-protagonist-narrator who has become a rich garment manufacturer. The theme of success is taken from American writers such as Howells, Frank Norris, and Theodore Dreiser. Cahan's masterpiece combines this American theme with the Jewish immigrant experience and Russian artistic sentiments. *The Rise of David Levinsky* is a mixture of realistic fiction, social history, social criticism, psychological realism, immigrant fiction, and business fiction, as well as a commentary on the American Dream.

The Rise of David Levinsky alleges to be a memoir written thirty years after the narrator arrived in America in 1885 with four cents in his pocket. It is divided into fourteen "books" in which David Levinsky looks back upon his life from the vantage point of his immense success as a garment manufacturer who has accumulated more than two million dollars. Despite this, this owner of a leading cloak and suit factory is not a happy man. Levinsky's entire self-revelatory story is told by himself in an intimate and sophisticated manner.

The first four books (approximately one-sixth of the novel) deal with David's life as a child and adolescent in Russia. He was born in Antomir, an impoverished city with a population of 80,000 located in the Northwestern Region of Russia. Ghetto life in this city embodied a sense of tradition that included the community values of learning, piety, and loyalty to faith and family. The small town atmosphere of much of Antomir emphasized the spiritual life of the community. In the city there were also a number of Westernized Jews who read modern books, wore modern clothes, and rejected religion. Their children attended Russian public schools where the classes were taught by Gentiles, associated freely with each other, and married for love.

David's father, a watchman, dies before he is three years old leaving him and his mother to make it on their own. They shared a basement room with three other families in the poorest section of town. David was brought up in dire poverty by his devoted, hard-working, and strong-willed mother who was determined that he would receive religious instruction despite their indigence. Her desire was for him to become a renowned scholar of the Talmud. She manages to raise enough money to send David to a private *cheder* where he would be taught the basics of Judaism and the Hebrew language. His mother was very kind and indulgent to him because she believed that he had already been punished enough in his life.

David was a fine student, but, when payments are late, the headmaster threatens to have him removed from the school. His mother promises to pay and struggles successfully to meet the school payments. Despite being a good student, David is subjected to verbal and physical abuse by the teachers who cannot take out their frustrations and aggression on the wealthier students. At *cheder* he was made to feel sharply the disadvantage of poverty as the teacher had little or nothing to risk in punishing a poor boy. As a result of his enduring abuse, humiliation, and hardship, not only does the young Levinsky excel academically, he also develops into a tough kid.

At age thirteen, David completes his *cheder* education and is encouraged by his mother to enter a *yeshivah* to begin his Talmudic education. After his Bar Mitzvah, he was admitted to a free Talmudic seminary as a scholarship student. While there he slept on the benches in the study hall and ate meals donated by people from orthodox households. His study of traditional religious texts prompted him to look at the world through the prism of Jewish philosophy. David exhibited great aptitude for holy study.

David meets and makes friends with Reb (Rabbi) Sender, a well-liked and bright scholar, who is supported by his wife while he devoted sixteen hours per day to the study of the Talmud. Sender perceives David's good nature and his will and determination with respect to his studies. Levinsky also befriends a young fellow student Naphtali, in addition to the older Sender. Naphtali was a diligent student two years ahead of David. He and David study together at nightly rights until morning worshippers arrive.

Beginning at age thirteen, David studied the Talmud for the next seven years. After graduating from *yeshivah* at age sixteen, he continued his studies at the Preacher's Synagogue as an independent scholar. Despite the warnings of Reb Sender and the cautionary teachings of the Talmud, Levinsky begins to experience an inner conflict between his religious instruction and his developing interest in the opposite sex. His mind began to be distracted by his sexual instincts as he was frequently tempted when he saw girls entering the synagogue. His childhood dislike for Red Esther, the daughter of one of the other families in his basement home, also changes to a perspective of curiosity and guilt.

Levinsky's passion for study is energized by his envy and dislike for a rival scholar, a Pole who has moved to Antomir and becomes a regular reader at the synagogue. David's jealousy is incited because the Pole has memorized five-hundred pages of the Talmud which he is able to recite by memory. Wanting to surpass these feats of learning, David begins to memorize large segments of the Talmud as a competition. Reb Sender questions David's motives when he finds out about David's actions.

At school, David watched and copied what other students did. Later in his life he would observe competitors who were successful in business, analyze their actions, and imitate them. Always the observer and analyzer, while a student, Levinsky reflected on why men who studied the Talmud so honestly and passionately were frequently indifferent to their own families.

Levinsky is harassed and attacked in the House Market on his way home from the synagogue during Passover by a group of gentiles celebrating Easter. When he gets home bruised and bleeding his mother sees his split lip and rushes to his defense against the bullies who had mocked and struck David. They break her skull and beat her to death. The murder of David's mother deeply unsettles the foundation of his world. As a result, others sympathize with David as an orphan and he moves into the synagogue in order to continue his studies. He frequently goes hungry but does eat in the homes of benefactors who customarily invite Talmudic scholars to share one meal per week with them.

Shiphrah Minsker, a rich Jewish woman, hears about David's situation and begins providing him with meals, clothing and money. Levinsky falls ill and is visited regularly by Shiphrah in the hospital. He is eventually taken into the hospitable Minsker home to live while her husband is away on business. Here he meets her attractive, modern, open-minded, and educated daughter, Matilda. The Minsker family thought of itself as being modern and enlightened. The children had been educated at Russian schools and acted like gentiles. It was here that Levinsky happened upon the modern world and assimilated many of its values.

David continues his studies but he is losing interest in the Talmud. Around the same time he finds out that his friend, Naphtali, had become an atheist. In addition, Matilda appeals to David to throw aside his old-fashioned ways and to obtain a real education at a Russian university. Matilda herself studied at a boarding school in Germany and at secular Russian schools. She teases David in Yiddish, a language that he does not know. He falls in love with this secular-minded young new Jewish woman who introduced him to new standards of love and sex. The naïve Levinsky fails to read her signals of sexual availability. He ultimately does kiss her and declares his love for her. She tells him he is crazy.

The circumstances of Jews living in Russia began to worsen after the assassination of Czar Alexander II. Anti-Jewish sentiment grew after the death of the Czar by socialist revolutions. After 1881, anti-Jewish riots were supported by, and sometimes even organized by, government authorities. As a result, many Jews took part in the "great New Exodus" from Russia to America. Matilda helped to turn Levinsky's thoughts toward emigration to America.

David is hungry for change and begins to embrace Matilda's idea that he should go to America. Instead of getting an education at a Russian university, he decides to go to America to work until he saves enough money to finance his studies. Matilda offers to finance his trip to America. When the Minskers hear that Matilda's father is returning from his business trip, Levinsky goes back to the synagogue to live.

David still has strong feelings for Matilda and has mixed feelings about leaving her to go to America. The pious Reb Sender is dismayed by David's idea to emigrate to America. He pleads with David not to forget that there is a God in America just as well as in Antomir. Matilda makes David take the money and she wishes him luck. He goes to the train station on the eve of the one year anniversary of his mother's death. There he is seen off by friends from the synagogue and Shiphrah, who gives him some food and money for his journey.

Books 5, 6, and 7 are primarily devoted to describing Levinsky's early years in New York City. Discussed are his continuing fall from chastity and piety, his attempts to learn English, and his introduction to work and the world of business. Even before departing Russia, David had begun to think of himself as no longer being a believer. His secularization had started to lead toward spiritual insecurity even before he left Russia. His estrangement from the *ethos* and life of Antomir began before he came to America where he continued to depart from his heritage into a new culture. Alienated from his former way of life, David was in a state of *anomie* and his orthodoxy was to further disintegrate.

In 1885 Levinsky boards a steamship headed for America and spends most of his time praying and thinking about Matilda. During the ocean crossing he experiences a sense of uncertainty, anxiety, homesickness, and desolation. On the trip he meets and befriends a fellow passenger, Gitelson, a shy, Yiddish-speaking tailor. When they arrive, the two wander around the city and Gitelson is recognized to be a tailor and is offered work. David continues to roam New York, attempts to sleep in a synagogue, and is told that things are different in America. All the while, people on the street regularly refer to him as a "greenhorn."

Mr. Even, a pious, older Jewish man, recognizes Levinsky to be a greenhorn and listens to David's story of his mother's death. The kindly synagogue member outfits David in some American-style clothes, buys him dinner, finds him a room, and gives him some money for some items to sell and for a haircut including the removal of his earlocks which are worn in front of each ear in accordance with the Biblical prohibition against clipping the hair at the temples. Mr. Even had felt pity for David and was intrigued by his knowledge of the Talmud. He asks David not to dismiss his religion or the Talmud.

David attempts to support himself as a peddler. With the money Mr. Evan has given him he acquires his first lodgings and a small amount of goods to peddle. At first he purchases dry goods but makes little profit selling them.

He switches to selling linens but he is not motivated to sell them and he becomes discouraged. His evenings are spent reading at the synagogue. Desiring to change his lifestyle and to cast off his Russian-Jewish characteristics, he eventually decides to shave off his beard. He wishes to escape from his past including his Jewish identity and his experiences in Europe.

Desiring to throw off the mantle of traditions and to blend into the American milieu, David rids himself of his earlocks and beard, remnants of his former way of life. He tries hard to copy the impious American culture and to erase the pious Jewish culture. He wants to transform from a greenhorn to become a real Yankee. To do this he memorizes American slang, attempts to eliminate his Talmudic gestures, and decides to attend night school. He knew that he could turn his Talmud-trained ability for mental work into the pursuit of a liberal education. To do this, he realized that he had to first earn and save sufficient money.

Levinsky observes, studies, and analyzes the actions and language of the other peddlers. David befriends another peddler, Max Margolis, who teaches him the tricks of the peddling trade and gives him advice about women. The older Max tells him that any woman can be won if a man knows how to go about it. David makes advances toward his first two landladies and one of them tells him that he is a "greenhorn no longer." He eventually loses his chastity with a prostitute. He begins to visit ladies of the evening including Argentina Rachaal who hailed from his hometown in Russia. This prostitute from Antomir taught David much about the realities of American politics. After these sexual experiences, he comes to understand why Matilda considered him to be so naïve. Although the fallen women repulse him, he continues to frequently visit them. He despises both them and himself.

David enrolls in a public evening school in order to learn and study English in an effort to Americanize himself. He finds that he enjoys the study of grammar. David masters good English rather easily and with pride. This night school education spurs his ambition to attend City College. At first, David dislikes his teacher, Mr. Bender, but he still attempts to copy his mannerisms. They develop an understanding and become friends. Bender decides to befriend Levinsky because of his enthusiasm and aptitude for learning. They have long talks about American history and politics. Along the way, David reads the Bible in English. Upon "graduation" from night school Bender gives David a copy of *Dombey and Son* by Charles Dickens. David reads this book and many others while neglecting his peddling business. Although he had escaped from his Orthodoxy, he had kept his love of scholarship and Talmudic intellectual curiosity.

Levinsky is having a hard time making it in America. He pays little mind to his peddling preferring to read or spend time at a music shop. He works for short periods at a variety of jobs which he either quits or is fired from. David finds himself pounding the pavement looking for work, often going hungry, living in substandard housing, and simply surviving from day to day.

At this point in the novel, Levinsky runs into Gitelson, the tailor who had been his companion on the journey to America. Gitelson had prospered as a tailor and advised David to seek work as a sewing machine operator in a cloak shop. Tailoring skill was lucrative in America. He offered to introduce David to an operator who would teach him the trade, and to pay him for David's tuition fee. David accepted Gitelson's offer and was apprenticed to a sewing machine operator.

Gradually Levinsky got used to the work and even enjoyed its processes. His skills improve as he earns money that he wants to use in order to attend City College. David even proposes marriage to Gussie, one of his co-workers in the factory, so that she could support him while he attended to his studies and to his business venture. The realistic Gussie perceives his insincerity and turns down his proposal in a brief and blunt letter. Levinsky's interests broaden and he developed a considerable passion for the Jewish theater. He frequently attended the theater with a new friend, Jake Mindels, the brother of one of the men David knew from the clothing field. David also meets Meyer Nodelman, a successful and wealthy manufacturer and the son of David's new landlord. David is hired for a short period of time to tutor Nodelman in English. When this mentorship ends, Levinsky returns to factory work.

Looking back at his life, Levinsky attributes his becoming a businessman and abandoning his desire to attend college to one single event—an accident at work. While having lunch at work, David opens a bottle of milk, which inadvertently slips out of his hands and spills onto a large order of silk coats. He is humiliated when his angry employer, Jeff Manheimer, chastises him, makes fun of his clumsiness, and calls him a lobster in front of the other workers. He tells David that the damages will be taken out of his pay. The embarrassment and his desire for revenge give David the idea of stealing Manheimer's best designs and entering business on his own. He sets his sight on pirating his employer's gifted designer and establishing a competing shop.

David's bold idea depends upon his ability to induce Manheimer's master-designer, Ansel Chaikin, to join him. Chaikin had the ability to accurately and easily make copies of popular fashions. Using his shrewdness and charm, David persistently discusses the business venture with Chaikin and his wife and eventually persuades Chaikin to go in with him. Levinsky had obtained a veritable treasure of information and suggestions for running a business from Meyer Nodelman, the son of his landlady. He effectively employs these in his new venture which operates on a very small budget. The new firm had problems getting credit, making rent payments for the shop, procuring appropriate sewing machines, producing samples, making sales, and so on. Using his "credit face" he obtains credit and aid from his acquaintances. After receiving credit from a consignment merchant, David is able to secure and fill an order from a firm out West for 500 cloaks. Unfortunately, the check does not arrive, as the firm out West has failed. The failure of the Western firm leads to the temporary end of David's commercial career and to the death of his academic dreams. Undeterred, Levinsky continued to aspire to make it in the business world.

Book 9, "Dora," the longest in the novel, is mainly about Levinsky's love affair with Max's wife and David's expanding business. Book 10, "On the Road," chronicles Levinsky in the role of a traveling salesman. These two chapters provide a lot of commercial details along with a description of how David attempts to dress and act like a sophisticated American imitating his buyers, yet still feeling inferior to his American-born customers.

Meyer Nodelman grants David a loan, but he still needs to obtain more cash. While seeking other lenders, a check arrives from the recovered and reorganized Western company. This enables Levinsky to resume his business operations, but first he had to convince Chaikin and his suspicious wife that he was to be trusted.

Levinsky had discussed his financial problems with Max Margolis (i.e., Maximum Max), his friend from early in his peddling days. Max listens compassionately and has David over to his home where he meets Max's wife, Dora, and their children. Max provides David with business advice and David becomes a frequent guest at the Margolis home, and eventually becomes a boarder there. David and Dora have long intimate talks and they fall in love. Although she admits that she loves him, she refuses for a long time to consummate their relationship. Ultimately they do physically come together and David is overjoyed and hopeful for their future together but Dora is remorseful and orders him to move out of the Margolis home.

Concurrently, Levinsky's business is flourishing. He could underprice major companies because the Orthodox East European Jewish tailors that he employed were willing to work longer hours and for lower wage rates in return for not having to work on Saturday, thus observing the Sabbath. Officially, Levinsky's firm had become a union shop, yet his men continued to work on non-union terms. Not only were they grateful for being able to take Saturday off, they were able to make considerably more money by working for non-union wages than they would in places governed by strict union rules. They could work any number of hours in David's shop and therefore, were paid a great many dollars. Levinsky also regularly illegally copied the designs of established manufacturers and specialized his clothing line on a few successful designs thereby achieving an economy of operations. As a result, he could afford to sell a garment for less than what was the production cost of the best-known cloak-houses. Levinsky sold fashionable clothes at low prices, thereby making stylish clothes readily available to most American women.

When all of the cloak-manufacturers formed a coalition and locked out their union men, Levinsky made a pretense of joining the industry-wide lockout, but secretly permitted his tailors to continue working, picking up the orders that the other manufacturers left unfilled. For a while, he gained a competitive advantage over other manufacturers who locked out the union workers. Worker agitation spread to his employees and they walked out on strike, leaving his shop practically closed.

Levinsky's contempt for the Cloak-maker's Union leads him to read Charles Darwin's *Origin of Species* and *Descent of Man,* and Herbert Spencer's *Sociology* and *Social Statics.* He also read a newspaper editorial that was inspired by the theories of the Struggle for Existence and the Survival of the Fittest. Viewing himself as one of the "fittest" and the union leaders as the "good-for-nothings," he coldly and shrewdly operated his business according to the principles of Social Darwinism. A businessman with an intellectual bent, Levinsky adopts the practical philosophy of Social Darwinism. David saw his business acumen as a direct result of his passionate study of the Talmud, which had developed his intellect and memory.

Public opinion became so strong that the manufacturers yielded, acceding to every demand of the union. The increased wage scales gave Levinsky greater advantage than ever because he was still able to hire men who were willing to trick the union organization. Every Friday his workers received pay envelopes containing wages calculated in strict conformity with the union's pay schedule. Then on the following Monday they would pay him back the difference between the official wage and the actual wage. By cheating the union in that manner, David could then undersell the larger manufacturers more easily than he had been able to do before the lockout and the strike. The low actual wage secretly given to the old-country tailors enables his business to make a great deal of money.

David hires his former teacher, Bender, as a salesman and he proved to be a dismal failure in that role. Fortunately, Levinsky decided to retain him as a bookkeeper and general manager and he developed great proficiency in these areas. This frees David to go on the road as a traveling salesman to find customers outside of New York City. He developed into an excellent and enthusiastic salesman who believed in the products he was selling.

Levinsky eloquently told buyers that doing business on a large scale was not always an advantage. He explained that big manufacturers had to pay for union labor and had huge administrative costs. He described his method for inexpensively getting the very best tailors. The old-fashioned, most skilled tailors loved their work and willingly worked long hours. David said that he treated them like family members and that they were able to earn much more than strict union members earned. He was able to get the best workers at the lowest wages. Because he did not have to pay union wages, his buyers receive lower prices.

Soon after Bender had been hired by David, they ran into Max Margolis as they were crossing a street. Max said that he wanted to speak to David about something, so Bender excused himself. He wanted to know the truth about David's relationship with Max's wife, Dora. Levinsky convincingly lies about the nature of his relationship with Dora. He and Max part as friends.

The road was a great school of business and life for Levinsky. He attempted to attain the vocabulary, ease, urbanity, and sense of gentility of the well-dressed Americans. Throughout the story David continues his Americanization process by imitating the buyers of his merchandise but he never does feel equal to them. At one point in the novel he speaks of his goal to be capable of "a convincing personation."

Levinsky's persistence and persuasiveness wins a huge business deal in St. Louis, which garners him national attention. He successfully tracks down Mr. Huntington, the head of the cloak and suit department of the Great Bazar, and talks him into placing large orders with him. David explains to the gentile buyer that he could undersell the German-American Jews primarily because the German-American cloak-manufacturer was mainly a merchant and not a tailor. As such, he was compelled to have a designer and a foreman whereas a Russian competitor such as Levinsky was a tailor and cloak-operator himself and, therefore, able to economize in ways that never occurred to the German-American houses. When marketing his garments, David declares himself to be the immigrant laborer that he primarily uses.

Chaikin wants to come back to Levinsky's firm and to be a partner again but David refuses to take him back. Chaikin went to work as a designer for another firm. Concerned with Chaikin's wonderful feeling for line, color, designs, Levinsky would buy copies of Chaikin's designs from tailors in plenty of time before the new cloak or suit was placed in the market. In this manner, and unknown to Chaikin, his designs were pirated and used in the service of David's business.

Levinsky survives the panic of 1893 and he expands his factory in the prosperous years that follow. He moves his office and factory to fine accommodations on Broadway with a large administrative staff. Becoming even more confirmed in his Social Darwinism, David looks at poor people with more contempt than ever before. Although wealthy, there were times when he recalled his unrealized dreams of attaining a college education, experiencing a qualm of regret. One day he came across Jake Mendels, his friend during the time when David was preparing for City College. Mendels had graduated from medical school and had opened a doctor's office. Seeing him elicited a pang of envy.

The final four books of the novel chronicle Levinsky's continuing business success and his failure to be happy as a human being. These books describe how David almost marries one woman whom he does not love, and of how he unsuccessfully pursues another woman whom he does love. During the last part of the novel many figures from his early days reappear but each reunion proves to be unsatisfactory and disappointing to his sense of nostalgia.

Meyer Nodelman and his wife introduce Levinsky to numerous unmarried young women but none of them interest him. Loeb, David's rival from the past who had been a "star" salesman in the clothing business, comes to work with him as a salesman. Not long thereafter, Chaikin enters Levinsky's employ as a designer. David heard that his first love, Matilda Minsker, was in New York with her husband to appear at a public meeting at the Cooper Institute to attempt to gain assistance for prisoned revolutionaries in Russia. When Levinsky arrived at the lecture hall to see her, she took stock of his mink overcoat and bourgeois deportment and dismissed him as a capitalist enemy. This event furthered David's hatred of socialists and other radicals.

At age forty, Levinsky becomes engaged to Fanny Kaplan, daughter of a rich, Orthodox Jewish businessman and Talmud scholar. Although he admires her lifestyle, he does not love her. Despite his atheism, he is drawn to the orthodoxy found in her father's home, which reminds him of his heritage. As a convinced free-thinker, Spencer's Unknowable had replaced Levinsky's God, yet religion now appeared to him as an indispensable instrument in the great orchestra of things. Just before he is to marry Fanny, David meets a young, beautiful, intelligent girl at a Catskill mountain resort that served as a marriage market. Her name is Anna Tevkin and he is attracted to her. Unfortunately for Levinsky, she has no interest in him.

David finds out that her father, Abraham Tevkin, is a former Hebrew poet whose works he and Naphtali found appealing back in Antomir. David ends his engagement with Fanny in order to pursue Anna by becoming friends with her father, who has abandoned his Hebrew poetry in order to become a real estate salesman.

After rush season, Levinsky was busy preparing to move his business to new quarters on Fifth Avenue near Twenty-third Street. This locale had become the center of the clothing trade. As David views the thriving garment district, he reflects on the benefits of capitalism and technology.

> The new aspect of that section of the proud thoroughfare marked the advent of the Russian Jew as the head of one of the largest industries in the United States. Also, it meant that as master of that industry he had made good, for in his hands it had increased a hundredfold, garments that had formerly reached only the few having been placed within the reach of the masses. Foreigners ourselves and mostly unable to speak English, we had Americanized the system of providing clothes for the American women of moderate or humble means. The ingenuity and unyielding tenacity of our managers, foremen, and operatives had introduced a thousand and one devices for making by machine garments that used to be considered possible only as the product of handwork.

> This—added to a vastly increased division of labor, the invention, at our
> instance, of all sorts of machinery for the manufacture of trimmings, and the
> enormous scale upon which production was carried on by us—had the effect
> of cheapening the better class of garments prodigiously. We had done away
> with prohibitive prices and greatly improved the popular taste. Indeed, the
> Russian Jew had made the average American girl a "tailor-made girl." (443)

Levinsky's new establishment occupied four vast floors and he employed a
large staff of trained bookkeepers, stenographers, clerks, and good-looking
Anglo-Saxon cloak models with good manners and good grammar. His new
place was the talk of the trade, and he received numerous letters of congratu-
lations from mill men, bankers, retail merchants, buyers, and private friends.
All of them had admired his success! Many visitors came to see his new
place of business including the kindly American commission merchant who
had been the first to grant him credit and Easton, a Philadelphia buyer who
had given him his first lesson in table manners.

Levinsky pursues Anna by befriending her father, praising his Hebrew
poetry, and investing in real estate with him. This gains him a regular presence in the Tevkin home. The Tevkin family members are Jewish intellectual
socialists. They call David "Mr. Capitalist" and ask him for money for their
causes. Levinsky overcomes his hatred of radicalism, gains some sympathy
for their socialist causes, and contributes to the children's radical undertak-
ings. The younger members of the family are atheists but their father, the
celebrated Hebrew poet, has become religious in his old age and requires his
family to celebrate Passover in the traditional fashion. David comes to understand that part of his unhappiness stems from his neglect of his Jewish
heritage after he came to America and went into business.

The Tevkin family members accept David into their household as a friend
of their father. Levinsky has located Tevkin's three books in Hebrew in a
library and can discuss them intelligently. The author is gratified because a
well-known businessman has taken an interest in his work. At this time, real
estate speculation has hit New York. David is attracted into it by Tevkin and
is almost financially ruined in the process. He would eventually recover with
the help of his friends and go on to amass even greater wealth.

One day when David arrived at his office he found Dora Margolis waiting
for him. The unhappily married woman no longer appeals to him because his
heart was full of love for Anna Tevkin. When Dora declares her love for him,
David is rather bored by her seriousness and her poor diction. At the Tev-
kins's traditional Passover *seder*, David professes his love for Anna and his
desire to marry her. She is stunned and coldly rejects him. Sick at his heart,
Levinsky had a crushing sense of final defeat.

In the last book of the novel, "Episodes of a Lonely Life," the rejected
Levinsky reasserts his hatred of socialists, discovers and recovers from the

losses incurred in real estate speculation, becomes even richer, and comes across many of his old acquaintances. At the end of the novel he is a lonely and unhappy man.

Shmerl the Pincher, a sadistic schoolmaster back in Russia, reappears as a ragged and feeble Lower East Side peddler. Levinsky sees Matilda at a theater benefit and she is much nicer to him on this occasion. He invites Gitelson, his ship brother twenty-five years earlier, to dine with him at the Waldorf-Astoria. The dinner is marred by the awkwardness and social distance between the two—one of them is a business success and the other is a failure. David also meets Gussie, the finisher girl to whom he had once proposed marriage, from time to time. She was now one of the oldest and most loyal members of the Cloak-makers' Union. Her devotion to the plight of her fellow workers prompts Levinsky into settling a dispute by giving partial concession to the workers' demands.

Levinsky's business continues to grow. He buys materials in enormous quantities at prices considerably lower than the general market prices. He invests at least half of his money in "quick assets," earning a higher return on them than the price he has to pay for borrowing funds. David also makes early payments to the mills gaining an "anticipation allowance" or discount at a rate higher than what money costs him to borrow at banks. Levinsky also owns a great deal of stock in the mills with which he does business generating a positive moral effect on their relations with his house. For similar purposes, he is a shareholder in large mail-order houses and department stores. He also financially helps retailers around the country who, in turn, tend to give preference to his house.

At the end of the novel the still unmarried Levinsky is lonely and unhappy. He concludes that his life is a case where success is a tragedy.

> There are moments when I regret my whole career, when my very success seems to be a mistake. I think that I was born for a life of intellectual interest. I was certainly brought up for one. The day when that accident turned my mind from college to business seems to be the most unfortunate day of my life. I think that I should be much happier as a scientist or writer, perhaps. . . . The business world contains plenty of successful men who have no brains. Why, then, should I ascribe my triumph to special ability? I should probably have made a much better college professor than a cloak-manufacturer, and should probably be a happier man, too. I know people who have made much more money than I and whom I consider my inferiors in every respect. At the height of my business success I feel that if I had my life to live over again I should never think of a business career. I can never forget the days of my misery. I cannot escape from my old self. My past and my present do not comport well. David, the poor lad swinging over a Talmud volume at the Preacher's Synagogue seems to have more in common with my inner identity than David Levinsky, the well-known cloak-manufacturer. (529–30)

Levinsky is not saying that a businessman's activities are not morally proper and worthy goals. He understands that innumerable individuals have satified their needs, actualized their potentialities, and attained their goals in the realm of business. He also realizes that one man's flourishing is not the same as another's. Personal flourishing is real, highly personal, and concerned with one's choices and actions. Each person is free to discern, select, and pursue their own goals including the career that is best for him in the context of his own existence. It takes practical wisdom to determine what is best for oneself when considering one's aptitudes, talents, likes, and so on. A person's work can be viewed as a calling—something that a man is meant to do. A calling is unique to the individual, requires the specific talent to do the job, and is accompanied by the enjoyment and sense of accomplishment, satisfaction, and renewed energy that its performance gives to the called person. At the end of the novel, Levinsky concludes that his choice of a business career was not the best choice for him. Also coming into play may be the fact his business "success" had been accomplished through the occasional use of unethical and illegal means. A legitimate businessman does not profit through force, fraud, deception, or other immoral means.

David's character appears to have been formed by his circumstances, hunger, dissatisfaction, sense of loss, yearning for fulfillment, thirst for change, ambition, ambiguous success, and, most importantly, his history of choices. Throughout the story we see the effects of these elements upon the character and inner life of the conflicted and self-absorbed narrator as he evolves from his Orthodox Jewish origins to become a financially successful, lonely, selfish entrepreneur who always feels inferior and never fully integrated into American society.

David lost his father early in his life, lived in poverty and squalor, and his devoted mother suffered a violent death. In addition, his many years of religious training involved sexual restraint and the absence of normal sexual relationships. His strong sense of loss and deprivation is heightened by his rebuff by Matilda, the abandonment of his religious and cultural heritage, the sacrifice of his dream of education for a business career, and his rejections by Dora and Anna. All of these are expressed in Levinsky's craving for wealth, intellectual freedom, sexual pleasures, access to women in society, and a wife and family.

Levinsky is attracted to women that he cannot have and contemptuous of those that he can have. The ones that he does want are either uninterested, married, or above him in culture, sophistication, or wealth. The women who do find him attractive do not appeal to him. He pursues unavailable women, prostitutes that he abhors, older women when he is young and young women when he is older. The few women he loves will not or cannot have him. The married women that he desires are unwilling to accept his attention and most single women find him to be socially unattractive. Of course, there are some girls at the end of the novel who see him as marriage material because of his great wealth. David's real passion is inwardly directed rather than outwardly directed. He is more interested in achieving images rather than reality. He desires a wife and a family but it is an ideal woman that he longs for and not a real one. Levinsky's sense of pleasure and power in his relationships with women tend to revolve around the use of language. For example, he asserts that he loves Dora but he reproaches her because of his ignorance of English and with his own command of it.

Preoccupied with his inner identity and his own feelings, David is insensitive to the perceptions of others and to reality itself. He values relationships and status that exist in his head rather than in reality. His self-identity depends upon his wealth and his imagined intellectual and social superiority. Levinsky admires the non-Jewish gentile world and attempts to copy gentile mannerisms and language. He saw life in America as a chance to have a fresh start and to remake himself in terms of some ideal image of what a successful American businessman should be like. David Levinsky's attempts at self-acculturation are remindful of Sinclair Lewis's George F. Babbitt's efforts at being an ideal social representative of the business class of Midwest America. In addition, like F. Scott Fitzgerald's Jay Gatsby, Levinsky tries to succeed in a world in which he is a stranger. All three of these characters are guilty of mistaking image and appearance for reality. As a result, they each lack authenticity or actualness. At one point in the novel, David observes that we are all, more or less, actors.

Once Levinsky is in the world of business all of his ideals and ethics are enthralled by the ethos of power and success. He yearns to impress people and to be recognized and praised by people who at one time thought themselves to be better than him. His superiority is confirmed when he employs former acquaintances like his former teacher, Bender, former competitor, Loeb, and former partner, Chaikin. He also becomes estranged from many people who helped him become rich. His hunger to relieve his dissatisfaction to escape and his past is strong and he is constantly striving to diminish it. David cannot escape from his old self and cannot reconcile his past with his present. His dual consciousness persists throughout the novel. He is unable to integrate the dichotomies in his life that had been Russian and American, traditional and modern, and religious and atheist. He is eager but unable to leave his past behind. Moreover, he sees no possibility of reconciling his dreams of the past and his activities of the present. Our complex "hero" is fraught with ambiguity. In the ironic end of the story his sense of triumph is paired with a sense of emptiness.

Chapter Six

Babbitt

Sinclair Lewis's Portrait of a Middle-aged Middle Class Businessman

Babbitt is Sinclair Lewis's satirical masterpiece about a middle-aged, middle class, Midwestern businessman in the 1920s. The story is set in the modern fictional city of Zenith which is a composite representation of typical American business cities of this era. Lewis's goal is to depict middle class life in a commercially-driven culture. In preparation for writing this novel, Lewis spent two years traveling and observing how business people think and act. This aided him in capturing a typical representative businessman in somewhat of a documentary manner—this character novel is a combination of materialistic realism and romanticism. In *Babbitt*, Lewis exaggerated the significant, noticeable attitudes of his American characters.

Zenith is portrayed as a modern city filled with automobiles, skyscrapers, and factories in which a "prosperity ethic" is at the root of its social norms. Believing that conformity is a function of commercial culture, Lewis depicts his typical small businessman as a compromising conformist. He emphasizes Zenith's social conformity and the residents' need for "boosterism"—building up one's own city in the hope of enhancing the social perception of it. This city even has a slogan—"Zenith, the Zip City-Zeal, Zest, and Zowie!" Residents of Zenith are characterized as materialists, primarily concerned with social status and appearance, hypocritical with respect to morality, un-cultured in art and music, and "religious" only to the extent that being so promotes the social status of an individual and his family.

Most of Zenith's 200,000 to 300,000 residents appear to live in standard-ized, comfortable homes filled with many modern conveniences. There seem to be no powerful independent industrial or financial tycoons in the city.

Lewis's message is that the age of creative industrial giants was over. Earlier business novels had focused on captains of industry who oftentimes tended to be very corrupt and unethical. In *Babbitt*, businessmen are only marginally dishonest and immoral. With a creed of prosperity and conformity pervading every aspect of society, Zenith's small businessmen become joiners who rely upon status symbols and public relations. Their goal is to conform to the norms of upper class society, social status, and peer pressure. It appears that their self-esteem can only be conferred on them by others.

George F. Babbitt is one such standardized businessman in the standardized city who has been living a life of conformity and seeming self-satisfaction. Lewis's novel documents Babbitt's increasing discontent with his shallow and sterile existence, his rebellion, his retreat, and his ultimate resignation. Lewis supplies the reader with a detailed view of Babbitt's transformation through descriptions of his trials, tribulations, and temptations.

Babbitt is a forty-six-year-old broker and partner with his father-in-law in a real estate firm. He lives with his family in the affluent Floral Heights neighborhood of Zenith where all of the houses are new and look the same. The Babbitt's home lacks the atmosphere of a real home being as impersonal as a room in a hotel. George is proud of his house because of its standardized interior decorations and architecture. For example, he is especially proud of his royal bathroom.

Myra, George's devoted but rather boring wife, had become a habit to him. However, he does appear to have a passionless affection for her. The Babbitts have three children—Verona (22), Ted (17), and Tinka (10). Verona leans toward economic radicalism. Having just graduated from college, she wants to do charity work, thereby contributing to society. Her father calls her a socialist for desiring "socially responsible" causes. Ted does not want to attend college. He would rather work in a factory.

Babbitt and his wife want to climb the social ladder. George wants to be popular and he desires expensive gadgets and other possessions such as appliances, cars, rugs, alarm clocks, toasters, and so on. He worships science, technology, and efficiency, and obtains the best advertised and mass produced products that he can find. Standardized advertised products are Babbitt's symbols and evidence of excellence. He worries about having the proper clothes, watch chain, tie pin, etc. Babbitt anguishes over and analyzes what to do in virtually every situation. Lewis is extraordinarily attentive to the details of George's life. Babbitt has a great number of friends and acquaintances, and one close friend, Paul Riesling. George has a desperate need for approval and does not have any original individual ideas. His political opinions are obtained from conservative newspapers and magazines, and advertising determines his preferences for goods. Babbitt's memberships in the Boosters Club, Zenith Athletes Club, Elks, Chamber of Commerce, and other groups are extremely important to him.

The first part of the novel follows Babbitt through a typical workday. This section leans toward social satire and emphasizes George as a social representative of the business class. The second part of the book shows Babbitt in a variety of settings including: on vacation; attending a business convention; campaigning for a conservative candidate for mayor; throwing dinner parties; delivering speeches; as a member of his church's Sunday School Committee; and so on. Throughout these sections, the author supplies caricatures of men in a great many fields of work including industrialists, politicians, poets, preachers, etc. Many of these chapters are loosely connected set pieces whose order could be changed without seriously harming the plot of the novel. These apparently randomly put together episodes portray a variety of aspects of American life—politics, social clubs, leisure, traditional religion, unorthodox religion, marriage and family, labor-management relations, bars, barbershops, and so on. These literary fragments provide both a sociological depiction of American life and a description of Babbitt as an individual rather than simply as a prototype. Parts two and three provide a personal narrative as Babbitt rebels, is disciplined, repents, and conforms.

The novel begins with a description of Babbitt's city and then switches to his dream life. He recurrently dreams of a fairy child who represents companionship and breaking away to a better life. His erotic dreams about this free-spirited girl contrast sharply with his mundane everyday business and family activities. It is no wonder he is in a bad mood when he awakens to go down to have breakfast with his dull but loyal wife, Myra. George is aware of the shallowness of his standardized life but he is not vocal about it.

George's closest friend, Paul Riesling, represents what is truly valuable to him. Paul had hopes of becoming a professional violinist but instead he went into the tar roofing business to support his shrewish wife, Zilla, who insults and infuriates people and then expects her husband to come to her defense. When Paul pretends not to notice when this happens, his wife accuses him of being a coward. Unlike George, Paul is able and willing to verbalize his dissatisfaction with his wife and his middle-class life. He frequently speaks of his desire to divorce Zilla.

When the social-climbing Babbitts throw dinner parties, they take all of the arrangements exactly from a woman's magazine. At his class reunion, George sees his highly successful classmate, Charles McKelvey, and invites him and his wife to a dinner party at the Babbitts's house. The party is not successful as the higher social class McKelveys are bored, leave early, and offer no return invitation. In addition, a less successful businessman than Babbitt, Ed Overbrook, invites the Babbitts to have dinner at his and his wife's home. George and Myra treat Ed and his wife with arrogance, incivility, and pretentiousness in much the same manner as the McKelveys had treated them.

George considers himself to have practical and flexible ethical standards. Although he engages in somewhat shady real estate deals, he proclaims his own morality and integrity and disparages the morality of his competitors and sometimes of his own employees. For example, Babbitt and his father-in-law are hidden investors in a housing development and they get local politicians and government officials to ignore regulations associated with the development. George says it is good to be honest, but not to be too unreasonably honest.

The novel views religion as a hypocritical means to attain social conformity. Both radical evangelists, Mike Monday and Minister Dr. Drew from Babbitt's Chatham Road Presbyterian Church, are in it for the money. Both of their churches are organized around business principles and they oppose socialism and unions. Socialism was said to be behind unions. By opposing unions, organized religion wanted to focus men's minds and energies to higher concerns. Dr. Drew delivers no substantive messages in his sermon, speaks of combining the cross and the dollar bill, and publishes a newspaper entitled "The Dollars and Sense Value of Christianity." Babbitt becomes a member of the Sunday School Advisory Committee of the church. Given the task of increasing Sunday School attendance, George approached his assignment as a public relations problem and hired a press agent to proclaim "the value of Prayer-life in attaining financial success."

Babbitt admires the work of T. Cholmondeley "Chum" Frink, an artist who is also a businessman. As a poet, he is the author of *Poemulations*, a syndicated daily newspaper column, and also the creator of "ads that add." Chum's poetry cannot be distinguished from his ads. Lacking consistency and integrity, he writes poems advocating the drinking of water rather than alcohol and then goes to parties where he drinks bootleg alcohol.

When George and Myra visit Paul and Zilla, Zilla hatefully criticizes Paul. George steps in to tell Zilla that she is nagging, bitter, and jealous, and appeals to her to permit Paul to go with Babbitt on a vacation to Maine away from their wives. The Maine vacation offers Babbitt some short-lived enjoyment but also makes him realize that his life in Zenith could be much better. Promising himself a new perspective on life as he travels home from Maine, George plans to read more, stop worrying about business, quit smoking, enjoy the theater, and attend more baseball games. None of these actualize as Babbitt's enthusiasm wanes and he returns to live the life of a typical middle-aged businessman in a culture dominated and saturated by commerce and consumerism.

Babbitt is chosen to deliver a speech at the convention of the State Association of Real Estate Brokers. In his talk, George says that real estate is a great profession and makes a case that real estate men should be called realtors. This elevates his social status and he becomes known as a great orator. In the world of politics, Babbitt is named to be a precinct leader, and helps Prout, a conservative businessman, to defeat Seneca Doane, a liberal/socialist politician.

Babbitt espouses inconsistent opinions. For example, he maintains that nobody should be compelled to join a union but that businessmen should be forced to belong to employees' associations and the Chamber of Commerce. The hypocritical Babbitt also praises hard work and frugality but he, himself, does not practice either one.

On a business trip to Chicago, George sees Paul with a middle-aged woman and discovers that Paul is having an affair. He keeps Paul's secret but he is concerned because he believes that Paul needs to maintain his social standing in the community. Paul needs to protect his reputation.

Shortly after George has been made vice-president of the Boosters Club, he discovers that Paul has shot Zilla during an argument. Zilla survives but Paul is sentenced to serve three years in prison. Paul's imprisonment is a tragedy for Babbitt. Destroyed by the loss of his friend's constant and loyal presence, George experiences a psychological crisis. Feeling alone, he begins to question his belief in the power of the dollar. Babbitt's world collapses and he sees his life as empty.

Longing for a more spirited life, George attempts to regain his pioneer vitality. Although his ancestors had been pioneers, he clearly represents a degeneration of pioneer ancestry. Remembering how his trip to Maine with Paul had made him feel manly and at ease, he makes a second trip accompanied by Joe, his preferred fishing guide who represented untamed independence to him. George is disappointed when Joe tells him that, if he had enough money, he would open a swell shoe store. The woodsman who had been admired by Babbitt for his primitive manner of living had also been corrupted by the culture of business.

Babbitt becomes dissatisfied with a life of conspicuous consumption and Chamber of Commerce propaganda. He no longer visits the Athletic Club, begins to criticize his pastor's sermons, and infrequently has lunch with Zenith's other businessmen. In time he repudiates his entire previous lifestyle by drinking, smoking, attending wild parties, espousing radical opinions, having a love affair, gaining bohemian friends, and so on. George fervently tries to escape into independence and individualism.

Babbitt begins to criticize the conservative opinions of his friends and to support causes that a right-wing businessman would never favor. He also takes the side of the strikers in a labor union dispute. He had discovered that he had compassion for the striking workers. He makes friends with Seneca Doane, the liberal politician that he had previously worked against, and discovers that he likes his liberal ideas. As a result, he enters the realm of liberal politics and publicly praises Doane. He begins to take the side of rebellion and to enter the world of the anti-establishment. Realizing that his time is running out, the middle-aged Babbitt is desperate to break out of his life of meaningless and complacent mediocrity.

George meets pretty middle-aged real estate client and widow, Tanis Judique, and goes to her house to fix a water leak. Thinking that he has found his fairy girl in real life, he turns to her for companionship and understanding. Viewing her as exactly what he needs, he has an affair with her and carries on with her unconventional and escapist bohemian friends known as the "Bunch." While his wife is away, Babbitt drinks and parties with Tanis and her friends. His behavior outrages his friends and associates who attempt to persuade him to come back to the fold but he refuses.

Zenith's leading businessmen ask Babbitt to join the Good Citizens' League, an organization intended to enforce conformity in business philosophy and to pressure individuals with liberal leanings to change their ways. On several occasions, George refuses to join this organization. As a result, the members of the Good Citizens' League boycott his real estate business and shun him in public.

Babbitt's friends continue to coax and coerce him into returning to his old way of life. Refusing to conform, George becomes even more unpopular, his business declines rapidly, and he is threatened with business ruin. He begins to realize that his attempts at nonconformity and individuality are futile and destructive of his life with his friends.

When Myra returns, she suspects Babbitt's dalliance. George admits to having an affair but convinces her that it is her fault. Admitting that she is also bored, she forgives him and allows him to redeem himself.

Babbitt is becoming disillusioned with his new lifestyle. Not only are the liberal lawyer-politicians actually more moderate, his perfect woman is actually not nearly what he thought she was. His life with the Bohemians is not much different given that the Bunch have their own rigid standards and conventions for their subculture.

When Myra becomes seriously ill with appendicitis, George realizes that he loves his wife and makes a complete break with Tanis Judique. He recognizes that there is great value in his marriage. His old friends offer him support during this ordeal and he is grateful to them.

Babbitt comes to understand that it is too late for him to revolt, and he gives up all rebellion. He realizes that by rebelling he had nearly destroyed all that he cared about including his wife and friends who welcome him back. He joins the Good Citizens' League and announces his distrust of Seneca Doane. By the end of the novel, he returns to his old life but he has been changed by his experiences. George has obtained a glimpse into another lifestyle and has become aware that he does not possess the inner resources to essentially change his conventional life to one of more independence. He says "They've licked me; licked me to the finish." He laments that he has never done a single thing that he has wanted to do.

Although Babbitt is incapable of changing the life that he had created, he still has hopes for his son to live a meaningful life. Ted announces that he has married Eunice Littlefield, the girl next door. He also states that rather than attend college, he wants to get into mechanics and perhaps become an inventor. Although the other family members are shocked and critical of Ted's decisions, George supports his son, takes pleasure in his son's defiance, and urges him to resist conformity and to try to give his life meaning and purpose.

Chapter Seven

"Who Is Henry M. Galt?"

A Review of Garet Garrett's The Driver

The Driver (1922) is a prime example of the literature of achievement. The author, Garet Garrett (1878–1954), had the ability to make economic, financial, and management processes come alive in novel form. Not only is *The Driver* a novel of high finance and Wall Street methods, it also paints a portrait of an efficacious and visionary man who uses reason to focus his enthusiasm on reality in his efforts to attain his goals.

As a financial journalist for several prominent papers, Garrett knew Wall Street well and wrote a series of novels portraying the morality of capitalism, production, and business activities. For many years, he exhibited his talents as a political commentator and essayist at the Saturday Evening Post. In fact, *The Driver* first appeared as a six-part series in the Saturday Evening Post.

The novel captures the essence of the progressive era of America that spanned the late nineteenth and early twentieth centuries. During this period, industrialization and a wave of immigrants altered the fabric of American life, which became increasingly urban, industrial, and specialized. This was a time of great social and economic development. During this formative period, America's agrarian society of farmers and small producers was transformed into an urban society in which the corporation became the dominant form of business organization. Steel and oil were in great demand and national transportation and communications networks were being developed. This was a period of seemingly boundless expansion that presented unprecedented opportunities to entrepreneurs and speculators. Wall Street was beginning to develop and railroads boomed as trains moved products from the resource-rich West to the East.

This was also a period of instability characterized by periods of boom and bust and the fact that not all citizens shared in the new wealth and optimism. Mark Twain called this period the "Gilded Age"—a period that was glittering on the surface but that was tarnished and corrupt underneath. This age saw the rise of populist reformers who blamed greedy robber barons and speculators for society's ills. Many people in society, especially those in government, were anti-business and anti-Wall Street and called for government intervention to cure the problems that had developed during the great industrial growth spurt of the late nineteenth century.

After the Panic of 1893, America suffered a severe economic depression and mass unemployment. In response to this economic adversity, in the winter of 1893–1894, Jacob S. Coxey, an American social reformer and populist leader from Massillon, Ohio, proposed a recovery program that included Congressional enactment of a large increase in the amount of legal tender in circulation that could be spent on public works, thus providing jobs for the unemployed. In other words, he advocated public works financed by fiat money. Coxey formed an organization called the Commonwealth of Christ and assembled an army of unemployed men. On Easter Sunday, March 25, 1894, he led an army of 100 unemployed men on a march scheduled to arrive in Washington, D.C. on May 1 for a huge demonstration petitioning Congress for measures to alleviate distress and unemployment. Coxey's Army wanted to demand from Congress a law by which unlimited prosperity and human happiness might be established on earth. They thought that people would work and be prosperous if Congress created an abundant amount of fiat or "democratic" money. Coxey's Army grew to only 500 participants who arrived in D.C. where the leaders were arrested and the army was quickly disbanded.

According to Garrett, naïve trust in the power of words to command reality is found in all mass delusions. For example, in 1894, populists pressured Congress to enact a bi-metallic system of money by declaring that gold and silver are equal in dollar value and that gold and silver dollars be interchangeable. The problem was that gold remained more valuable to people, prompting them to hoard gold or to sell it in Europe. As a result, the Treasury's gold fund was continually depleted.

The nameless first-person narrator of *The Driver* is a reporter for an undisclosed newspaper who follows Coxey's Army to Washington, D.C. This correspondent-narrator is selected by a group of forty-three reporters to send accurate reports regarding the march of Coxey's Army to Mr. Valentine, president of the Great Midwestern Railroad headquartered in New York City. The narrator, who acquires the nickname of "Coxey," gains a position as personal secretary to Valentine and meets Henry M. Galt, a Wall Street speculator who has an intense interest in the Great Midwestern. After meeting Galt, "Coxey" becomes Galt's friend and a constant presence in Galt's business and personal life. It is through the eyes of this reporter-narrator that readers understand the career, struggles, and evolution of a little-known Wall Street speculator and risk-taker to king of Wall Street and to a potential economic dictator of the United States. Unfortunately, Garrett also includes a disappointing, confusing, frustrating, and mostly irrelevant subplot dealing with Galt's family.

Galt, an eccentric and brilliant broker, floor trader, and member of the stock exchange, believes in the future of the Great Midwestern Railroad, continually buys stock in it with his and his family's money, and becomes one of its largest stockholders. He knows more about the Great Midwestern than anyone else, including its president, Mr. Valentine, a weak, inefficient, and non-confident man who runs the business into bankruptcy.

Although Valentine is appointed as receiver, Galt intelligently and diligently studies records, data, and statistics to develop a strategic plan of reorganization to save and rebuild the Great Midwestern. His creative plan encompassed finance, physical resources, and business policy, reflected his great knowledge of the railroad and its properties, and was embraced by the Board. He thereby exhibited how invaluable he was to the railroad.

Galt knew that, after the reorganization, he would be one of ten men in the boardroom and that "everything else follows from that." Not only does he become a member of the Board of Directors he also manages to get himself elected as its chairman using his influence with several men who were indebted to him. The Great Midwestern Railroad Company thus lives on and progresses under the new name of the Great Midwestern Railway Company. In time, Galt would overthrow Valentine, thereby also becoming the company's president.

Galt overcame obstacles by driving ahead with aggressive insensitivity and fanatic intentness, all the time keeping focused on his goal and taking practical rational steps in its pursuit. He harshly dismissed employees who hindered the company and rewarded employees who advanced it. Carefully calculating his every action, Galt continually persisted to improve the railroad. He made huge investments in assets including new tracks, engines, cars, rails, land, road improvements, and equipment. He carefully considered the relative merits of different kinds of equipment, operational problems, the cost of capital, upkeep, and so on. Galt employed an innovative profile map identifying bad grades. As a consequence, he developed better routes by cutting steep grades and by reducing or eliminating curves. Galt ultimately rebuilds the railroad from end to end. Through his intelligence, hard work, and determination, he was able to take a failing company and revitalize it. One of his key moves was to issue new securities using the proceeds to invest in the reconstruction of the Great Midwestern. He later used the company's profits to buy large interests in other companies. Through the reinvestment of profits he was able to make his railroad stronger.

Unlike many other businessmen, Galt did not begin by asking how his company can be made to earn a certain rate of profit. Rather, he asked how the Great Midwestern can be built into the greatest transportation company in the world. He knew that if that were done, then the profit would take care of itself.

Galt was committed to reality and action and the need to transform ideas into concrete form. He worked on the premise that once something happened, it becomes an irreversible fact, and that every other fact in the universe must adjust itself to that one fact. In other words, a man must use his unique attribute, reason, to apprehend the natural order by which he is bound. It was evident that Galt had confidence in his capacity to deal with the world through the implementation of appropriate and efficacious ideas and measures.

Galt invested all of himself, as well as all of his savings, into the Great Midwestern. He had a tremendous work ethic as evidenced by his passionate expenditure of time and mental and physical effort in the unwavering pursuit of his dream of building a great railroad. Galt had the power to move men's minds, to persuade them, to command them, and to reward them. He had the power to imagine what could be, to bring his vision into reality, and to create wealth. He was seen as an elemental force. Regarding Galt, the novel's narrator says, "The sight of inspired craftsmanship is irresistible to men."

After rebuilding the Great Midwestern, Galt led the company into other ventures such as buying controlling interests in other railroads as well as in investment and insurance companies. Two such companies were the Orient and Pacific Railroad and Security Life Insurance Company. As a result, he and his family became rich.

Galt wins, creates his empire, and makes enemies in the process. He was satiric and had the power to irritate people. In addition, he has no use for public opinion or government. He was contemptuous of politics. Galt knows nothing about society's views and does not care about them. He had no time for the press and did not engage in public relations. Galt greatly underestimated the force of public opinion. As a result, his family faces social ostracism, Wall Street turns against him, and he is attacked under the antitrust act that had been enacted as special interest regulation to protect less-efficient firms.

Galt's family gains some acceptance and Galt is able to take actions to reverse the decline in the price of the Great Midwestern's stock. An alarmed Congress resolves to investigate Galt and his business dealings and summons him to appear before a Committee of the House. Of course, as expected by now by the reader, Galt defends himself magnificently. He tells the Committee that he is a farmer who farms the country, fertilizes it with money, sows it with more money, reaps profits, and sows the profits back again.

Galt was then asked by the Committee if he, as chairman of the finance committee of Security Life Insurance Company, recommended that securities of the Great Midwestern be purchased. He answered yes and explained that he did not know of a better investment. He was then asked about the disgruntled minority shareholders of the Orient and Pacific who were upset with the Great Midwestern for exercising the power of a majority shareholder. Galt simply explained that he was willing to buy them out at any time.

Galt went on to explain that he built his empire by buying a bankrupt company and equipment, property, and stock in other companies when they were selling at low prices. He bought things that nobody else wanted, saw what others did not see, worked hard, managed well, and created great wealth. At this point he announces that in the next year he would be spending $500,000,000 (an amount equal to half the national debt at that time) for double tracking, grade reductions, new equipment, and larger terminals. Galt's testimony turns public opinion overwhelmingly in his favor.

Galt suffers a stroke and collapses after his ordeal with the committee. His health deteriorates and he becomes bed-ridden. Still, his mind was clear and he continued to build for the future. He even had his maps and charts drawn on the ceiling so that he could see them. His dream for a pan-American railroad connecting the North and South American continents survived him in the form of an idea. Galt dies a well-respected hero.

It is interesting to note that the character of Henry M. Galt was modeled on nineteenth-century railroad czar and turnaround specialist, Edward H. Harriman (1848–1909). Harriman had bought a seat on the New York Stock Exchange at age twenty-two. By 1883, he sat on the board of the Illinois Central and initiated its huge expansion program. In 1898 he took over and rescued the Union Pacific, a property in receivership and near collapse, and shortly thereafter purchased the Southern Pacific and Central Pacific and saved the Erie. It was Harriman who established standards for locomotives, cars, bridges, structures, signals, and so on.

Although *The Driver* is flawed by its sketchy characterization and its bewildering and extraneous subplot involving Galt's family, it is still to be recommended for the portrait it paints of a hardworking, visionary, passionate, loyal, and competent businessman and for the sense of the "drive of the age" that it conveys. It is certainly not in the same class as *Atlas Shrugged*, but what is? It is a good and quick read and I recommend it to you. After a long absence, it has fortunately been brought back into print by the Ludwig von Mises Institute.

Chapter Eight

F. Scott Fitzgerald's *The Great Gatsby*

The Great Gatsby (1925) is one of the most important works in American literature. This novel is the crowning achievement of F. Scott Fitzgerald's career. The monumental novel explores the American Dream as it exists, changes, and withers in a period corrupted by easy money, dishonesty, and pure greed. *The Great Gatsby* is simultaneously a story about greed, excess, unrequited love, tragedy, material consumption, pleasure, morals, hope, success, entitlement, judgment, obsession, reinvention, ambivalence, skepticism, faith, inherited wealth vs. earned wealth, the old rich vs. the new rich, betrayal, and much more. Fitzgerald is able to masterfully and meaningfully unify all of the above. His use of words, phrases, and symbols all support the novel's pronounced feeling of unity. The author develops the plot slowly, progressing toward a violent, dramatic incident and ironic and melodramatic conclusion.

The story takes place during the summer of 1922 and is told by Nick Carraway who moved from the Midwest to West Egg, Long Island in order to learn about the bond business. He had decided to abandon his family's hardware business in order to sell bonds in New York City. West Egg is wealthy but unfavorable compared to East Egg, the more fashionable side of Long Island. Nick's social connections to East Egg include his distant cousin, Daisy Buchanan, and her husband Tom, Nick's classmate at Yale. Nick is twenty-nine years old when the story begins.

Nick provides F. Scott Fitzgerald's voice as both "objective" narrator and participant in the story and is the focal point of the action. He is forthright, tolerant, and willing to reserve judgment. Other people confide in the middle-class Nick, a good listener, who has the ability to read people and situations. The sober and reflective businessman with Midwestern values observes and helps the other characters. This everyman point-of-view character embodies the reader and sets the moral tone of the story.

Nick goes to East Egg to visit Daisy and Tom Buchanan. Daisy exudes a superficial aura of sophistication, charm, grace, wealth, and aristocracy. She is actually shallow, often bored, wants to be constantly entertained, and loves luxury, money, and leisure. Tom is a powerful, imposing, and arrogant man who likes to push people around. Both are small-minded, intellectually empty, and morally indifferent. These representations of "old money" portray social grace and elegance to others, are concerned with social appearances, and neglect concern for others.

While there, Nick meets professional golfer, Jordan Baker, who has also had a privileged life. She is an attractive, cynical, self-centered young woman who represents the "new woman" of the 1920s. She is a fundamentally dishonest realist who cheated in order to win her first professional golf tournament. Jordan informs Nick that Tom has a lover in the valley of ashes, a gray industrial dumping ground between West Egg and New York City. It appeared that Daisy knew that her husband was unfaithful. Jordan and Nick will develop a romantic relationship throughout the story.

When Nick returns home, he gets a glimpse of his wealthy and mysterious neighbor, Jay Gatsby, who is staring intently at a green light across the Sound. The green light is at the end of Daisy's dock. Nick has rented a cottage on the lavish estate of the enigmatic Gatsby who hosts opulent weekly parties for the rich and famous. Throughout the novel, it is almost always through Nick, or in relation to him, that the reader learns the details of Gatsby's life. Fitzgerald defers most information about Gatsby until somewhat late in the story thereby maintaining and suggesting an atmosphere of mystery. Whereas Nick can be considered to be a solid character, Gatsby is more of an obscure creation.

One day Nick goes along with Tom to meet his mistress, Myrtle Wilson, a frumpish, overweight married woman whose husband, George, runs a gas station and second-rate auto repair shop in the valley of ashes. Nick accompanies Tom and Myrtle to New York City where they party at an apartment that Tom keeps for their affair. While there, Myrtle and Tom fight about Daisy and Tom slaps and breaks the nose of the argumentative Myrtle who stubbornly taunts Tom by constantly repeating "Daisy."

People tend to just show up for Gatsby's parties but Nick waits until he receives an invitation before he attends one of them. When he arrives he spots people who are famous in so-called speak-easy society and notes how food and illegal liquor are served lavishly to the attendees. He sees Jordan there and they meet Gatsby, who appears to be an observer more than a participant in the parties. Gatsby is frequently called away to take long-distance business-related telephone calls. Nobody seems to know where he hails from or how he has made his money. Gatsby talks to Jordan alone and she is astonished by what he has to say about himself. Jordan relates what she has heard to Nick, who slowly and enigmatically discloses the details of Gatsby's life to the reader.

Gatsby had revealed to Jordan that he and Daisy had been in love with one another in Louisville in 1917 and that he was still deeply in love with her. Many army officers including Gatsby, an obscure second lieutenant, had courted Daisy. The two fell in love and she promised to wait for him. Having heard Daisy say "poor guys shouldn't think of marrying rich girls," Gatsby insisted on waiting until he had a lot of money before they would marry.

Daisy did not keep her promise. Instead she met and married a man who could give wealth, social standing, and attention—the wealthy, powerful, and influential Tom Buchanan. Daisy apparently did have second thoughts about forsaking Gatsby. Before the bridal dinner, she became intoxicated and persisted at reading and re-reading a letter that obviously was from Gatsby and explaining that she had changed her mind. In the end, she went through with the wedding.

Since Gatsby heard of Daisy's marriage, she became his sole desire and every avenue he pursued in life was for the purpose of winning her back. He bet that time would bring them back together and he devoted his life to achieving this reunion. Gatsby had made his fortune and bought his house across the Sound with the goal of getting Daisy back. His wild parties are attempts to get her attention, to impress her, and to revive the love he once shared with her. As a man driven by a consuming passion, Gatsby creates a luxurious atmosphere and persona for Daisy's romantic and hedonistic enjoyment, hoping to draw her to him. His end game is the love of Daisy. He takes no pleasure in his possessions given that his intention is solely to attract her attention. At night, Gatsby appears in his garden staring at a single blinking green light which is the symbol of his hopes and dreams for the future. For Gatsby, Daisy is the promise of fulfillment that lies beyond the green light that glows every night on her dock.

As the summer progresses, Nick and Gatsby become friends. One day they go together into the city where they meet Meyer Wolfsheim, a professional gambler and Gatsby's link to organized crime. Wolfsheim claims personal responsibility for fixing the 1919 World Series. Wolfsheim hints at the questionable business deals that exposed Gatsby's racketeering activities and tells Gatsby that their business ventures in Philadelphia and Detroit are in trouble.

Although Nick knows that Jordan is dishonest, he sees her on a regular basis. He describes himself as "one of the few honest people he has ever met." Later that same day Jordan tells Nick what Gatsby had revealed to her about his past. Nick is the natural link that will reconnect Gatsby and Daisy and Jordan informs Nick that Gatsby would like Nick to invite Daisy to his cottage for tea, and Gatsby, himself, would just show up unexpectedly. Gats-

by thinks that it is now time to turn time backward to recapture his relationship with Daisy.

On the day of the reunion, Nick's house is impeccably prepared due to the
detail-oriented Gatsby. The get-together is an awkward and strained affair
between the equally shy and uneasy couple. After a while they relax and
become more comfortable with one another, leaving Nick to feel like he is an
intruder. As the meeting progresses, the reader is in the position of believing
in the equal possibility that Gatsby will and will not be able to recapture the
past by winning Daisy back.

The concept of time plays a significant role in *The Great Gatsby* with its
many references to sun dials and other methods of measuring time. For
example, the reunion takes place exactly in the middle of the novel in a
timeless and static scene that connects the past and the present. The party
moves to Gatsby's house where he proudly displays his mansion, gardens,
pool, furniture, and clothes. At one point, Gatsby leans against the mantle
and a clock precariously wobbles back and forth on its edge, eventually
regaining balance and not falling. The hesitating, teetering clock eventually
comes to rest on the mantle suggesting that it may indeed be possible to
rekindle the past in the present. At the same time, all those present imagine
that they see the clock shattered on the floor, thus implying the improbability
of bringing the past into the present.

At this place in the novel, Nick provides much of Gatsby's story to the
reader. His original name was James Gatz and his parents were poor farmers
in North Dakota. He attended St. Olaf's College in Minnesota but he dropped
out after two weeks because he despised the janitorial work he was doing in
order to pay his tuition. He changed his name at age seventeen. Gatsby had
met Daisy while training to be an officer. While working on Lake Superior,
Gatsby became acquainted with wealthy mining entrepreneur, Dan Cody,
who became his mentor. Cody hired Gatsby to work on his yacht. As the
millionaire's personal assistant, he traveled around the continent three times
with Cody. Cody told Gatsby that a person can have anything he wants if he
has money. When the old miner died, Gatsby became an entrepreneur who
accumulated money quickly. Now around thirty, Gatsby is rumored to be
involved in illegal activities such as gambling, alcohol, and trading in stolen
securities.

The love affair between Gatsby and Daisy has rekindled. We learn that
Daisy and Tom are planning to go to one of Gatsby's parties. While Nick
flirts with other women, Daisy and Gatsby go to Nick's yard in order to be
together privately. After the party is over, Gatsby tells Nick about his past
with Daisy and explains his five year plan to recapture the experience of past
perfection with Daisy. As the summer progresses, Gatsby and Daisy frequently see each other and their affair evolves.

On one occasion, Nick and Gatsby travel to East Egg to have lunch with Jordan and the Buchanans. Tom notices that Daisy pays particular attention to Gatsby and that Gatsby stares at Daisy with unconcealed passion. The suspicious and angry Tom suggests that the group drive into New York City to take a room at the Plaza Hotel. Gatsby and Daisy go in Tom's coupe. Tom, Nick, and Jordan drive Gatsby's new yellow car and they stop at Wilson's garage. Wilson has just learned about Myrtle's affair but he does not know who the man is. Wilson tells Tom that he was selling his business and taking Myrtle, whom he knew to be unfaithful, out west away from the city. Tom is disturbed as it appears that he may be losing both his wife and his mistress.

While at the hotel, Tom hassles Gatsby about his interest in Daisy and declares that Gatsby is a criminal involved in bootlegging and other unsavory illegal activities. Accused by Tom of trying to steal his wife, Gatsby announces that Tom is right and that he wanted Daisy to leave Tom for him. By turn, Daisy sides with each man. Ultimately, she states her allegiance to Tom. The confrontation had convinced her to reject Gatsby once and for all. Learning of Gatsby's unethical behavior, Daisy is not willing to stand by her love for him. The authoritative Tom orders her to go back to East Egg with Gatsby in Gatsby's car proving that Gatsby has no way of harming him.

On the way back, Tom, Nick, and Jordan saw that an accident had occurred near Wilson's garage. They stopped to investigate the accident and saw the dead body of Myrtle. She had been struck and killed by a hit-and-run driver in what was obviously Gatsby's yellow car. They return to East Egg where Nick meets Gatsby outside the Buchanan's home. When Nick accuses Gatsby, Gatsby tells Nick that Daisy had been driving but that he plans to take the blame. He explained to Nick that a woman had run out as if she wanted to talk to someone in the yellow car. Apparently, Myrtle looked out the window and rushed out thinking that she had seen Tom in the yellow car that he had been driving earlier. The inexperienced driver, Daisy, hit her and drove away.

In the valley of the ashes there is a giant advertising billboard portraying the fading bespectacled eyes of Dr. T. J. Eckleberry, an oculist who presumably is no longer in business. For the unglued Wilson, the advertising sign suggests the existence of a personal and omniscient God compelling him to strike vengeance for his wife's death. These empty eyes with glasses become and mean whatever the onlooker in the novel attributes to them. The novel does not provide any concrete evidence nor make the case explicitly that the eyes are a symbol of a watchful God. At the most, the vacant eyes can be considered to be a "floating symbol."

When an author creates an authentic symbol, he typically illustrates an idea in the action of the story and then uses a symbol to bring the abstract idea down to the observational level. It is best when the writer has the reader experience particular concrete actions in order to have enough information to inductively derive and understand the principle involved. The author then uses a symbol to represent the abstraction. In *The Great Gatsby* it is clear that Fitzgerald did not include the existence of an observant God in the actions of the story. The connection only exists in the mind of one of the characters, the upset George Wilson.

The distressed Wilson searches for the driver of the "death car" as the newspaper called it. He approaches Tom, whom he had seen in a yellow car earlier that day and Tom reassures him that it was not him in the yellow car. Tom discloses that Gatsby is the owner of the hit-and-run car and redirects Wilson to Gatsby's residence where the readily identifiable car still sits. At approximately 2:00 pm Gatsby decides to take a float in his pool. Having traced the yellow automobile to Gatsby, Wilson appears in the estate and sees Gatsby floating on a rubber mattress in his pool. He shoots and kills Gatsby and then himself. Wilson's misunderstanding had led him to take revenge on the wrong person.

Nick ends his relationship with Jordan and makes the arrangements for Gatsby's small funeral and burial. Very few people are in attendance. None of Gatsby's racketeering associates make an appearance. Neither do the Buchanans. When Nick talks to Tom he learns about Tom's part in Gatsby's murder. Tom tells Nick that Wilson had visited him and forced him to divulge the owner of the car.

At the inquest, neither Daisy's guilt nor Tom's affair with Myrtle are brought out. The insincere Daisy lets Gatsby take the blame for Myrtle's death. She is not at all remorseful for her role in the accident. The Buchanans let Gatsby take the fall with no concern or sorrow. Tom and Daisy go away, with no forwarding address, at least until things calm down.

Tom and Daisy are unlikeable and unpleasant literary characters with little moral or mental substance. As Nick says: "They were careless people, Tom and Daisy—they smashed things and creatures and then retreated into their money or their vast carelessness or whatever it was that kept them together, and let other people clean up the mess they had made."

Jay Gatsby's father, Henry C. Gatz, travels from Minnesota for his son's funeral. Gatsby's father is an unrefined and simple man who is astounded by what his son had made for himself. He shows up with evidence of Gatsby's adolescent aspirations—a youthful manual of self-improvement. He brings with him a worn-out old copy of a *Hopalong Cassidy* book that has a "schedule" that his son had written on the flyleaf:

Rise from bed	6:00 am
Dumbbell exercising and wall-scaling	6:15–6:30
Study electricity, etc.	7:15–8:15
Work	8:30–4:30

Baseball and sports	4:30–5:00
Practice elocution, poise, and how to attain it	5:00–6:00
Study needed inventions	7:00–9:00

GENERAL RESOLVES

No wasting time . . .
No more smoking or chewing
Bathing every other day
Read one improving book or magazine per week
Save $5.00 (crossed out) $3.00 per week
Be better to parents

To Gatsby's father, the above list which he has shown to Nick means that Gatsby was bound to get ahead. He explains that his son was always making resolves and trying to improve his mind. The schedule was seen as imposing purpose, discipline, and order on the conditions of Gatsby's life. Throughout his life, Gatsby had created goals for himself but he had unfortunately devoted himself to an unattainable one.

Nick decides to return to his slower-paced roots in the Midwest after he learns how shallow the elite and the rich can become. He had sat on the fence, attracted to the lavish, fast-paced, fun-filled, extravagant lifestyle, but at the same time, finds it damaging and morally empty. He has social aspirations and is partially taken in, for a while at least, by his social superiors. Nick contends that he is honest, but comes to admire and cater to Gatsby, a man who breaks rules and laws. In addition, he does not tell Tom that it was Daisy who had been driving the car that struck Mrs. Wilson. Nevertheless, Nick is full of interior rules and, although he is attracted by the lifestyle of excess, pleasure, and corruption, he possesses the moral decency to restrain himself from full participation in the pure pursuit of pleasure. Nick, who is simultaneously in and out of the game, is both fascinated by Daisy's charm and contemptuous of her moral hollowness. Nick's conscious moral instinct is to condemn Gatsby, but his imagination is engaged by his romantic readiness. At the same time, Nick has contempt for and faith in Jay Gatsby. As a matter of hope, Nick tends to reserve judgment throughout most of the novel.

Nick has a more discerning view of life and is more objective than the other characters in the story. He sees that the contest between Gatsby and Tom is a struggle between illusion and reality. Nick understands that the brutal and arrogant Tom has the nature of reality on his side and is thus destined to win. Nick roots for the romantic Gatsby although he realizes that Gatsby's idealism is doomed in a confrontation with the reckless, wealthy businessman. Throughout the novel, we witness Nick's moral growth from an inexperienced, uninitiated Midwesterner to a wiser, more mature person who is able to sense the complexity in other people and in life overall. Nick loses his innocence and gains a new and deeper philosophical perspective on life. He is both enchanted and repulsed by the variety of life that he has witnessed. Although Nick is attracted by the allure of wealth, he morally disapproves of the sometimes corrupt, empty lives of those who attain wealth. He is saddened and repelled by the infidelity and unrestrained behavior that he sees, along with the lack of morals, loyalty, and concern. Nick symbolically decides to return to the Midwest to escape the morally polluted culture of New York and the East Coast. The forthright Nick had come east to make a legitimate fortune in the bond business, but he is to return disillusioned to the Midwest.

The Buchanans embody a sense of entitlement. Tom is a hypocritical, sexist, and racist bully who represents gross sensuality and unclear thinking. He has no moral misgivings about his affair. He pushes people around and constantly interrupts people's conversations. Daisy exists on two separate levels in the novel—as what she really is and how she exists in Gatsby's vision of her. She is actually cynical, spoiled, ruthless, and vacuous as well as superficially charming, graceful, and sophisticated. She reveals her true colors when she runs down Myrtle without stopping. Her bad driving becomes a moral statement in the novel.

Jay Gatsby is a character of epic grandeur and mythical proportions. Although he stands for romantic belief, hope, and the myth of the second chance, he had failed to realize that he would be unable to recapture the past. Suspended between his memories and his dreams, he is guilty of optimistic over-estimation of what he is capable of achieving. We are all a bit like Gatsby, proceeding forward toward the future but experiencing the pull of our past.

Resembling an actor who views life itself as a stage, Gatsby believed in his Platonic conception of himself and in his illusions. Lacking the powers of discrimination, he did not succeed in seeing through his own phoniness or that of his acquaintances. Not only had Gatsby not set a proper goal, he also did not select proper means. He was incapable of advancing to the elite social class that is found in East Egg. He was willing to resort to illegality in order to satisfy his dreams. He employed illicit activities in his pursuit of his inner vision of, and longing for, the ideal. Given that Gatsby is true to his invented self, he is, in one sense, the embodiment of the American Dream.

The American Dream was originally about individualism, discovery, and the pursuit of happiness through one's flourishing as a human being. It was about a person's desire to create a better life for himself and his family. By the 1920s, it had become, for many people, the belief that one only needs to have money and to be a powerful social figure in order to have achieved it. This new inauthentic version of the American Dream consisted of a drive to making easy money, having the finest possessions, and treating other people as possessions. *The Great Gatsby* portrays the decline of the moral culture, particularly in the eastern states during the reckless 1920s, a time period of prohibition, speak-easies, greed, crime, and hedonism.

The novel focuses more on the decline or mutation of the American Dream than it does in how to achieve it. It focuses on the affairs that people have, the pursuit of empty pleasure, and the lies and criminal activities that people use to obtain wealth. A genuine American Dream would be achieved through dedication and hard work as it was in America's romantic western past and not in the unromantic eastern present. Still, the great novel is at least a partial dramatic affirmation in fictional terms of the American spirit in the midst of a corrupt culture.

Chapter Nine

An American Romance

King Vidor's Epic Film of Immigration and the American Dream

The advent of railway and steamship transportation during the mid nineteenth century started a mass intercontinental and transcontinental migration unequaled before or since. Between 1860 and 1920, more than forty-five million people left overpopulated Europe with over half of this number arriving in the United States. Many of these immigrants progressed with the industrial expansion of America. They learned English, worked hard, made good, and were successfully assimilated into America.

King Vidor's epic 1944 film, *An American Romance*, chronicles a Czech immigrant's rise from humble beginnings to a position of wealth and power. When Stefan Dangosbiblchek arrives at Ellis Island in 1898, he is almost sent back when he does not have enough money to pay the entrance fee. His moving protest convinces a sympathetic interpreter/immigration official to sign his papers. He must make it to Minnesota to meet his cousin, Anton Dubschek, who has a job for him. He embarks on a 1,000 mile walking journey from Manhattan to the Mesabi Range in northeast Minnesota. On his way he performs odd jobs in exchange for food and shelter. When Steve Dangos (the Americanized form of his name) arrives in Minnesota he wants to begin work immediately and is amazed at how much money he will get for digging and collecting iron ore. His first job pays six dollars per week of which he gives Anton two dollars per week to repay him for buying the ticket for his boat ride to America.

Steve and Anton move further west to obtain better paying mining jobs. Steve is fascinated with the iron and steel industry and wants to learn how to read and write so that he can learn about iron and steel production. He wants to learn all he can about iron ore and its uses. He wants to know where it goes after it leaves the mine and to understand how iron ore gets turned into steel. Steve asks local Irish schoolteacher, Anna O'Rourke, to teach him to read English. She teaches him how to read and acquaints him with the encyclopedia. In time, Steve and Anna fall in love.

Steve attends a Fourth of July picnic filled with beer, music, baseball, and patriotic speeches. One speaker says that America is a land of unbounded opportunity in which anyone's son can become president. The highly motivated Steve asks "Is that true?" He was always looking for better opportunities to flourish and to achieve his American Dream.

Steve plans on continuing to work at the Mesabi mine in order to be with Anna. She reminds him of his ambitions and encourages him to pursue his dreams elsewhere. When the last railroad car is leaving with the last of the ore mined during the summer and fall months, he goes along with the iron ore by rail to Duluth and then travels by freighter to Chicago where he finds work in a steel mill. He does this by sneaking into a mill, where he picks up a shovel and begins working. A manager comes by and asks who he is for payroll purposes. Steve gets a job as a "goggle man" and almost dies due to a spill of molten steel. He asks Anna to move to Chicago and they marry and start a family. Their first child is a girl, Tina. Ever the patriot, Steve names his four sons after American presidents: George Washington, Thomas Jefferson, Abraham Lincoln, and Theodore Roosevelt.

As Steve gains promotions, he learns each new stage of the steel-making process. He becomes a foreman of rolling ingots where he analyzes the process and makes changes to make it more efficient. He takes a risk and doubles production by simultaneously passing two slabs of hot steel through the process. A persistent and passionate student, Steve learns the details of how iron ore, coal, coke, and limestone are combined with men's labor to produce steel. He was a friendly co-worker who would stand at the gate of the mill at the end of the workday on Christmas Eve to wish each worker a Merry Christmas.

Steve saved enough money to buy a car in 1918, which was the year in which his oldest son, George, graduated from high school. The car breaks down on the family's way to hear George's valedictory speech. Steve becomes curious and disassembles the car in order to figure out how it works. This incident thus ignites Steve's desire to learn all he can about automobiles. He subsequently spends a lot of time taking the car apart, reassembling it, and improving it.

George delivers a moving valedictory speech in which he talks about the future and how proud he is to be an American. George enlists in the army and says that for his graduation present he wants his father to become an American citizen. Steve studies diligently in order to obtain his citizenship. On the day that Steve is scheduled to take his test, the family receives a telegram saying that George has been killed in World War I. The grief-stricken Steve keeps his promise, takes the test, and becomes an American citizen.

Steve continues to rebuild and upgrade his car, making it safer and faster. He used many steel parts and installed an ignition starter to replace the hand crank. George's former literature teacher, Howard Clinton, stops by to offer Steve and Anna his condolences and to bring them some of George's poetry from school. Steve invites Howard to test-drive his rebuilt car. They are arrested for traveling eighty miles per hour and Howard suggests that there are prospects for George's car in Indy car racing. They go to Indianapolis to race the car, have a wreck, and end up in the hospital.

The two entrepreneur-inventors develop the Danton Safety Six which has a steel top and a suspension-mounted engine. The steel roof protects passengers in the event the car is rolled over, and the added suspension keeps the car from shaking when it is running. They move their families to Detroit, create the Danton Auto Company, and build a prototype to present to a large automobile manufacturer who is interested in acquiring the design and patents, but not in actually producing the car unless or until a car with similar features is introduced by a competitor.

Rather than having their design shelved by the large car company, Steve and Howard decide to continue to improve their prototype car and to enter it in an upcoming New York auto show. Steve's cousin, Anton, provides much needed financial help at this time by supplying the money needed to start the business and to produce the prototype. At this auto show, Howard locates financial backers who are willing to invest five million dollars in Steve and Howard's company in order to produce the Danton Safety Six. Steve becomes a motor magnate with stockholders and autoworkers.

Teddy, Steve's youngest son, graduates with an engineering degree from college, and goes to work for his father's company. Teddy insists on starting at the bottom of the company so that he can learn about all aspects and levels of the business.

Years later, Teddy plays a major role in the unionization of Danton's employees. Although the working conditions were good, the workers wanted a union for security reasons. They wanted to make certain that they would have their jobs and receive fair wages and treatment regardless of who was heading up management. Conditions changed over time in the United States and employees relied more on large corporations than on farms and small businesses. Times have continued to change and today (2013) we often see unions demanding more benefits than a company can afford to pay (e.g., in the automobile industry).

Despite having empathy for his employees, Steve stubbornly objects to a union maintaining that it is the owner's responsibility to take care of his employees. He argues that he had built the company and that he has always treated all of his employees well. He sees no need for a union and says that management will lose control of the company as time goes on. Steve perceived that he was the only person who built the company, ignoring the contributions of others such as Howard, Anton, and Anna. He saw himself as a self-made man.

The workers walk out, refusing to work until the board agrees to meet with the employees. After a bitter three-month strike, the board meets with every member, except for Steve, convinced that having a union would benefit both the workers and the corporation. Teddy had spoken on behalf of the workers and reminds his father that it is not his company and that he has a responsibility to the stockholders. Steve is disillusioned and believes that he has been betrayed by Teddy, Howard, and Anton. He retires and goes to California for a long-overdue honeymoon with his wife, Anna.

Steve and Anna settle in California until Pearl Harbor is bombed and Teddy informs Steve of a deal in which Danton will manufacture bombers for the American government for use in World War II. Steve and Teddy are reconciled and reunited when Teddy asks his father for help in the manufacture of warplanes.

An American Romance is a fine film portraying how an immigrant's hard work, courage, determination, persistence, and ability to take risks can lead to the achievement of his American dream. It is also an epic of steel, documenting the entire steel process from the mining of iron ore to the making of steel to the manufacturing of automobiles and airplanes. In addition, it is a film filled with much American propaganda as evidenced by: the Fourth of July celebration; the naming of Steve and Anna's male children after American presidents; George's speech and his enlisting during World War I; Steve's gaining of citizenship; and, most of all, the making of bombers for use in World War II.

Director King Vidor had to deal with several problems during the production of the film. First of all, during World War II there were no passenger car assembly lines in operation. As a result, Vidor had to borrow cars from Chrysler, take them apart, and reassemble them in a simulated assembly line. In addition, costly post-production editing and scene rearrangement led to thirty minutes being removed from the film. Vidor thought that the cuts in the film would come from the documentary scenes in the film, but that film footage was already attached to the music. The cuts came out of the dramatic portion of the film, and the re-edited final version emphasized the documentary and technical aspects of the story rather than the personal drama. Despite these cuts, the end result is an inspiring film of American capitalism as a system of unbounded opportunity.

Chapter Ten

Arthur Miller's *Death of a Salesman*

A Case of Self-Delusion

One of the best known fictional depictions of business is Arthur Miller's 1949 play, *Death of a Salesman*, which tells the story of a traveling salesman who has reached the end of his road. Several fine films have been made of this drama, and in 1984 Dustin Hoffman starred in an acclaimed revival of it. The story is told through the mind and memory of the weary, confused, and pathetic salesman, Willy Loman. In his early sixties, he has worked for thirty-four years for Wagner Company and wants to believe that he is vital to the company's operations in the New England area.

The action takes place in New York and Boston over a two-day period. The play involves a succession of scenes that flow freely through time. The times of the play fluctuate between the somewhat distorted and distant past and present. The majority of the action occurs in the Loman's home.

The story begins with Willy returning from an extended Florida sales trip to his home in Brooklyn. The exhausted salesman daydreams, has difficulty remembering, and cannot distinguish between the present and his memories of the past. He hallucinates and his mind shifts rapidly between past, present, and his imaginings, with all three seeming real to him. In his mind, reality merges with his recollections. The worn-out salesman nearly wrecks his car and when he arrives home he tells his wife, Linda, about his wandering mind and his near accident. She tells Willy that his mind is overactive and that he needs to rest. In an attempt to persuade him, Linda suggests to Willy that he should ask his boss, Howard Wagner, for a selling job in a New York show-room so that he would not have to travel. Howard is the son of the man who hired Willy many years ago. Willy says that he will talk to Howard. He then complains about Biff's lack of success. Willy has long envisioned Biff becoming a successful, well-known, and loved businessman.

Willy's sons, Biff and Happy, are upstairs and can hear Willy talking to himself. Neither son is successful and both are unhappy with their jobs. The aimless Biff has lived his life as a worthless drifter for many years. He had been a great athlete in high school but did not attend college because he failed math in high school. He has learned from his father that being well-liked is more important than being academically superior. Biff is caught between his love for his father and his need to get away from his father's influence on him. Happy is a charismatic womanizer who enjoys the appearance of success. Happy lives in Biff's shadow but he has adopted Willy's value system. Willy is unequal with his sons as he tends to praise Biff and to ignore Happy. Sharing Willy's capacity for self-delusion, Happy wants to emulate his father in order to get attention.

Biff's notion of the American Dream is to go out West to run a ranch. While still upstairs, he and Happy discuss buying a ranch together. Downstairs, Willy is daydreaming about episodes from the past—Biff stealing a football while in high school; his sons visiting him in Boston; his return from a trip and telling his boys that he will open his own business someday that will be bigger than Charley's business; his neighbor Charley's son, Bernard, telling Willy that Biff is failing math and needs to study; Willy commenting that Bernard and Charley are liked but not well-liked, and so on.

Willy recollects a conversation in which he brags and exaggerates his sales and commissions earned to a younger Linda. She recalculates much lower numbers and realizes that he has inflated them in order to feel and to appear more successful. Linda feeds into his delusion by reassuring him. Willy remembers complaining about his physical appearance and Linda tells him that he is attractive. Aware of her husband's evasions and weaknesses, Linda loves Willy, is loyal to him, and constantly comforts and supports him. Linda tries to keep her family intact. As a realist, she is the authentic leader of the Loman family. Willy then recalls "the Woman" with whom he had an affair. The vision of the woman disappears and Willy realizes Linda is mending her stockings, a symbol of Willy's infidelity because he had given stockings to the Woman. She tells Willy to remind Biff to return the stolen football. The older Happy goes downstairs to hear Willy expressing his regret about not joining his brother Ben in Alaska. Ben ultimately became rich when he discovered a diamond mine in Africa.

Willy's close friend and empathetic neighbor, Charley, comes over to play cards. Charley offers Willy a job that he turns down. Willy then imagines that he is talking to his brother Ben who has recently passed away. To Willy, Ben is the personification of glamor, success, initiative, and self-reliance. The confused Charley departs and Willy asks Ben for advice. Linda appears and Ben meets her. Willy remembers asking Biff and Happy to steal lumber supplies to remodel the porch. Bernard rushes in to announce that the watchman is chasing Biff as he attempts to steal supplies.

As the play returns to the present day, the brothers have come downstairs to discuss Willy's behavior and ramblings with Linda. She tells Biff and Happy that Willy has been put on straight commission and that he has been consistently borrowing from Charley to make ends meet. Linda admonishes her sons for the way they treat and talk about their father. She says to give Willy respect or not to come home. Biff states that Willy is a fake but he does not elaborate. Linda tells her sons that Willy has attempted suicide.

Willy hears his wife and sons talking, enters, and argues with Biff. Happy announces that he and Biff might go into the sporting goods business. As a result, Willy cheers up and gives Biff advice on how to conduct himself when he interviews with Bill Oliver. Later, Linda asks Willy what Biff has against him.

Act II begins the next morning with Willy getting ready to go to ask Howard Wagner for a non-traveling position in New York. At breakfast, Willy expresses anger about the high price of appliances. Linda tells Willy that his sons are taking him to dinner that evening.

Willy arrives to ask Howard to reassign him to a position in New York, but Howard is preoccupied with his new recording machine. The second-generation owner barely pays any attention to Willy's request and is intent on showing off his new recorder. Pointing out his many years of faithful service to the company, Willy makes his plea to Howard. Willy intimates that he once was a successful salesman. Of course, the truth is that he had never been a good salesman. Howard says that no such position is available. Willy raises his voice and reminds Howard that he played a role in naming him. Willy bases his appeals to his employer on his images of the past.

Willy relates to Howard how legendary salesman, Dave Singleman, inspired him to enter the sales field. At the age of eighty-four, Singleman could go to a town, simply make a number of phone calls, and obtain numerous orders, without leaving his hotel room. He told Willy that selling was the greatest career that a man could ever have. Unlike Willy's brother Ben, Singleman represented success that he saw as potentially attainable by him. He died the noble "death of a salesman" in the smoker of a train while on a business trip. When Dave died, hundreds of salesmen and buyers attended his funeral. Willy had wrongly attributed Singleman's success to his person-ality traits rather than to his well-developed sales strategies and tactics.

Howard fires Willy saying that he wants Willy to take some time off. He says that he does not want Willy to represent the company any longer. He adds that he has been "meaning to tell" Willy that for a long time. Willy brings about his ultimate dismissal himself by going to meet with Howard. Howard had both ignored and carried Willy for a long time. He recently did put Willy on a straight commission, but he had not been totally honest with

Willy, with himself, or with reality. A manager should give each person what he deserves and Willy's always poor sales had been getting even worse. Howard had waited too long to level with Willy. When a manager is honest and just with an employee, then it is more likely that the employee will be more honest with himself. It is essential for a manager to give each employee what he deserves. Such a perspective on justice recognizes that good job performance brings values for the company into existence and that poor job performance does not do so. Both the person receiving just treatment and the company bestowing that treatment profit from that practice. Willy should have been evaluated objectively and justly throughout his career. It would then be more likely that he would have followed a career more suited to him.

Memories of Willy's past fill his mind. As Howard departs, Ben enters and Willy asks him for advice. Ben offers Willy a job in Alaska. This offer presented a crossroads to Willy early in his life—he could either pursue a career as a salesman or join his adventurous brother. The younger Linda enters and reminds Willy of his sons, his sales job, and the success of Dave Singleman. Willy's mind switches to his memories of Biff's final football game. Bernard and Happy are excited about the game. Willy speaks optimistically to Biff about the game. Charley arrives and teases Willy by acting as if he is unaware of the game. Willy's imaginings disappear when he arrives at Charley's office. Charley's secretary asks the mature Bernard to calm Willy down.

Bernard is about to leave for Washington, D.C. to present a case to the Supreme Court. Curious about Biff's lack of motivation and success, Willy asks Bernard why Biff has always been such a failure. Bernard says that something changed in Biff following his visit to Boston to see Willy right after high school. The defensive Willy states that he is not to be blamed for Biff's lack of success. Charley arrives to send Bernard off to Washington and Willy asks Charley for more money than usual because of his insurance payments. Once again, the empathetic neighbor offers Willy a job. The insulted Willy turns it down but eventually admits that he had been fired. Charley admonishes Willy for always wanting to be well-liked and angrily gives him the money. The well-intentioned Charley continued his practice of giving Willy a free handout. As a result, Willy had no incentive to change by finding a job to which he was more suited.

At Frank's Chop House, the restaurant where Willy is to meet his sons, Happy assists the waiter, Stanley, in preparing a table. Biff enters and Happy introduces him to a call girl that he is flirting with. The distraught Biff says that he waited for six hours to see Bill Oliver and that Oliver did not even remember him. During his ordeal, Biff had realized that he had not been a salesman for Oliver but had only been a shipping clerk. It appears that Biff had recollected his father's misconception that Biff had been employed as a salesman for Oliver. Biff tells Happy that after he left he went back to

Oliver's office and stole one of his fountain pens. He tells Happy that he has stolen himself out of every job that he has ever held.

When Willy enters the restaurant, Biff attempts to tell him what transpired when he went to see Oliver. Willy interrupts and says that he had been fired that day. Biff tries to complete his story but Willy keeps breaking in with his own comments. Biff blows up at his father for his inattentiveness.

At this point, Willy begins reliving the past. He remembers Bernard telling Linda about Biff failing math. He then recollects Bernard telling her that Biff was going to Boston to see Willy. The restaurant conversation in which Biff is attempting to explain what happened intermittently comes back into focus. Biff claims that Oliver is discussing with his partner the notion of supplying Biff with money. This renews Willy's interest and he begins to ask delving questions. Biff yells at Willy who becomes very confused. Willy thinks about Boston, the Woman, trying to hide her in the bathroom, the Woman's laughter, Biff finding out about the Woman and calling Willy a fake, Oliver, and so on. Ultimately, Biff rushes out of the restaurant and Happy leaves with two girls.

Returning to the present, Willy recognizes that he is still in the restaurant with the waiter, Stanley. Willy wants to locate a seed store and Stanley gives him directions to one. Willy returns home to plant a garden at night. He appears to think that by planting the seeds he is establishing the worth of himself and his labor. Willy is discussing his suicide plans with Ben. Biff finds his father planting seeds in the garden with a flashlight. They argue, but reconcile somewhat, and Biff attempts to say goodbye. Happy goes to the Loman's kitchen looking for Willy and finds his mother there. When Biff comes inside the house, Linda berates her sons for forsaking their father.

Ben comes back into sight and reminds Willy of his $20,000 insurance policy. In Willy's mind his suicide would provide his family with money, would prove that he was a success, and would symbolize some sort of unity of the generations. Willy's car speeds away as he leaves to kill himself believing that, because of his popularity, a lot of people would attend his funeral.

The Requiem to the play takes place at Willy's graveside. The only people at his funeral were the two boys, Linda, Charley, and Bernard. At the service, Biff declares that Willy had the wrong dream and the empathetic Charley tries to provide Willy with some dignity by saying that he was a victim of his profession. The attendees felt a mixture of sadness, anger, and relief.

At the end of the play, the truth-seeking Biff acknowledges his failures and changes his life's path. Accepting himself, he decides to move out West to seek his dreams of freedom and adventure. Realizing that he needed to change and to make his own decisions, Biff saw Willy's death as a symbol for his new beginning. Happy, on the other hand, decides to follow in Willy's footsteps to try to become a success in the New York business world. He will attempt to validate his father's life (and death). At the funeral, the sobbing Linda tells Willy that the family is now "free and clear."

The original title of Miller's play, "The Inside of His Head," refers to how Willy's mind wanders between reality, flashbacks, and delusions. His mind wanders because he has lost control over his life just as he lost control of his car in the beginning of the story. Throughout the play the connections between the salesman's inner fantasy world and external reality grow ever more volatile and unstable as evidenced by his dreamlike ongoing inner dialogue with a variety of characters in which the past merges with the present.

Willy is truly a "low man" who is forced to face his failures as a salesman, father, and husband. For the most part, the audience (or readers) of the play can only imagine how or why he became what he is. What is known is that Willy imagines himself to be someone that he could never be. He desperately wants to believe that he is well-liked, a great salesman, a good father, and a devoted husband.

Willy believed that attractive, well-liked salesmen are destined for success. He was obsessed with how he appeared to others. As such, he was a failure according to his own standards. It is apparent that Willy's career recollections are exaggerated and that he never was a good salesman. In his prime he was at best a poor to mediocre salesman who claimed to be admired by many people.

Putting his faith in personality, Willy ignores the American success tradition that is based on virtues, character development, and hard work. For him, commercial success is attainable through one's popularity and charisma. He dreamed of being like Dave Singleman. Willy thought that being popular and having a good physical appearance meant that a person would attain his American Dream. It is apparent that his career strategies were based on a false set of beliefs. He was obsessed with the superficial qualities of attractiveness and likeability.

Willy appears to have been obsessed with his goal of being known as a great salesman rather than with actually being a great salesman. He takes little or no delight in the activity itself. He did not love the drudgery of his work. Willy never even mentions what it is that he sells. He was unable to adapt to the ways in which his firm conducted business. He could not connect with a new generation of customers. Willy believed that his old style and techniques could succeed. He did not learn from his mistakes.

Willy spent his life pursuing the wrong dreams for him. The wrong dream slowly possessed his life. One's dream needs to be based on the reality of hard facts. Discernment is needed to determine what one is both good at doing and loves doing. Willy did not have such self-awareness. He did not pay attention to himself.

Throughout the play, it is apparent that Willy is wonderful at working with his hands. Good at carpentry, he makes many home improvements, puts up a living room ceiling, builds a porch, and fixes things that need to be repaired. He was happy when he was working with cement. Unfortunately for Willy, he was unimpressed with such physical labor and always pictured himself as being a great salesman.

Chapter Eleven

John P. Marquand's *Point of No Return*

John P. Marquand's *Point of No Return* (1949) takes a long and detailed look at the life and career of the novel's main character, Charles Gray. The author skillfully dramatizes the social constraints and personal limitations of a post-World War II pure-bred Bostonian businessman. Representing its times, *Point of No Return* also emphasizes and illustrates an individual's response to employment in a business organization. Our hero is shown to be, at least partially, socially restricted by the rules and norms of social systems that limit his responses in various situations. His upbringing in a small town, circumstances, and the culture and climate of his place of employment all serve to limit his autonomy and decision-making. Charles's life story is told at a leisurely pace and includes a meticulous and detailed description of upper class culture in a small New England town that has an intimate class structure. The first part of the novel provides background on his current life and introduces his family and some of his co-workers.

Charles (Charley) Gray, our protagonist, is a conservative and earnest upper middle class banker in his forties. The story is told from his point of view. He lives with his wife, Nancy, and their two children, nine-year-old son Bill, and their daughter, Evelyn, who is six. They live in Sycamore Park in the suburbs of New York in housing appropriate for young professionals. The Grays have a nice house that they could not quite afford and their children attend private schools. Although they are financially overextended, Nancy dresses in the manner of the upper class. They have memberships in a local country club and employ a live-in maid.

Charles has returned from World War II to retake his position as assistant vice-president in the trust department of the old, small, traditional Stuyvesant Bank of Manhattan in 1947. In the beginning of the story we see Nancy driving Charles to the train station. All the way they engage in affectionate

and good-humored conversation. Charles had met Nancy shortly after starting in the bond department of Stuyvesant Bank. He had been assigned the
task of delivering papers to the law firm of Burrell, Jessup, and Cockburn
where Nancy was employed as a legal secretary for Mr. Jessup, one of the
firm's partners.

Charles is not quite upper class. He attended Dartmouth rather than Harvard like so many of his co-workers. After working for a period at Stuyvesant
Bank, Charles had enlisted in the service where he served as a Colonel in the
Air Force. Later in the book, we learn that he had enlisted as a tribute to his
brother Sam who had been killed in wartime activities.

Charles is hoping for a promotion and is competing with a co-worker for
a vice-president position at the bank. Charley's mentor, Arthur Slade, the
youngest vice-president at the bank, had died six months before in a plane
crash when he was returning from a West Coast business trip. Charles is at a
pivotal point in his career and is hoping to be appointed as Slade's replacement. It was Slade who had recruited Charley for his first position in Stuyvesant's bond department.

Charley's rival for the vice presidency is Roger Blakesley who is sharp,
gregarious, sneaky, and flashy. Roger was a well-dressed name dropper who
frequently and quickly displays his Harvard connections. They are competing for a position that only one of them can attain. We do not learn whether
Charley or Roger becomes the fifth and youngest VP of the bank until the
very end of the novel. Charles sees Roger as a fine representative of a
businessman who appears to represent everything that the bank president
would be looking for. Blakesley and his wife, Molly, belong to the same
country club as do the Grays.

Roger is quick to tackle projects. Charles feels that both Roger and he
were equally well qualified. Unlike Charles, Roger had not gone to war. He
stayed behind to move up within the bank's hierarchy. Both are assistant vice
presidents in the trust department and have experience in almost all areas of
bank operations. Both are bright and are good with customers. Charles is
concerned but he is not discouraged. Anthony Burton, the bank's president,
appears to like Charles and he frequently appoints him to carry out important
tasks that the president would normally have done himself. This gives the
appearance that he is preparing Gray for the upcoming position.

There is a hierarchy of trains for the bank's managers. All of the top-level
executives rode the later 8:30 am train. In addition, it was a big occasion
when Burton asked an employee to call him Tony. Burton had asked Charles
to call him by his first name. Nancy and Charley thought that this was a
positive sign with respect to the pending promotion but they soon learned
that Roger also called him Tony. Then they wondered who was asked first.

Charles was first introduced to Stuyvesant Bank on a trip with his father
to New York. The bank was located in a former private dwelling. Stuyvesant

Bank was an old bank with old values that emphasized customer service. It was a family bank that had handled some wealthy families' accounts for generations. There were many tax experts employed there and the bank had been named executor for many wills and estates. The bank's wealthy clients were particular about the manner in which they are treated. Charles and the other bank employees had developed priestly ascetic, untouchable attitudes in dealing with them. They were personally committed to the bank's affluent clients and they worked hard to establish a relationship of trust with them.

The bank's employees were taught to separate their own financial problems and lives from their positions in which they were expected to be professional counselors, confidants, and friends of their customers. As a result, the bankers tended to develop sort of split personalities. During work a bank employee would discuss investing large sums of money only to return home to face his own mundane concerns. On the train each morning Charles would begin to forget his family and to start thinking about the bank.

> In time this gave you a split personality since you had to toss your own problems completely aside and never allow them to mingle in any way with those of clients and depositors when you reached your desk at the Stuyvesant. At your desk you had to be a friend and confidant, as professional as a doctor or a lawyer, and with an intelligent perspective for almost anything. Anthony Burton had once said that this attitude was one's responsibility toward society. Though personally Charles had never felt like a social worker, he felt this responsibility. He was already forgetting Nancy and the children, already assuming his business character, when he said good morning to Gus, the doorman on the sidewalk outside the Stuyvesant. (28)

A person's success at Stuyvesant Bank was indicated by the placement of his desk. The floor plan and location of each employee's desk denoted each one's ranking and status within the organization. The desks were positioned in line with an assessment of each person's title, rank, dedication, and loyalty. Charley occupied one of two flat mahogany desks located in a kind of no-man's land between the roll tops of the officers and the flat top desks of lower executives and secretaries placed outside the teller cages. Roger sat at the other flat mahogany desk. A green rug extended from the officers' desks and ended just past the desks of Charles and Roger. This formed a systematic and orderly restricted zone. Arthur Slade's roll top desk had been vacant since his tragic death. Even the tellers, office assistants, and secretaries had desk placements that indicated their rankings within their classifications.

Charles is a good, steady, and hard worker who is waiting patiently to hear who would be the next VP. However, the intelligent and sensitive Gray is not satisfied with his life. He is searching for his true, individual self and engages in a great deal of soul searching and reflection regarding how he had reached this point in his life. His mid-life crisis involves both curiosity and regret with respect to how his life might have been if he had taken a different path.

Charles feels like a prefabricated executive whose entire life has been "contrived" and predictable. Although he is a successful and efficient working professional, he has no sense of self-fulfillment. He is troubled because he is unable to experience pleasure or a sense of "flow" in his work. He is not flourishing and he is not happy. Charles does not share the passion for banking that Tony Burton exhibits as displayed in the following exchange between the two.

> 'Yes, sir,' Charles had said. 'I'm just beginning to see that everything fits into banking somewhere.' 'Everything,' Mr. Burton had said. 'Everything. You see banking basically is only how to use extraneous knowledge. I like to think of banking as being not only the oldest, but, well, the most basically human business that there is in the world, for it deals with all the most fundamental hopes and aspirations of human beings. In fact, I don't like, honestly, I don't, to think of banking as a business or even as a profession. Banking—it may startle you a little that I say this, but I'm right, I know I'm right—banking, for a good banker, is an art.' (18)

During one particular business day Charles is reminded twice of his youth and upbringing in Clyde, Massachusetts, a beautiful static village and fictional representation of Marquand's hometown of Newburyport, Massachusetts. Charles runs into anthropologist, Malcolm Bryant, an acquaintance from long ago back in Clyde. Bryant had gone to Clyde to conduct a sociological study. Bryant, who possesses no social skills and who treats people as scientific phenomena to be observed, had written a book about Clyde entitled *Yankee Persepolis*. It was a study of a typical New England town, its culture, and it social implications. He explains that the title means "where the Persians worshipped memories."

Bryant explains that in his book he had divided Clyde into distinct social classes such as upper, middle, and lower. He then subdivided them into upper-upper, middle-upper, and lower-upper and used the same subdivisions for the middle and lower classes. Neighborhoods, family names, and street names were only thinly concealed. One of the main indicators of what class a person belonged to was the street on which he lived. Bryant gives Charley a copy of the book and he discovers that the Gray family was classified as part of the lower-upper rung on the social ladder. This was partly due to the fact that Charley's father was a poor money manager. Charley's parents did not have sufficient wealth for a higher ranking in this caste system, but they both came from respectable families. Charles's maternal grandfather was a doctor and his paternal grandfather was a judge.

A second reminder of Clyde comes when Roger proposes a new client who is using his holdings in a Clyde rope company, Nickerson Cordage

Company, as collateral for a potential loan. Burton remembers that Charles was from Clyde and asks him to return to his boyhood home to investigate the firm. The thought of going back to Clyde is intimidating to Charley and resurrects suppressed feelings and memories that he had kept buried for years. These memories are of what events and people helped to form who he is today. While there, he would be required to encounter and answer questions from people who he had not seen in a long time.

A great deal of *Point of No Return* is devoted to a retrospective look at Charley's life in Clyde. Through a long narrative recollection we watch him grow up in the beautiful, static New England community of Clyde. Marquand provides the reader with a painstaking exploration of Gray's past. Through flashbacks we view Charles as thoughtful, sentimental, and kind. These flashbacks relate to his youth, friends, relationship with his father, family life, first romance, and so on. Even before he left for Clyde, Charles began to reminisce about past people and events and their lasting effects on his life.

This trip to Clyde is potentially the decisive factor with respect to whether or not Charles would receive the promotion to VP. He realizes that he could not turn down Tony's request without jeopardizing his chances. On the evening before the day he was to return to Clyde, Charley's memories took him from his childhood through his departure from Clyde. Marquand's flashback technique provides a detailed explanation of life in Clyde from the 1920s and into the 1940s. Through these flashbacks and his upcoming visit with residents of Clyde, Gray evaluates his life as he progresses from a small town Massachusetts boy to his current status as a Manhattan banker.

Clyde was a conservative suburb of Boston located on a river by the ocean. Charley's family was headed by his father John, an unfocused and unstable man, who liked to gamble in the stock market. Charles's mother, Esther, was disappointed by her husband but maintained some faith in his abilities. Charley's brother Sam frequently complained about his father's habits of not making good on his promises and of his compulsive speculation in the stock market. Dorothea, the only female sibling, had little ambition and simply wanted to marry well.

The pleasant but irresponsible John Gray promised much but delivered little. He loved his wife and children and was not a bad father. He was well read but had failed to complete his Harvard education. Reckless in his investing, Charles's father was a bad role model who harshly criticized the system. He had a sense of independence with respect to others in the community. He was a venturous but likeable rogue who paid no attention to convention.

Charley loved his father but he did not want to be like him. Unlike his father, Charley is reliable, responsible, steady, ambitious, purposive, and a hard worker. He had learned well from his father's mistakes. However, in the end of the novel he does come to agree with his father that he exists as a member of various systems the terms of which restrict his autonomy and limit his actions.

Charley's father would disappear for days in Boston speculating in the stock market. He never knew when to cash out. He always wanted to make more money. At one point, Charley's aunt passes away and leaves a large amount of money to Charley's father who invested it in the stock market. On many occasions Charles urged his father to set up trust funds for his mother and sister but that never happened.

Another important event that affected Charley's life and tarnished his memories of his hometown was his relationship with Jessica Lovell, a rich young lady who is out of his social league. The Grays lived on Spruce Street and the Lovells lived on Johnson Street. The people on these two streets belonged to different country clubs and rarely mingled with one another. Clyde's streets are segregated by the castes of their residents. Jessica Lovell came from old money and lived on Johnson Street with her widowed father and spinster aunt. The Grays came from the middle-upper class and lived with similar families on Spruce Street. Society in Clyde is intricately structured and Charles metaphorically hails from the wrong side of the tracks.

Charles and Jessica's love affair began at the annual firemen's muster where Malcolm Bryant is studying folk customs. Their relationship was kept very quiet and Jessica's father was rather disappointed with it because Charley's family did not come from the same social class that the Lovells come from. In fact, when Charles and Jessica developed feelings for one another Mr. Lovell tried his best to separate the two. While he did not openly treat Charley badly, he certainly was not welcoming to him. He attempted to make Jessica feel guilty about liking Charles and took his daughter on extra-long vacations to Europe and other locations.

In order to prove to Mr. Lovell that he was an appropriate suitor for Jessica, Charles invested a $5,000 inheritance in the stock market and built it into $50,000. He believed that this would provide the financial foundation necessary to marry Jessica and to squelch her controlling father's objections. In addition, Charley resigned from his job in the accounting department of Wright-Sherman, the local precision metal parts company in Clyde, and went to work in Boston. With John Gray's help he landed a job there with E.P. Rush and Company, an investment firm. In time, Mr. Lovell realized that there was not much he could do to keep Jessica and Charles apart so he agreed to their engagement.

For a while, Mr. Gray did well with his investments. While the stock market soared, Charles's father earned a lot of money. He purchased a Cadillac, refurnished the house, hired servants, gave donations, rented a boat, joined a country club, and so on. He was trying to show the townspeople that his family was at long last thriving financially. Unfortunately, the stock market crashed in 1929 and he lost everything. He had been determined to reach a sum of $1,000,000 before getting out of the market.

Charley's father fell apart after the stock market crash and apparently committed suicide. After the crash, Charles found his father dead. There was a bottle of pills nearby and suicide was suspected. In an effort to salvage his father's reputation, Charley added his $50,000 to his father's estate. This ended the possibility of marrying Jessica and he abandoned his courtship of her. After Mr. Gray's death, Mr. Lovell told Charles that the engagement could not continue. He did not want his family's name to suffer any damage because of being associated with the Grays. Not only was the scandal of the suicide a factor but Charles's adding his $50,000 to John Gray's estate made Charles unable to financially support a woman of Jessica's standing.

After the engagement was broken off, Charley left Clyde for good, quit his job in Boston, and went to work for Anthony Burton at the Stuyvesant Bank in New York. In addition, Charley's mother moved to Kansas City to live with Dorothea and her new husband, Eldridge Sterne.

Charley's trip to Clyde resurrects a lot of suppressed feelings and thoughts. He realizes that he has some slight regrets and wonders what his life would have been like if he had taken a different path. He apprehends that, although he had pride in his hometown, he would not have been able to advance professionally there. By the time Charles returns to New York, he has convinced himself that Roger will get the vice presidency.

Charles has come to view his life and career as preprogrammed. He realizes that his life has come prefabricated and that he, like Anthony Burton, is a perfect Platonic image of a banker rather than being a banker with a unique individual identity. He sees his own character as being subsumed by the bank itself.

> The Stuyvesant was the aggregate of the character of many individuals, who merged a part of their personal strivings and ambitions into a common effort. He only knew that in the end it was stronger than any one person. In the end, no matter what the rewards might be, a part of one's life remained built into that complicated structure. . . . They were all on an assembly line, but you could not blame that line. It was too cumbersome, too inhumanly human for anyone to blame. (478–79)

Charley and Nancy are invited to dinner for four by Tony Burton at the Burton mansion by the sea. It is at this important dinner that Charley is to find out his fate with respect to the potential promotion. Early in the evening Tony says that he hopes that they will continue to be friends no matter what might occur in the future. This makes Charley suspect that he will not get the promotion and, as a result, he feels free. Charles and Tony walk to the study, away from their wives.

As they walk to the smaller room from the dining room, Charley is some-how remembering his entire career. It was amazing that his thoughts could move so far afield in such a short space of time. He was like a defeated general withdrawing to a prepared position. He could still sell the house at Sycamore Park. Suburban real estate was still high. They could move to a smaller place. There would be funds enough to educate Bill, and there was the trust fund of his mother's which would revert to him eventually. He would never have his present reputation but he would have the commercial value of an educated wheel horse, if he knew his place. He would never have to try so hard again. "'It's over,' he said to himself as he walked across the hall. 'Thank God, it's over.' It was the first time he had felt really free since the moment he had met Jessica at the firemen's muster." (554)

Thinking that he is not going to get the promotion, Charles feels personal-ly liberated. In the next instant this feeling ends when Tony tells him that he has won the promotion. Charles is stunned when he learns that he has earned the job. Burton had concluded that Charley is the best man for the job. He wants to hear Charley's opinion of Roger and how he thinks that Tony should let him down. Charley tells Tony that Roger was good at his job, but that he does not like Roger or his personality. Burton is surprised that Charles ever had any doubt that he would get the position.

Charles realizes that he never had any real control of the situation. Tony had never even considered Roger Blakesley for the position. He had never recognized any conflict or competition between Charles and Roger. Charley makes no decision as his triumph was decided for him. It was the benevolent system that decided that the passive Charles was the best candidate for the vice presidency. This resolution followed the established pattern of his entire life. He has always been a conservative, honest man of character who defers to the system. Charley realizes at the end that the entire inter-office rivalry for the vice presidency was not real at all. He sees that his freedom of choice was limited and that he had never left the continuum of his life. There was always some kind of order and a large range of circumstances that affected the path of his life. He sees patterns repeating themselves with the present extending and repeating the past.

Charles would accept the position as soon as it was approved by the board of directors of the bank. His wife, Nancy, is proud, confident, and ready for the challenge. People would view Charley as a steady, reliable, hard-work-ing, honest, and loyal employee who was rewarded for his efforts. Charley foresees another car, a bigger house, a more exclusive country club, and an enhanced professional friendship with his employer, Tony Burton.

Although on the surface things turn out well for Charles Gray, all is not for the best. His promotion to VP both delights and disturbs him. Although he gets the promotion, he finds no joy, satisfaction, or sense of fulfillment in it. Something is missing. It may be that he does not find his work intrinsically satisfying and challenging as Tony Burton does. He does not experience a sense of flow in his work.

His "success" does not make him happy. Perhaps he could have been happy if he had pursued another vocation, if he had lived his life differently, or if his past circumstances had been different. After his promotion, the past still rests on his shoulders. His discontent and doubts remain the same. He has attained what he had dreamed about long ago but the reality is not equal to his earlier dreams. Charles continues to be a man in search of his true self. At the end of the story he still has a sense of his life as contrived or preassembled.

Chapter Twelve

Henry Hazlitt's *Time Will Run Back*

A Tale of the Reinvention of Capitalism

Henry Hazlitt's novel, *Time Will Run Back*, was originally published in 1951 as *The Great Idea*. It teaches that if capitalism did not exist, then it would be necessary to invent it. It makes the case that the discovery of capitalism is one of the greatest triumphs of the human mind. In his nonfiction works Hazlitt is a master with respect to making economics understandable (e.g., *Economics in One Lesson*). In *Time Will Run Back* he skillfully uses fiction to illustrate his teachings on economics. He makes his points although the book was not written as an economic treatise. The book has a good story line to keep the readers interested.

In *Time Will Run Back* the author creates a hypothetical future in the year 2100 that might have been if Soviet influences had spread throughout the entire world. The novel depicts a future where the whole world is ruled by a communist regime. All traces and artifacts of the ancient capitalist world have been wiped out. All of the history, including books, music, etc. that could evoke capitalist ideas or question socialist ones were destroyed or kept in secret places where only the highest members of government have access to it. History prior to the creation of the communist Wonworld was not to be remembered. Wonworld is the fictional country comprised of all of the territories of the world ruled under communism. Top government officials had fabricated new history books for the masses. The premise of the novel is that all of the political and economic writings of the past (except for that of the Marxists) have been totally destroyed and that, consequently, the hero is required to create out of his own mind the ideas that actually have taken generations of economic thinkers to develop and to refine.

The plot is based on the unraveling of a socialist/communist system and the rediscovery and triumph of capitalism. It foreshadows events in Russia, China, and other countries. Highlighting the inadequacies of a centrally planned economy, the novel argues that under world totalitarianism, the world would not only stop progressing but would also decline economically, technologically, and morally.

Time Will Run Back can be classified in a genre that includes works like Edward Bellamy's *Looking Backward* (1888), Yevgeny Zamaytin's *We* (1921), Aldous Huxley's *Brave New World* (1932), Ayn Rand's *Anthem* (1938), and George Orwell's *1984* (1949). The style and settings are remindful of the novels by Orwell and Huxley. Both Orwell and Hazlitt delimit the linguistic capacities of individuals through new languages, Newspeak and Marxanto (a combination of Esperanto and Marxian concepts). These languages restrict ideas and give more control to the government. Interestingly, *Time Will Run Back* reverses the situation described in *Looking Backward*. These two novels are great candidates for back-to-back use in college courses.

The story is told mainly from the perspective of Peter Uldanov, son of Stalenin, dictator of Wonworld. Peter was raised by his mother in the Bermudas, far away from his father's influences. He was taught by teachers and in subjects that his mother chose. Peter was well-educated in math, science, and music but was taught nothing about politics and economics. He was a bright young man who could think for himself. Having received a well-rounded education, Peter would later be able to make his own judgments with respect to political economy. Peter was fond of classical music and had a passion and talent for playing the piano.

When Peter was very young, his father and mother disagreed when it came to politics and economics. In fact, Peter's mother was seen to be a threat to communism who needed to be silenced. Stalenin exiled her and Peter to Bermuda. Stalenin was a true believer in Marxism who wanted to prove to his wife that his beliefs were correct. He wanted to challenge Peter's mother's ideology and to demonstrate that it was wrong. She subsequently passed away before he could do so.

Peter receives a letter from his ruler father summoning him back to Russia. Peter has grown up knowing very little about his father. Stalenin, who is getting old, is in poor health, and is, in fact, dying. He wants Peter to study politics and economics and to become his successor. When Peter meets his father he is surprised that he is not as large and imposing as the propaganda signs portray him to be. He informs Peter that he is very ill and that he wants Peter to be his successor. Peter declines and says that he is not ready because he knows nothing about Marxian history, politics, and economics. Stalenin explains that his current would-be successor, Bolshekov, would kill Peter, who would be a threat to him, because he was Stalenin's son and because he was not brought up under the communist ideology. As a result, Peter agrees to study Marxian politics and economics. In addition, early on in the novel, Stalenin has Peter imitating his signature in case something happened to Stalenin, such as another stroke.

Bolshekov, number two in Wonworld's ranking system, is Stalenin's rival who constantly conspires to be the next ruler. Stalenin shrewdly assigns Bolshekov to teach Peter about their political and economic system. Bolshekov is not aware of Stalenin's real intentions. This intelligent plan is an attempt to keep Bolshekov from assassinating Stalenin and Peter. The plan does create some turmoil as Peter pushes boundaries and tests waters by asking questions that no one else would ever dare to ask. Normally, questioning anything is punishable by death. Thinking outside the box, Peter learns about Wonworld's Marxist ways, is confused from the beginning, and questions the socialist teachings. The inexperienced but bright Peter perceives that there is something wrong under socialism. Peter's unconventional ways of thinking anger Bolshekov who is completely dedicated and true to Marxist teachings.

Peter learns about government production methods and motivation through fear. All people, even Stalenin himself, live in fear in Wonworld. Under communism in Wonworld, there is an immense hunger for power by any means. Everybody is told to be a spy on their neighbors. Each person's duty is to report any incidences of nonconformance with the party's rules. People are just numbers and are referred to by their respective numbers. People are assigned where to live, with whom to live, and with whom to work. Jobs are simply assigned to individuals who had no choice in the matter. There are long workdays with people being marched to and from work each day. Living conditions are miserable with people packed into rooms as tightly as possible. There is no privacy. Government propaganda is everywhere. People are taught to believe and not to question whatever the government officials tell them. If a person publicly disagrees he will suffer severe repercussions. Peter is told that certain ideologies no longer exist and that the "truth" is whatever is good for the communist state. There is a single party called the Politburo that devises five-year plans. Peter witnesses arbitrary economic control procedures and the repression of the population. He begins to think about the ramifications of nationalization and collectivization.

Society in Wonworld is made up of protectors, deputies, proletarians, and social unreliables. The protectors make up one percent of the population and are the top level officers. The deputies (intellectuals, managers, and technology experts) comprise about ten percent of the population. It is only the highly ranked members who are treated well and are granted special privileges. Social unreliables are the twenty percent of the people who have committed crimes or who are incapable of being good proletarians. The proletarians, who make up the remainder of the population, are the so-called "rulers" of the nation. Marxist doctrine proclaims the emancipation of the proletariat, the oppressed class under a previous ideology.

Bolshekov steps down from educating Peter, and number three, Thomas Jefferson Adams, an American, is appointed to continue Peter's education in the ways of the state in Wonworld. As an American, Adams has similar fears of Bolshekov as does Peter. Peter and Adams form a bond and the pleasant and patient American becomes Peter's ally and best friend. Through their Socratic-style discussions they discover the workings of production, incentives, prices, profits and losses, ownership, markets, the meaning of money, entrepreneurship, and so on.

While Bolshekov was away Peter was made a member of the Party—only about one in every ten Protectors was so honored. A little later Stalenin tells Peter that there are two records labeled X and Z that are kept in a safe, and he gives Peter the combination to the safe. Record X is to be broadcast over the entire Wonworld network if Stalenin has a stroke that incapacitates him. Record Z is to be broadcast immediately in the case of Stalenin's death. Soon thereafter, Stalenin arranges for Peter's election to the Politburo. He is admitted at the bottom as number thirteen. Early in the novel, Peter had met and befriended Edith Maxwell, a librarian, and her father, John Maxwell. After Peter's appointment to the Politburo, they are taken away by secret police and Peter tries desperately to find them but he fails to do so. It is not until the last part of the novel that their fates are revealed.

Stalenin suffers a debilitating stroke, forcing Peter to act quickly to ensure his safety. He opens the safe and pulls out envelope X which contains a record that Peter and Adams rush to the Central Broadcasting Station where it is played over the airwaves. The recording of Stalenin's voice says that he will no longer make public appearances but instead will work quietly by himself to make the state more prosperous. He says that Peter will act as his deputy in his absence. This keeps Bolshekov out of power, and Peter and Adams are safe at least for the time being. Bolshekov is named to be head of the Army and Navy, but Peter took the Air Force for himself so that number two would not control all of the powerful military forces.

Adams tries to convince Peter to have Bolshekov killed so that Peter does not have to fear for his own life. Peter declines to take that brutal and degraded action. He says that it is not worth living in a society that is based on violence. Bolshekov decides to hold a parade in order to showcase his military power. Just before the parade an announcement is made on the radio that Stalenin has made Peter number 1-A and that he would rank just below number one. The announcer adds that this man has the wholehearted endorsement of number two, Comrade Bolshekov. Of course, Bolshekov is infuriated when he hears the news.

Part two of the book, called "Groping," consists of many dialogues and debates between Peter and Adams as they attempt to figure out and correct the problems of communism and to implement economic improvements. These discussions and attempts carry over into section three of the book titled "Discovery." Peter and Adams increase their understanding as they see their errors in addition to learning from unanticipated results as the reforms elicit emergent behaviors in the population. Adams is Peter's sounding board and makes sure that Peter thinks things through before any decisions are made.

Peter and Adams discuss how coordination and synchronization failures result from a centralized planning system. They deduce that a centrally directed economy cannot solve the problems of economic calculation and that without private property, free markets, and freedom of consumer choice, no solution to the problem of economic calculation is possible. They conclude that it is impossible for anyone to manage everything effectively and efficiently. No single person or board can have knowledge of what is concurrently going on everywhere in the economy. In a centrally planned system it is impossible to measure the real costs of things and the extent of wasted resources.

They discuss the benefits of having a legal system that is separated from executive power and how a person should be considered to be innocent until proven guilty. Peter wants to introduce a new system to put an end to oppression and fear. They consider the necessity of the rule of law, where the law must be general and abstract, known and certain, and equally applicable to all people. Under the rule of law everyone would be bound by the rules, including the government. They reason that the existence of general rules plus the functional distribution of state power would lead to a smoothly functioning social order. Peter and Adams examine the advantages of majority rule, democracy, and periodic free elections. As an experiment, they hold small free elections in France, but the voters are suspicious and tend to vote for who they think the government officials support.

Peter and Adams agree that the key to a better society is freedom, including freedom of choice for workers and consumers, freedom of the press, and freedom even to criticize the government. Under the current system anyone who opposes or criticizes the government is dealt with immediately and harshly. Peter wants people to be free so that they would have more initiative to be productive at work. He wants people to have options to choose which goods, and how much of each good, they could acquire. He realizes that freedom brings out the best in people.

Peter says that in agriculture workers should be able to enjoy profit from the surplus that they produce. He also notes that people are issued ration coupons that allow them to purchase specific amounts of particular goods. He decides to implement a new ration coupon plan in which every individual is permitted to trade coupons with others to meet their own needs and wants. Markets shortly appear as Peter's coupon trading scheme creates the phenomenon of market prices. People are better off and happier as a result. Peter had sown the seed for what will become money in the future.

Peter and Adams learn that a market economy evolves as a voluntary association of property owners when people are free to trade to their mutual advantage. They view the market as an effective communicator of data and prices as transmitters of knowledge that economize the amount of information required to produce a given economic result. Prices are a mechanism for carrying out the rationing function and are a fast, effective conveyor of information in a society in which fragmented knowledge must be coordinated.

They envision the market as a social process that derives from conscious, cooperative, and purposeful individual exchanges of people's ration tickets. Through trial and error, competitively determined market prices permit individuals to assess the relative value of scarce means and alternative uses in competing applications and alternative uses of goods and services. The pricing process, a social process, is accomplished through the interaction of all valuers within the society. The social function of the price system is to promote the use of knowledge in society by making calculation possible. Calculation is necessary for a person to determine the best allocation of his scarce resources. Peter and Adams conclude that private property, the market, and money are prerequisites for the mental tool of rational economic calculation. Prices are expressed through the common denominator of money.

Peter and Adams reason that rational central planning under socialism is impossible. Without market-based prices, decision making by central planners would be irrational and arbitrary. A centrally planned economy would be unable to allocate resources rationally. Socialism destroys the incentive of profits and losses, private ownership of property, and the benefits of competition. They also figure out that Marx's labor theory of value was mistaken. Marx had held that the value of commodities is solely determined by the amount of physical labor used in making them. He thought that only labor produces the surplus over costs from which capitalist profits derive. Our heroes conclude that others, such as owners and managers, also contribute toward the generation of profits.

Peter and Adams step by step dismantle controls and slowly, gradually, and incrementally move Wonworld toward having a free market economy. In doing so, they increase their understanding as they see their mistakes and learn from unanticipated results. Bolshekov is not at all pleased by what is happening. He sends an assassin who kills Stalenin. Peter and Adams quickly broadcast a message recorded on record Z making Peter the next dictator. The angered Bolshekov attempts to kill them and they escape to America with the help of the Air Force. There, Peter has the opportunity to implement his economic ideas in a new country called Freeworld.

Peter becomes the leader of Freeworld and establishes private ownership of the means of production with ownership of companies evidenced by what came to be known as shares—this leads to the establishment of markets for shares of stock. Peter saw that private property was essential for the preservation of individual freedom. When property rights are respected and protected, a person is able to keep and enjoy the product of his labor. Corporations evolved as voluntary associations and as private property. People came to understand that men have an inherent right to form a corporation by contract.

Peter and Adams had already learned back in Wonworld that it is prices, articulated through the common denominator of money that makes economic calculation possible. In Freeworld they observed money, in the form of gold, emerge from the domain of directly exchanged commodities. Money originates on the free market when a specific commodity is no longer valued only as a consumer good or a producer good but also as a medium of exchange. Gold became currency because it is stable, nonperishable, and noninflationary. Gold, as a measure of price, became the commodity by which all other commodities would be valued without using roundabout procedures. After a certain time period, money certificates became money substitutes (i.e., claims to a definite amount of money payable and redeemable on demand that circulates indefinitely).

A market system soon evolved. Freeworld developed a market economy as a voluntary association of property owners for the purpose of trading to their mutual advantage. Peter and Adams understood that a market economy is a necessary condition for a free society. People who became known as enterprisers began to create new products and services, new businesses, new production methods, and so on. The market process became a competitive process through which profit incentives induce competing producers to find better ways of serving customers. People started to lend money, thus earning interest, to risk-taking enterprisers so that they could create in the hope of making profits. Some people came to envy and resent the enterprisers. Our heroes observed that it is simply a fact of human existence that some individuals are more capable than others, that some individuals work harder than others, and that some individuals are better at creating wealth than others. This is not a matter of injustice.

Peter even reinvents Adam Smith's term, "invisible hand" to explain how things work in a free economy. He and Adams marvel at how competitors compel each other to cooperate more effectively with the buying public. Successful competitors are those who best cooperate with, or satisfy, others in society. They understand that profits indicate that a person has served his fellow men by using resources to produce a product or service at costs below the value people place upon the product or service. They also realize that losses indicate that a person has failed to serve his fellow man effectively and efficiently. Profit provides risk-takers with incentives, serves as a guide for allocating resources, supplies a reward for serving other people, and serves as a measure of effectiveness in the use of resources to satisfy customers.

Peter and Adams eventually learn the fate of Edith and John Maxwell. In one of his speeches, Bolshekov tells of the execution of two traitors who had committed acts of sabotage and treason at the direct order of arch traitor, Peter Uldanov.

Going back to their discussions, Peter and Adams discover the nature of interest. They note that creditors don't force loans on borrowers who pay interest voluntarily. They conclude that interest is the economic expression of a positive time preference (i.e., that people prefer to have something sooner rather than later).

The years passed and a state of war still existed between Wonworld and Freeworld. However, it was a war of propaganda rather than a war of battles and bloodshed. Adams exhorts Peter to attack Wonworld before Bolshekov attacks Freeworld but Peter hopes to convince Wonworld that Freeworld's system is the better system.

Peter and Adams continue to debate topics such as selfishness, altruism, charity, generosity, competition, etc. They are against state charity because the only way the state can "help" people is to give them wealth taken from someone else. Only people who are allowed to keep what they have earned have the means to be benevolent, compassionate, and charitable. The obligation for charity is that the benefactor owes it to himself, not to the recipients. Freely-given charity may be considered as perfective of a person's capacity for cooperation and an embodiment of that capacity.

After five years Bolshekov decides to attack Freeworld. During the first strike, Peter is injured and spends many weeks in the hospital. Edith Robinson is the nurse who takes care of him after he was injured in the attack on the White House. Eventually they fall in love and they marry.

While Peter was in the hospital, Adams brilliantly conducted the military operation of the war, but he did not fare as well in the economic sphere. Adams had called in all of the gold coins and replaced them with warehouse receipts promising to pay actual gold on demand. Then, to finance the high cost of the war, Adams issued more engraved warehouse receipts for gold even though there was no additional gold to back such issuances. Inflation had resulted. Peter explained that instead of printing additional money Adams should have allowed the system time to adjust. Adams had also tried to remedy the inflation by fixing prices, another flawed action.

Peter explains that inflation, a monetary phenomenon, consists of expanding a nation's money supply by adding something other than real money (i.e., gold). Fiat money, backed only by government decree, produces general price increases. Such an increase in the money supply necessarily dilutes the purchasing power of money. He also notes that price controls in the form of price ceilings end up producing shortages of products. The nature of price controls (i.e., maximum or minimum prices) is to control and force people to do what the government wants them to do. Prices maintained by artificial mechanisms necessarily contain misinformation, inhibit the feedback that permits transactors to communicate, and create market distortions that harm producers and consumers.

Freeworld is incomparably superior to Wonworld with respect to war production. As a result, Wonworld surrenders and the war is over. A constitution is written and a democracy is created. Peter decides not to run for election and appoints Adams to assume the leadership of the Freedom Party. For a while it looks like an eloquent candidate, who proposed a "Third Way" between capitalism and socialism, might win. In the end Adams's party wins and he asks Parliament to name Peter as the first president.

Time Will Run Back has been out of print for a long time, but it is now available online and in printed form. Reading this tale of political intrigue in a grim, socialistic future is a fine way for people to learn the principles underpinning a free market society.

Chapter Thirteen

Executive Suite

A Story of Corporate Success and Succession

For over a quarter of a century, Cameron Hawley had two simultaneous successful careers—as a businessman and as a writer of short stories in magazines such as *The Saturday Evening Post*, *McCall's*, and *Good Housekeeping*. For several years, he was an advertising executive in Minneapolis. This was followed by a twenty-four-year career at Armstrong Cork Company in Lancaster, Pennsylvania, where he worked in marketing, product development, and product testing. He published his best known business novel, *Executive Suite* (1952), a year after retiring from Armstrong. He wrote three more business dramas: *Cash McCall* (1955), *The Lincoln Lords* (1960), and *The Hurricane Years* (1969).

Cameron Hawley provides an honorable and favorable account of the majority of businessmen in his excellent, suspenseful, and engaging 1952 novel, *Executive Suite*. A 1954 film adaptation of the book stays rather close to the novel but is a bit more negative in its depiction of people in business. Both the novel and film have a Randian feel reminding one of an Ayn Rand novel. Overall, both versions provide a realistic and positive image of the businessman, show the actual machinations and politics of corporate life, communicate the drama and romance of business, and make excellent business school case studies.

The story begins with Avery Bullard, president of Tredway Corporation, in New York to determine if an outside person would be right for the vacant position of executive vice-president. Bullard was fifty-six years old in the novel but only fifty-three in the film. He had just met with Bruce Pilcher and Julius Stiegel, president and chairman of the board, respectively, of Odessa Stores to discuss this position.

Bullard had lacked sufficient foresight to create a succession plan and to select an executive vice-president soon after the death of executive vice-president, John Fitzgerald. Many months had gone by without appropriate actions being taken. It had taken pressure from investment fund executives for Bullard to give serious attention to the development of a succession plan. He had been too busy building the company to have given consideration with respect to who was going to run it after he had retired.

After meeting with Pilcher and Stiegel, Bullard wires his loyal and professional secretary, Erica Martin, in Millburgh, Pennsylvania, and asks her to call an executive meeting for six o'clock that evening. Bullard had decided to present a new business proposition at this meeting to see how his various vice-presidents reacted to it. Based on their respective performances, he was going to select one of them to be his executive vice-president. The efficient Erica Martin notifies the executives of a last minute meeting. Perceptive of office politics, she adeptly handles the dilemma of the order in which she informs the executives of this meeting.

As Bullard hails a taxi, a catastrophe occurs—he suffers a cerebral hemorrhage just outside of Pilcher's building. Bullard is not identified immediately because his wallet had been picked up by a passerby who took the cash it held and discarded it. All that is known to the authorities is that there is a John Doe with the initials A.B.

In the film version, it is George Caswell, Tredway board member and head of a stock brokerage house, who witnesses Bullard's death. He decides to sell Tredway Stock short with the intention of repurchasing it at a lower price after Bullard's demise became publicly known. The success of Caswell's scheme depended upon Bullard's passing being announced after Caswell borrowed and sold Tredway shares but before the news of Tredway's strong quarterly earnings report (of which he is aware) is announced to the public. The use of such knowledge is indicative of insider trading. Only then could he buy back and replace the borrowed stock at a price lower than the one at which he had sold it. It is interesting to note that in the novel it is Bruce Pilcher, rather than Caswell, who first sees Bullard's dead body and who schemes to sell Tredway stock short. Pilcher, a candidate from a competing company who Bullard has been considering for the executive vice-president position, is severely chastised by his colleague, Julius Stiegel, for this devious stock scheme.

At the six o'clock meeting, no one knows yet that Bullard is dead. In the film, it is Caswell who phones a number of hospitals and eventually finds a short article in the Friday evening paper about a John Doe with the initials A.B. in the morgue. Caswell then phones the police and informs them that Avery Bullard is the unidentified man in the morgue. However, in the novel, the woman who picks up Bullard's wallet feels guilty and calls the police after she reads the small piece in the paper. Either way, news of Bullard's death spread as the evening goes on. With the death of the king and the lack of a succession plan, the story shifts to the jockeying that takes place among five executives vying for the throne: Loren P. Shaw, VP and Comptroller; Frederick W. Alderson, VP and Treasurer; Don Walling, VP for Design and Development; Jesse Grimm, VP for Manufacturing; and J. Walter Dudley, VP for Sales.

Loren P. Shaw, vice president and comptroller, takes the lead to establish his power immediately after finding out about Bullard's passing. He takes it upon himself to release positive financial information to the press and to set a date and time for Bullard's funeral. Shaw's quick thinking keeps Tredway stock from declining. Because the company has until Monday, quarterly financial reports are sent out in Saturday's newspapers, thus ensuring that Tredway's stock price would not fall. Shaw's immediate action gains favor throughout the company as well as with customers and suppliers.

Alderson and Walling are proactive but not as much as Shaw is. When they arrive at Tredway Tower they are surprised to find that Shaw had already released a statement to the press and the financial statements for the last quarter so that the stockholders would not lose faith in the company with the death of Bullard and sell their stock. Shaw's plan worked and, as a result, Caswell (in the film) was unable to repurchase the stock that he had sold short.

When Alderson and Walling arrive to find Shaw making such decisions without consulting the rest of the board, Alderson is infuriated because he knows that Shaw disrespects Bullard. Alderson and Walling are in agreement in not wanting Shaw to be president. Shaw is a planner and is excellent in the areas of cost control, finance, budgeting, and so on. He seems to have an answer for almost every situation. He is concerned with the company's profits and with satisfying stockholders. He is not concerned with the quality of the products and argues that the (low) priced merchandise has an important place in Tredway's profit structure. Shaw is unimaginative and not particularly concerned with the morale of the plant employees. He lacks long-term vision and does not see the big picture for the company. Alderson and Walling blame Shaw, the efficiency expert, for making Bullard recently lose sight of the Tredway tradition of quality products.

Shaw is a skilled, calculating, ambitious, and politically astute businessman who is relentless in his efforts to climb the corporate ladder. In the film he is depicted as a ruthless and manipulative schemer who blackmails Caswell and Dudley. Shaw makes a deal with Caswell that if Shaw is elected, then Caswell will get back the Tredway shares he sold short at the price at which he had sold them. In addition, having spied on Dudley, Shaw catches him in an affair and blackmails Dudley for his vote. In the novel, there is no reason to blackmail Caswell and Shaw merely contemplates blackmailing Dudley for his vote.

Walling initially champions Alderson, Bullard's right-hand man for a great many years, for president. Alderson has the most tenure of the various vice-presidents but he does not believe that he will be able to defeat Shaw. Although he has the background, he does not think that he is the right fit to be president. Alderson says that a younger man should take over. Alderson, Tredway's longest-serving executive and Bullard's perennial second-in-command, does not think that he has the passion and drive to succeed as president. He also firmly believes that he is incapable of performing the job as well as Bullard had done. The seasoned Alderson had been with Bullard from the beginning.

Before Avery Bullard was president of Tredway, Oliver Tredway had been the head man. He had built a large corporate office building, Tredway Tower, in Millburgh, Pennsylvania, a small city where Tredway was the major employer. Its carillon rang loudest in its Executive Suite. Bullard took over as president after Oliver Tredway committed suicide because of impending financial disaster. After Bullard assumed the presidency, the people of Millburgh looked at the tower with admiration and respect. In Millburgh, everything seemed to center around Tredway Tower, the tallest building in town.

Avery Bullard began at Tredway as a salesperson, but he also became a designer and a production specialist. He was an insightful man of superlative talent and keen business sense who had a commanding presence and the loyalty, admiration, and respect of his employees. Luigi, the elevator operator and Bullard's best friend, idolizes him, as does executive secretary, Erica Martin, as well as most of the vice-presidents. All of the vice-presidents were affected by him as he was personally involved in each of their areas. As a hands-on president, he desired what was best for each of his vice-presidents. Bullard had assembled a team of executives by capitalizing on their individual strengths and by keeping each vice-president focused on his own special area. He was a one-man-show who did not share his views and thoughts with the entire executive committee. Although each executive knew about his particular areas and what Bullard wanted from him, there was no brainstorming among the executive team members. The executive committee was not a team. Each vice-president wanted Bullard's approval but was not concerned with what the other VPs thought of their performance.

Bullard had selected vice-presidents who had strengths and abilities in their specialties. He, on the other hand, as president, had to have knowledge and make decisions with respect to all of the areas of the business. Each VP had in-depth knowledge of his own area but none of them understood the company as a whole. Although Bullard was highly intelligent, charismatic, and had a powerful personality, he could perhaps also be looked at as manipulative. A master of psychology, he knew each of his VP's talents, ambitions, motivations, desires, and personalities so as to be able to predict their reactions and behaviors and, at times, to play them off against one another. Most of the time, however, he simply kept each VP focused on his area of specialization.

Bullard, as the "one man" in the operation, valued building the business more than he valued personal relationships, marriage, family, etc. His affair with Julia Tredway, daughter of Oliver Tredway, had ended badly as Bullard could not balance the challenges of work life and personal life. Julia had broken down after her father's suicide. She is now embittered because Bullard loved the company more than he loved her.

Despite his immense intelligence, Bullard overlooked the importance of having a corporate succession plan. If a succession plan had existed, then we would have had a very different story or perhaps no story at all. Bullard thought he would be with the company for nine more years. If he had named a successor or had a succession plan he would have, in a sense, been able to control, to a certain degree, what happened to Tredway even after his demise.

Alderson and Walling had noticed a recent progressive weakening of Bullard's drive for constant improvement. He recently lost his way and was losing ground to the competition by producing a low quality line of furniture compared to that which was previously produced.

At first, Don Walling had wanted to support Alderson for president but Alderson declines. Walling, a family man, initially considers himself to be too young for that position. As an engineer, he is more interested in developing new ideas, manufacturing processes, and innovative products.

Alderson and Walling then turn to production man, Jesse Grimm, one of Bullard's favorites, but they learn that he intends to retire soon. Grimm had decided to retire prior to Bullard's death and had planned on announcing it the following week at a board meeting. Grimm was selected by them because Alderson believed that Dudley and Caswell would choose Shaw due to their business relationships and friendships. Grimm, who considered himself to be a "real production man," was ready to take early retirement and hated Walling, the young production man and "boy wonder," for trying to be like Bullard. He tells Alderson that he will vote for any of Alderson's recommendations except for Walling. When Grimm had originally built his factory in Millburgh, he had been worried that Bullard would permit Walling to interfere. What happened was that Bullard detained Walling in Pittsburgh and Grimm was left free to build the factory his way. Recently, Grimm takes delight when Walling's experiments fail. Walling attributes his failed experiments to the absence of proper equipment that is a consequence of Shaw's cost-cutting measures.

J. Walter Dudley, the affable and social sales and people person, knows how to entertain and is the most-liked executive in the firm. He is cheating on his wife and is not a serious candidate for president. Even if he were, at least in the film version, he is being blackmailed for his vote by Shaw who catches

Dudley having the affair when he was supposed to be on a business trip to Chicago. In the film, Shaw informs Dudley that nothing will be mentioned if he supports Shaw for the top job.

Walling was initially uninterested in gaining the presidency. He would rather develop new products and more efficient manufacturing methods. In addition, Walling's wife, Mary, resented Bullard's influence over her husband and wanted him to leave the company. Walling did not want to work for Shaw and came to realize that only Walling himself had the pride and passion to run the company. His wife tries to talk him out of vying for the presidency and urges him to go out on his own. Walling explains to his wife Shaw's focus on cost-cutting and the bottom line at the expense of the company's quality, innovation, and creativity. Walling tells her that his new process finally works but that it cannot be implemented because of a budgetary directive issued by Shaw. Shaw's decisions keep Walling from implementing his design concepts. Walling wants to improve existing products and to research new designs.

Throughout his career, Walling has kept a balance between work life and family life and has toiled alongside the plant workers. He takes pride in his work and is concerned about the well-being of the employees. He listens to the factory workers who are dissatisfied with the quality of the products they are producing. He knows of long-time factory employees who refuse to work on Tredway's low-quality furniture line and take a pay cut to avoid working on that line. He knows that people are motivated by pride in their accomplishments and not solely by money. He wants all of Tredway's employees to take pride in selling quality products to loyal customers and to stand behind these products. Walling wants the company to reinvest profits to develop quality products that elicit the pride of the employees. He wants to relive his earliest experiences with the company by building the best possible products. This approach will benefit customers, employees, and shareholders alike.

Walling realizes that the key to victory is the vote of board member Julia Tredway. He approaches her to seek her support by convincing her that he is the right man for the job. The unstable Julia does not seem to care about money, stock, or the future of a company that has torn her life apart and has caused her so much sadness. Walling's plea convinces Julia to support him in the novel but not in the film version. Unfortunately, in the film version, she had already given her proxy to Shaw thus empowering him to vote her shares at the board meeting. Shaw's fatherly sympathy easily persuades the fragile and emotional Julia who is devastated by the death of Bullard. Just before the meeting, although angry and grieving, Julia changes her mind, tears up the document she had given to Shaw, and goes to the meeting in Executive Suite to vote her shares for herself.

In the film, Alderson phones Walling's wife and asks her to let Walling know that he has been detained while picking up Grimm at the train station and wants to have the vote postponed until the two of them arrive. She nearly sabotages her husband's chances by not giving him the message. Feeling guilty, she later goes to Executive Suite to support her husband's desire to be president and to ask him to forgive her.

Shaw begins the meeting without all of the board members present because he fears that they may have plotted against him just as he has plotted against the others. Dudley nominates Shaw and the first ballot is inconclusive because one member has abstained. The first vote leaves Shaw one vote short because Caswell (not Julia) has abstained.

In the film, Alderson and Grimm arrive in time to hear Walling's passionate and motivational oration. In the novel, Alderson uses the drive time to clear up a misunderstanding that Grimm had about Walling. Walling is a dynamic character who has changed and developed into a creative, charismatic, strong, decisive, and visionary leader with a future-orientation, much like Bullard had been. Walling now displays characteristics that had been descriptive of Bullard.

Walling's impassioned speech applauds high quality production, recognizes the importance of employees, and promises growth of the company. He says that men do not work for money alone. They require work they can take pride in. In his speech, Walling speaks of Bullard and how he had changed over time. He says that the pride of one man is not enough to run a company. He believes that Tredway is currently sacrificing quality and failing to take pride in its products. He wants to get back into the business of building quality furniture. He says that the plant workers want to do their best and to take pride in their work. Men have to take pride in what they are doing. In the film version, he shows his dissatisfaction with the low-cost KF line by picking up a table and breaking it, thus making a compelling argument against producing sub-par products. He argues that the men in the factory need pride and that the company should not compromise the furniture's beauty, function, and value. Walling observes that Grimm wants to take pride in craftsmanship and that Dudley wants a quality product to sell. Walling wants to bring the company back to its former greatness.

Walling shares his recollections of Bullard in this excerpt from this boardroom speech in the novel:

> He was never much concerned about money for its own sake. I remember his saying once that dollars were just a way of keeping score. I don't think he was too much concerned about personal power, either—just power for power's sake. I know that's the easy way to explain the drive that any great man has—the lust for power—but I don't think that was true of Avery Bullard. The thing that kept him going was his terrific pride in himself—the driving way to do things that no other man on earth could do. He saved the company when everyone else had given up. He built a big corporation when everyone said that only small corporations could succeed. He was only happy when he was doing

the impossible—and he did that only to satisfy his own pride. He never asked
for applause or appreciation—or even for understanding. He was a lonely man
but I don't think that his loneliness ever bothered him very much. He was the
man at the top of the tower—figuratively as well as literally. That was what he
wanted. That is what it took to satisfy his pride. . . . He never realized that
other men had to be proud, too—that the force behind a great company had to
be the pride of more than one man—that it had to be the pride of thousands of
men. (332–33)

Toward the end of the film, Walling explains it like this to Julia Tredway:

The force behind a great company has to be more than the pride of one man. It
has to be the pride of thousands. You can't make men work for money alone.
You starve their souls when you try it. And you can starve a company to death
the same way. Avery Bullard must have known that once, but he'd become a
little lost these last few years. The company had been saved; there was no
more battles to win. Now he had to find something else to feed his pride—
bigger sales, more profits, something. And that's when we started doing things
like this—the KF line.

In his closing speech in the film he says:

We'll have a line of low-priced furniture, a new and different line—as different from anything we're making today as a modern automobile is different
from a covered wagon. That's what you want, Walt, isn't it—what you've
always wanted? Merchandise that will sell because it had beauty, function, and
value—not because the buyer likes your scotch or think that you're a good
egg. The kind of stuff that you, Jesse, will feel in your guts when you know it's
coming off your production line. A kind of product that you will be able to
budget to the nearest hundredth of a cent, Shaw, because it will be scientifical-
ly and efficiently designed. And something you will be proud to have your
name on, Miss Tredway.

Walling's speech wins the hearts and minds of all of the board members,
including Shaw, Walling chooses Shaw to be his executive vice-president
and to help him keep his feet on the ground. Both Walling and Shaw are right
and they need one another. The company can both have a quality product and
produce it in a cost-effective manner. Walling and Shaw shake hands and
become working partners with each bringing his specific strengths and perspectives to the boardroom.

   Until the company's succession crisis, Tredway's executive group had
never acted as an effective team. Because there was no executive vice-president to take charge, they were forced to come together and ultimately to work
as a team.

   The idea of the importance of time constraints, pressures, and deadlines in
business permeates *Executive Suite* from beginning to end. The film begins

with the ominous ringing of the chimes in Tredway Tower above the streets of Millburgh, Pennsylvania. Perhaps they were tolling for Bullard who was experiencing his last moments of life on earth. In the novel, the date and time are given, thus counting down the last minutes of Avery Bullard's life and leadership of his company. He had let months go by without adopting a succession plan or appointing an executive vice-president. The short-selling of Tredway stock depended upon the timing of the sale and repurchase of it. When Shaw immediately takes the reins and issues favorable financial information, the stock price does not go down. There is great time pressure to find a successor for Bullard. The film version ends as it had begun, with the ringing of the chimes of the bells of Tredway Tower. This time, however, the ringing was hopeful of a great future for this company.

Chapter Fourteen

Cash McCall

The Story of a Heroic Corporate Raider

Cash McCall (1955) is a novel by Cameron Hawley that is positive about business and free-market capitalism. It explores many of the same themes as does Ayn Rand's *Atlas Shrugged* but it is not nearly as philosophical. Like *Atlas Shrugged*, *Cash McCall* is populated with a range of good and bad characters. It is also a 1959 film starring James Garner and Natalie Wood. Despite some changes in the details, the film is very similar to the book.

McCall is a notorious financial maverick and mysterious millionaire who buys depressed companies, makes changes to them, and sells them to make profits. He acquires companies in order to sell them rather than to operate them. He adds value by making companies more effective and/or by taking advantage of overlooked opportunities. Cash McCall's name has become legendary and he has become the subject of much gossip, rumor, and innuendo. Many people call him a pirate and believe that he is an evil, unprincipled, and immoral man. Others are jealous and envious of him. Throughout the novel the reader, as well as characters in the book, discover the true character of McCall, what he represents, and what he stands for.

In the novel we meet the weary Grant Austen, who is worn down by the responsibilities of running his company, Suffolk Moulding, a small family-owned plastics company. The only two owners are Grant and his daughter, Lory. Although Grant Austen appears to be in a rut and is not a great businessman, he is not exactly ready to retire. However, he does fear that he is in danger of losing a vital contract.

Austen's largest customer, Andscott Instrument Corporation represents around sixty percent of Suffolk's business and wants Suffolk to produce a new, larger television cabinet. In order to do so, Suffolk would need to install a new press costing a quarter of a million dollars. General Danvers, And-scott's president, threatens to take all of his business to another company if Suffolk does not do as he says. Later in the novel we discover that Danvers was bluffing about moving his business elsewhere—he knew he could not because of certain patents that Austen owned.

While reading a newspaper, Grant Austen sees an ad that gives him the idea of selling his company. He discusses this idea with his daughter, Lory, and then he tells Gil Clark, a management consultant with Corporate Asso-ciates, that he is contemplating selling his business and retiring. During their discussion, Austen did not disclose to Clark the precarious situation that Suffolk was in with Andscott. He wants to create the image that he simply wants to retire. Gil estimates to Austen Clark that two million dollars would be an extraordinary amount to receive for his company. In a later conversa-tion in the novel, Will Atherson, President of Freeholders Bank and Trust Co. of Philadelphia provides Austen with a similar estimate of Suffolk's value. Atherson, who has worked with McCall, tells Austen that he could be lucky to get that amount.

Gil Clark is a young management consultant with integrity who under-stands the moral and practical value of capitalism, business, and careers in business. He realizes that business can improve human existence through the production of increasingly better products that contribute to the fulfillment of individuals' lives. In the beginning of the novel Clark does not know that McCall owns the consulting firm that he works for.

Harrison Glenn, Gil's boss and President of Corporate Associates, sug-gests Cash McCall to Gil as a potential buyer of Suffolk and arranges for Gil to meet with McCall over lunch. In the beginning of the story Gil is skeptical and has a negative impression of Cash based on hearsay. He thought that McCall was a person who would not hesitate to throw an entire community out of work if it meant making a quick profit. This attitude was soon to change to approval when he meets with McCall and sees him in action.

When Gil meets Cash he finds him to be a moral businessman and a true gentleman who treats all parties in a business deal with justice and fairness. Cash inform Gil that he is the owner of Corporate Associates. Impressed with Gil's character and business, Cash offers him a job as his assistant.

Gil explains to Cash that he has no objection to making money. In re-sponse, McCall proclaims his agreement with this view: "In case there is any doubt in your mind, Gil, I don't belong to the better circles. I'm a thoroughly vulgar character—I enjoy making money." (153)

Cash then scolds America for its ambivalence regarding capitalism and business:

> We have a peculiar national attitude toward money-making. . . . We maintain
> that the very foundation of our way of life is what we call free enterprise—the

profit system. We're so serious about it that we'll fight to preserve it—literally go to war—but when one of our citizens shows enough free enterprise to pile up a little of that profit, we do our best to make him feel that he ought to be ashamed of himself . . . it still strikes me as something of an anomaly that here, living under the profit system—fighting and dying to defend it—we've come now to regard the accumulation of profit as a crime against society. It's gotten to the point now where the only way a millionaire can expiate his sin is to endow a charity or a cancer research foundation. (154)

McCall does not condone the government's numerous and arbitrary tax laws and other regulations but he abides by, and adapts to, and profits while so doing: "I don't make the rules Gil, I only play the game. I never thought much of the kick-for-point after touchdown, either, but as long as it's in the rule book, that's the way the game is played" (164).

Will Atherson, McCall's banker and friend of Grant Austen, was advising Austen regarding what to do with his company and tells Austen that he thought that Cash McCall might be interested in buying the company. Of course, Gil Clark has already brought the possible acquisition of Suffolk Moulding to McCall's attention.

Atherson calls Cash to tell him about Austen's company and mentions that Austen is meeting his daughter, Lory, at three o'clock in the lobby of the hotel where Cash resides. Lory and Cash had a brief romantic relationship in Maine prior to the events of the novel. Cash and Lory spot each other in the lobby at the hotel—she had no idea that McCall was the person interested in buying the company.

Lory and Grant Austen go with McCall to his apartment to discuss the possible sale of Suffolk to McCall. There Lory, an illustrator of children's books, sees the frontispiece drawing she had done for a novel hanging on his wall. The drawing was clearly a portrait of Cash McCall. Austen makes Cash aware that he and Lory are the sole stockholders in the company and McCall informs Austen that he is the owner of Corporate Associates where Gil Clark had worked and who has been advising Austen on business matters. Cash wants to make certain that Austen is aware of the potential for bias in Clark's business advice. Cash explains that he had discussed the possible purchase with Clark and that Atherson's suggestions to Austen of McCall as a potential buyer are just coincidences. Austen states that he is only willing to accept money, not stock, for his company. General Danvers of Andscott was interested in buying Suffolk but he was only able to offer stock in exchange for the company. Austen fails to inform McCall about the possibility of Andscott pulling out its business. Cash offers Austen two million dollars and the deal is sealed by a handshake.

Lory Austen for years had wanted to be independent of her parents and the sale proceeds of her ten percent ownership in Suffolk (i.e., $200,000) could at least provide her with financial freedom. In turn, Grant Austen's wife, Miriam, yearns to be free of her daughter. Possessing an unhealthy jealousy of her daughter, Miriam wants to have Grant all to herself. She resents the late night talks about business in which Lory and Grant frequently engage. Miriam does not know that Lory also dreads their late night talks. Lory wants to travel to Italy to develop her talents as an artist. Miriam views McCall as potential marriage material for Lory.

McCall calls upon Gil Clark to take over the management of Suffolk during the transition phase and while he searched for a potential buyer of the company. Winston Conway, a highly competent and experienced lawyer, has observed that Cash is a trader whereas Gil is a builder. Gil comes to understand that not many people, not even the employees, realize what companies, and how many companies, that McCall owns. For example, McCall owns Lockwood Reports, a firm that collects information on individuals and companies. These reports do not contain information that is illegally obtained—all of its contents are available legally and publicly. Background checks are conducted but an ethical line is drawn so as not to invade the privacy of individuals (e.g., no wiretapping). Lockwood only engages in ethical intelligence gathering.

Gil sees Cash as a respectable and honest man who does not abandon his beliefs and morality in his personal life and in his business life. McCall knows that to be truly successful a man cannot sell his soul to make a profit. In his business deals McCall seeks out win-win situations. Cash's intentions with regard to Suffolk Moulding are highly respectable. He tells Gil that he knows he could have acquired the company for less than he offered. In Cash's words, "There's only one way that I can get a wallop out of a deal like this, Gil. And that's by knowing that I haven't dug money out of another man's hide" (211).

The lawyer, Winston Conway, speaks to Gil about McCalls honesty, openness and morality: "Yes the practice of law would be much more pleasant these days if there were few more gentlemen of Cash McCall stripe—and I use the word gentleman in its true meaning. They're becoming rare, you know, men who recognize the difference between a thing being morally right and legally right" (227).

Grant Austen is not the best husband or father, and recently has not done that well in business. He tends to suppress his wife and daughter. He is not able to delegate at work and has been unable to move his company forward. He is loyal to incompetent employees and once he has sold his company, he finds that this loyalty is not reciprocated to him. Austen's former employees ignore him as soon as he sells the business. Austen views life in terms of a series of win-lose outcomes. After he sold his company, he was free to try to mend his family relationships. Unfortunately, the sale of Suffolk leads him to lose his self-direction and self-identity. Austen has always gained his self-worth from his status in society and his membership in the business community. A man of low self-esteem and self-confidence, Austen views and judges himself through the eyes of other people. Unknown to Austen, McCall arranges for someone from Washington to invite Austen to be a member of a committee of U.S. businessmen who would give advice to Latin American companies. Austen becomes a wealthy man liberated from his company but still rather dependent upon others for his sense of worth.

Cash McCall is not yet forty. Vibrant and self-assured, he tries to stay anonymous, deals with secrecy, and values his privacy. He keeps his ownership interest in various companies quiet and only divulges his ownership when he believe that someone has the right to know about it. Only Cash's advisors can contact him. He surrounds himself with high caliber people and has the ability to discern and develop new talent. Cash lives in a penthouse suite (an entire floor) at the top of the Hotel Ivanhoe, and has a direct phone number that bypasses the hotel switchboard. He also has a country retreat home that is surrounded by mountains and that overlooks a waterfall. Having made his first million dollars before he was thirty, McCall flies a remodeled B-26 ex-military bomber. His two residencies complement the two sides of his personality. His penthouse symbolizes success and his secluded countryside retreat symbolizes freedom in his personal life.

Maude Kennard is the effective, detail-oriented, power-seeking, and ambitious manager of the hotel where McCall resides. At first she views Cash as an irritant to her because of his wealth and ability to obtain whatever he wants. She changes her mind about McCall when she eventually concludes that he owns the hotel. She becomes very interested in him (perhaps even romantically), pursues him, and toward the end of the story, tries to damage him. Cash of course has no interest in her. She even attempts to attain a Lockwood Report to gain information about him.

Miriam Austen wants her daughter to spend time with McCall. Lory drives Cash to the airport and he talks her into getting on his private plane. They embark for his private estate where he explains to her that he had fallen in love with her in Maine and that he should not have called off their relationship. He realizes that he had made a mistake when he did not pursue her when she showed up at his cabin. He tells her that he has been searching for her ever since. He had thought that he was not ready for a serious relationship. He had always seen himself as being too busy to fall in love. Cash and Lory decide to get married. The jealous Kennard attempts to get revenge when she finds out.

Gil begins managing Suffolk Moulding and discovers that Suffolk owns the patents to the machines that produce Andscott's products. When Cash returns, Gil tells him about the valuable patents that General Danvers needs to run his business. These patents are now McCall's property. Gil and Cash now realize that because of these essential patents, Danvers needs to continue to do business with Suffolk. Danvers is upset about Cash's purchasing Suf-

folk. Danvers was prejudiced against McCall because Cash had sold to Andscott a cabinet plant it had offered to Andscott a year earlier for half the
price. McCall is able to capitalize on these patents, an overlooked detail that
could have kept Austen from being pressured by Andscott. Even if Danvers
had really wanted to pull his business from Suffolk he would not have been
able to continue in business.

McCall is now in a position to make a significant profit on the purchase
and sale of Suffolk Moulding. General Danvers attempts to buy Suffolk for
300,000 shares of Andscott stock valued at three million dollars so that he
can retain the patents. McCall initiates a plan in which he can potentially gain
control of both Suffolk and Andscott. He begins by personally buying another 200,000 shares of Andscott on the market. Andscott gives 300,000
shares of stock to Cash through Cash's Gammer Corporation.

Cash has learned that a medical research foundation established by Hor-
ace Andrews has a large block of Andscott stock. The foundation depends
upon Andscott dividends for funding its research projects and no dividends
have been paid for the last four years. Cash wants to add the foundation's
proxy to the half million shares of Andscott that he has acquired, thus giving
him ownership control over Andscott and Suffolk. Gil sets up a meeting with
Dr. Martin Bergmann, head of the research foundation. Gil finds out that
Bergmann supports Cash and wants him to take a strong interest in the
management of Andscott. Bergmann needs Andscott dividends and he believes that Andscott desperately needs a new president. Ultimately, Cash
finds a president for Andscott but keeps Danvers as Chairman of the Board.
Despite their previous run-ins, Cash, ever the professional, recognizes Danvers's talents and offers him that important position. McCall also sends Gil to
Andscott for a new career as Vice President of Research and Development.

Trouble begins to brew when Harvey Bannon, President of Cavalier
Chemical Company and a member of Andscott's board, divulges to Grant
Austen that Andscott is giving 300,000 shares of stock worth approximately
three million dollars to Cash (through Cash's Gammer Corporation) for Suffolk. Austen is furious because he thinks that McCall has duped him and
made a fool of him by turning right around to sell Suffolk to Andscott at a
one million dollar profit. On top of this, Maude Kennard discovers that Cash
did not own the Hotel Ivanhoe and that he planned on bringing a woman into
his life and it was not her. The jealous Kennard had also overheard details of
McCall's business deal with Andscott. She attempts to gain revenge by un-
professionally telling Austen that he is being taken advantage of by Cash.
Kennard also discusses what she overheard about Cash's business deal with
lawyer Clay B. Torrant.

The infuriated Austen seriously considers a lawsuit against McCall. He
suspects that Gil Clark, Harrison Glenn, Will Atherson, Winston Conway,
and others are all part of the "McCall gang" and conspired against him.

Austen appears to forget that he had wanted cash rather than stock. What had actually occurred was the result of a number of remarkable coincidences involving the above individuals—there was no conspiracy. The parties involved all agree that they would be willing to give Austen back his company if that was what he wanted. Cash and the rest of the "McCall gang" are willing to reverse the sale.

Cash goes to see Austen to see if he can clear up matters. Lory reminds her father that Cash had been upfront from the beginning and told him that he owned Gil's company. During the conversation between the Austens, Lori, and Cash, all of the evidence is presented and explained and the air is cleared. Austen then understands what really transpired. Austen realizes that it was he who had not been forthcoming when he had withheld information about the potential loss of a major customer. He also remember how happy he had been with the price he received, how Cash had suggested that he receive legal counsel, and how Cash had asked him if he was certain he wanted to go through the deal. In the end, Cash is shown to be an ethical financial maverick who finds the romantic relationship that he had been lacking.

Chapter Fifteen

Sloan Wilson's *The Man in the Gray Flannel Suit*

Published in 1955, Sloan Wilson's *The Man in the Gray Flannel Suit* was universally acclaimed and captured the authentic mood of post-World War II America. This old-fashioned social novel was a massive national best seller and was made into an award-winning film in 1956 starring Gregory Peck as Tom Rath, Jennifer Jones as his wife Betsy, and Frederic March as Ralph Hopkins.

The novel paints a realistic portrait of what life was like in the early 1950s for the typical middle-class family. Portraying the roles of men and women of the time, it brings home to today's reader how the culture has changed since the days when men would go off to work and women would stay home to take care of the children. *The Man in the Gray Flannel Suit* supplies a journalistic depiction of many period details of the era and of corporate life including William H. Whyte's "organization man." The novel successfully embodies the spirit of the pure 1950s including conformity, political inactivism, conflict avoidance, and the primacy of the nuclear family.

Tom Rath is a pleasant thirty-three-year-old Harvard graduate with a complicated past including emotional scars from his wartime actions, sorrow for a comrade lost during a battle, regret and pain from a lost love affair, and apprehension and wonder with respect to a child he is not certain that he had. Battling the mental anguish of a man who served in war, the cautious and reticent Tom lacks confidence but nevertheless seeks a comfortable living and a restoration of order in his life after the chaos he has experienced.

Tom holds a monotonous, unexciting job as assistant to the director of the Schanenhauser Foundation which finances scientific research and the arts. Living in a modest house for the last seven years with his wife, Betsy, and their three children, Tom takes the same train to New York City each day to perform a job that rarely varies and experiences a predictable social life. His children are fascinated by (perhaps addicted to) television and rarely have an interest in anything else. Betsy dislikes and feels trapped in their Westport, Connecticut home and would much rather live somewhere else. Tom essentially goes through the motions while his socially ambitious wife tries to figure out how to make their lives better.

After Tom left the army, he began working at Schanenhauser Foundation at the request of his grandmother. It is unlikely that he would be promoted soon and he did not aspire to climb very far up the corporate ladder. However, he knows that he needs to earn more money to care for his wife and children and to keep them comfortable and happy. Betsy wants to find a better home and presses Tom to find a higher paying job. Betsy is optimistic, enthusiastic, and eager to upgrade to a nicer house. The Raths are members of the "Greatest Generation" who survived the Great Depression during their teen years and who now want to prosper economically, have their children attend good schools, and have a nice home in the suburbs.

Tom has been unable to communicate with his wife after his war experiences. He has not come to terms with the decisions he had made and the things he had done during the war years. Tom experiences disturbing and horrific flashbacks to when he was a captain and a paratrooper in World War II. He had killed seventeen men in combat and, in one instance, he killed a young German soldier in order to gain the warmth of his coat.

While in Rome, Italy, waiting for transportation to their next mission in the Pacific, Tom and his best friend, Hank Mahoney, decide to go to town to find some girls to spend the evening with. He meets a young, beautiful Italian girl, Maria, and falls in love with her. Tom had been honest with Maria about his marriage and open with respect to his feelings for her. Their affair had only lasted seven weeks and Tom had never been happier. When he leaves, she tells him that she thinks she is pregnant with his child and that she hopes that she is.

Later, Tom accidentally kills his best friend, Mahoney, in what could be classified as "friendly fire." While engaging in combat, Tom mistakenly throws a grenade and kills his friend who dies in his arms. He has never recovered emotionally from what happened to him overseas including his guilt over the killings, his affair with Maria, and the possibility of an illegitimate child. Tom apparently needs to come to terms with these war-time situations in order to somehow correct the psychological damage he has undergone. He clearly suffers from what today would be called post-traumatic stress disorder (PTSD). His wife only knows that somehow he has changed and has not been the same since he has returned from the war. Betsy assumes that the war compelled him to grow and that this new, uncommunicative man was a reflection of his maturity.

Tom's friend, Bill Hawthorne, tells him about the possibility of a public relations position opening at United Broadcasting Corporation that would pay more than his current job does. With the increased compensation, the Raths could afford to buy a new home. Betsy thinks that Tom should speak to his grandmother about the job because she believes that she might be able to influence UBC. Tom's current position with the Schanenhauser charitable foundation was directly attributable to his grandmother and to the Rath family name, given that Tom's grandfather had been a state senator. He served one term as a state senator in Hartford but spent the rest of his life accomplishing very little. Living in the past, Tom's grandmother had delusions of grandeur and perceived her deceased husband to have been more accomplished than he actually was. She also believed Tom's father, Steven, to have been a success, but he actually had not been one. Steven had worked for a financial firm but was let go after two years. He was killed in a suspicious car crash that very well may have been a suicide.

Tom is wary of change and is uncomfortable applying for this vague and ill-defined job at UBC. As part of the initial interview process, Tom is asked to write his autobiography in one hour's time finishing with the sentence: "The most significant fact about me is . . . the unforthcoming young man finishes fifty minutes early and simply says . . . the most significant fact about me is that I am applying for a position in the public relations department, and after an initial period of learning, I would probably do a good job" (14).

The introspective Tom Rath reflects on the four totally unrelated worlds in which he exists. There are: (1) the ghost-ridden world of his grandmother and his deceased parents; (2) the best-not-remembered world in which he had been a paratrooper; (3) the matter-of-fact world of places like UBC and the Schanenhauser Foundation; and (4) the world populated by his wife and kids. Although he thinks that there must be some way in which these worlds are related, he thinks that it would be best to consider these as totally separate from one another.

After several interviews, Tom is offered a position at UBC but at a lower salary than he expected. After haggling over the salary, he accepts the position as special assistant to the president of UBC, Ralph Hopkins. Tom's initial assignment is to help Mr. Hopkins write a speech that he will deliver to a large group of physicians and other medical professionals that would inspire them to develop a national committee on mental health awareness issues and to recognize that Hopkins is the right man to take charge of the committee. Despite his title, Rath actually has to report to Bill Ogden, Hopkins's right-hand "yes man." Tom realizes that working on such a special project could be risky if Hopkins losses interest in it or if the committee does not come into existence. While working for the charitable foundation, he was able to spend a significant amount of time with his family but he finds out that he no longer has that luxury after beginning work with the network.

While working on this project, Tom encounters two distinct and opposite management styles. The humorless and resentful Ogden seems to be jealous of Rath, focuses on negative criticism, and verbally degrades Tom's efforts without offering any advice other than by saying that the speech is too boring. We could easily say that Ogden, the man that Rath reports to, is less than helpful. Hopkins focuses on positive reinforcement, always politely thanks Tom for his efforts, emphasizes collaboration, and makes Tom feel valued and willing to expend extra effort. Of course, after praising Tom's efforts, Hopkins still sits down with him, picks the speech apart, and offers many detailed suggestions for revisions. Tom becomes frustrated as he submits a great many drafts of the speech and each one of them is rejected.

While Tom is still adjusting to his new job, he finds out that his grandmother had fallen and had broken her thigh and her pelvis. She unwillingly goes to the hospital and requests Tom to meet with her estate lawyer, Mr. Sims, who tells Tom that he is the sole beneficiary of her estate. She dies only eight days after she had fallen. She had told Tom that she wants him and his family to live in her home and to make some provisions for her long-time caretaker and butler, Edward Schultz.

Betsy decides to take responsibility for her own happiness and for that of her family. She begins to change the family dynamics by having the family members have breakfast together and to attend church as a family every Sunday. Her program of family self-improvement also includes getting Tom involved in local politics, selling her despised house, and becoming a real estate entrepreneur herself. When Tom's grandmother passed away, she left a home on twenty acres of land and a carriage house. Betsy develops grand plans for the house and the land. She wants to subdivide the land, develop small lots, build houses on them, and sell them to make money. She does some research and finds out that there may be trouble with zoning laws but the optimistic Betsy is not deterred.

Tom's new job, his grandmother's death, and his wife's plans for the estate unsettle the psychologically fragile Tom Rath as he is traveling to his job in New York. He thinks back to the war and to the words that had a marvelous soothing effect on him. When he jumped out the door of a plane he would say to himself, "It doesn't really matter." Then, as he began to open his parachute, he would think, "Here goes nothing." Finally, as he was about to land he would say, "It will be interesting to see what happens." He finds that these three catch phrases still hold their power, as he feels relaxed by the time the train arrives in New York.

When Tom goes to work, he recognizes the elevator operator as a man who was with him during the war and who knows of the events that have affected Tom's life. The man is Caesar Gardella, a fellow paratrooper with

Tom in World War II. Gardella knows of Tom's affair with Maria because he dated, and eventually married, Maria's cousin, Gina. Tom and Caesar do not reunite right away but eventually Tom learns from Caesar that Maria did have a son. He tells Tom that things are not going well for Maria and her son. She had married a local shop owner who is now deceased. Caesar and his wife send Maria money each month and they hope that Tom will also do so. Betsy has no idea about the affair or the child, and Tom's first instinct is to conceal the boy's existence from her. Tom knows that he will not turn away from his responsibility, but he has the dilemma of deciding when and how to tell Betsy about the situation.

Another problem develops when the caretaker, Edward Schultz, claims that Tom's grandmother had promised the estate to him in appreciation of his service and dedication. This subplot threatens the Rath's ability to upgrade their living quarters and their plans to subdivide the adjacent land. Probate Judge Saul Bernstein is brought in to settle the dispute. Although the will explicitly states that Tom is the sole heir of the Rath estate, Edward has a signed but unwitnessed piece of paper saying that the house is to be his. As a judge of the probate court, Bernstein is concerned with the orderly disposition of papers rather than with people.

When Tom's inheritance is in doubt because of the counter-claim, Judge Bernstein goes out of his way to investigate the other claimant and uncovers his dishonesty. Exceeding his duties and prerogatives as a judge, he engages in some detective work to discover that the caretaker had been embezzling. He finds out that Schultz has been lying and falsifying documents for a long period of time in order to obtain extra money. The judge finds out that the servant went shop to shop to ask the shop owners to substantially (i.e., by twenty percent) pad bills so that he would get additional money on top of the compensation he was receiving for his duties. In turn, the storekeepers would receive a kickback. Judge Bernstein meets with Edward and his lawyer and accuses him of padding the household bills. When the dishonest butler is confronted with the judge's evidence, the litigation comes to a quick end. A contract is proposed that would absolve the servant from being sued for padding the bills and, in turn, he would forfeit his claim to the house.

Ralph Hopkins is a wealthy, well-respected businessman and empire builder who is surrounded by "yes-men." Totally committed to his work, Hopkins has made consistent decisions throughout his career, thereby building a great company and making a great deal of money. His every decision has bolstered his career goals at the cost of his relationships with his wife, son, and daughter. While he focused on climbing the corporate ladder, he missed many opportunities with his family. The multi-talented, agreeable, polite, workaholic schedules appointments for every waking moment and does not see his family for weeks at a time. Hopkins explains that the world is built by two types of complementary men: (1) the great men who are willing to do whatever it takes to build an organization; and (2) the men who work for an organization from nine to five. He understands that nothing can be achieved without both types of men. It is obvious that Hopkins is the kind of man who loves to work and whose happiness depends upon his work.

Hopkins's disconnection between his work life and his family life is reflected in his daughter's actions. She parties constantly, runs around with older, inappropriate men, and does not work nor attend college. Hopkins and his distraught wife learn that she has eloped with a man her father's age. We also discover that Hopkins and his wife no longer live together.

Hopkins likes Tom Rath, who reminds him of his late son who had been killed in combat during the war. Hopkins has had a difficult time coping with his son's death. His son had made an honorable choice by enlisting even though he knew that his father could have pulled the appropriate strings to produce a commissioned position in the service.

Tom finds that it is not easy to write the speech to help Hopkins present the mental health proposals as successive versions of the speech are rejected. He begins to question the value of the work in his new job. Tom also feels strange "giving away" his writing as though it is not his own work. However, he does realize that keeping his job and meeting Hopkins's expectations are more important considerations than receiving proper recognition for what he had written.

After many extensive revisions of the speech, Tom is taken off the project and the speech is given to someone else, leaving Tom with grave doubts about his future with UBC. Subsequently, Hopkins asks Tom what he thinks about a new version of the speech that had been written by another individual. As a result, he is able to look at it objectively for the first time and sees it as boring, superficial, filled with slogans, preaching to the choir, and offering no concrete proposals for improving mental health. The speech reiterated what the doctors already know. It seems to appeal to the fact that mental health is important rather than to the need for a mental health committee. Betsy reads the speech and concurs with her husband's assessment of it.

Tom is torn with respect to how he should respond to Hopkins about the quality and tone of the speech. He wants to say: "I'm sorry but I think that this speech is absurd. It's an untrue repetition of the obvious fact that mental health is important. You've said that over and over again and finally turned it into a cheap advertising slogan. If you want to form a mental-health committee, why don't you find out what needs to be done and offer to help do it?" (193).

Tom thinks that he can't talk to his boss like that and expect to hold on to his job. He considers telling the man what he thinks he wants to hear. Betsy wants Tom to be honest and to have integrity and self-respect, but he realizes that it is not easy when one doesn't have security, money, and other jobs waiting for him. Tom decides that the responsible thing to do is to be honest with Hopkins about the speech.

Tom gains the respect of Hopkins when he tells him what he honestly thinks of the speech. Tom persuades Hopkins that the approach to the speech is all wrong. It misrepresents Hopkins's qualifications to head the campaign. He should be viewed as what he is—an intelligent and responsible layman who can bring doctors and a committee of publicity men together. Tom urges Hopkins to propose practical ways to initiate a mental health program rather than simply repeating how important it is to have such a program. Hopkins appreciates Tom's insights and honesty and thinks that Tom is on to something.

Hopkins delivers his speech in Atlantic City and asks the doctors if there is anything the public could do to help them conquer the mental health problem. He says: "We laymen must make sure we have a broad understanding of the problems physicians face and the physicians have the tools they need to find solutions" (217). He concludes by saying:

> There is a possibility that some organization might be formed, similar in purpose to the March of Dimes, to subsidize research on mental disease, but, beyond that, to banish unreasonable fear. In such an effort, the medical profession would have to take the lead. I think you can be sure that those of us whose business it is to transmit information to the public will do everything we can to help. (218)

The speech goes well and Hopkins receives many requests to start the committee.

Hopkins asks Tom to be his personal assistant after the speech is delivered and Tom accepts and moves into Hopkins's outer office. He had been honest and is rewarded for it as Hopkins takes Tom under his wing. He discovers that being Hopkins's personal assistant entails working a lot more hours than he wants to work and spending a great deal of time away from his family. He finds his new position to include an indefinite and ever-growing set of responsibilities.

Hopkins rewards Tom's integrity by offering him the job of setting up and heading a separate but affiliated organization in Los Angeles, California. Tom tells Hopkins that he is not like him and that he does not want to work all of the time. He turns down this significant promotion with a similarly significant raise in compensation in order to become more of a nine to five person. He had decided to find a less demanding job which would offer him both dignity and more time with his family rather than attempt to be a top businessman by accepting a high-pressure position. In his words:

I don't think I am the kind of guy who should try to be a big executive. I'll say it frankly: I don't think I have the willingness to make the sacrifices. I don't want to give up the time. I'm trying to be honest about this. I want the

money. Nobody likes money better than I do. But I'm just not the kind of guy
who can work evenings and weekends and all the rest of it forever. I guess
there's even more to it than that. I'm not the kind of person who can get all
wrapped up in a job—I can't get myself convinced that my work is the most
important thing in the world (251).

Rather than run the corporate rat race, Tom Rath is willing to take a
satisfactory comfortable position on the sidelines. His renunciation is the
modern-day equivalent of Herman Melville's Bartleby's "I prefer not to."

Hopkins is a good and kind man who is compassionate and understanding
of why Tom chooses not to wrap himself up completely in business. Hopkins
says that he appreciates Rath's honesty and that there are a lot of good
positions where it is not required for a man to put in an inordinate amount of
work. He said:

> I think we can find something for you. . . . How would you like to go back to
> the mental-health committee? That will be developing into a small, permanent
> organization. I'm thinking of giving my house in South Bay to be its headquar-
> ters. That would be nice for you—you wouldn't even have any commuting.
> How would you like to be director of the outfit? The job would pay pretty
> well. I'd like to think I had a man with your integrity there, and I'll be making
> all the major decisions." (252)

After Tom turned down the great opportunity, his tolerant boss has surpris-
ingly offered him a comfortable mid-level position.

After Tom says that he would be grateful for that, Hopkins suddenly
turns, faces him, and says: "Somebody has to do the big jobs! . . . The world
was built by men like me! To really do a job, you have to live it, body and
soul! You people who just give half your mind to work are riding on our
backs!" (252). Tom responds that he knows that and Hopkins immediately
regains control of himself and tells Tom that he thinks that Tom has made a
good decision. He tells Tom that he needs men like Tom who can keep a
sense of proportion.

Betsy has decided to make a housing development out of the land on the
estate consisting of several rows of homes running parallel to the waterfront.
To do this, permission needs to be obtained from the zoning board. At the
same time, the town is facing the public matter of a bond issue to support the
construction of a new elementary school. Both projects involve change, and a
number of the town's residents did not want the town to change. The issues
of the housing development, the new school, and town change and expansion
are inextricably interrelated. If the people won't build new schools, then the
town cannot bring in a lot of new families. The local electorate votes to tax
itself more dearly in order to have a better school, and the village authorizes
an exception to the zoning laws permitting the Raths to turn their inherited
land into a commercial development.

Tom regains confidence and control over his life when he tells Betsy about the perils of war, his love affair with Maria for love, companionship, and passion, and the child that was born from that affair. He explains to Betsy that his mindset during the war was that it was quite likely that he would not return home from the war. She becomes hurt and angry, speeds off in the car, calms down, and returns the next day. Tom wants to accept responsibility by helping Maria and her son. Together, Tom and Betsy agree to send one hundred dollars to them each month. They work things out through Judge Bernstein and they tell him that they eventually want to establish a trust fund for the boy. Bernstein is touched and does not charge the Raths for his services. Tom and Betsy are reconnected and seem to be closer together than they have ever been before. Although Betsy was stunned and felt betrayed at first, the news opens up their ability to communicate with one another and makes their relationship stronger and healthier.

The Man in the Gray Flannel Suit is about making choices, accountability, self-awareness, self-control, integrity, and achieving balance and order in one's life. Tom goes from passive anonymity to become a self-conscious, self-empowered individual capable of making honorable decisions. Throughout the story he is on a path of self-discovery. By the end of the novel, he is able to connect his life as a paratrooper in World War II, his work life, and his family life of suburban domesticity.

At one point in the novel, Tom declares that money is the root of all order. Later on he rejects the notion that happiness is only attainable through the accumulation of material possessions. He chooses not to be on the fast track to financial success. He does not aspire to do the things necessary to be on top. He realizes that he would be happier working less and being more involved with his family. Tom's virtues of honesty, integrity, and so on are rewarded in Sloan Wilson's benevolent society. Tom Rath concludes that he may not be able to do anything about the world, but that he can set his own life in order.

Chapter Sixteen

Atlas Shrugged

An Epic Story of Heroic Businessmen

In *Atlas Shrugged* (1957) Ayn Rand presents her original, brilliant, and controversial philosophy of Objectivism in dramatized form. This novel articulates a theoretically consistent, systematic, and intellectually-sound defense of capitalism; expounds the principles of traditional liberalism, voluntary cooperation, and individual freedom; and exposes the errors of collectivism and coercion. *Atlas Shrugged* is the philosophical and artistic capstone of Ayn Rand's novels.

Atlas Shrugged characterizes business and businessmen in a favorable light by emphasizing: the possibilities of life in a free society; the inherent ethical nature of capitalism and the good businessman; the strength, courage, integrity, and self-sufficiency of the hardworking businessman; and the entrepreneur as wealth creator and promotor of human progress. Teachers can use this great novel to promulgate the conceptual and moral foundations of a free society to their students. *Atlas Shrugged* is a powerful tool to educate people with respect to a just and proper political and economic order that is a true reflection of man and the world properly understood. This novel has a strong emotional impact, portrays a positive sense of life, and serves as a blueprint for the future and potential source for social change.

Atlas Shrugged shows the businessman's role as potentially heroic by celebrating the energy and opportunity of life for men of talent and ambition to make something of themselves. This superb novel teaches that acts of courage and creativity consist of having integrity rather than in blind obedience and in inspiring others instead of following them. *Atlas Shrugged* portrays the business hero as a persistent, original, and independent thinker who pursues an idea to its fruition. Rand's masterpiece dramatizes the positive qualities of the businessman by showing the triumph of individualism over collectivism; depicting business heroes as noble, appealing, and larger than life; and by characterizing business careers as at least as, if not more, honorable, as careers in medicine, law, or education.

Atlas Shrugged is beginning to be taught in colleges and universities in a variety of courses. It is being used in the classroom to study the moral foundations of capitalism and commerce and related topics in philosophy, economics, free enterprise, management, business, and other areas. This novel provides an excellent base for teaching issues in business, business ethics, economics, and political and economic philosophy. The use of *Atlas Shrugged* aids in moving between abstract principles and realistic business examples. The novel serves as a link between philosophical concepts and the practical aspects of business and illustrates that philosophy is accessible and important to people in general and to business people in particular.

Atlas Shrugged fosters a spirited exchange of ideas among students in the classroom as many students respond strongly and positively to this novel and its heroes. The novel presents the pursuit of profit as thoroughly moral, makes the discussion of capitalism intellectually legitimate, provides a powerful critique of socialism, and challenges the prevailing beliefs of our culture. Students are impressed with *Atlas Shrugged*'s prophetic nature. It portrays the United States economy collapsing due to government intervention and regulation, politicians placing the blame on capitalism and the free market, and the government countering with ever more controls that further the crisis. Government intervention is shown to discourage innovation and risk-taking, and the novel portrays how regulations in a mixed economy are made with political interest groups lobbying the government which grants favors to those who have the most votes, political pull, or influence.

Atlas Shrugged possesses striking narrative power and manifests the essentials of an entire philosophical system. It is a model of integration among theme, story, and characters. Its most extraordinary quality is its integration with every event, action, and character serving both dramatic and philosophical purposes. *Atlas Shrugged* is a very intentional novel with every detail designed to mean something by the author. Even the philosophical speeches are integrated with the events of the story. The lengthy philosophical speeches are integrated components of the plot, make explicit the principles dramatized throughout the actions of the novel, and move the story forward.

Ayn Rand formulated her characters in *Atlas Shrugged* with reference to philosophical principles and premises. She presents no random details and focuses on the essentials to understanding each character. Each character serves a purpose and the author skillfully matches characters against each other. Rand presents her characters as parallels and contrasts. In this story of human action, the author ties physical actions to the values of her characters.

The actions of the novel support philosophical moral principles through the purposeful progression of events. The reader sees values embodied in concrete form in the world. The most crucial events are dramatized. Rand also effectively uses flashbacks and symbolism as supplementary techniques. There are no "floating symbols" as the author typically illustrates an idea in action and then uses a symbol to bring abstract subject matter down to the observational level. In her strongly ironic novel, Rand also effectively alters and adapts some famous Greek myths in order to tell these from an Objectivist viewpoint. By changing them, she challenges their traditional meanings and infuses them with new meanings reflecting her revolutionary worldview. Another one of her techniques is to contrast the universe of the men of reason and the men of unreason in consecutive scenes.

This both anachronistic and timeless story takes place in the not-too-distant future in a slightly modified United States where there is a Head of State instead of a President and a National Legislature rather than a Congress. American society is crumbling under the impact of the welfare state and creeping socialism, and most other nations have already become Communist People's States. Most companies are owned and run by individual entrepreneurs. A somber mood and sense of dread permeate a society that is filled with government interference and political corruption.

The story is an apocalyptic vision of the last stages of a conflict between two classes of humanity—the looters (non-creators) and the non-looters (creators). The looters are proponents of high taxation, big labor, government ownership, government spending, government planning, regulation, and redistribution. They include politicians and their supporters, intellectuals, government bureaucrats, scientists who sell their minds to the bureaucrats, and liberal businessmen, who, afraid of honest competition, sell out their initiative, creative powers, and independence for the security of government regulation. The looters are impervious to reason and believe that the prime movers will always come to their aid and save them. The looters believe that by expropriating the wealth of the creators they will gain an unearned moral status and self-esteem.

The non-looters—the thinkers and doers—are the competent and daring individualists who innovate and create new enterprises. These prime movers love their work, are dedicated to achievement through their thought and effort, and abhor the forces of collectivism and mediocrity. The battle is thus between the non-earners who deal by force and "profit" through political power and earners who deal by trade and profit through productive ability. *Atlas Shrugged* is a story of the struggle between people with contradictory visions, values, and moralities.

Atlas Shrugged illustrates that there are good and bad businessmen and that businessmen don't always act virtuously. There are two kinds of businessmen—those who lobby government for special privileges, make deals, as well as engage in fraud and corrupt activities, and the real producers who succeed or fail on their own. Rand's business heroes are independent, rational, and committed to the facts of reality, to the judgment of their own minds, and to their own happiness. Each of them thinks for himself, actualizes his potential, and views himself as competent to deal with the challenges of life and as worthy of success and happiness. *Atlas Shrugged* makes a great case that the businessman is the appropriate and best symbol of a free society.

Production is the means to the fulfillment of men's material needs. *Atlas Shrugged* masterfully illustrates that the production of goods, services, and wealth metaphysically precedes their distribution and exchange. The primacy of production means that we must produce before we can consume. Production (i.e., supply) is the source of demand. This means that products are ultimately paid for with other products. Rand shows that, because life requires the production of values, people in business are heroic. The heroes of *Atlas Shrugged* find joy in taking risks and bringing men and materials together to produce what people value.

Atlas Shrugged chronicles the rise of corrupt businessmen who profit by dealing with dishonest politicians. They avoid rationality and productivity by using their political pull and pressure groups to loot the producers. The looters exploit the creators in both physical and spiritual concerns. They attack the self-esteem of the producers by advocating the morality of altruism which holds that the pursuit of happiness is a source of guilt. The looters employ need, weakness, and incompetence as a demand on the creators. They deem it to be acceptable to receive altruistic "gifts" if a person is weak, suffering, or incompetent. Rand is scathing in her indictment of these villains who would rob the creative thinkers who are responsible for human progress and prosperity.

Government intervention discourages innovation and risk-taking and obstructs the process of wealth-creation. In *Atlas Shrugged* the producers' minds are shackled by government policies. Lacking the freedom to create, compete, and earn wealth, the independent thinkers withdraw from society. This is Rand's recommended response to the bureaucratic assault of the entrepreneurial spirit. Whereas the theme of *Atlas Shrugged* is the role of the mind in human existence, the plot-theme is the men of the mind going on strike against an altruistic-collectivistic society.

Atlas Shrugged delineates government intervention as the great enemy of the businessman. Rand details how government intervention into private markets produces costs and unintended consequences more harmful than the targeted problem itself. Socialistic bureaucrats attempt to protect men from their own minds and tend to think only of intended, primary, and immediate results while ignoring unintended, ancillary, and long-term ones. Government-produced impediments to a free society are shown to include taxation, protectionism, antitrust laws, regulation, welfare programs, inflation, and more.

The plot is built around several business and industrial executives. The beautiful Dagny Taggart, perhaps the most heroic female protagonist in American fiction, is the operating genius who efficiently runs Taggart Transcontinental Railroad, which was founded by her grandfather. Her brother James, president in title only, is an indecisive, incompetent, liberal businessman who takes all the credit for his sister's achievements. Dagny optimistically and confidently performs Herculean labors to keep the railroad running despite destructive government edicts, her brother's weaknesses, the incompetence of many of her associates, and the silent and inexplicable disappearance of society's competent industrialists. Free of inner conflict, Dagny is passionately creative and comfortable with respect to her fundamental relationship to existence. She is a model of synthesis, unity, and mind-body integration. Dagny is an engineer and the operating vice-president of a transcontinental railroad who deals with every industry and every policy of the looters. Because of her integrating context, she has contact with every industry, thus permitting the reader to see the total collapse of modern industrial civilization.

As both society and her railroad are disintegrating, Dagny attempts to rebuild an old Taggart rail line. In the process, she contacts Hank Rearden, a self-made steel tycoon and inventor of an alloy stronger and lighter than steel. Rearden, Dagny's equal in intelligence, determination, and sense of responsibility, becomes her ally and eventually her lover. They struggle to keep the economy running and ultimately discover the secret of the continuing disappearance of the men of ability.

John Galt, a messiah of free enterprise, is secretly persuading thinkers and doers to vanish mysteriously one after the other—deserting and sometimes sabotaging their factories before they depart. Galt explains how desperately the world needs productive individuals, but how viciously it treats them. The greater a person's productive ability, the greater are the penalties he endures in the form of regulations, controls, and the expropriation and redistribution of his earned wealth. This evil, however, is only made possible by the sanction of the victims. By accepting an underserved guilt—not for their vices but for their virtues—the achievers have acquiesced in the political theft of their minds' products. Galt masterminds his plan to stop the motor of the world by convincing many of the giants of intellect and productivity to refuse to be exploited any longer by the looters and the moochers, to strike by withdrawing their talents from the world by escaping to a secret hideout in the Colorado Rockies, thus leaving the welfare state to destroy itself. The hero-conspirators will then return to lay the groundwork for a healthy new social order based on the principles of laissez-faire capitalism.

Galt, the mysterious physicist who is also a philosopher, teacher, and leader of an intellectual movement, has invented a motor that can convert static electricity into useful but inexpensive kinetic energy. He chooses to keep his invention a secret until it is time for him and the other heroes to reclaim the world. For two-thirds of the novel, Galt exists only as a plaintive expressive—Who is John Galt? He has been in hiding, working underground as a laborer in the Taggart Tunnels, while recruiting the strikers.

One of the key hero-characters is Francisco d'Anconia, aristocrat, copper baron, and former lover of Dagny, who prefers to destroy his mines systematically rather than to let them fall into the hands of the looters. Another is Ragnar Danneskjöld, a philosopher turned pirate, who raids only public, nonprofit commerce ships in order to return to the productive what is rightly theirs.

The men of ability fade out of the picture and are labeled traitors and deserters by Dagny and Hank, who remain fighting at their desks. Ironically, because they have not been told of the conspiracy, Dagny and Hank are even battling their natural allies—the ex-leaders of the business world who have gone on strike. The result is that not only is there dramatic conflict between the good and the bad, there is also conflict between the good and the good. Dagny and Hank, the primary creators, are philosophically against the looters, but in action they support them. Also, existentially Dagny and Rearden oppose Galt and the other strikers, but philosophically they agree with them.

Dagny pursues one of the deserters by plane to a valley deep in the Rockies, crashes, and accidentally discovers John Galt's headquarters—the Utopian free-enterprise community created by the former business leaders along with several academicians, artists, and artisans. They have set up Galt's Gulch (also known as Mulligan's Valley) as a refuge from the looters and moochers of the outside world.

Galt's Gulch is the hidden valley that is the Atlantis of *Atlas Shrugged*. This paradigm and microcosm of a free society consists of a voluntary association of men held together by nothing but every man's self-interest. Here, productive men who have gone on strike are free to produce and trade as long as they observe the valley's customs. In this secret free society, enshrouded by the crumbling interventionist one, each individual is unencumbered in the pursuit of his own flourishing and happiness.

Dagny is the last hero, except for Hank, to reach Galt's outpost. While there, she listens to the logic of Galt and his associates and falls in love with Galt, who represents all that she values. Inspired by the vision of Rearden, who continues to search for her and to battle the looters, she decides to return to a world in shambles. Dagny and Hank refuse almost to the end to accept Galt's plan and stubbornly fight to save the economy. John Galt returns as well so that he can look out for her and be there when she decides she has had enough.

Mr. Thompson, Head of State, is scheduled to address the nation regarding economic conditions when he is cut off the air and preempted by John Galt, who, in a three-hour speech, spells out the tenets of his rational philosophy. He tells the citizens that the men of the mind have gone on strike, that human beings require freedom of thought and action, and that they must reject the code of self-sacrifice.

Dagny inadvertently leads the looter-politicians to Galt. They capture him and, in an attempt to save the crumbling economy, they offer him the position of Economic Dictator, which he promptly refuses. They take him prisoner and torture him, but the torture machine breaks down. Then, in a melodramatic confrontation, Galt is rescued by the Utopian entrepreneurs, and the looters are vanquished. Galt, Dagny, and the other men of the mind return to the valley, rewrite the Constitution, and add a clause stating that Congress shall make no law abridging the freedom of production and trade. At the end of the novel, just before going back to rebuild the world, Galt symbolically traces the sign of the dollar in the air.

Atlas Shrugged is an achievement of intricate structural composition and integration. The titles of its three major sections pay tribute to Aristotle, correspond to his basic philosophical axioms, and accomplish a thematic goal by implying something regarding the meaning of the events and actions in the respective sections of the novel. In part 1, called Non-Contradiction, there is a numerous series of strange and apparently contradictory events and paradoxes with no discernible logical solutions. In part 2, Either-Or, based on Aristotle's Law of Excluded Middle, Dagny faces a fundamental choice with no middle road—to continue to battle to save her business or to give it up. Part 3, A is A, is based on Aristotle's Law of Identity. In it, Dagny and Rearden (along with the readers) learn the true nature of the events and all of the apparent contradictions are identified and resolved. The Aristotelian laws of thought are not simply how we must think in order to gain knowledge. They are also ontological laws that pertain to the fundamental nature of reality. All that exists must comply with these principles.

The major plot of *Atlas Shrugged* is the story of the strike. Rand provides clues throughout parts 1 and 2 regarding the existence of the strike and, through the use and emphasis of subsidiary surface plots she is able to keep the major plot hidden and to reveal the strike only in a step-by-step retrospective manner. The secondary plots include: (1) Dagny Taggart and Hank Rearden's struggles to save their respective companies and industries primarily through the construction of the John Galt Line, and (2) Dagny's quests to find the inventor of the revolutionary motor and to find and stop the destroyer who is draining the brains of the world. There are observable and unobservable lines of action in the novel. We see our heroes striving to construct the John Galt Line and searching for the inventor of the motor. We also see the looters, their policies, and the effects of their policies. What is not discernible is John Galt removing the men of the mind from the world and relocating them to Mulligan's Valley. The link between these two spheres of action is Eddie Willers who unknowingly feeds information to John Galt, disguised as a low-level worker with whom Eddie has lunch.

Until this point we have discussed *Atlas Shrugged* from a big picture perspective. We now turn to a more detailed look at the purposeful progression of events of this long and complex novel.

The story begins in a devastated New York City with empty stores, closed businesses, crumbling buildings, and the disappearance of capable workers. Feeling a sense of dread and doom, Eddie Willers, assistant to Dagny Taggart, Vice President of Operations of Taggart Transcontinental Railroad, walks the streets of this city in decay. As he approaches the Taggart Transcontinental Building, a beggar asks him "Who is John Galt?" Eddie confronts the company's president, James Taggart, regarding the replacement of the crumbling tracks of the Rio Norte Line which serves the Wyatt oil fields and the other industrialized areas of Colorado, America's last booming industrial center. Wyatt has devised a method for extracting oil from shale. Dagny runs things and carries Jim who is preoccupied with evading responsibility.

While on a Taggart train named the Comet, Dagny hears a young brakeman whistling a tune which he describes as Richard Halley's Fifth Piano Concerto. He becomes evasive when Dagny points out that Halley only wrote four concertos before his mysterious disappearance. A faulty signal stops the Comet and Dagny gives orders with respect to the stopped train. Realizing that good men are becoming hard to find Dagny plans on promoting a promising young engineer, Owen Kellogg,

Dagny meets with Jim regarding the ordering of new metal rails for the Rio Norte Line. James wants to use rails supplied by his friend Orren Boyle, a liberal businessman who runs Associated Steel and who is constantly delaying delivery of the rails. Dagny prefers to use Rearden Metal, a revolutionary alloy stronger and lighter than steel. Denounced by metalurgists, the metal that took industrialist Henry (Hank) Rearden ten years to develop, had not yet been tried commercially. Dagny, who has studied the metal, accepts responsibility and tells Jim that the Boyle order has been cancelled and that Rearden is to supply the rail.

When Dagny meets with Owen Kellogg he unexpectedly resigns. Dagny calls Halley's publisher and discovers that, indeed, he had only written four concertos. These events are the first of many mysterious and seeming contradictions that confront the heroes of *Atlas Shrugged*.

Hank Rearden pours the first heat of Rearden Metal and reflects on his accomplishment and his life as he walks home from his mills. When he arrives at his home he finds a gathering that includes his wife, Lillian, his brother, Philip, his mother, and family friend, Paul Larkin. His family members berate him and attempt to make him feel guilty because of his work.

Hank has feelings of obligation to his manipulative wife and mother and to his ungrateful brother. Hank gives his wife a bracelet made from the first pouring of Rearden Metal for which his family members reproach him as egotistical. Lillian ironically refers to it as the chain by which Hank holds them all in bondage. Hank agrees to have an anniversary party and he gives Philip a huge amount of money for one of his liberal causes. Hank discusses the political situation with Larkin, who warns him about the loyalty of Wesley Mouch, Rearden's Washington man.

In a meeting at the top of a skyscraper in a cellar-like, windowless, bar room, James Taggart conspires with Wesley Mouch, Orren Boyle, and Paul Larkin to sacrifice Dan Conway and Hank Rearden. They agree to use their political power and connections to crush Taggart Transcontinental's only competition in Colorado, Dan Conway's superb Phoenix-Durango Railroad, and to strip Hank Rearden of his ore mines. They also discuss Mexico and the San Sebastián Line built by Taggart Transcontinental to serve the San Sebastián Mines. The novel then discusses the careers and history of Dagny and James Taggart. Dagny rises because of her productivity and James because of his Washington ability. Eddie Willers is then shown in the underground employee cafeteria talking with a nameless worker. At this point in the novel neither Eddie nor the reader know that the worker is John Galt, the ultimate hero of the story.

Eddie tells Dagny that McNamara, Taggart Transcontinental's and the country's best contractor, has quit and vanished. The San Sebastián Mines and Line are nationalized and James Taggart takes credit before the board of directors for the decision to strip the lines of any valuable assets. As a part of the deal agreed to in the cellar-like bar room, the National Alliance of Railroads passes the Anti-dog-eat-dog Rule which ostensibly places a ban on "destructive competition" by granting seniority to the oldest railroad company in a given region of the country. Its real purpose is to put Dan Conway's Phoenix-Durango Railroad out of business. Dagny encourages Conway to fight the rule but Conway gives up.

Ellis Wyatt and the other Colorado industrialists are now forced to use Taggart Transcontinental for their transportation needs. In order to handle this business, Dagny must quickly rebuild the Rio-Norte Line. Wyatt confronts Dagny with an ultimatum. Dagny and Hank then discuss their plans to rebuild the line using Rearden Metal.

The San Sebastián Mines are revealed to be worthless and a fraud. Dagny makes an appointment to confront Francisco. While Dagny walks over to see Francisco at the Wayne-Falkland Hotel she recalls her childhood friendship and later romance with Francisco and the d'Anconia family history. She remembers his purposefulness and ability and how he unexpectedly turned into a playboy. Dagny is bewildered because she knew that Francisco had been brilliant and productive just two years earlier. Dagny asks Francisco about his motives and he tells her that he intentionally wanted to ruin his investors like James Taggart, Orren Boyle, and others who attempted to ride on Francisco's coattails. He deliberately caused the San Sebastián disaster knowing that it would harm Wyatt Oil, Taggart Transcontinental Railroad, d'Anconia Copper (his own company), and other companies.

At the Rearden's anniversary party a variety of intellectuals all support the pending Equalization of Opportunity Bill. The guests reduce men to instinct and are against free will, logic, melody, plot, and property rights. They damn the values and virtues that Hank Rearden embodies. Francisco arrives at the party, approaches Hank, and thanks him for his values and virtues. He also warns Hank that his freeloading family members have a weapon that they are using against him. Hank is grateful to Francisco but still is suspicious of him. Dagny trades her diamond bracelet to Lillian for the one made with Rearden Metal.

The reader is shown that the exploiters are men like James Taggart, Wesley Mouch, and Robert Stadler whereas the exploited are individuals like Hank Rearden, Dagny Taggart, and Ellis Wyatt who fail to understand the nature of the evil looters whom they face. Dagny and Hank endeavor to rebuild the Rio Norte Line and Hank designs an innovative bridge of Rearden Metal that combines a truss with an arch. Dagny refuses to debate Bertram Scudder on his radio show regarding the safety of Rearden Metal. Her brother James had tried to talk her into appearing on Scudder's program.

Dr. Potter of the State Science Institute attempts to obtain the rights to Rearden Metal but Hank refuses. Potter offers Hank a great deal of government money. The SSI attempts to bribe and threaten Rearden to keep his new metal off the market because of the "social damage" it will cause to steel producers (like Orren Boyle) who can't compete with him. The SSI alleges potential weaknesses in the metal and, as a result, the public begins questioning its safety. Dagny reads about SSI's denunciation of Rearden Metal and makes an appointment to see Robert Stadler, the head of the institute, to see if he will retract SSI's damaging and unproven allegations. Stadler refuses because he does not want SSI to look bad. Stadler, the theoretical physicist, has contempt for practical technology. He tells Dagny about the failure of the three most promising students that he had taught at Patrick Henry University. Two are Francisco d'Anconia and Ragnar Danneskjöld, the pirate, and the third is probably now some "second assistant bookkeeper."

The Railroad union forbids its employees to work on the Rio Norte Line and the stock price of Taggart Transcontinental plummets. Dagny decides to take a leave of absence to construct the Rio Norte Line on her own. As a result the "John Galt Line" is born. This is the name that the defiant Dagny gives to her new railroad. If her efforts are successful, then she will turn the line back over to Taggart Transcontinental. Dagny seeks investors for her new company, asks Francisco to purchase John Galt Line bonds, and he refuses.

James Taggart had previously used his political friendship with steel producer Orren Boyle to influence the National Alliance of Railroads to pass the Anti-dog-eat-dog Rule. In turn, Boyle employs Taggart to use his influence in Washington in order to strip Hank Rearden of his ore mines, delivering them to Paul Larkin, who would provide Boyle with the first chance to obtain the ore. Taggart uses his Washington connections to pass the Equalization of Opportunity Bill which forbids any one person or corporation from owning more than one type of business concern. Although the stated rationale for this antitrust legislation is that it is unfair to permit one individual or corporation to own several types of business enterprises, the hidden agenda is to allow Boyle's Associated Steel to compete with Rearden Steel. This new antitrust law forces Rearden to surrender his subsidiary coal and iron ore mines. The law prohibits Hank from using the mines that supply raw materials to make Rearden Metal.

Rearden and the other Colorado businessmen invest in the John Galt Line. Dagny and Hank are becoming strongly attracted to one another. Hank complies with the Equalization of Opportunity Bill and sells his ore mines to Paul Larkin and his coal mines to Ken Dannager, a Pennsylvania coal producer and friend of Hank. Rearden gives an extension to Taggart Transcontinental on its rail payments. The John Galt Line is completed before its deadline. The John Galt Line is denunciated as unsafe and the union attempts to stop the first run of the line. Every Taggart engineer volunteers for its first run. Dagny and Hank ride in the locomotive on the first run to Colorado which is a resounding success. They have dinner at Ellis Wyatt's home to celebrate. They make love for the first time that night and their romance begins.

The morning following Hank and Dagny's night of passion, Rearden condemns them both for their low urges but Dagny is happy for what happened. She regards having sex with Rearden as being noble whereas he considers it to be low and base. She realizes that sexual attraction is based on the mutual admiration for each other's values and other qualities. Despite his condemnation, Hank resolves to continue what he considers to be their depraved affair. James Taggart meets Cherryl Brooks, an innocent shop girl and hero-worshipper, who admires achievement and thinks that Jim is one of the people responsible for the John Galt Line's success. Dagny returns ownership of the John Galt Line to Taggart Transcontinental. Wesley Mouch is appointed to head up the Bureau of Economic Planning and National Resources.

Hank and Dagny decide to take a vacation together. They drive around the country looking at abandoned factories. At the Twentieth Century Motor Company in Wisconsin they discover the remnants of a motor that is capable of extracting static electricity from the atmosphere and converting it into usable kinetic energy. They are shocked to find such a revolutionary invention on a scrap heap in an abandoned factory. Dagny and Hank vow to find the inventor of the motor.

Dagny searches for the inventor of the motor in Rome, Wisconsin where she speaks with Mayor Bascom and other city officials about the Twentieth Century Motor Company. When she speaks to Eddie Willers, he tells her that politicians want to pass laws that would destroy industrial production in Colorado. Through the proposed legislation others would be able to cash in on Colorado's success, perhaps crippling many Colorado enterprises in the process. Paul Larkin betrays Rearden by shipping the ore to Orren Boyle in compliance with the crooked deal arranged in the skyscraper-cellar-bar room some time ago.

Dagny's search for the inventor of the motor leads her to the widow of former chief engineer of the Twentieth Century Motor Company's research department. Mrs. Hastings tells Dagny that her husband's young assistant had invented the motor. She doesn't know him but provides a clue that leads Dagny to a remote local diner in Wyoming. The cook there knows who the inventor is, but will not tell Dagny who he is. Dagny is surprised to learn that the cook making hamburgers is the great philosopher, Hugh Akston, a former professor at the Patrick Henry University, who had retired many years before. Akston talks about his three star pupils. He will not explain why he left the teaching profession and tells her that "contradictions do not exist" and that if she encounters a paradox she should check her premises because one of them is wrong.

When Dagny returns to Cheyenne she finds that a new series of directives and taxes have been placed on the Colorado industrialists. The Colorado Directives were intended (at least officially) to help with the national emergency by forcing Colorado to share the suffering. The directive was actually due to the efforts of economic interest groups who wanted the industrially successful state of Colorado to force its profitable firms to redistribute their earnings. Dagny rushed to see Ellis Wyatt in Colorado but she is too late. The defiant Ellis Wyatt had set fire to his wells and has disappeared. As the Colorado situation worsens, other industrialists will retire and vanish. Mouch's Colorado Directives will hasten the retirement and disappearance of many Colorado industrialists who had created productive enterprises and who are forced to carry less competent businessmen with them. The Colorado Directives put Wyatt Oil and other companies out of business and will ultimately wipe out the Rio Norte Line.

Colorado's economy continues to collapse as many of the state's industrialists are vanishing. Dagny has therefore been forced to cut trains on the Colorado schedule. In her attempt to either find the inventor of the motor or a person who can reconstruct it, Dagny has another meeting with Robert Stadler. She shows him the fragmentary notes left by the inventor. Looking at the motor and the remaining pages of notes, Stadler realizes the extraordinary accomplishment in the field of theoretical physics that the inventor had made. He is also baffled as to why a man with such a great mind would waste his time making a practical motor. Stadler recommends a young scientist at the Utah Institute of Technology to work on reconstructing the motor. The physicist, Quentin Daniels, has refused to work for the government. Stadler tells Dagny that he once knew a John Galt.

The government passes a ruling with respect to the amount of Rearden Metal that can be sold to each customer and the government bureaucrats send a young college graduate to monitor Rearden's activities as Deputy Director of Distribution. His name is Tony but the workers dub him the "Wet Nurse." Hank is approached and ordered to supply 10,000 tons of Rearden Metal for the mysterious Project X without telling him what the project is. Hank refuses and tells the agent from the State Science Institute, the "Traffic Cop," that the government has the guns and could use them to seize his metal if it wanted it. Hank understands that his "voluntary cooperation" is needed in order to give the appearance of a moral transaction. The government needs Rearden to pretend that he is not being coerced. The agent's shocked reaction makes Hank realize that the looters require his sanction and that he should continue to refuse to grant his sanction in the future. Later Hank and Dagny discuss the nature of sanction.

Dagny begins to believe that there is a destroyer who is systematically eliminating the men of the mind. Hank secretly sells more Rearden Metal than legally permitted to Ken Danagger. Jim Taggart marries Cherryl Brooks and Hank Rearden accompanies his wife, Lillian, to the wedding reception. Francisco arrives and announces that the new order of the world is the "aristocracy of pull." It is replacing the aristrocracy of money. He later makes a speech praising the virtue and morality of money and production.

In his "Money Speech" Francisco says that money is made possible only by men who produce. Money is a tool of exchange which presumes productive men and the results of their activities. He explains that wealth is the source of money and that money is the effect, rather than the cause, of wealth. He points out that production initiates the demand for other products and services—production is the source of demand. Francisco notes that money should be an objective standard of value tied to reality in order to act as an integrator of economic value. An objective standard requires an objective commodity such as gold.

Francisco approaches Hank at the reception and says that he wants to morally equip him for his self-defense. Rearden is attracted to Francisco's ideas despite having contempt for the apparent manner in which he is living. Francisco warns Hank not to deal with d'Anconia Copper. He then loudly announces that his company is having problems. This incites panic among the crooked investors in d'Anconia stock who realize that they will be losing money.

Hank takes Lillian to the train station after the wedding celebration and he then spends the evening with Dagny. Lillian confronts Hank about where he slept that night. She has discovered that he is having an affair but she does not know who the woman is. Hank admits to the affair but will not divulge the woman's identity. Lillian plans on using her knowledge of the affair and on Hank's sense of guilt to control him.

Hank is visited by Floyd Ferris of the State Science Institute who attempts to blackmail Rearden into agreeing to sell Rearden Metal to the institute. He says that Hank Rearden and Ken Danagger will be put on trial for the illegal sale of Rearden Metal if Hank does not sell his metal to the SSI. Hank refuses and the government brings charges against them.

Eddie Willers and the unnamed worker (i.e., John Galt) discuss in the Taggart Cafeteria Dagny's suspicion about the existence of a destroyer and how she is afraid that Ken Danagger will be the next industrialist to disappear. Dagny makes an appointment to see Danagger and travels to Pittsburgh to talk to him. Dagny waits for several hours in the outer office while Danagger is speaking to someone else. Dagny attempts to convince Danagger to stay but he tells her that he is quitting and that he will not give her the reason for his doing so.

Francisco visits Rearden at his mills and asks why Hank puts up with all of the suffering. He wants to know what is so worthwhile to remain in business under such crippling conditions. Francisco talks about the ideas of moral sanction and opposing moral codes. There is a furnace breakout and the two magnificently fight the fire side by side. Francisco helps to save Rearden's furnace and during the ordeal Rearden saves Francisco's life. Rearden asks Francisco to finish the question he had been asking. Francisco understands that this is not the right time to continue that discussion. He knows the answer—it is Hank's love for his mills.

At Thanksgiving dinner, the night before Rearden's trial, Hank confronts his brother Philip and frees himself of the guilt that he has felt toward his family. At his trial Hank says that he does not accept the court's authority or their moral and legal premises. He says that he will offer no defense because he does not perceive his sale to Danagger to be a crime. Using Francisco's words, he states that he has the right to produce and sell any quantity of his metal to whomever he wants as he sees fit to do so. Rearden explains that the government does not have the right to compel and that the trial is simply an institutionalized attempt to seize his metal. The judge fines him and suspends the sentence as the crowd applauds and cheers.

Rearden visits Francisco at his hotel suite. He tells Francisco that he admires his intellect but deplores his depraved playboy lifestyle. Francisco says that his playboy image is a façade or camouflage. He says that in his entire life he has only loved and slept with one woman. Francisco then leads a discussion of the nature and meaning of sex and money.

Hank tells Francisco that he has placed an important order with d'Anconia Copper. Francisco is taken aback, goes to the phone, but stops. In that moment of indecision, Francisco had the power to prevent some disaster affecting Rearden to occur. He tells Hank, by taking an oath to the only woman he has ever loved, that he is Rearden's friend despite what might happen in the future. A few days later Ragnar Danneskjöld sinks d'Anconia ships carrying Rearden's supply of copper. The angry Rearden feels a sense of great betrayal.

The ships of the world's last copper producer, d'Anconia Copper, continue to be sunk by Ragnar Danneskjöld. Because no copper arrives in America, electrical appliances cease to be produced there. In addition, Hank Rearden fails to deliver Rearden Metal rail needed to replace Taggart Transcontinental's disintegrating mainline track. The Atlantic Southern Bridge collapses leaving Taggart Transcontinental as the only path across America. Because of the copper shortage, Taggart's track continues to deteriorate, train wrecks take place, and companies using Taggart Transcontinental to transport their goods go out of business. The Taggart Board meets to formally close the John Galt Line (i.e., The Rio Norte Line) and Francisco is waiting to talk to Dagny after the meeting. Dagny and Hank go to Colorado for the closing of the line that had been so important to them.

James Taggart is at the mercy of the government, the railroad unions that are demanding wage increases, and his customers demanding rate reductions. Jim desperately needs information that he can trade to the government so that he will be able to keep his shipping rates at their current levels. He conspires with Lillian Rearden and appeals to her for help. He knows that she wants to destroy her husband. She discovers that Hank is traveling by train under a phony name and concludes that he must be traveling with his mistress. She goes to confront Hank, realizes that her husband's lover is Dagny, and is devastated and terrified. Hank refuses when Lillian demands that he give Dagny up.

The government enacts Directive 10–289 that has the purported purpose of stopping the country's decline by freezing the economy in its present state. Comprehensive central government planning is to be used to maintain the status quo. This directive will allow top government officials and politically connected businessmen to retain their power and to enhance their control over the economy. Directive 10–289 mandates that all workers remain at their current jobs, that no business is permitted to close, and that all patents and copyrights be "voluntarily" turned over to the government. It also forbids the introduction of new products and innovations and requires firms to annually produce a number of goods identical to the number produced during the preceding year. In addition, the directive freezes all wages, prices, and profits and requires every person to spend the same amount of money as he did in the preceding year. This directive prevents businesses from adjusting expenses and making other strategic and tactical decisions. The directive also establishes a Unification Board to hear all disagreements stemming from the new laws. The Board's decision on any issues that emerge will be final. Because appeals for exceptions can be made to the Unification Board, the buying and selling of economic favors are the logical result. In response to the directive, more people each day fail to show up at work.

Dagny resigns in response to Directive 10–289 and retreats to a family cabin in Woodstock when she reflects on the nature of purpose and on her conflict with respect to going back to work or not. Dagny confides her whereabouts to Eddie. Hank does not resign. He knows that he has two weeks to sign the Gift Certificate turning the rights to Rearden Metal over to the government and he wants to be there to refuse to do so. The Wet Nurse offers to look the other way and to cover up anything that Rearden does to break the new laws.

Floyd Ferris visits Hank and tells him that Lillian had told him about Hank's affair with Dagny. Ferris says that the government has evidence of the affair and will make it public if Hank does not sign the Gift Certificate. Hank thinks about morality, his love for Dagny, and his guilt for not divorcing Lillian immediately and making public his love for Dagny. In order to save Dagny's reputation he signs the Gift Certificate. He will not let her suffer for his errors.

Eddie tells the worker in the Taggart cafeteria that Dagny has quit and that she is staying in a mountain lodge in the Berkshires. Furious at his wife for disclosing his relationship with Dagny to the looters, Hank moves out of his house and into an apartment. He instructs his lawyers that Lillian is to receive no alimony or property settlement. Walking home one evening he is approached by the pirate, Ragnar Danneskjöld, who attempts to give him a number of bars of gold in partial repayment for the unjust income taxes he has paid over the years. The pirate explains his purpose as a man of justice. Rearden rejects the gold but later saves Ragnar from the police.

The Taggart Comet, full of passengers, breaks down and a replacement diesel engine cannot be found. Politician Kip Chalmers demands a nonexistent engine. All that can be found is a coal-burning engine that is unsafe to go through a long tunnel. Many Taggart employees evade responsibility for the decision to use the coal-burner and disaster occurs. All those aboard the train are asphyxiated in the tunnel and an army munitions train runs into the stalled Comet resulting in an immense explosion.

Francisco shows up at the cabin where Dagny is staying. He tells her that he was one of the first men to quit, that for twelve years he has deliberately, systematically, and slowly been destroying d'Anconia Copper, and that she too has a right to quit. Francisco introduces the notion to Dagny that she is enabling her enemies, the looters. While they talk, the radio announces news of the Taggart Tunnel train wreck disaster in the heart of the Rocky Mountains making transcontinental traffic impossible. Dagny rushes back to New York, resumes her duties, and reroutes trains utilizing the tracks of other railroad firms. She finds that her brother, James, has his letter of resignation ready (just in case).

Dagny goes home to her apartment and that evening Francisco visits her to try to convince her to leave her railroad. Hank shows up and is enraged to see Francisco who he thinks has betrayed him. Francisco realizes that Dagny is Hank Rearden's mistress and tells Rearden that Dagny is the woman he loves. Hank slaps Francisco who, exercising great self-restraint, does not retaliate. Dagny fears that Francisco might break and kill Hank. After Hank slaps Francisco, she says that Francisco was her first lover.

Quentin Daniels sends a letter to Dagny telling her that he is resigning. He refuses to work under Directive 10–289. Dagny calls him and he agrees to wait for her to visit him. Eddie arrives at Dagny's apartment, sees Rearden's initialed robe, and realizes that she is sleeping with him. Later Eddie eats dinner with the worker (John Galt) in the cafeteria. He tells the worker about Daniels who has been working on the motor and that Dagny is going to Utah to talk with him before the destroyer takes him away. Eddie also reveals to the worker that Dagny and Hank Rearden are having an affair.

Dagny is traveling cross country to Utah when she sees a hobo hitching a ride in her car. She rescues the tramp and invites him to have dinner with her. During their conversation, he tells her that he used to work at the Twentieth Century Motor Works Company and that he and other employees there had come up with the phrase "Who is John Galt?" some twelve years ago. The hobo, Jeff Allen, then relates the story of the Starnes heirs' small scale socialist experiment in which the employees as a group voted to decide the needs of each worker as well as the expected production of each laborer based on an assessment of his ability. The result was predictably that, when earnings are not based on productivity, incentives diminish, production plummets, and bankruptcy results. The tramp tells Dagny that the first man to quit was a young engineer named John Galt who vowed that he would stop the motor of the world.

The train stops suddenly and the crew deserts in the middle of nowhere. A "frozen train" such as this is becoming common because men have no legal way to leave their jobs. Dagny spots Owen Kellogg, the young engineer who quit early on in the story, who tells her that he is going on a month's vacation with his friends. Dagny leaves with Owen Kellogg to walk down the track to phone for help and leaves Jeff Allen in charge. She gives instructions to Kellogg, walks to a small airfield, rents a plane, and flies to Utah where the airfield attendant informs her that Quentin Daniels had just left with a man in another plane. Dagny realizes that this man must be the destroyer. She races after that plane in hers and crashes in the mountains.

Dagny's injuries are not serious but she does lose consciousness. When she awakens and opens her eyes she sees John Galt who is both the inventor of the motor and the man who is removing the men of the mind from the outside world. All of the great men who have disappeared are there. They are on a strike of the mind against an oppressive code that worships incompetence and altruism. She is taken to Galt's home where she could be considered to be a guest and/or a prisoner. She is taken on a tour of the valley where Galt's motor supplies the power for the residents' appliances and for a ray source that hides the valley from detection. Ragnar and Galt are concerned about Francisco who is late in arriving. When Quentin Daniels shows up he says that a great many people in the outside world, including Hank Rearden, are looking for the wreckage of Dagny's plane. Francisco finally arrives, sees Dagny, and is relieved.

Dagny stays at Galt's home where she works as a servant in order to pay her debts due in gold for the expenses that she has incurred in the valley. Dagny and Galt are strongly attracted to one another but they stay in separate rooms because she is still a scab. Although she falls in love with Galt who has watched her and loved her for years, she is still his enemy until she decides to join the strike.

Dagny has dinner at the home of Midas Mulligan where she meets the industrialists, scientists, philosophers, inventors, artists, and so on who reside in what is called "Galt's Gulch," "Mulligan's Valley," or "Atlantis." At that dinner the purpose of the valley's residents is formally revealed along with the history of the valley that was established by Mulligan. Each resident in turn proclaims his reasons for joining the strike. Dagny realizes that she will need to make a choice with respect to becoming a striker and staying in the valley or returning to the outside world to continue battling the looters.

For a month Dagny voluntarily works as Galt's housekeeper and cook. Hank Rearden is continuing to search for Dagny, and Francisco wants to contact him to let him know that she is all right but John Galt refuses. Most of the strikers live in the outside world for much of each year but they all spend the month of June together in Galt's Gulch. Dagny accompanies Hugh Akston's three students to their annual reunion at Akston's home.

Francisco believes that he has lost Dagny to Hank Rearden, not realizing that John Galt is the man whom she has sought for her entire life. Galt knows about Dagny and Francisco's history together and that Francisco is still in love with Dagny. Francisco invites Dagny to stay at his home during her last week in the valley. Dagny asks Galt to decide and he says no because he realizes that such an action is against the self-interest of all three of them. At the end of the month Dagny decides to return to the world because she still thinks there is a chance to defeat the looters. She cannot give up her railroad.

She believes that her values are still possible to achieve in the outside world, that she can save the railroad, that the looters love their lives, and that she can persuade them to see the truth. John Galt returns as well so that he can watch over Dagny and be there when she decides to join the strike. Galt drops Dagny off in the outside world.

Robert Stadler is called by Floyd Ferris to attend a public demonstration of the previously top secret Project X, a new weapon that uses sound waves to cause terrible destruction over a radius of 100 miles. Its purported purpose is to provide public security. Project X is revealed and demonstrated. Stadler is horrified by its effects yet he still goes along and sanctions it by delivering a speech that Ferris had prepared for him.

Dagny returns to New York and phones Hank who is totally surprised by her call. She finds out that the railroad industry has been nationlized under the Railroad Unification Plan. The Director of Unification is looter-politician Cuffy Meigs. The plan is actually James Taggart's desperate scheme to keep Taggart Transcontinental from going out of business by means of existing off its competition. The plan provides that the total profits of all railroad companies be allocated according to the number of miles of track each owns instead of according to the amount of service that each supplies.

James Taggart attempts to get his sister to appear on Bertram Scudder's radio program to make a speech reassuring the public that the railroad industry is not failing. She refuses but Lillian Rearden tells Dagny that the government bureaucrats know about her affair with Hank and that they will announce it to the public if she fails to appear on Scudder's show. In response to this blackmail attempt, Dagny appears on the show and proudly proclaims that she had been Hank Rearden's lover and that Rearden had been blackmailed into signing the gift certificate turning over the rights to Rearden Metal to the government.

Dagny goes to her apartment and finds Hank waiting there for her. Rearden realizes that she has met her true love during her absence because during her speech she spoke of their affair only in the past tense. They discuss their plans to fight the looters. Hank wants to talk to Francisco, the man that is helping him to escape from the looters' altruist ethics.

Eddie Willers tells Cherryl Taggart the truth about who it is that runs Taggart Transcontinental—she finds out that it is Dagny rather than her husband. Over the years of their marriage she had already formed doubts with respect to his moral character and his role in the railroad. Jim brags and wants to celebrate his "achievement" of a crooked political deal in which the nationalization of d'Anconia Copper will make him a great deal of money. Recalling the details of their marriage, Cherryl confronts James and asks him why he married her. She wants to know what motivates him. They argue and she leaves. Cherryl visits Dagny and apologizes.

Lillian Rearden arrives and appeals to James Taggart to use his political power to stop her forthcoming divorce from Hank which will leave her penniless. He tells her that he does not have the power to prevent the divorce. Lillian then has sex with James in an effort to hurt her husband one final time while she is still his wife. Cherryl returns, hears a woman's voice, and knows that her husband has been unfaithful. James tells Cherryl that he will not grant her a divorce. He says that he married her because she was worthless and he felt sorry for her. She does not believe him. Cherryl now understands that James is a nihilistic killer of the good. He sought to destroy her because of her ambition and virtues. Unable to destroy the men of the mind, James turned his hatred of the good on the poor shop girl and hero-worshipper. Cherryl runs out of the house and commits suicide by jumping into the river where she drowns. Cherryl's fatal error was that she thought that James was Dagny.

The unreason of the looters is exemplified by James Taggart who is anti-effort and has the need to feel superior. He is on the death premise. He evades, rationalizes, and disregards his responsibility to think. He wants his consciousness to control reality. James thinks that all he has to do is to "want" something. He wants to be rich without earning wealth and to be loved and admired without earning the right to be loved and admired. Jim is motivated by his hatred of good men and his desire to kill them.

A copper shortage drastically affects Taggart Transcontinental and other companies. At the very moment Chilean legislation nationalizes d'Anconia Copper, Francisco simultaneously destroys every property belonging to his company. There is nothing left for the looters to take. Francisco disappears after destroying his holdings. The Washington planners attempt to placate Rearden, his divorce trial goes through smoothly, and the Wet Nurse warns him that something is up. He says that the Washington bureaucrats are planning to impose a new restrictive policy on Rearden Steel but he does not know what it is. The politicians are sneaking their men into Rearden's factories. Both Philip, Hank's brother, and Tony, the Wet Nurse, appeal to Hank for a job. He turns Philip down because he is not competent and tells Tony that he would hire him gladly and at once but the Unification Board won't allow him to do that.

Politicians no longer even pretend that they are working for the public good. Instead they use their political power to create their own personal fortunes. They even divert freight trains as political favors. Cuffy Meigs sends freight cars necessary for the Minnesota wheat house to Ma Chalmers's soybean project in Louisiana. She is the mother of Washington politician, Kip Chalmers. The result is the rotting of the much needed Minnesota crops.

A copper wire breaks in the Taggart Terminal causing its signal system to go down. Dagny rushes to the tunnel, calls for help from another railroad, and decides to improvise a lantern scheme to signal and move the trains manually using her track workers. During the emergency, Dagny spots John Galt in the middle of a group of unskilled workers. After she issues orders to the workers, she goes into the tunnels and Galt follows her there. There they make love for the first time. Afterward, they talk and he tells her that he will be killed if she unintentionally leads the politicians to him.

The steelworkers union asks for a raise but the Unification Board refuses making it sound like the rejection came from Hank Rearden. The government "accidentally" attaches all of Rearden's money making it unavailable to him. His property is seized on trumped up tax charges. His family does not want him to quit and vanish so his mother visits him and beseeches him to stay (and to sacrificially provide them with financial help).

Hank goes to New York to meet with the looters including Mouch, Holoway, Lawson, Ferris, and Jim Taggart. They tell Rearden that they are prepared to launch a new Steel Unification Plan that is patterned after the Railroad Unification Plan. Under the plan all of the steel companies' earnings are to be rewarded according to the number of furnaces each owns. Because Orren Boyle has a great many idle furnaces, he would be paid for almost double his actual output. In turn, Rearden would be paid for less than half of his actual output. Both the Railroad Unification Plan and the Steel Unification Plan require companies to produce according to each one's ability with the profits allocated according to each firm's needs.

Rearden tells them that, no matter what his output is, he will go broke under that plan. They tell him that "you'll do something." They expect him to make the irrational work. He now understands their nature and the fact that he has been supporting them—he has sanctioned their view of existence. He rejects their plan and drives back to his mills in Philadelphia.

As he approaches his mills he hears gunfire and sees a mob. His mills are under attack. He comforts the dying Wet Nurse who was attempting to defend the mills against the government thugs who had infiltrated his workforce. Rearden is attacked and is hit in the head with a pipe but an unknown worker saves him. The worker is Francisco who had been working undercover as "Frank Adams" in Rearden's mills. It was Francisco who successfully organized the workers' resistance and defense of the mills. When Hank regains consciousness in the infirmary he is reunited with Francisco who finishes telling him what he needed to hear. Rearden retires, vanishes, and joins the strike. At long last, Hank is freed from the grasp of the looters.

The people of America learn that Hank Rearden has quit and the country falls into even greater chaos and is near collapse. The government has announced that Mr. Thompson will speak to the country over the radio on November 22 to discuss the crisis and his plan to remedy it. Instead John Galt overwhelms the radio signals and takes over the airwaves.

A scheduled national broadcast by the Head of the State is interrupted by Galt, who, in a three-hour speech, spells out the tenets of his philosophy. Among his many provocative ideas is the notion that the doctrine of Original Sin, which holds man's nature as his sin, is absurd—a sin that is outside the possibility of choice is outside the realm of morality. Another provocative idea is that both forced and voluntary altruism are evil. Placing the welfare of others above an individual's own interests is wrong. The desire to give charity, compassion, and pleasure unconditionally to the undeserving is wrong.

Galt explains that reality is objective, absolute, and comprehensible, and that man is a rational being who relies upon his mind as his only means to obtain objectively valid knowledge and as his "basic tool of survival." The concept of value presupposes an entity capable of acting to attain a goal in the face of an alternative. The one basic alternative in the world is existence versus non-existence. A is A—existence exists. "It is only the concept of 'Life' that makes the concept of 'Value' possible." An organism's life is its standard of value. Whatever furthers its life is good and that which threatens it is evil. It is therefore the nature of a living entity that determines what it ought to do.

Galt identifies man's life as the proper standard of man's values and morality as the principle defining the actions necessary to maintain life as a man. If life as a man is one's purpose, he has "a right to live as a rational being." To live, man must think, act, and create the values his life requires. Because a man's life is sustained through thought and action, the individual must have the right to think and act and to keep the product of his thinking and acting (i.e., the right to life, liberty, and property).

He asserts that because men are creatures who think and act according to principle, a doctrine of rights ensures that an individual's choice to live by those principles is not violated by other human beings. All individuals possess the same rights to freely pursue their own goals. These rights are innate and can be logically derived from man's nature and needs—the state is not involved in the creation of rights and merely exists to protect an individual's natural rights. Because force is the means by which one's rights are violated, it follows that freedom is a basic good. Therefore, it follows that the role of government is to "protect man's rights" through the use of force but "only in retaliation and only against those who initiate its use."

Galt's speech explicitly ties together all of the ideas previously dramatized in the actions, descriptions, and dialogues in the novel, leads to Galt's eventual capture and the story's climax, hastens the collapse, and makes the rebuilding of society easier. Galt's speech is necessary in order to understand the climax of the novel. When the looters hear his speech, they realize that he is the best thinker in the world and thus search for him in order to enlist his help in saving the deteriorating economy. It is the speech that moves Galt from mythical to concrete status in the novel. The events and actions prior to the speech provide the inductive evidence needed to derive the principle that "the mind is man's tool of survival." By then the reader and the American people in the novel have seen the men of the mind in the world, their gradual disappearance, the effects of the looters' policies, and the resulting crumbling of the world. It is through this speech that Galt demonstrates the value of the men of the mind. Galt's long speech is warranted because the detailed and complex events previously presented concretize the message given in his speech. The knowledge contained in Galt's speech is what convinced the strikers earlier in the novel to abandon their firms and to retreat to Galt's Gulch.

The philosophy of the morality of life embodied in the speech is what the producers needed to hear and accept in order for them to realize their own greatness and to stand up against the looters. It is the right moment for the speech as the strike has served its purpose. It was not delivered until the American people were ready to hear it. In large part, Galt's Objectivist statement is addressed to the common but rational listeners in an effort to gain their support by going on strike themselves. Galt tells them that the world is perishing from the morality of death (i.e., sacrifice) which requires the renunciation of the mind, about the existence of, and reasons for, the strike; about the existence of a proper, rational morality of life and reason; and that they need to withdraw their moral approval (i.e., sanction) of the morality of death.

After hearing Galt's speech, Mr. Thompson wants to negotiate a deal with him. When Thompson asks what to do, Dagny tells him to have the looters give up power, but they will not do that. Stadler suggests that Dagny will lead them to Galt. The desperate government officials seek John Galt. They want him to become the country's economic dictator so that the men of the mind will return and rescue the government. The looters broadcast repeated appeals in their attempts to reach Galt. Fearing for Galt's safety, Dagny looks up his address on Taggart's payroll records and goes to his apartment. He tells her that it is extremely likely that the government officials had her followed. He says that they will torture her in order to force her to go along with their wishes if they discover what they mean to one another. He tells her to "betray" him and to take the side of the police when they arrive, which she does. They arrest Galt, take him to the Wayne-Falkland hotel, and attempt to convince him to take charge. He, of course, refuses. Stadler is summoned and meets with Galt. Stadler wants to have Galt killed!

There are riots in California and one of the warring groups has taken over a rail station there with the result that Taggart Transcontinental is unable to provide cross-country transportation. Eddie Willers goes there to see if he can restore order. While he is in California, the looters announce that they will reveal the details of the "John Galt Plan" to save the economy. Galt is ordered to the ballroom to make a speech at a televised press conference.

When they parade him before the TV cameras, he turns sideways to reveal a hidden gun that was pointed at him and exclaims, "Get the hell out of my way."

Robert Stadler hears the press conference over the radio and realizes that, caught between the looters and the men of the mind, he has nowhere to go. If the looters win he will be under their control and if Galt wins he will be turned away as a traitor to the mind. Stadler decides to establish his own domain and drives to the Project X site in Iowa hoping to use that weapon to create his own kingdom. He gets past the guards and spots the drunken Cuffy Meigs at the controls of Project X. Meigs had the same idea and had beaten Stadler to it. They struggle and the weapon goes off creating mass destruction for hundreds of square miles and killing everyone at the facility, including Stadler.

Robert Stadler, a man of great intelligence and Director of the State Science Institute is the novel's Plato-like character who holds a theoretical versus applied science split. He is a cynical and brilliant theoretical physicist and intellectual elitist who believes that most people are corrupt, stupid, and incapable of virtuous behavior and that only a rare handful of men are open to reason. Stadler is contemptuous of applied science and material production. He is a thoroughgoing Platonist who thinks that the human mind, reason, and science exist on a higher realm that has nothing to do with life on earth.

Stadler resorts to the extortion of citizens to finance his theoretical noncommercial projects. Why would a man with such a great mind tragically turn to the use of brute force to get the funding he desires? The answer is that Stadler concludes that his work must be sustained through government force because he thinks that reason is impotent in the world. Because he wants unearned material wealth for his laboratory, he aligns himself with the statist brutes and looters and their barbarous methods. Stadler thinks that the role of the mind is to deal with a higher realm of reality that is divorced from this world and that, therefore, the mind is inefficacious in dealing with this world. He deduces that brute bodily power is dominant in a world in which most people are irrational, emotional, and impervious to reason. Because most individuals can't appreciate science, he needs a state-backed science institute to force people to finance his research. John Galt recognizes that Stadler, his former professor at Patrick Henry University, is a traitor to the mind and breaks with him when he endorses and joins the State Science Institute. At one time, Stadler would say that the phrase "free scientific inquiry" was redundant. He later insists that government is necessary to conduct scientific inquiry.

Stadler, a man once with a great mind, chooses to renounce the mind by throwing in with the force-wielders and, in the end, is destroyed by his own power-lust. Stadler is doomed once he turns his mind over to the brutes. He is destroyed because he mistakenly thinks that he can survive by joining the power-lusters. At that point, the men of the mind become his enemy alongside the looters who always were his enemy given that Stadler, at least in the beginning, was one of the thinkers. Ultimately, Stadler has nowhere to go. Toward the end of the novel he realizes that, if Galt and the other men of the mind are victorious, he will be repudiated as a traitor to the mind and that, if the looters win, he will be shackled to the irrational brutes.

The looters take Galt to a small concrete structure in the State Science Institute where they torture him with a series of electrical shocks provided by the Ferris Persuader. The generator breaks down and Galt tells them how to fix it. Dagny has called Francisco who left a phone number to call in case such an event occurred. While Dagny is getting ready to look for Galt, she receives a call telling her that Taggart Bridge crossing the Mississippi River was destroyed by the explosion of Project X. She tells the caller that she does not know what to do and goes to join Francisco. Dagny has finally decided to join the strikers.

James Taggart, while attempting to break John Galt, realizes that his life has been devoted to destroying the good. Trying to evade his own evil, he breaks down and collapses. Taggart always desired the unearned regarding both physical and spiritual concerns. He does not have any positive ambitions or purpose. He only wants political influence and the opportunity to destroy. He seeks to destroy value because it is value. Although he wants unearned money, he does not view money as a value. Being on the death premise, his goal is to destroy the values required by life. Taggart desires a world in which reason and purpose are not required to survive and flourish in it. Rebelling against life and existence, he conceals his nihilism even from himself. He fabricates and simulates concern with values that promote life. He is under the illusion that obtaining wealth and "success," without effort or rational thought, will give him moral status and self-esteem. Ultimately, the self-deceived Taggart's desire to steal became a desire to destroy value even though such destruction will result in the loss of his own life.

Upon entering the State Science Institute, Dagny shoots a guard who refused to decide what he should do. She along with Francisco, Ragnar, and Rearden invade the premises and free Galt from his torturers. With the rescued John Galt they travel by plane to Galt's Gulch. As they pass over New York City the lights of the city go out. Having saved the Taggart station in California, Eddie Willers is heading back home on the Comet when it breaks down in Arizona and the members of the crew cannot fix the engine. The passengers and the crew, except for Eddie, leave with a passing covered wagon. Eddie refuses to give up and stays with the marooned train. He cannot let go of the railroad. Eddie's fate is bleak but uncertain. He cannot repair the train but he does have great friends like Dagny and the other heroes who will certainly do their best in attempting to find him. Back in the valley

John Galt declares an end to the strike and announces that it is now time for the men of the mind to return and rebuild society.

Atlas Shrugged concretizes through hierarchical, progressive, and inductive demonstration Rand's systematic philosophy of Objectivism. In her great novel she dramatizes grand themes and presents an entire and integrated view of how a man should live his life. She primarily does this by illustrating the steady growth in knowledge, understanding, and appreciation of the strikers' motives on the parts of Dagny Taggart and Hank Rearden. As they form successively higher abstractions and conceptualizations and draw conclusions, the alert reader is able to concurrently gain a wider and deeper perspective on the novel's events.

Part 1 tells the story of Dagny Taggart's greatest accomplishment, the construction of the John Galt Line, and of its paradoxical consequences. Part 2 contrasts two opposite moral codes and the effects of each, tells of Hank Rearden's progressive liberation from guilt, and explains Dagny's conflict stemming from her mistaken premises regarding the looters and the strikers. In part 3 Rearden and Dagny grasp more abstractly, fully, and deeply the state of the world and how they should act in it. Let's take a closer look at these two characters.

Dagny, like Hank, is a self-initiator who goes by her own judgments and is the motive power of her own happiness. Unlike Rearden, she does not feel guilty for her achievements. She understands that the world lives because of the work of the prime movers and then hates them for it. Dagny recognizes that the creators are expected to feel guilty for their virtues. Of course, the creators are guilty only of not claiming their moral virtue and values.

Dagny does not fully understand the world's situation and is conflicted because of this lack of knowledge. From her perspective, the strikers are giving up and she sees that as dishonorable and as a form of capitulation. Of course, at one point of the novel, Dagny is on a "mini-strike" of her own when Directive 10–289 is passed. For most of the story, Dagny is on the "wrong track" by believing that the looters love their lives and that they want to live. She thinks that she can persuade them to see the truth and that she can win the war. Throughout Part Three she progressively comes to realize that the looters are irrational and do not value their lives. This begins to become apparent to her when she meets with Mr. Thompson and the other looter-politicians.

Throughout most of the novel, Dagny believed that she was right to go on. She needed to check her premises. She ultimately realizes that the looters do not value her products or those of the other producers. By the end of the story, she understands what motivates the looters. By then she understands the contradictions in her principles and the need to go on strike. She realizes that there is no chance of winning in the world of the looters.

Dagny has a fuller and more explicit conception of morality than Rearden does and is more morally consistent than he is. Her error is that she does not fully understand the looters' moral code and motives. Their motives become fully clear to her when they want to torture and/or kill Galt rather than to switch course and rescue themselves. Prior to this point, she believed that the looters would eventually comprehend the uselessness of their policies and would concede.

Hank Rearden, a great industrialist who accepts the mind-body dichotomy, is the primary human instantiation of Atlas in the novel. He is a master of reality whose erroneous surface ideas do not corrupt his essential character and subconsciousness in terms of his psychoepistemology. Although Rearden's words and ideas sanction an unearned guilt, his actions belie his words. Down deep he does not believe the notion of the mind-body split.

Hank and the other industrialists are the worst victims of the conventionally accepted altruist-collectivist philosophy. It is the mistaken sanction of the men of ability that paves the way for the parasites and statist looters who want the creators to produce for the world and then to suffer for doing so. A moral code based on altruism and the idea of a mind-body split holds the creators guilty because of their greatest virtues. Once Rearden and the other producers gain an understanding of the looters' evil and of the importance of their own morality, they will obtain the sense that life is about accomplishment and joy rather than about suffering and disaster.

It is under the tutelage of Francisco and Dagny that Rearden slowly awakens to the truth; comprehends the nature, causes, and interrelationships between his personal and work-related problems; understands the motives of the looters and his family; and realizes his own virtues and values. They are able to provide Hank with a moral sanction and lead him to realize that he has been guilty in accepting a wrong moral code and of giving the looters and his family a moral sanction based on the wrong code of morality. Throughout much of the novel, he needed to attain a belief in his own morality and in his right to self-esteem.

Hank's decision to go on strike takes a long time to develop. Until his discussion with the looters regarding the proposed Steel Unification Plan, he thought that the looters would ultimately be rational. After the confrontation, Rearden drives back to his mills, happens upon the dying Wet Nurse, is saved by Francisco (disguised as worker "Frank Adams"), and listens to Galt's logic as delivered to him by Francisco. In the next chapter he disappears to Mulligan's Valley. Now seeing the truth, he recognizes that he must give up the world in order to save it.

For much of the novel Dagny and Hank considered the looters' evil policies to be self-defeating. They did not understand that they are not impotent if they are empowered by the good. It was only the producers' toleration and tacit acceptance of the looters' moral code that made the devastating results possible. In order to be able to effectively battle their enemies, Dagny and Hank had to come to understand how they were complicit in their own victimization. The moral code of self-sacrifice had been used against, and accepted by, the creators who had been made to feel guilt for their achievement and wealth. This is the "sanction of the victim" moral principle.

Rearden's exploitation is more extreme than Dagny's. She has an explicit awareness of morality that he does not have. Rearden questions his right to his own happiness and self-esteem and she does not. He partially accepts altruism and does not explicitly understand that he goes by a moral code in his work life. He does so implicitly because his work life exemplifies morality as it leads to production, life, and life-enhancing values.

There have been many good philosophical novels and good business novels, but none have been as brilliantly integrated and unified as *Atlas Shrugged*. *Atlas Shrugged* is arguably the greatest combination of philosophy, business, and literature written to date. Ayn Rand's presentation of businessmen as heroes makes this novel virtually unparalleled in the history of literature. This great novel is currently being brought to the big screen in the form of a trilogy of films. Part 1 was released in the spring of 2011, part 2 was released in the fall of 2012, and part 3 will follow in 2014.

Chapter Seventeen

Sometimes a Great Notion

The Story of a Family Who Would Never Give an Inch

Ken Kesey's novel, *Sometimes a Great Notion* (1964), is a complex and integrated historical background and relationship study of the Stamper family, a prideful logging clan living in Wakonda, Oregon. This big story involves a man, his family, a town, the country, a period of time, and the effects of time. All of the elements of the novel including its characters, events, settings, symbols, and so on, are integrated and oriented toward the themes of independence, individualism, and self-sufficiency. The novel teaches that a person should have the right to try to be as big as he believes it is in him to be. *Sometimes a Great Notion* was made into a 1971 film directed by and starring Paul Newman. In Britain this film about generations of loggers was called *Never Give an Inch*.

At the beginning of the twentieth century, Jonas Stamper had traveled from Kansas to Oregon to pursue his American dream of becoming a successful pioneer in the promising new Western frontier. Jonas begins to construct a large frame house on a bank of the Wakonda Auga River. Overcome by the potential of the Oregon climate and wilderness to overpower and destroy men, the intimidated Jonas leaves his family and goes back to Kansas.

Jonas's son, Henry, takes command, finishes the house, and commences a continual battle to keep it from being washed away by the mighty river. Stamper House stands on a dangerous peninsula on a river bend. All of the other homes in the vicinity are eventually destroyed by the waters. Henry refuses any help from others in the community and declines to join the Wakonda Co-op or any other community association. By 1961, the independent, stubborn, and fierce Henry is widely recognized as the patriarch of the long-resented Stamper clan. His motto is "Never Give an Inch." In the novel, the house built on the river will come to represent family tradition, the river will symbolize the eroding effects of time, and Henry will epitomize the family's link with its pioneering past. Henry is a man of habit whose philosophy is "to keep on going."

Hank is Henry's oldest son. A man of integrity, he is loyal, honest, and courageous, and possesses a strong will and personality. The toughest man in the region, Hank was an all-state football player and a veteran of the Korean War as a Marine. Like his father, Hank is tough, obstinate, self-reliant, and independent. He is the only character in the novel who is able to swim across the river, his most powerful and relentless adversary. The aggressive and vital Hank becomes the leader of the family and has numerous clashes with members of the community and his own family. Throughout the novel he is portrayed as a heroic small businessman who is able to deal with and withstand a variety of pressures.

Hank's mother dies when he is only ten years old and Henry goes off to New York City to find another wife. Henry returns with a youthful new wife, Myra. The beautiful, twenty-one-year-old, Stanford-educated Myra prefers an urban environment and becomes unhappy in a household of loggers. She and Henry have a son, Leland, who is sensitive, intellectual, and has low self-esteem. Henry pays little attention to Leland as he is apparently satisfied with one son in his image. When Leland was born Hank was already twelve years old.

Myra seduces Hank when he is sixteen years old. The young Leland views them in bed together through a hole in the wall. Psychologically damaged by the incident, Leland hates, fears, and envies his half-brother, Hank. Henry never finds out about the affair and Hank never realizes that Leland knows about his secret affair with Myra. Aware that she is unsuited for the tough life of a logging wife, Myra decides to leave for New York with Leland when he is twelve years old. A dozen years later, she commits suicide by leaping off a tall building. The intellectual Leland has been pursuing doctoral work in English literature at Yale. Having troubles with his studies, he becomes paranoid, turns to drugs, and he too attempts suicide, but is unsuccessful.

The major action of the story occurs during a period of several weeks in 1961. At that time Hank and his cousin and best friend, Joe Ben, are running the Stamper family's logging business. Henry does what he can but has recently been injured and wears a cast on one side of his body. Having captured the market, the big lumber corporations have been putting pressure on the smaller companies and the union. The Stamper family owns and operates a company that does not have a union—Hank only hires family members. Henry's goal is to keep the family logging business alive.

The small town is dying due to the introduction of the gas-powered chainsaw, which has reduced greatly the need for manual labor. As a result, the union loggers go on strike demanding the same pay for shorter hours in response to the decreasing need for manual labor. The union is striking against Wakonda Pacific Lumber Company, a regional mill. The union leaders and members want the Stampers to close down their family-owned, non-union shop believing that it was the Stamper's duty to support the strike as a sign of solidarity for this small town. The union's message is one of brotherhood and interdependence.

The Stampers decide to continue to work and to cut and to supply trees to the regional mill in opposition to the striking unionized workers. They supply all of the lumber that the union laborers normally would have supplied from their union shops if the strike had not occurred. Accepting the contract to supply the big lumber company with logs is the opportunity for the Stamper family to gain great wealth. Signing this contract with Wakonda Pacific is the break they had been waiting for. The Stampers also understand that backing the union would damage their own non-unionized family business. To Hank and the other Stampers, the union represents mediocrity and conformity. These small businessmen are thus eager to confront the union.

The union has the backing of the whole town except for the Stampers. This does not sit well with the union workers who feel betrayed. The Stamper family's decision to keep working prevents the strike from ending because there is no good reason for Wakonda Pacific to negotiate and to resolve the dispute when the Stampers are doing all of the work that the unionized workers would have done. This large corporation can only meet its own contracts by dealing with men like Hank Stamper, a man of his word.

With Henry still injured, the family needs additional labor and, as a result, Hank sends for his half-brother, Leland, who is doing graduate work back East. Leland receives the card from Oregon just after he has unsuccessfully tried to commit suicide by gassing himself. His suicide attempt had blown up all of his possessions including the dissertation that he was writing. He was in a lot of trouble as he could not pay his hospital bills and his landlord was suing him for destroying his home. He decides to travel back to his roots in the Oregon timberlands to help with the logging business and to gain revenge against Hank. He has never forgiven Hank for what happened between Hank and his mother and for not going to his mother's funeral. The bitter and vengeful socialist-leaning intellectual wants Hank to pay for the things that he had done. The insecure Lee hates Hank's strength and self-sufficiency.

Floyd Evenwrite, the local union leader, has been envious of Hank's strength since high school. This fierce, blustery, impulsive, and unintelligent man wants to stop the Stamper family from fulfilling its contract and will use violent and illegal means to sabotage the family's efforts. Evenwrite sends for Jonathan Draeger, a union representative from California, to aid him.

Draeger is well-educated, confident, manipulative, rational, and coldly-cal-
culating. The cruel and destructive Draeger takes the offensive through trickery, subterfuge, and patience. He fervently believes in communal values and
hates the ideas of self-determination and freedom. Draeger is convinced that
all people behave according to predictable patterns. Together, Evenwrite's
fury and Draeger's machinations provoke the feelings of the community
members against the Stampers.

Leland arrives and the Stampers teach him to cut down trees. The Stampers do not make up a totally happy family. There are many confrontations
among them. In this family the men do the talking and the women remain
quiet. Lee has a very different view of life than do the other Stamper men. He
believes that women are equal to men and that everyone's voice should be
heard. He finds he has a great deal more in common with Viv, Hank's wife,
than he does with the men of his family. Leland devises a plan and cam-
paigns to seduce and sleep with Viv which he eventually does. During the
stay, Lee and Viv grow even closer as he recognizes and acknowledges her
unhappiness because she is not appreciated by the others in the house.

The Stampers will not succumb to the demands of the union workers to
cease working so that they can gain the benefit of higher wages. One of the
townspeople, who is Hank's friend and union member, pleads with Hank to
stop working during the strike. He says that if the Stampers don't stop then
he will commit suicide pretending it was an accident thereby gaining insurance proceeds for his family. Hank refuses while exhibiting no emotions.
His friend later follows through with his suicide. Hank is determined by
principle to fulfill his commitment to deliver the logs.

After a football game at a community picnic turns into a brawl between
the Stampers and the other townspeople, the union workers sabotage some of
the Stampers's machinery. Hank retaliates by going to the union office with a
chainsaw to cut Evenwrite's desk in half. The union members also attempt to
vandalize the Stampers's collected logs. When one of the union workers falls
in the water, Hank jumps in to save him. The Stampers's determination to
succeed is demonstrated when their transportation equipment is destroyed
and Hank and Henry decide to cut trees closer to the river thereby eliminating the need to transport them. This strategy unfortunately and ultimately
will result in the accidental deaths of Henry and Joe Ben as described below.

Henry had recovered sufficiently to rejoin the logging efforts. As Hank is
cutting down a tree, it splits vertically down the middle with half crashing
backward toward the forest and the other half landing in the river. The
portion of the tree that fell on land severs Henry's arm in the process. The
section that fell into the water lands on Joe Ben pushing him toward the
bottom of the river.

Lee drives the mortally wounded Henry to the hospital and Hank attempts
to use the chainsaw to free Joe Ben but it runs out of oil. With no axes to be

found, Hank valiantly but unsuccessfully attempts to save Joe Ben. As the river rises, the tree shifts and Joe Ben gives up his struggle and drowns. In an ironic twist of fate, the chainsaw, an important cause of the strike itself, fails and results in the death of the optimistic, hard-working, well-liked and loyal Joe Ben.

Viv feels trapped and her love for her husband, Hank, wanes as she comes to understand her place in the household. Like Myra, Viv begins to think that there must be better ways in which to spend her life. She is eventually seduced by, and has an affair with, Lee. Hank sees them through the same hole that Lee had used as a young boy to witness the sexual relationship between his mother and Hank. As a young child, Leland saw his mother in bed with Hank and has bitterly resented his half-brother ever since.

A fist-fight showdown between Hank and Leland ends in a draw. Hank apologizes for sleeping with Lee's mother and explains that, because of the age difference, Hank was not taking advantage of Lee's mother, Myra. The brothers come to somewhat of a truce. Lee also discovers that Hank has been sending money to his mother for many years.

At this point in the story Hank appears to be ready to give in to the union demands. This has negative effects on the community, and the townspeople are saddened. His giving up would disillusion the residents of the community and would destroy their assurance in confronting life's challenges. The novel thus illustrates how a heroic free individual with strength and integrity, like Hank, has a positive effect on the community. The community benefits from Hank's free expression of his self-interest.

By this time, Henry and Joe Ben have been killed, the mill has been partly burned down, and the boathouse has been dynamited into the river. It is at this point that Hank, the strong and stubborn idealist, decides not to give in and gets ready to steer the logs down the river by himself. Lee joins Hank on the tugboat and they pilot the boat and four large rafts of logs past the disbelieving townspeople. Viv leaves Hank just as the two brothers begin the log drive. On the boat sits Henry's severed arm with all the fingers bent and tied down except for the middle one. This defiant gesture is aimed toward the union members gathered on the side of the river. It represents the strength of men to defeat, at least temporarily, overwhelming forces.

Sometimes a Great Notion illustrates the value of a family sticking together. Hank, the product of a frontier culture, has a strong will and work ethic and leads his family in fighting for what they believe. He is a man of integrity who has a strong sense of kinship. In association with his family, Hank is able to withstand a variety of pressures including the forces of nature, (i.e., the river and the forest), social pressures exerted by the townspeople, the conformist pressures brought by the union, and the need to fulfill their logging contract. Hank represents the joy of an unyielding will in his quest to deliver the logs to the Wakonda Pacific Lumber Company.

Lee has abandoned his sheltered academic life in the East to affirm himself as a man. At first he is uncomfortable with his new duties as a logger. Because of his lack of knowledge of the business he feels out of place and distant from his family. After working with his family for a while he discovers a common ground with them in the activity of logging which demands strength, skill, and courage. By the end of the story he has learned the values and virtues of family, work, and self-reliance.

This fine tale of independence, individualism, and family has been made into a 1971 film. The roles and actors include: Hank Stamper (Paul Newman), Henry Stamper (Henry Fonda), Viv Stamper (Lee Remick), Leland Stamper (Michael Sarazin), Joe Ben Stamper (Richard Jaeckel), Floyd Everwrite (Joe Maross), and Jonathan Draeger (Roy Poole).

Chapter Eighteen

Wilfrid Sheed's *Office Politics*

A Lesson About Organizational Conflict

Wilfrid Sheed's 1966 novel, *Office Politics*, was the runner up for the National Book Award in that year. It tells the story of interpersonal conflicts and intramural jockeying for editorial power among the staff of a small, bimonthly liberal journal called *The Outsider*, similar to political magazines such as *The Nation, The New Republic*, and *Commonweal*. Sheed himself had been the drama critic for the *Commonweal*. The circulation of *The Outsider* had steadily decreased from 27,000 subscribers down to 21,000. Office politics is about power and advantage. Because office politics is a fact of life and a necessary component of the functioning of any organization, this novel is relevant to the contemporary workplace.

Both the magazine and the building in which it is located are in decline. The office itself is a shabby, nearly windowless assortment of divided rooms somewhere on the East Side of Manhattan, New York. The walls are peeling, the furniture is falling apart, and a filing cabinet blocks the fire exit. The walls are dark and dirty and the elevator is slow and noisy. The conditions of the cramped, drab office reflect the mood of the novel's characters.

The magazine espouses "radicalism with responsibility" but its interchangeable, dull content always seems to come out the same. The ignoble routine of producing the journal has turned the once idealistic editors into depressed cynics. The result is a wide separation between the liberal political rhetoric appearing in *The Outsider* and the values and shallow worldviews of the editors themselves.

The inertia of the magazine's editorial culture had set in over a long period of time. *The Outsider* had a powerful managing editor who could suppress views against his interests and restrict any debates as to editorial content. As a result, bad conflict had increased along with organizational listlessness. Although the associate editors fight constantly over what is included in an issue and who gets to approve the final copy, the head editor always gets his way. Each of the editors' attempts to translate his own views into what he wants the others to think is in the best interest of the journal. The editor's unwillingness to delegate and his domination of every aspect of the business has led to the desire for change among the staff members.

The main characters are editor Gilbert Twining, two long-time employees, associate editors Brian Fine and Fritz Tyler, and recently hired junior editor, George Wren, the primary character in the story. There are also several minor office characters in the novel including accountant and office manager Olga Marplute, advertising director Philo Sonnabend, drama critic Wally Funk, and Brian Fine's nephew, Sam Thirsby, who is brought in to help out later on in the story. Gilbert Twining controls all of the office employees and each of them engages in, and is confronted with, rivalry and disloyalty to one another. In their efforts to attain power, they conspire, connive, gossip, back stab, maneuver, and engage in self-serving posturing. They take actions directed toward the goal of serving their own perceived self-interest without regard for the well-being of others or of the organization. The employees occasionally share ideas among themselves but rarely voice their opinions to Twining out of fear of being rejected. Each one thinks he has a solution to the problem of declining subscriptions but they are all reluctant to take their ideas to the maestro. Let us now take a brief look at the history and personalities of these characters.

Gilbert Twining is a reserved, British-born editor in his early fifties who was hired to edit *The Outsider* when Frank Tippitt, founder of the journal, stepped down from running its day to day operations. Twining had been the youngest editor to head the successful English magazine *The Watchman*. Twining had attended finishing school and was able to intimidate his employees with his superior attitude and his cultured English speech and demeanor. He is manipulative, calculating, and pragmatic, and has a keen instinct for discerning people's weak points. It follows that he is able to adjust his approach to each specific individual and situation. In tune to the thoughts and feelings of his staff, the flexible Twining adapts his managerial approach to particular circumstances.

The neurotic Twining constantly thinks that someone is sabotaging him in an attempt to usurp his power. He works to manage everyday conflicts and real and imagined threats to his authority. He must constantly control his editors' maneuverings. Maintaining a Machiavellian management style, Twining manipulates his employees in his efforts to create the journal to his image. He runs a tight ship, plays mind games, and runs things his way. He is in complete charge of every aspect of the magazine. Although the members of his editorial staff are unhappy, they also praise him. They complain about him but they also respect him and admire him and do what he wants to be done in the manner in which he wants things done. They refer to him as a great editor, a first-rate man, and always a gentleman. He is called maestro, captain, commander, admiral, commandant, and so on. Despite his authoritarian style, the charming British expatriate maintains the ability to take his employees out for drinks after work.

Flashbacks in the novel reveal that Gilbert suffers from wounds experienced as a young child when the young Twining was bullied and tormented by other children, especially by his cousin, Richard. The grownup Twining has low self-esteem and is shy and awkward with women. He frequently goes to the park to watch pretty girls but he does not have the confidence or courage to speak to them because he fears being ignored and rejected. Twining is married to a soft-spoken woman named Polly who tends to change subjects in order to avoid confrontations.

Brian Fine is the publication's most senior editor having held his position when Gilbert Twining was hired for the chief editorial position. At that time, Fine thought that he had a chance to become the magazine's senior editor. The unmarried Fine is chubby and small, somewhat humorous, and not liked or respected by his fellow co-workers. Ironically, he enjoys their company. Fine is an insecure schemer who is certain that he can improve *The Outsider* when he gets to a position of power. Suffering from self-delusions of grandeur, the high-strung, frustrated associate editor is bitter about the way that Twining is running the journal and he wants to change things around. He believes that editorial meetings are necessary in order to obtain consensus before each issue of the journal is finalized. Fine complains about the lack of delegation of duties and maintains that Twining will not permit the others to grow professionally.

A number of years ago, Twining had given Fine what Twining thought was constructive criticism, but Fine interpreted the criticism as condescending. In addition, he felt emasculated and became enervated when Twining drastically edited and shortened one of his pieces of writing. Fine half-despised Twining. In turn, the perceptive Twining believed that Fine had a personal vendetta toward him.

Another associate editor, the thin and sarcastic Fritz Tyler, is a social climber and a cynic. He had worked at *The Outsider* for four years and had been introduced to Gilbert Twining by Gilbert's wife, Polly, who had been a college friend of Tyler. When Fritz was first hired, Twining treated him as a confidant and went drinking with him much like he does now with the newly hired George Wren. The power-hungry Tyler wants to take control of the journal. To help him do this, he has aligned himself with, and began dating, Mrs. Harriet Wadsworth, one of the largest financial supporters of *The Outsider*. In order to further his career, Tyler acquires a rich mistress who has designs on being a drama critic. Tyler wants her to purchase a controlling interest in the publication's stock.

George Wren, the protagonist of the novel, was hired as the number four editor three months before the story begins. A long-time reader and admirer of *The Outsider*, George left a better paying position at CBS because he believed in the importance of the magazine's liberalism. He thought that the journal's ideals and principles were worth working toward and fighting for. Not only did he join the company because of what it stood for, he also wanted the opportunity to work with the highly regarded Gilbert Twining.

Wren, the newest employee, tries at first to remain neutral, to avoid negativity, and to have a positive view with respect to the potential of the publication. It is not long before each of the three senior editors shows his feelings about the others with George. He becomes the confidant of Gilbert Twining and unwillingly spends many evenings going to bars and listening to Twining's stories about his childhood and his distrust of anyone at the journal because he thinks that the others are conspiring against him. During drinks after work, the head editor tries to know George and to decide how, and if, he is going to fit into the organization.

The reduced salary causes some distress in George's marriage of three years to his wife, Matilda, with whom he has a young son, Peter, the joy in his life. Not only does Wren have to deal with office politics, he also has to listen to the disapproval of his wife when he arrives home later after drinking with his boss. Work is affecting Wren's family life as he is frequently arriving home late which does not provide a lot of time to spend with his wife and son. At home he attempts to communicate with his wife regarding the difficulties he experiences at the office. George senses that Matilda dislikes both the magazine and its lead editor who control a great deal of George's time.

Because there are no specialists in this small magazine, Wren is quick to learn all aspects of the business. Our middle man is both impressed and disappointed with the editor who runs the magazine with an iron fist. He concludes that a shakeup in style might be needed in order to get more readers. George has come to realize that Twining has maintained the same behind the times style ever since his arrival at the journal.

Olga Marplate is a frumpish miser who is in charge of accounting, considers herself to be the office manager responsible for office discipline, and is a bully to the secretaries. Her goals are to adopt stricter office rules and to redecorate the office. Philo Sonnabend both sells advertising space within the journal and advertises the journal itself. He is never given any real responsibility and his ideas are ignored and/or vetoed by Twining. He is offended by how Twining treats his office staff. This generally agreeable man with a disheveled appearance is poorly treated by all. The sensitive Wally Funk is the magazine's drama critic. His writing tends to be flamboyant and exuberant and thus requires frequent editing. Sam Thirsby, the incompetent nephew of Brian Fine, is hired in the middle of the story and is an unneeded addition to the staff.

Gilbert Twining has a heart attack while on a business trip to California. His employees are shocked to hear that he had suffered his heart attack while he was in bed with a woman he had met at the hotel bar. They do not seem to be very concerned with Twining's health, preferring to view the situation as an opportunity to take command. They do not know if, and when, he would ever return to work. Each person becomes power-hungry and attempts to make alliances to gain some kind of advantage. Backstabbing, disloyalty, backroom manipulation, and outright confrontations occur after Gilbert's heart attack. More specifically, George Wren gets drawn into the plots of Brian Fine and Fritz Tyler to dethrone Twining.

Without consulting anyone, Brian Fine takes full editorial authority upon himself to run the journal and to delegate duties. Although Fritz Taylor is also eager to take control, he is not very concerned because he thinks that Fine is destined to fail. Fine seems to have begun his time at the top with good intentions to perk up the magazine and to increase its readership. He thinks that he will remain in the editor's post once his ideas for meetings, consensus, and other improvements are implemented and applauded by readers and stockholders of *The Outsider*.

Fine holds editorial meetings which are intended to elicit input from Tyler and Wren. They become bored when Fine ignores their suggestions. As a result, Fine concludes that those meetings are unsuccessful and unneeded. Fine also attempts to form alliances with Olga Marplate and Philo Sonnabend. Changing the office décor is the top priority for Marplate, the office manager, who shocks Fine by wanting to spend way too much money on unrealistic office beautification. Fine also listens to Sonnabend's extravagant and dreadful advertising schemes that would very likely not produce any additional revenue.

Despite the fact that the employees complained about Twining's managerial approach, his methods are copied during his absence. Fine shuts down new ideas just as Twining had done and everyone continues to perform their duties in their comfortable, routine, familiar ways. The situation in *Office Politics* illustrates just how hard it is to transform a firm's climate (i.e., its policies, practices, and procedures) and culture (i.e., its deeply held values and beliefs) which are inextricably interconnected and mutually reinforcing.

The pressure of the job gets to Brian Fine and he fires Wally Funk, the drama critic, and replaces advertising director, Philo Sonnabend, with his inept nephew who would serve as Fine's assistant. The interim editor also attempts to gain financial backing for the magazine from Olga Marplate, who refuses and sees his action as a letdown of their friendship. Throughout his tenure as editor, Fine becomes ever more defensive, controlling, rude, and argumentative.

Brian Fine has much the same editorial standards as does Gilbert Twining. As a result, he edits the magazine as closely to the way that Twining would have edited it. When the next issue reaches the market it appears almost identical to any other issue that Twining had put together. Fine's subsequent issues are also little different from Twining's. George Wren observes that, in Twining's absence, Fine has become just like Twining.

All the while, Fritz Tyler continues to date the magazine's chief financial banker, Harriet Wadsworth, in his efforts to gain both financial and editorial control. Tyler makes a huge error when he permits her poorly written vacuous reviews to appear in the journal He had reasoned that she would buy more stock in the publications and use her ownership power to hand him the editorship if he made her the theater critic for the magazine. Knowing how bitter and angry Twining's wife, Polly, is regarding the circumstances surrounding her husband's heart attack, Fritz talks her into giving him control of her shares of stock, thereby harming her husband and boosting Tyler's chances to obtain control of the magazine.

George Wren had promised to write Twining a letter four months ago but he had never done so. Having viewed the conflicts and power struggles that had taken place during Twining's absence, the angry George decides to write Twining detailing exactly what had transpired and how things were at the office. George wants to see what that would lead to.

The charismatic and articulate Twining returns to Manhattan to resume command after reading George Wren's letter. He takes George along with him to make a series of weekend visits to the members of his staff. The insecure Twining fears that the others are gunning for permanent takeover of his top position so he decides to restore order. He uses George's comments about the other employees in front of him in these awkward encounters.

They first pay a late night visit to Brian Fine. After some small talk, Twining congratulates Brian for doing a creditable job keeping the magazine going in his absence. He then says that he did notice a few things in one of the issues that Brian had edited. Twining had filled the pages with red marks and proceeded to cold-bloodedly wear Fine out with a torrent of minor criticisms until three o'clock in the morning. By then, Twining had humbled and intimidated Fine into unintelligible repentance.

The next day Gilbert and George visit Wally Funk, the magazine's drama critic, who had been replaced during Twining's absence. Twining apologizes to Wally and flatters him by praising his effusive and passionate writing in order to get him to come back to the magazine. Of course, Twining added that a drudge like himself was necessary, at times, to trim his exuberance. Next, Twining visits Philo Sonnebend, the magazine's long-time advertising manager, treats him with respect, allows him to vent, apologizes for his treatment, and talks the resentful Philo into returning to work at *The Outsider*. Gilbert is also very pleasant when he and George visit and listen to the concerns of Olga Marplate, the office manager. As a result of Twining's charm, Olga is even friendly to Wren, whom she did not really like at all.

Twining still has to put Fritz Tyler back in his place. After some boring chit chat, Twining tells Tyler that "Harriet Wadsworth does not own the magazine, you know" (291). Fritz smiles and tells Gilbert that she owned thirty-five percent and that Twining's wife, Polly, "used to own" twenty-five percent, which she had sold to Harriet. He adds that "Harriet has the stocks, and she wants me to be editor" (292). Telling Tyler that we shall see about that, Twining calls Harriet who says that she would be delighted to see Gilbert, George, and Fritz.

At first, Twining avoids any discussion about the magazine, instead engaging the woman's vanity with name-dropping and gossip about wealthy and famous people that they know. After he had sweet-talked her to death, he finally turns the conversation toward the magazine. He tells her she is not talented as a drama critic and implies that only someone as low and self-serving as Fritz Taylor would let her embarrass herself by not being truthful with her. Gilbert makes sure that she understands that he would never use their friendship for his own purpose as Fritz had been trying to do:

> You're no good at that kind of thing, you know . . . I could tell you that you were, of course, but you wouldn't really respect me for that, would you? I'm in the magazine business, not the flattery business. You know as well as I do that people with money are seldom told the truth. Many so-called friends encourage them to make fools of themselves." (300–301)

After Twining talks Harriet out of being a drama critic and backing Fritz Tyler, both George and Gilbert go home and think about the situation at the journal. After having watched the entire staff being manipulated by Twining, Wren ends up ready to quit his position at the magazine. The tired Twining comes to terms with the fact that Polly is likely to leave him. He thinks about the magazine and concludes that George is the most logical next editor of *The Outsider*. It may be that Twining stayed away from the office as long as he did as a test to see who might make a good successor to him. He did think that George going with him to visit the various employees could serve as a hurried apprenticeship for him.

Wren visits Twining and tells him what he thinks of Twining's bullying, manipulating, flattering, and catering to his employee's various weaknesses. He calls Twining a cold-blooded bastard, says that he did not want to receive the "treatment" from Twining, and tells him he did not want to get into a fencing match with him because he was too good of a talker. George tells Gilbert that he was somewhat responsible for the fiasco at the office and for the lousy people there. Twining had left a confused situation behind with no clear succession plan. George had been shocked by what he saw and tells

Gilbert that people are brought down, rather than improved, when they are around him. He does not want to be around Twining because he knows that Twining will play on some strain of his character.

Despite George's criticism of him, Twining tells him that he would be the next editor of *The Outsider*. He says that George can take over and make changes with his help. He also explains to George that he had no master plan to control his staff and that his strategy and tactics depended on what each member tells him in a given situation. George says that he is not the man for the job but that he wants to part on good terms.

When George leaves, the weary Twining thinks that he needs to develop a new plan. He concludes that all promising young people eventually end up like Fritz Taylor and Brian Fine. After he rests for a while he sees Polly. They talk about the last few days and they make up. She forgives him and changes her mind about getting a divorce. She wants to stay with him.

In the end, Twining decides that he still wants to keep George at the magazine. He offers George the job of editor-in-chief and says that he will not interfere in any way at all. At the end of the novel, George is undecided about whether or not to accept the offer.

The novel *Office Politics* is a great vehicle to bring up discussions about conflict and office politics as it realistically portrays these issues in the workplace. Some conflict is natural, can be beneficial, and can improve organizational effectiveness and decision making. However, at some point it can become dysfunctional and can cause organizational decline. Managers need good judgment to permit "good" conflict without letting it escalate into "bad" conflict. The same can be said with regard to office politics which are a natural part of the interactive process of working together toward individual and organizational goals. Good office politics can help to build positive relationships and mutually beneficial alliance, and to get things done. Bad office politics include actions aimed at advancing one's self without consideration for the good of others or the organization itself.

Chapter Nineteen

The Franchiser

Stanley Elkin's Tale of a Man Who Wanted to Costume the Country

Stanley Elkin's *The Franchiser* (1976) is a synthesis of Elkin's own health crisis of multiple sclerosis (MS) with national phenomena of the 1970s such as the energy crisis and the growth of franchises. Ben Flesh, the protagonist and main narrator, shares Elkin's disease as he crisscrosses the country in his pale-blue Cadillac, visiting, opening, closing, and relocating a variety of franchises. Throughout the novel, the author provides analogies between Flesh's physical problems and those of American society in the mid-1970s. Although most of the story takes place during the mid-70s, it covers a period ranging from 1940s to the 1970s.

Much of this road novel is organized around three trips Ben makes to check on his franchises. The novel is presented as a number of diverse and seemingly unrelated episodes. Elkin supplies the reader with a number of linked stories from Ben's past and present in a series of darkly comic and moving encounters of Ben with his employees, business associates, road people, and his adopted family, the Finsbergs. Along his highway journeys, Flesh meets a multitude of interesting characters.

The novel is replete with long monologues, ramblings, and meditations on life, death, and the places Ben visits and the people he meets during his travels. These are narrated through flashbacks that are not chronologically presented. Elkin skillfully presents this episodic plot structure in coherent form that subsumes and reconciles the novel's parallels, overlappings, juxta-positions, and metaphors that imply or embody each other. By the end of the novel both Ben and the reader are able to discern the lines of his life coming together to form a pattern.

Ben Flesh was born in 1928. His parents died in an automobile accident when he was sixteen years old and serving in the military; both the U.S. army and the Red Cross had failed to inform him of this tragedy. When he returned home on furlough he found out about their demise that had occurred a month before. Obtaining a compassionate leave from the military, he enters the Wharton School of Business.

During his junior year at Wharton, Ben is summoned to his godfather's hospital bedside. The godfather, Julius Finsberg, was Ben's father's business partner and he wants to make amends and reparations for cheating Ben's father out of his share in a theatrical costuming business. Julius bequests Ben the ability to borrow money at the same rate that the prime interest rate is on the date of Julius Finsberg's death. Although, he is leaving his money to his children, he believes he is giving Ben something more valuable. This action would serve to his clear his conscience before he died.

Flesh thus gains the ability to obtain loans from Finsberg's bank, at the prime rate, whatever it would be on the date that he dies, no matter how high it may climb thereafter. The loan or loans are never to exceed the value of the money left to the surviving children. The principal and the interest are to be guaranteed by them on a pro-rata basis up to and until Ben's first bankruptcy. The prime rate was 1.45 percent on four to six month commercial paper on the date of the Finsberg's death.

Julius Finsberg and his wife, Estelle, had nine sons and nine daughters in the form of four sets of triplets and three sets of twins. Every child was initially the same possessing the same looks, mannerisms, gestures, voices, and tics. The only difference was that each one had one esoteric physical malady. All of these multiple-birth siblings had show business names.

Throughout the years, Ben Flesh cared for his god-cousins and their investments. Ben likes helping them and consistently shows compassion and loyalty to them. He becomes forever tied to this bizarre group. He becomes sentimentally attached to them and becomes the benefactor, leader, father figure, lover, and annoyance to various members of the clan. One of the god-cousins suggested that Ben should invest in a Howard Johnsons because all of the Finsbergs love ice cream and because all of the Howard Johnsons are identical, just as the children are identical. When he does invest in a Howard Johnsons he begins his crusade as a franchiser (although technically he is a franchisee) who invests in a variety of reduplicative franchises. Over the years, Ben uses the Finsberg family funds to invest in more and more franchises. His franchises include Howard Johnsons, KFC, Dairy Queen, Radio Shack, Fred Astaire Dance Studio, Baskin-Robbins, Mr. Softee, and many more. He, of course, does not run the day-to-day operations of the establishments but instead hires proxies to run his businesses for him.

America was transformed by franchises during the second half of the twentieth century and Elkin's "hero" was somewhat of a pioneer in that change. A businessperson can buy the right to operate a business under a national franchise and is subject to its oversight. A franchise can be viewed as a method of transferring a business format with minimal financial investment. A franchise is the local embodiment of a national business. It is able to increase output, create jobs, and diffuse innovations around a system of outlets. The increased competition from franchises adds to consumer choices and leads to lower and stable prices. Franchising is a means to efficiently distribute goods and services and to provide a consistent level of quality of standardized goods. A franchise is the means to reach consumers with homogenized tastes, values, and lifestyles with a single marketing message and to satisfy them with a predictable and standardized product or service. Franchises tend to efficiently produce reliable, low-cost products and services.

Of course, there are critics who decry the loss of humanity in the production process due to franchising's standardized approach. They fear cultural homogenization, the loss of local culture, a uniformity of lifestyles and cultural symbols, and the dehumanization of workers who are not required to think because of the existence of standardized rules, practices, and procedures. They understand that standardization has its economic purpose but they also claim that it is esthetically dangerous.

Ben Flesh is unconcerned with the negative aspects of franchises. On the contrary, he applauds franchises and pursues the homogenization of the entire country. He wants to see the same brands, stores, and logos scattered all over the United States. His noble cause is to make America look like America. Ben believes that franchises are the face of the nation. He wants to contribute to the uniformity and structure of American culture. His goal is to normalize life for everyone. He wants to build America in the image of his own undifferentiating vision. Ben's goal is to impose uniformity upon space through his franchises. His commercial vision represents certainty and stability.

The Franchiser is about a man who wants to costume a country with all of its familiar, ubiquitous neon logos and symbols. Ben wants to be the man who makes America famous. He has a zeal for making money by implementing his vision of uniformity. Ben glorifies consumer culture and the standardization of American life. He calls himself a true democrat who would quell distinctions, obliterate differences, and common denominate until people would recognize that it was America everywhere. He looks forward to a time when it will be impossible to distinguish the outskirts and suburbs of one American city from those of another American city. Ben wants to homogenize the United States by proliferating identical franchises around its landscape. When places are identical a person can never really know where he is. Today, of course, we can use our GPS as we drive along the interstate highways and notice how most of the stops and exits look familiar and similar.

Ben wants to help people purchase what they want or need. He wants to satisfy "consumer necessity and the universalized appetite." Fascinated by the variety of the world, Ben sees the franchiser as a person who is able to cooperate with, and contribute to, the miracle that is in the world. He knows that people consume so that they can live and pursue their visions of happiness. Ben sees the world as a wonderful place of infinite opportunities. He wants to make the world's miraculous possibilities available to all people. He understands that the franchisers along with other private businesses can provide for all people luxuries which formerly would only have been available to very wealthy individuals.

Ben states that he was born without goals, obsessions, drive, or personality. He believes that, at age forty-eight, the print of his own personality had never developed. However, he does experience pleasure because of the needs of other people. He believes that he is motivated by his need to do good, rather than by his ego. One such need is to keep the Finsberg family financially secure. He is animated to service others through the interest borrowing privilege he inherited from Julius Finsberg. Ben wants people to think communally the way he does rather than thinking only of themselves. Recognizing that he has no good thing of his own, Ben concludes that he should place himself in the service of those who have good things of their own. Happy to learn that he could purchase names of men with good things of their own, Ben teams up with them to live his franchised life under the corporate trademarks, symbols, and logos of others.

With no identity of his own, Ben tries to become the characters found in his franchises. He attempts to assimilate the personalities of his franchises. He proceeds to buy more and more people's names. There are no franchises named Flesh's. He sets out to purchase men's names as if to borrow their identities. As a franchiser, Ben is a man without a consistent self who teams up with the available.

As a franchiser of many businesses, Ben is like a theatrical producer who has several shows running concurrently on Broadway. He views franchising as a particular manifestation of theatrical costuming. Ben wants to costume the country. He desires to supply the nation with its visual props.

Ben Flesh brings Plato's supramundane world of ideas and essences down to earth. He explains that people read shapes, symbols, logos, trademarks, and so on. People are shape-orientated and symbol-dominated. He says that we have a preliterate culture in which objects are differentiated by these shapes and sizes. Unlike Plato's essences, they are not located in another dimension. They are real and available in the here and now.

Ben spends his days on the road traveling from city to city. He is an enthusiastic and dynamic man in motion practicing "shuttle finance" as opposed to high finance. Ben is a franchiser/entrepreneur on a limited scale. He is a Yankee Peddler of the 1970s who found a way of pursuing his individual business interests within the world of gigantic corporations. Ben wants to leave a legacy and sees franchising as the way in which he can do that. He wants to share his organized, organizing, other-directed vision of the homogenization of culture and society. He wants to spatially unite and standardize the country.

In *The Franchiser* the author embeds the idea that capitalism is preferable to socialism. He portrays the private businessman as a strong individual who can resist control of the static state. The novel illustrates that the act of becoming is vastly better than a state of being. Elkin's vision is of an individual who has concern for the community rather than a vision of an isolated individual. The private businessman is a catalyst who sets things in motion—he is a dynamic self-starter, doer, and producer. By identifying himself as an individual with natural rights, the businessman also learns to respect, value, and treat other people as individuals.

Individualism and independence liberate voluntary interdependence. Self-reliant and capable people realize that more can be accomplished by working together than by working alone. People can combine their efforts with the efforts of others to achieve even greater success and happiness. Genuine communities arise when people are free to form voluntary associations to pursue their individual and mutual interests. *The Franchiser* depicts the business realm as a cooperative system of value-seeking individuals who produce and trade for mutual advantage.

Ben becomes ever more responsible for the eighteen exotically diseased Finsberg children after Estelle, Julius's wife, passes away. He becomes head of the family because he is the eldest. There is a parallel between the virtually identical Finsberg children and Ben's franchises. Early on in the story we perceive both as associated with solidarity, unity, stability, certainty, consolidation, and sameness. The twins and triplets are interchangeable just as the individual franchises of a given brand are interchangeable.

Ben loves business and franchising but he is not very good at these activities. He does not have a sense of self that is needed in order to translate his ambitions into achievements. He drives cross country to monitor his oftentimes outdated and poorly located businesses. He frequently does not think through his ideas and consequently makes bad business decisions. For example, Ben opened a car wash in a slum area where few individuals owned cars and where half of the cars that existed were destined to be repossessed. He also opened a Radio Shack in a town where television reception was bad and a Fred Astaire Dance Studio in a part of town where people were afraid to walk in the streets. In addition, he opened an ice cream shop in the cold north and in a neighborhood where very few kids resided. Then there was his refusal to update a dry cleaning business that was likely to have prospered if it had new equipment.

Ben also had ridiculous hiring practices. For example, he offered a hitch-hiker a job managing one of his franchises. He also tried to hire an ex-convict and told him that he did not require any references. He trusted everyone including strangers. Ben preferred to give opportunities to random others. He wanted to help people off the street. He liked to hear people's stories, to tell them his stories, and to help them out.

Ben was not concerned with regulations and legal barriers and would sometimes resort to the bribing of officials. For example, when attendance at his Cinema I and Cinema II movie theaters had declined, Ben decided that he wanted smoking to be permitted in the first ten rows of the theater. He encouraged the usher to smoke as a way of informing customers that it was acceptable in the theater even though it was not permitted by law. Ben told his employees to pay off inspectors and commissioners if they registered complaints. Ben's good point is that smoking should be permitted in a given establishment if the owner and everyone attending had no problem with it.

Ben's nomadic lifestyle does not lead to relationships and leaves him isolated. He needs to be loved and accepted and turns toward the Finsberg community. He even wants to be buried with the Finsbergs. Throughout his manic odyssey he is focused on providing for this strange clan. He is lonely and wants to be part of the family. His sister lives in Maine where her husband works as a fund raiser for Colby College. Given Ben's need to belong and for family, it is not surprising that he donates $100,000 so that the college will keep her brother-in-law employed.

At a certain point in the novel Dr. Wolfe informs Ben that he has multiple sclerosis (MS)—the progressive sensory deterioration of his demyelinating nervous system. This crippling disease is destroying Ben's ability to feel and to distinguish one sensation or object from another sensation or object. Ben's last name takes on a touch of irony as his flesh is now failing him. Dr. Wolfe tells Ben that he will have periodic remissions but also that the disease will always come back and worsen. Ben will go in and out of remissions and will likely be plagued by numbness and other symptoms.

Ben's health crisis takes place just when the country is experiencing difficult times. People are experiencing the aftermath of the Vietnam War. There are also energy problems as evidenced in rolling blackouts and brown-outs and in gas shortages. In addition, interest rates are high, and inflation rates and unemployment rates are running together resulting in new phenom-enon called "stagflation." Until then people believed that there was a consis-tent negative, or inverse, relationship between the rate of inflation and the rate of unemployment. There was thought to be a trade-off between the inflation rate and the unemployment rate. Economist Milton Friedman ex-plained that inflation and unemployment tend to run in the same direction in the long run because people will not continue to suffer from a "money illusion." They realize the truth that then may not have been an increase in demand and that the additional "demand" is actually a result of the government's expansionary monetary and fiscal policies.

Both Ben and his country are ill and running out of energy. His life, illness, and personal decline mirror problems at the national level. There is a metaphoric analogy between the microsystem that is Ben's body and the macrosystem that is America. The future of his own body is reflected in cities and towns that have to deal with massive heat waves, power shortages, brownouts, gas lines, and so on. The country's problems affect Ben's franchises. For example, his Mr. Softee ice cream franchise literally melts because of the energy crisis and has to be closed.

As a result of his disease Ben becomes bi-polar. When he was in remission he is euphoric and experiences mania, rage, and exaltation. When the MS becomes more active he is depressed and cannot taste food or sense temperatures. While in periods of remission he has a perspective on what he wants from life and is motivated to achieve his goals. He wants to build a new America and is driven to move his businesses toward unity as his body is being torn apart by his disease.

Ben knows that he is running out of time. He is motivated because his body is falling apart on him. He understands that his life is a series of remissions during which he can work and create. Ben feels his mortality directly and at one point exclaims "I want my remission back!" The point the novel is making is that all people are eventually betrayed by their bodies and have to battle against deteriorating health and lost opportunities in their efforts to attain their life purposes and to achieve their happiness. Throughout the story Ben is learning that life itself is a franchise and that people live from remission to remission.

The Finsberg children begin experiencing a series of tragic events. The family begins to fall apart when one of the children commits suicide thereby destroying their perfect symmetry of nine girls and nine boys. For the longest time all of the children had looked similar. This begins to change the night of the suicide. The family unravels and grows apart as the twins and triplets are no longer exactly alike. The children begin dying of bizarre causes at an alarming rate. The fractures in the family mirror and symbolize the physical decline of Ben's health, his franchises, and power-depleted America. Early in the novel the Finsbergs have a collectivized "we are all in this together" attitude. Their solidarity dissipates as their health deteriorates. They are not as fond of Ben as they were when they were younger. He fulfilled their needs then but now his franchises are failing and he is becoming a burden to them.

Ben's goal of making America look like America through his franchises collides with social, economic, and cultural forces found in the country in the 1970s. He still wants to organize and synthesize, and pushes on even though his franchises are failing. Although he is drawn to organization, consolidation, and plenitude, he sees chaos, deficiency, deterioration, and death all around him. Despite this and the fact that he knows that he will shortly be confined to a wheelchair, he continues to establish his franchises.

The last part of the book relates Ben's final last attempt to build a lasting enterprise—a carefully calculated Travel Inn for families traveling to Disney World. The location in Ringgold, Georgia was selected according to set of coordinates based on driving time from various locations to Disney World. Ben gambled on the idea that people would stay there. He planned the location of his motel with great deliberation because he desperately wanted to translate its success into a restoration of the Finsbergs and the revitalization and justification of himself.

As Ben begins closing some of his businesses, the Finsbergs ask to see his financial statements. The failure of some of his franchises leads them to pull their money out in an effort to stop losing money. They say they can no longer provide Ben with the prime rate of interest. They will no longer back his dealings including the Travel Inn project, which ends up costing Ben over a million dollars. They offer to let him stay with them but he chooses to go it alone on the road. Ben takes out a loan putting up all of his franchises as collateral in order to complete his pet project, which was plagued with labor strikes and cost overruns.

Ben discovers that the new national fifty-five miles per hour speed limit has significantly changed the distance and times upon when his Travel Inn is based. The location he chose is no longer an exact midway point on the southern path from northeastern population centers to the recently established Disney World in Florida. His Travel Inn proves to be a failing business.

While Ben is striving to establish his last franchise we see him progressively changing from being an other-directed human being to being an inner-directed person more concerned with the disintegration of his body. He realizes that each man is ultimately alone with his own needs—the self is primary. He learns that a man of flesh cannot live in the sphere of the ideal.

However, at the very end of the novel we perceive that Ben has not completely given up his commercial and community worldview. He takes an inventory of his life and sees that he is part of everything. He maintains his deluded idea that he is the consolidator of the country and has an image of himself spanning from coast to coast.

> Ben Flesh himself like a note on sheet music, the clefs of his neon logos in the American sky. All of his businesses he'd had, The road companies of Colonial Sanders, Baskin-Robbins, Howard Johnsons, Travel Inn, *all* his franchises. Why, he belonged everywhere, anywhere. . . . And ah, he thought, euphorically, ecstatically, this privileged man who could have been a vegetable or miner-

al instead of an animal, and a lower animal instead of a higher, who could have been a pencil or a dot on a die, who could have been a stitch in a glove or change in someone's pocket, or a lost dollar nobody found, who could have been stillborn or less sentient than sand, or the chemical flash of someone's else's fear, ahh. Ahh! (342)

Chapter Twenty

Glengarry Glen Ross

A David Mamet Word Play

David Mamet's 1984 Pulitzer Prize winning play, *Glengarry Glen Ross*, is about the struggles of four shady small-time salesmen in a small branch of a larger real estate company located in Chicago. Taking place over two business days, the play portrays the dog-eat-dog world of real estate and the ends ruthless salesmen will go to in order to sell overpriced and undesirable land to uninterested and reluctant potential buyers. The cutthroat conniving salesmen resort to trickery, bribery, deceit, lying, and theft. This dark play successfully illustrates the social Darwinistic nature of the shady world of real estate in a big city and the Darwinian rules of the desperate salesmen's game. The title of the play refers to two unattractive and overvalued parcels of Florida land—Glengarry Heights and Glen Ross Farms. Mamet's play was also made into a fine 1992 film which incorporated two additional scenes.

The author, Mamet, had worked for a year in a Chicago real estate office where he observed salesmen's noble but often pathetic efforts to sell unwanted real estate. There he heard the coarse and vulgar language that depicted the high pressure felt by the agents. Mamet had first-hand experience of both the desperation and exhilaration of the salesmen's calling. He knew how they talked and incorporated much obscene and unprofessional language into the play's dialogue. Abrasive and pungent language is shown to constitute the jargon of the salesmen's trade. Such language also measures and connotes the intensity of the salesmen's quests.

Mamet shows how hucksters use language to con customers and each other. He employs sporadic conversations and erratic speech patterns to convey their thoughts and personalities. Mamet illustrates that language is a con man's tool and that conversation can be used to persuade, convince, and lie.

His characters use language and storytelling in order to survive in their
dismal and dreary situations and to exalt that survival. Mamet's characters
define themselves through their language and discourse. Each character's
ability or inability to sell is essential to his identity and relationships to the
others.

The original play is set in two locations—a rundown Chinese restaurant
across the street from the shabby real estate office, and the dingy office itself.
The appearance of both the restaurant and the office sets us up for the dark-
ness, gloom, and sense of despair of the salesmen themselves. The three
scenes of Act I take place in the restaurant, and Act II entirely takes place the
following day in the office. The film version is fairly true to the play with
two scenes added. One scene shows one of the salesmen making an unsuccessful sales call at someone's home. The other scene effectively adds a new
character who threatens the salesmen at the beginning of the screenplay
version. Blake (played by Alec Baldwin), a slick troubleshooter from downtown, is sent to shake up the salesmen.

The very first scene of the film version is valuable by making explicit
much of what is subsequently illustrated, explained, or implied in the suc-
ceeding events of the play. The film begins with an emergency meeting in the
shabby real estate office. Blake, a tough emissary sent by downtown bosses
Mitch and Murray, delivers a "pep talk" to the salesmen. He tells the salesmen that they are all fired and that the only way to get their jobs back is to
close enough deals in the sales contest he is instituting. Blake is arrogant,
pompous, and takes pleasure in demeaning the salesmen. He delivers his talk
in unprofessional, negative, and vulgar language. He cracks the whip by
pitting the salesmen against each other in a sales contest. They will be fired
unless they get "on the board." There is an ever-present chalkboard in the
front of the office that consistently reminds them of the contest at all times—
it is literally in their faces.

Blake informs them that the winner will get a Cadillac, the second place
finisher will receive a set of steak knives, and the rest of them will be fired.
He says that each of them will be given two leads by Williamson, the office
manager, and that they had until the next morning to turn them into sales.
The salesmen know that the leads are old and worthless and two of them,
Dave Moss and Shelly Levene, complain that they are old leads. Blake's
attempts to "teach" the salesmen how to sell merely amount to repeating two
acronyms—ABC (Always Be Closing) and AIDA (Attention, Interest, Decision, and Action).

The first scene in Act I of the play shows Shelly "the Machine" Levene
attempting to persuade John Williamson, the sales manager, to give him
some of the premium leads locked up in the office. Williamson has 500 good
Glengarry leads that are only to be distributed to "closers." The desperate and
despairing Levene pleads, brags, flatters, bullies, and attempts to bribe the

office manager in order to obtain the leads. Levene tries to bribe Williamson by offering him fifty dollars for every lead plus twenty percent of the profit made. The unsympathetic, heartless, and impassive office manager says he wants his money up front.

Levene, a great salesman in the past, needs money to pay for his sick daughter's medical bills. As a tragic figure who boasts about his past accomplishments, Levene brings to mind the character Willy Loman in Arthur Miller's 1949 play *Death of a Salesman*. Viewed by Williamson as expendable, Shelly, the worn-out sagging old timer, has been on a losing streak not having made a sale in months. Levene attributes his misfortunes on the economy and the lack of quality leads that Williamson gives him. He views Williamson as a naïve, incompetent, sadistic, and bureaucratic young man with no sales experience.

Williamson takes orders from Mitch and Murray, the downtown sales bosses. The uncharismatic and ruthless sales manager resorts to fear and intimidation and is not respected by the salesmen. They despise both Williamson and the system under which they work. Lacking in leadership skills, the spineless Williamson is a stooge for the main office downtown who has never had to live by his wits as a salesman on the front line.

In scene two of Act I, Dave Moss and George Aaronow are at the Chinese restaurant engaging in a conversation about the unfairness of the distribution of the leads. They are offended by the company's disrespect for its employees. In order to get the good leads one had to make sales and in order to make sales one needed to have the good leads. The angry and ruthless Moss shares his idea of stealing the leads and selling them to a former colleague and current competitor, Jerry Graff, who is in business for himself. The bitter, intimidating, and aggressive Moss wants the timid, reserved, and soft-spoken Aaronow to break into the office and steal the leads. Moss informs Aaronow that even if he did not participate in the robbery he would still be an accessory before the fact because he had talked to Moss about the robbery plot—for the salesmen it appears that talking implies action. He tells Aaronow that if he breaks in himself he will name Aaronow as an accomplice.

Ricky Roma, the star of the sales force, is also at the Chinese restaurant. Roma is a subtle, smooth, instinctual, and informal salesman who does not need a list of hot prospects to make sales—for him every person is a potential customer, even bar strangers. Roma is able to improvise according to his sense of each occasion. He works magic on potential customers by avoiding the hard sell and by getting the potential clients to trust him. Roma has the knack of persuading customers to purchase what they neither need nor want. He knows how to use language (often vulgar) to sell his point. He expertly employs language to engage prospective buyers in small talk, thereby placing them at ease. The charming Roma thinks out of the box and uses his finesse to manipulate his target. Roma's sales acumen embodies the art of selling.

He knows how to get the potential customer to trust him. Of course, he does not really care about the customer but he has the ability to make the customer believe that he cares.

At the bar in the Chinese restaurant, Roma spots James Lingk and identifies him as a great target. Observing Roma in action permits us to experience vicariously the salesman's thrill of the chase. He shows us how talk can transfer needs from the salesman to the potential customer and power from the potential customer to the salesman. Realizing that Lingk does not believe he enjoys or is in control of his life, Roma engages in a philosophical monologue in which he talks about the meaning of life, risk-taking, and seizing the moment. Roma plays to Lingk's insecurities.

Approaching Lingk as a friend, Roma talks about opportunities and questions the idea of morality. Creating a comfortable setting for Lingk, Ricky uses vulgar language to proclaim the absence of absolute morality in the world and the responsibility of each person to be the master of his own fate. Roma never stops talking, suggests outrageous and extravagant opportunities, and gets Lingk to actually believe that he is his own man. The ace huckster gets Lingk to buy land that he can't afford. Roma does not even consider if he is doing anything wrong—he just does his job the best way that he knows how to do it.

Act II takes place the following morning at the shabby real estate office which consists of four desks, a coffee pot, the chalkboard, and a couple of windows. The office is disheveled and the leads, telephones, and some contracts had been stolen.

Williamson and Aaronow are in the outer office and Moss is being interrogated by a police detective named Baylen. When they arrive, both Roma and Levene believe that they have closed deals from the night before but their deals have not really been closed. Moss emerges from the inner office and is outraged by the way that the detective has treated him. The hot-headed Moss hears Levene raving about his successful deal and storms out. Moss's anger appears to be a charade to make him look to be uninvolved in the office break-in.

Shelly is heartened by his successful sale. When he enters the office he thinks that he is the new leader in the competition. Levene boasts about the $80,000 plus sale he made the previous night to Bruce and Harriett Nyborg. The self-secure Ricky Roma congratulates the sagging old-timer on the sale. When he hears about the robbery, Ricky is concerned about whether or not his deal from the night before has been processed.

James Lingk enters the office to renege on the deal he made with Roma. His wife does not approve of it. Knowing that he has three business days to change his mind, he wants to make certain that the contract has not yet been filed and that his check has not been cashed. Roma informs Lingk that neither event has occurred and that there is plenty of time to back out of the deal if he really wants to do so. Roma suggests that he and Lingk meet on Monday to discuss the situation knowing that by then it will be too late to cancel the deal.

Roma teams up with Levene to make it appear that Roma has an important satisfied client, a senior vice-president of American Express, who has bought property from Roma and who has to be rushed immediately to the airport. Roma and Levene improvise to mislead and manipulate the tearful, pathetic customer who came to the office to demand a refund. Ricky admires Shelly for his spontaneous ability to cleverly play their con game. He only had to give Levene a few cues regarding how to proceed.

Williamson emerges from his office to ruin Roma and Levene's team effort. The inexperienced office manager misreads the situation. He mistakenly thinks that Lingk is upset by the disorder of the office and reassures Lingk that the deal has gone through despite the robbery and that the contract has been processed and the check has been deposited the night before. At that point, Lingk realizes that he is being scammed. He leaves upset proclaiming that he is going to report Roma to the Attorney General.

Roma blows up and is furious with Williamson for sabotaging the deal. Levene joins Roma in berating and vilifying the office manager. After Roma goes in for questioning by Officer Baylen, Levene gets himself into serious trouble by telling Williamson that he should not have lied about having processed the deal and having cashed the check. Everyone knows that it was the office manager's policy to nightly take the checks to the bank and to file the contracts. As luck would have it, the previous night Williamson failed to do so. The only way Shelly could have known that was if he had been in the office the night before. Williamson is thereby tipped off that Levene was the guilty party who had robbed the office.

The office manager knows that Levene is guilty. Levene attempts to deny the crime but eventually folds, admits his guilt (and that of Moss), begs for mercy, and attempts to bribe Williamson. He admits to selling the leads to Graff. To add to Levene's woes, Williamson tells Levine that the Nyborgs's check is no good and that they are a crazy old couple who simply like to talk to salesmen. He had purposely given Shelly the worst possible leads. Levene asks Williamson why he is reporting him to the police and the office manager responds, "Because I don't like you." Levene had begun the day with pride believing that he had made a major sale but he certainly did not end the day that way.

Roma exits the interrogation, praises Levene, and attempts to convince Levene into being his partner so that he can share in the commission. Williamson has revealed Levene and Moss as the thieves to the detective. Shelly goes in to confess to Baylen just as Ricky is telling Levene how much he admires him. There is no closure at the end of the play. The selling goes on as we observe Ricky heading back to the Chinese restaurant.

Mamet's character-centered play portrays a passionate, dismal, brutal world in which all of the characters are tragic figures. One moment a salesman praises a colleague and the next moment he betrays him. Teamwork is only evident among the salesmen when they conspire to bamboozle a customer or to steal from the company. The salesmen attempt to sound confident when they are on the phone but they are actually haunted by despair and desperation. They talk to make a living and most of the time they try to hide the truth. They appear to be addicted to what they do and exhibit the desire to manipulate. The main purpose of their talking is to claim power over others or to withhold power from them. They lie that they are in town for only a few hours, that there are only a few lots left, and so on. Playing roles and living by their wits seem to come naturally for these salesmen. We could say that the characters themselves are, in fact, actors.

The reader might wonder if these salesmen are naturally deceitful scam-artists who are attracted to their profession or if their organizational climate requires them to act the way they do. There is no loyalty or trust by or to the organization. The salesmen are driven by the bosses to participate in a dog-eat-dog cutthroat competition. Leadership, if any, is boss-centered and Theory X oriented. The salesmen are not mentored. There is no goal clarification or participation and the employees are in no way empowered. They fear punishment and the only motivation provided is negative—the chance to keep their jobs. A leader should be able to motivate his subordinates through the joint formulation of goals and the facilitation of the attainment of their goals. The organization has no people-centered practices or policies. There is no talk about providing value to the customers.

This play can be looked at as a description of a new kind of American salesmanship, a detective story with a surprise ending, and as a dogfight for power, domination, and survival. The excellent film adaptation includes a fine ensemble cast: Ricky (Al Pacino), Shelly (Jack Lemmon), Blake (Alec Baldwin), Dave (Ed Harris), George (Alan Arkin), John (Kevin Spacey), and James (Jonathan Pryce).

Chapter Twenty-One

Wall Street

Oliver Stone's Zero-Sum Vision of Capitalism

Wall Street is a 1987 American film directed by Oliver Stone with the screenplay co-written by Stone and Stanley Weiser. The film strongly reflects Stone's artistic vision, "zero-sum" conception of capitalism, and view of the effects of the industry's culture on ethics. The filmmaker presents the high pressure world of the stock market and depicts how an individual can be swept up in greed and power while forgetting who he really is. The film represents Stone's radical critique of the capitalist trading mentality and the get-rich-quick culture of the 1980s. This morality play follows the rise and fall of a persistent young man from an ambitious, low-level, cold-calling stockbroker to the protégé of a wealthy and unscrupulous corporate raider to defendant in a criminal case involving securities fraud and insider trading. A film such as this one can significantly affect public opinion, and *Wall Street* attempts to get the movie-goer to believe that capitalism is inherently corrupt and that the securities industry is a rigged game dominated by high-rollers who can manipulate stock prices.

Wall Street takes place in New York City in 1985. Bud Fox (played by Charlie Sheen) is an ordinary young guy which is precisely what he does not want to be. He wants to be on top of the world. As a junior stockbroker, he works the phones at the brokerage firm, Jackson, Steinem, and Company, soliciting new clients. The struggling junior account executive spends his time cold calling and pitching stocks to high income individuals on a list. Bud calls people he does not know to try to get them to buy stocks that he has not analyzed.

Bud spends frivolously and is not concerned with paying back his student loans. At the beginning of the story, he takes a financial hit when one of his

clients defaults on a large sum of money. Told by his boss that he will have
to personally cover these losses, Bud is forced to borrow money from his
father, Carl Fox (played by Martin Sheen), a hard-working, self-made blue-
collar worker. Bud's father represents to him everything that he does not
want to be. The elder Fox is an airline maintenance foreman and mechanic at
BlueStar Airlines and is his union's president. When Bud goes to ask his
father for a loan, Carl unwittingly and casually makes Bud aware that the
Federal Aviation Administration (FAA) has absolved *BlueStar* of responsibility for an accident that had occurred in a previous year. The not-yet-
public favorable ruling concerning the crash will not be announced publicly
for the next few days.

Bud is persistent in trying to get the attention of his hero, Gordon Gekko
(played by Michael Douglas), a powerful, rich, successful, influential corporate raider. Wanting to change his life quickly, he yearns to be a player, to be
associated with the ruthless, legendary, egotistical Gekko, and to be part of
his inner circle. Desiring to move into the fast lane, Bud idolizes Gekko, the
savvy, amoral, and cutthroat powerbroker who he believes can lead him to
the top.

Lou Mannheim (played by Hal Holbrook) is Bud's senior colleague and
floor manager at Jackson and Steinem. The old school Manheim attempts to
mentor Bud by repeatedly warning him that there are no shortcuts and that he
should stick to the fundamentals. This wise veteran stockbroker counsels
Bud that get rich quick artists are destined to fail. This old man father-figure
from the office is highly respected and has had a long career of steady
performance. He is concerned with Bud's welfare and tries to look out for the
interests of both the employees and the company. This character is based on
Oliver Stone's father, Lou Stone, a stockbroker during the Great Depression.
The movie *Wall Street* was made as a tribute to him.

Bud gains access to Gordon Gekko's office by finding and exploiting
information. He discovers Gekko's birthday and that he loves Cuban cigars.
Bud convinces the secretary to allow him to speak to Gekko for a brief period
of time. Assuming that Gekko wants to invest in stocks with long-term
growth potential, he suggests several stocks from his short list that fundamental analysis has revealed to be undervalued by the market. Gekko is
unimpressed and is uninterested in Bud's recommendations based on sound
fundamentals. He tells Bud that the stocks he is pitching are dogs with fleas.
Gekko wants information and is not interested in creating long-term value
from building or restructuring. He tells Bud to tell him something that he
does not know. His goal is to make money by buying and selling stocks
based on insider information and/or by taking over companies and liquidating them.

The desperate Bud then mentions the inside information about the positive FAA ruling in *BlueStar*'s favor that has not yet been announced. This

interests Gekko and he places an order for *BlueStar* stock, thus becoming one of Bud's clients. Gekko understands that he can buy that stock at a low price and watch it rise after the announcement is made public. The huge profits made by Gekko on this transaction are due to the fact that other investors did not know about the favorable FAA decision.

Investment valuation theory (also called capital markets research) in general and the efficient markets hypothesis (EMH) in particular state that the market for securities is efficient if security prices reflect fully and promptly all currently available information. There are three forms or levels of this hypothesis:

The weak form states that security prices fully reflect information implied by the historical sequence of prices. This means that all information that has caused a stock's price to change or fluctuate in the past has been incorporated into the stock's current price. This form has been confirmed by research.

The semi-strong form, which has been generally supported by research, states that stock prices fully reflect all publicly available information about the firm.

The strong form says that security prices fully reflect all public and private (i.e., privileged or insider) information. This form has not been supported by research.

The relevance of the support of the semi-strong form and the non-support of the strong form of the EMH is that the market is inefficient with respect to insider information and that excess or abnormal earnings could be obtained by trading on the basis of such information. Because of this, the Securities and Exchange Commission (SEC) has the goal of information symmetry. The SEC wants to have information available publicly as soon as possible in order to minimize the possibility for the use of insider information. It is explained that, when inside information is used to the advantage of specific individuals, other participants lose. The effect is the transfer of wealth from some investors to others. Trading on inside information is generally illegal. Proponents of insider trading laws want to have a level playing field when it comes to people's ability to gain financially in the stock market.

Illegal insider trading occurs when those possessing confidential information use the special advantage of that knowledge to gain profits or to avoid losses in the stock market to the detriment of the source of the information and/or to conventional investors who buy or sell stock without the advantage of the confidential information. More particularly, a person who receives information from an inside tipper is legally liable if he knew (or had reason to believe) that the tipper had breached a fiduciary duty in disclosing the inside information and the tipper received a direct or indirect personal benefit from the disclosure. The implication is that anyone who possesses inside information is required to either refrain from trading or to disclose the information publicly. Potential illegal traders include officers, directors, and employees and their friends, business associates, family members, and other tippees who traded based on the confidential information.

Morally, insider trading is not always wrong. There is nothing wrong with learning of opportunities ahead of time. People need to be free to gain information and to make deals based on not-yet-published knowledge with respect to business opportunities. It is the potential for profits that motivates men to discover and use new information before it becomes widely known to others. It is certainly permissible to use information that is accidentally acquired or obtained in the absence of fraud or theft. If an individual has a fiduciary duty (i.e., a prior contractual obligation) to keep particular information confidential or if the information is stolen, then there are questions of both morality and legality that need to be investigated. It is not that information comes from the inside, but the fact that a fiduciary duty has been breached or that the information has been stolen or extorted, that makes an action wrong.

Insider trading laws are technical and hard to define and apply. For example, did Bud illegally share the information that he accidentally obtained regarding *BlueStar*? Although Bud did not profit directly by investing in *BlueStar* stock, he did use the information to gain a client who made money on that stock. He also earned a commission on that transaction. What about Bud's father, Carl? Did he have a prior fiduciary obligation to *BlueStar* to keep the information about the FAA ruling confidential? Is he guilty of breaking insider trading laws? After all, his son did benefit due to the use of that information and, in a way that could be construed to constitute an indirect benefit to Carl himself, who has long supported his son and who has recently loaned him money. Then there is Gekko himself who has based his career on finding out things that other people do not know. He routinely enlists a large network of individuals to seek out and feed him valuable private information so that the SEC would have a difficult task linking him to any one source.

Gekko invites Bud to have lunch with him and to play squash. He gives Bud some money to manage as a test to see how well he would do investing. Gekko's money is invested by Bud in *Terafly*, one of Bud's suggested companies, and money is lost as a result. Gekko says that money was lost because Bud did not have a family member on the board like he did at *BlueStar*. Craving inside information, Gekko tells Bud to "get information" rather than to "send information." He wants to invest in sure things. Contrary to what Gekko states, there are no sure things even when one possesses inside information. It is possible for there to be a rival out there with even better information.

Gekko is not portrayed in the film as all bad all of the time. The charismatic corporate raider is able to sense the mood of a crowd and knows how to play to their feelings. He appears to be confident in, and to believe in, his own message when he speaks to the stockholders of *Teldar Paper*, one of his takeover targets. His speech hints at why corporate raiders like himself can provide a positive service. The speech scene gives Gekko, as well as other corporate raiders, an opportunity to legitimize their actions. Gekko states:

> *Teldar Paper* has thirty-three different vice-presidents, each making over two hundred thousand dollars a year. . . . You own *Teldar Paper*, the stockholders, and you are all being royally screwed over by these bureaucrats with their steak lunches, golf and hunting trips, corporate jets, and golden parachutes! . . . Our paper company lost $110,000,000 last year, and I'll bet half of that was spent in all the paperwork going back and forth between all those vice-presidents. The new law of evolution in corporate America seems to be "survival of the unfittest." Well, in my book, you either do it right or you get eliminated. . . . The bottom line, ladies and gentlemen, as you very well know, is the only way to stay strong, is to create value, that's why you buy stock, to have it go up. . . . It's you people who own the company, not them, they work for you and they've done a lousy job of it. Get rid of them fast, before you all get sick and die. I may be an opportunist, but if these clowns did a better job, I'd be out of work. In the last seven deals I've been in, there were 2.3 million stockholders that actually made a pretty profit of $12 Billion. . . . I am not a destroyer of companies, I am a liberator of them. The point is, ladies and gentlemen, that greed for a lack of a better word, is good. Greed is right. Greed works. Greed clarifies, cuts through, and captures the essence of the evolutionary spirit. Greed in all its forms, greed for life, for money, for love, knowledge, has marked the upward surge of mankind. And greed—you mark my words—will not only save *Teldar Paper* but that other manufacturing corporation called the United States of America.

Gekko assigns Bud to discover the current financial interest of Sir Laurence Wildman (played by Terrence Stamp), Gekko's British nemesis and big time arbitrageur, with whom Gekko has battled before. Gekko's chief rival is an investment magnate who has changed his ways and is now concerned with building and growing productive businesses that deliver goods and services. He used to be occupied with liquidating businesses and selling off their assets piecemeal. He now speaks for the good forces of capital markets and condemns the superficiality of the get-rich-quick character of Gekko's business model.

Bud spies on Wildman in order to uncover the latest deal that he is working on. He learns that Wildman is attempting to gain a controlling interest in *Anacott Steel*, a company that he wants to rejuvenate and turn around. Gekko wants to start a bidding war in order to force Wildman to pay more in acquisition costs than he would have had to otherwise pay. Gekko buys a large amount of stock and then sells it to Wildman at high prices. Bud helps Gekko raise the price by asking other traders in his company to buy *Anacott* stock and by phoning the *Wall Street Chronicle* with the tip, "Blue Horseshoe loves *Anacott*."

Wildman is forced to purchase Gekko's shares in order to complete his control of *Anacott*. Gekko used the information uncovered by Bud in order to gain revenge on Wildman and, at the same time, make a considerable profit. Gekko took a large position in *Anacott* as its stock price climbed the charts. When Wildman buys Gekko's share, Gekko makes millions of dollars. The additional money that Wildman had to pay could have gone into product development and capital improvements.

Bud is promoted at Jackson-Steinem because of the large commission fees made from Gekko's trading. In addition, he is relocated to a private office. Gekko also rewards Bud for his good performance and increases his authority as he continues to obtain useful insider information for Gekko. Bud receives many perks and in-kind rewards, becomes wealthy, and acquires a penthouse and a beautiful blonde interior decorator girlfriend, Darien Taylor (played by Darryl Hannah), a former girlfriend of Gekko himself. He has been admitted into Gekko's inner circle of high living. Gekko takes the fresh-faced naïve young stockbroker under his wing and seduces him by allowing him to have a taste of what his life is like and to reap some of the benefits of it.

Bud goes over to the dark side when he crosses over to the arena of gaining information by any possible means. He uses his co-workers as a means of getting Gekko what he wants by both obtaining information from them and by giving them information for their own clients. Bud buys, bribes, and shares information about deals with his merger and acquisitions lawyer friend, Roger. These actions can be interpreted to involve a type of theft of information from the lawyer's clients. In one scene, Bud spies for Gekko and steals information by posing as a cleaning worker, breaking into and entering the office of Roger's employer, going through the files, and copying them with a scanning device. Bud is unconcerned when Gekko's lawyers give him limited power of attorney papers to sign and tells Bud that Gekko will have "no official knowledge" of Bud's dealings. He does not conceive of the possibility that he is being used as a pawn or front man and that the paper trail would end with him.

Bud has an idea to buy *BlueStar Airlines* and to expand it with himself as president. *BlueStar* is not popular with its unions and appears to be ripe for a takeover. Bud wants to restructure *BlueStar* and to work closely with the unions. He wants to make the company profitable by cutting costs and ex-panding into new markets. Bud goes to Gekko with a Larry Wildman-type plan to purchase *BlueStar* and turn it around. Bud has a survival plan to save the airlines that includes modernization, cost cutting, inventory management, advertising, and expansion of hubs to compete with the major airlines. Bud believes that a positive sum relationship can come about between *BlueStar* and Gordon Gekko.

Bud believes that he has persuaded Gekko to buy *BlueStar Airlines*, to keep it, and to turn it around. Bud and Gordon meet with the various union leaders to try to convince them to have their members take temporary pay cuts during the reorganization period. Bud's father, Carl, one of the union heads, dislikes and distrusts Gekko. Bud's dad is uncomfortable dealing with Gekko, sees through the smoke and mirrors of Gekko's presentation, and believes that something is just not right. He foresees a zero-sum transaction as the likely result of making a deal with Gordon Gekko. Carl Fox is the only union president to refuse to vote in favor of the takeover. As a result, union support is obtained for the deal.

Carl's warning proves to be accurate when Bud happens upon a meeting that he was not invited to and learns that Gekko is planning to liquidate *BlueStar*. He wants to dismantle the company and to sell it off piece by piece. It becomes clear that Gekko had never intended on implementing a "survival plan" in the first place. He had deceived Bud as the representatives from all of *BlueStar* constituencies. Realizing that Gekko has betrayed him, the furious Bud Fox cuts off his business relationship with the corporate predator and resolves to foil Gekko's plans and to show his loyalty to his father. He also breaks up with Darien. Bud's father has a heart attack and Bud has an emotional hospital reconciliation scene with him in which he promises to save the airlines. He has decided to use the ruthless techniques that he learned from Gekko against the former mentor himself.

Bud goes to Larry Wildman to pitch his survival plan for *BlueStar*. He convinces the Englishman to undercut Gekko. Bud asks Wildman to be a white knight by purchasing the company in order to keep it from being liquidated. He and Wildman make a deal in which Bud will initially take steps to run up the price of *BlueStar* stock. Bud, Wildman, and other brokers from Bud's firm drive the price up as Gekko is trying to buy the stock. Having taken a large position in *BlueStar*, Wildman sells all of his *BlueStar* stock at high prices just as Gekko is continuing to buy all of the stock that he can at those high prices. Bud and his broker friends also start selling their shares. At the same time the union backs out of the deal. All of these actions cause the stock price to plummet. Gekko is forced to sell his shares and takes a huge hit once the others start selling their shares to Wildman who becomes the firm's new majority stockholder. Gekko takes his losses only to find out that Wildman was able to acquire the company at very low per share prices. Gekko realizes that he has been had, having to pay high prices and to sell at low prices, while not ending up with the company that he was after.

In the meantime, Bud's illegal activities have attracted the attention of *Stockwatch* and the SEC. There is a somber mood in the offices of Jackson-Steinem the next morning when Bud goes to work to a host of averted glances. He is summoned to the manager's office and the police and SEC investigators are there to arrest Bud for insider trading and conspiring to commit stock fraud in connection with a deal separate from that of *BlueStar*. Bud is handcuffed and escorted out of the building.

Gekko and Bud confront one another in Central Park where Gekko physically assaults Bud, who is wearing a wire recording device in the hopes of incriminating Gekko. Gekko recounts everything that he has done for him, how he taught Bud the tricks of the trade, and the illegal actions that he has taken. Bud turns over the recording device that he was wearing to the federal authorities and Gekko's connection to Bud's illegal acts are made known due to his self-incriminating statements.

While riding in a car to go to Bud's court appearance, Bud's father tells him he did the right things in saving the airlines and in exposing Gekko. He advises Bud to produce and to create rather than living off the buying and selling of other people. As he has done throughout the story, he continues to lecture Bud on the necessity of ethical values. The film ends with Bud walking up the steps of the courthouse to face punishment for his crime.

At the end of the film it is not apparent that Bud has located his moral compass. He seems to be a moral relativist who is sorry because he was caught. He still needs to develop a value system and moral barometer of his own. In the end, he does seek redemption from his father but that is only an initial step in the right direction.

The story can be looked at as a battle between good and evil for Bud's soul. Throughout most of the film, Carl and Lou are ineffectual good mentors and Gekko is an effective evil mentor as an apostle of greed and immorality. Bud's salt of the earth father preaches the values of honor, hard work, and pride in one's accomplishments, but Bud considers him to be old-fashioned and unaware of what it takes to succeed in today's business world. Lou, the office sage, is full of high-sounding aphorisms but does not offer any concrete advice that can directly help Bud. Jackson-Steinem does not have an official leadership or mentoring program and simply relies on broker competition, examples of sales leaders, and advice from old pros like Lou. Bud does not see eye to eye with either of these would-be role models. However, Bud is impressed with Gekko's seductive and larger-than-life qualities and view that money is the measure of success. As a consequence, we have a story of an eager young man, impressed by a successful older man, tempted by him, and betrayed by him. He then turns the table on him. Gekko, a distorted type of father figure to Bud, does not turn out to be a good role model for him.

The overall moral of Oliver Stone's story is that producing and creating are good, and that making profits on the buying and selling done by others is not good. Stone has Gekko proudly proclaim, "I create nothing, I own." Stone seems to believe that capitalism is a zero-sum game. He does not understand that wealth can be created, not just transferred around. The film also paints a distorted picture of takeovers by focusing on one that liquidates a going concern by deceitful means, thus destroying jobs. It is a fact that many takeovers create values by imposing discipline on unsuccessful corporate managers. Stone's *Wall Street* gives a favorable nod to labor unions and government that he believes save companies from ruthless and corrupt capitalists.

Chapter Twenty-Two

Tucker: The Man and His Dream

Tucker: The Man and His Dream is a 1988 film starring Jeff Bridges, directed by Francis Ford Coppola, and produced by George Lucas. Preston Tucker, a combination of genius and con artist, was one of the most visionary, ambitious, innovative, charismatic, and flamboyant entrepreneurs of the twentieth century. He, as well as the other characters, are portrayed in a rather cartoon-like manner in this movie.

Tucker is introduced in the film as a family man in Ypsilanti, Michigan who had a long history of ideas. During World War II he had anticipated the need for and designed a fast, lightweight, bullet-proof, armored combat vehicle with a special gun turret for the U.S. military. The car was rejected because it was too fast, but the car's gun turret was adopted by the government.

Tucker had read survey results revealing that eighty-seven percent of the American people desired to purchase a new car whenever World War II would end. These results bolstered his dream that he would design and manufacture a futuristic and innovative automobile with many safety features. A firm believer in free-market capitalism, Tucker is convinced that he can challenge the industrial giants by producing the "car of tomorrow today." His dream car would have a rear-mounted engine, seatbelts, a pop-out windshield, shatter-proof glass, fuel-injection, disc brakes, double torque converters (replacing transmissions and clutches), padded dashboards, moving fenders, and an aerodynamic body style.

Tucker hires an agent, Able Karatz, to raise the capital needed to fund the project. Karatz does not believe that Tucker's idea has a chance to succeed. He is skeptical because he thinks that the Big 3 (Ford, General Motors, and Chrysler) would do all they could to derail Tucker's innovative design ideas.

Tucker promotes his vehicle even before a prototype is built. He uses advance advertising to pre-sell his car. Working with a writer, Tucker runs a flashy article in *Pic* magazine. Believing what they read, people send in inquiry letters from all over the country. Within a week, over 150,000 letters are received in response.

Karatz arranges a meeting between Tucker and Floyd Cerf, a conservative stockbroker, to discuss the possibility of raising the required capital. Tucker's entrepreneurial spirit and charisma convinces Cerf to come on board. Cerf explains that popular, powerful, and confidence-inspiring people with big Detroit names are needed to sit on the board of directors. Along the same lines, he brings in Robert Bennington, an experienced executive in the auto industry, to run the company. Bennington and Tucker were to have a tumultuous relationship because each of them failed to read the contract and thought that he had complete control over how the car would be manufactured.

Karatz locates a Dodge plant in Chicago where B-29 engines were built for the war effort. Tucker arranges a meeting with the War Assets Administration in his efforts to rent the surplus plant. At a meeting with government officials Tucker serves rare roast beef and shows slides of bloody automobile accidents while describing his car's safety features. During his presentation to the War Assets Administration, Tucker chides the Big 3 for not adopting such safety features. This gets back to the Detroit automakers, thereby fueling their negative reaction to Tucker.

Tucker is given permission to lease the giant war production plant in 1946 but he is required to agree to difficult terms requiring him to raise 15 million dollars and to produce a prototype within sixty days. In addition, Tucker has to manufacture fifty cars within one year of the plant opening in order to continue to lease the plant. Promising a car that did not exist, Tucker issues stock, sells dealer franchises, and makes advance sales of cars in order to build a car that is just an idea and a picture in a magazine.

Tucker and his team only had sixty days to build a car, whereas it normally took a company like Ford nine months to go from model to prototype. Alex Tremulis, Tucker's chief design engineer, worked diligently with mechanics and members of Tucker's family to produce the prototype. Tucker blames the Detroit automakers when he is unable to purchase clay, steel, and other necessary materials. He decides to meet with Michigan's Senator Ferguson to discuss the matter. Ferguson keeps Tucker and Karatz waiting and gets called away quickly to his next meeting but not before he warns Tucker to keep out of the automobile manufacturing business. It is obvious that the senator knew about Tucker's reckless comments about the Big 3.

The actual production of the prototype was a lot more difficult than Tucker had envisioned. He had no sound plan for producing it. The hastily assembled prototype was produced from cannibalized parts from junk cars and an airplane. The engineers experienced problems with the rear engine, double-torque converters, and the fenders. The fabled double-torque converters were replaced with a Cord transmission and the moving fenders were superseded by moving headlights. In addition, there was no fuel injection. During final production, the car falls almost killing the engineer. On the day of the unveiling, the car is not even close to Tucker's original conception. Over one thousand people turn out to see the far from functional car. The prototype keeps breaking down before it reaches the stage and it has no reverse gear. A fire starts backstage and disaster is averted, but a security guard who was a spy for Senator Ferguson supplies that information to the Big 3. Somehow, the unveiling is a success as Tucker pulls off a "smoke and mirrors" presentation.

Tucker is sent on a publicity tour which keeps him away from the company's decision-making processes. While Tucker is away, Bennington and the Board make many changes to the Tucker Torpedo. During this period, Bennington eliminates many features and makes substitute design changes. Hiring other engineers to develop new specifications, Bennington eliminates the rear-mounted engine, fuel upgrades, and seat belts. He also increases the height of the car and lengthens the wheel track. In addition, the price of the car is doubled because steel cost Tucker's company twice as much as is charged to the Big 3. Tucker's wife goes to a board meeting and demands to know why these changes were made. She is told that Tucker could do nothing about them because the agreement gave all control to Bennington.

Tucker is furious when his wife tells him about the changes being made. While Tucker and Bennington argue about whose company it is, Tucker receives a phone call from Howard Hughes. When they meet, Hughes suggests a near-bankrupt helicopter factory where Tucker would obtain steel and an aluminum helicopter engine for his car. The Tucker family moves back to Ypsilanti and begins producing the car in a barn. When the car is completed it is taken to a racetrack and ran for twenty-four straight hours. The car is pushed to the limit, is rolled over, and is able to start with the driver walking away from the car. Once the car was road-tested, Tucker takes his production team back to the Chicago plant. Bennington then threatens to bring a breach of contract lawsuit against Tucker.

Forty-seven Tucker Torpedoes had been assembled when Tucker hears about an SEC investigation of him on the radio. The factory had been bugged and Tucker was being followed by government agents. Karatz phones Tucker to tell him that policemen in two cars were waiting outside Tucker's home to arrest him. Seeing an opportunity, Tucker leads the police on a chase while driving a new Tucker automobile in front of more than one hundred reporters who are waiting at the courthouse where the chase ends.

Tucker is charged with twenty-five counts of mail fraud, five counts of SEC violations, and one count of conspiracy to defraud. Tucker faces the possibility of 155 years in prison for making false promises about revolutionary designs. He is accused of fraud for selling dealerships without first having a car. The SEC charges that Tucker kept money for himself that he had raised from outside investors. Tucker's potential conviction will rely on proof that he had never intended on building the car from the outset.

Karatz, who had once been convicted of bank fraud, resigns because he is afraid that his criminal record will prejudice the jurors. His resignation does not prevent the prosecutors from attacking him about his past bank fraud and jail time. Bennington, as well as all the other members of the board, resigns, and the plant closes. The SEC confiscates the company's files. Production stops during the investigation and the delay financially ruins the company. The trial itself lasts about six months.

Tucker's family and friends manufacture the last three cars to ensure that Tucker has lived up to his part of the contract. The fiftieth car was finished a week before the deadline and all fifty cars were lined up in front of the courthouse during the trial. In the film, Tucker asks that the jury be able to go to the window to see the cars, but the judge rules that evidence was no longer admissible. Tucker delivers an impassioned speech in his own defense:

> The prosecution claims that I never had any intention to make any cars. . . . But according to the law if I tried to make the cars, even if they turned out no good, even if I didn't make them, if you believed I tried, really tried, I'm not guilty. . . . I'm not guilty because it's not against the law, thank God, to be wrong or stupid. . . . When I was a boy, I used to read all about Edison, the Wright Brothers, and Mr. Ford, they were my heroes. Rags to riches wasn't just the name of a book. It was what the country was all about. . . . We invented the free enterprise system, where anybody, no matter who he was, what class he belonged to, if he came up with a better idea about anything, there was no limit to how far he could go. I grew up a generation too late I guess because now the way the system works, the loner, the dreamer, the crackpot who comes up with some crazy idea that everybody laughs at that later turns out to revolutionize the world, he's squashed from above before he even gets his head out of the water because the bureaucrats, they'd rather kill a new idea than let it rock the boat. If Benjamin Franklin was alive today, he'd be thrown in jail for sailing a kite without a license . . . if big business closes the door on the little guy with the new idea, we're not only closing the door on progress, but we're sabotaging everything we fought for, everything the country stands for.

Tucker is found to be not guilty, but the delay and bad press causes the company to be unable to resume production and forces it into bankruptcy. The film shows that he is acquitted despite the fact that the SEC had falsified a set of books indicating that Tucker raised money to build the company and kept it for himself. The SEC had failed to seize the records that Mrs. Tucker kept while the prototype was being built. She could have proven the SEC to be wrong but her proof was not required as Tucker was exonerated of fraud charges. Tucker continues to be portrayed as a visionary innovator at the end of the film and he outlines his idea for a small, non-electronic refrigerator that could be used to store milk in Third World countries.

The film is Capraesque with a twist—the small guy does not win in the end as his company is unable to reopen. The film is a combination of fact and speculation. In actual fact, there is little evidence that the Big 3 controlled a senator from Michigan, cut off Tucker's supply of steel, instigated an SEC investigation, and tampered with the courts. The film emphasizes the existence of a Washington power play and conspiracy rather than Tucker's questionable business methods. For example, each Tucker car was handcrafted at a very high cost per automobile produced. He did not know if the car could be manufactured on an assembly line at a reasonable cost per car.

Tucker was not totally honest. He overpromised and advertised features that he could not deliver. He misled shareholders and sold dealerships before a prototype was completed. Tucker claimed that his safety features would save thousands of lives and he announced that he would put the Big 3 out of business. Tucker had an idea and virtually no money. His sole asset was a leased surplus war factory. It makes sense that he would come to the attention of the Big 3 and the SEC. He brought on the battle himself. The SEC used Tucker's dubious and creative financing methods and business practices against him.

Tucker failed to read his contract with Bennington and found himself, for a while, not controlling the company. Tucker did not have a proper management team for his new endeavor. A man like Bennington was more suited for the running of an established firm. Of course, Tucker was told that he needed to have proven automobile executives like Bennington on his board if he had any chance of success. Bennington also had not read the contract and believed that he had the authority to modify Tucker's design plans. He later found out that, according to the contract, he had signed on to manufacture the car as Tucker had designed it.

The film implies that Tucker's inability to purchase steel is because the Big 3 controls the supply. Another possibility is that steel suppliers simply favored selling to the established automobile companies rather to a small competitor like Tucker who might not have the wherewithal to pay for it.

The film emphasizes the idea that big businesses and government bureaucrats can make it extremely difficult for innovators to create products that actually reach markets. Competition can be stifled by established firms and the government. The film promotes the notion of a government-based conspiracy to halt the development of Tucker's new car. Tucker is shown to underestimate the influence and power of the industry leaders and crony capitalists. In other words, there is no place for a little guy like the beleaguered Tucker who is a victim of the collusion of power from Detroit and

Washington, D.C. In the film Tucker is championed as a heroic, visionary, and infectious dreamer and symbol of the American can-do spirit.

Chapter Twenty-Three

David Lodge's *Nice Work*

A Tale of Two Cultures

David Lodge has written a series of three campus novels—*Changing Places* (1975), *Small World* (1984), and *Nice Work* (1988). The third study of the academic community, *Nice Work*, combines elements of the campus novel and the industrial novel genre with Elizabeth Gaskell's *North and South* (1855) as its particular literary model.

The setting of the novel is the industrial heartland of Thatcherite England in 1986. The fictitious city of Rummidge, based on the real city of Birmingham, is located in the industrial midlands also known as Britain's contemporary rust belt. Rummidge is a dirty manufacturing town filled with factories, railways, and heaps of scrap metal. The economy is in sharp decline and there is a great deal of unemployment. In contrast to the factories, there is also Rummidge University which is clean, well-maintained, and serene with beautiful green grass, lakes, and trees. On the downside, the University is beginning to feel the pressure of Margaret Thatcher's severe funding cuts to the university educational system. There is a separation of town and gown with two cultures simultaneously inhabiting this area of contemporary Britain. *Nice Work* provides a portrait of the austere Thatcher years as seen through the eyes of two very different individuals. It is also the story of an unlikely relationship between two essentially different and apparently incompatible characters.

Leaders in the government have decided that intervention is necessary to encourage a sense of mutual understanding between academia and industry. The government therefore designates 1986 as "Industry Year" and develops a Shadow Scheme to lessen the ivory tower image of universities and to bring academia and industry together. To celebrate the Industry Year of 1986,

239

companies and universities are to sponsor a manager and a professor to be paired together one day per week. As part of the program, Rummidge University is to send a professor to shadow a designated manager every Wednesday for a term of eight weeks. To achieve this end a university lecturer in literature and the managing director of an engineering firm are thrown together against their will. Neither one is interested in participating in the program.

The program is mandatory for Vic Wilcox, managing director for J. Pringle and Sons Casting and General Engineering, a recently acquired small, troubled part of the Engineering and Foundry Division of the conglomerate Midland Amalgamated. The hard-working Wilcox was hired to turn the company around. The short and aggressive Vic worked his way up from humble beginnings, is proud of what he has accomplished, and is resentful of the Shadow Scheme's imposition on his time.

From the outside it appears as if Vic has an ideal life with his wife, three kids (Raymond, Sandra, and Gary) and upper middle class home. His good life has been stagnating. Vic is bored with his personal life and is no longer attracted to his wife, Marge, whom he felt had become complacent. Marge is a homemaker who enjoys shopping and reading self-improvement books. She actively takes steps to enhance her attractiveness to Vic but he does not notice. He views his children as not living up to their potential. Vic does not approve of their work ethic. He is disappointed with his eldest son who at twenty years of age dropped out of college and parties every night. Vic's daughter does not even want to attend college.

Vic knows that he is good at his job, has a great work ethic, and firmly believes in capitalism. His favorite saying is "there is no such thing as a free lunch." He is passionate about buying and supporting British-made products. The favorite part of Vic's day is his twenty-five-minute commute to work. His British-made Jaguar is one reason he finds enjoyment in his morning commute. Vic seems to have some form of narcissistic attachment to his car. While driving he can relax and listen to the type of music that he likes. His favorite music combines female voices and a slow tempo.

Dr. Robyn Penrose is a temporary lecturer in English literature and women's studies at the University of Rummidge. Robyn is appointed to participate in the Shadow Scheme because she is the most likely teacher to agree to do so and also because she is the most knowledgeable faculty member regarding industry. The passionate postmodernist and feminist had settled for a position as a temporary lecturer. This was a position that could be cut at any time. Robyn desperately seeks full-time employment but budget cuts seem to be making that nearly impossible. A permanent teaching position would be "nice work" if she could get it. She thinks that getting involved with the Shadow Scheme may help to enhance her chances at future full-time employment at Rummidge. Robyn has her Ph.D. from Oxford University in Cambridge where she specialized in nineteenth-century industrial novels. Of course, she had never been in a factory just as Vic had never read a literary classic. Robyn is ignorant of the real condition of contemporary industrial England. In a classroom lecture presented early in the novel she reveals her ideological positions, thus predicting her likely reactions to contemporary British manufacturing.

The intelligent, strong-willed, independent Robyn had been born in Australia but was, for the most part, raised in England. She came from a family of academic scholars—her father was a history professor. Robyn's on-again, off-again boyfriend, Charles, lectures at the University of Suffolk in the Comparative Literature Department. They began dating while they attended Sussex University. They spend their weekends together in Rummidge. The bland Charles holds many of the same views that Robyn holds.

The postmodern Robyn believes that character is a bourgeois myth, an illusion created to reinforce the ideology of capitalism which she despises. Robyn believes there is a strong link between the rise of the novel and the rise of capitalism. She views the deconstruction of the classic novel in the twentieth century as reflecting a crisis in capitalism. She also is a proponent of semiotic materialism where symbols and signs are associated with language. As a feminist, she tends to wear loose-fitting and dark-colored clothing to make sure that she does not become an object of sexual attraction. Although she is attractive, Robyn will not use that fact to move ahead in her career. This ardent feminist is devoted to the study of repressed women in the Victorian industrial novel.

As a deconstructionist, Robyn attempts to devalue and dismantle the logic by which a specific system of thought preserves its integrity. Deconstructionists claim that words are inadequate for defining reality. They argue that language intercedes between the reader and the ideas. According to them everything is simply perspectival and there is not a fixed way of discovering linguistic meaning. Deconstructionists try to understand how the media and vocabulary used to represent ideas fail to mean the same thing to all people. Deconstruction is thus a technique for uncovering multiple interpretations of texts. Certainty in textual analysis is impossible and there is no way to assess the validity of competing interpretations. It follows that when critics analyze a work of literature, they do not analyze what the writer originally meant but rather what the reader interprets from the work. As the idea of author has lost its significance, the reader's context becomes paramount. The reader creates the book's reality. Deconstructionists like Robyn do not understand that there is, in fact, life outside the text. Deconstructionists argue that reason is simply an attempt at "metanarrative" (i.e., an attempt to control societal values). Literature and language are therefore seen as becoming means for enforcing a specific ideology on others for the purpose of exploitation.

As a postmodernist, Robyn believes that reality is socially constructed and that pluralism is a fact of reality. Postmodernists express disbelief in metanarrative. They display disdain for the modern ideas of rationality, linear progress, and a right way to do things. They find fault with systems of thought that try to explain the world. Postmodern themes include: (1) the attainment of universal truth is impossible; (2) no ideas or truths are transcendent; (3) all ideas are culturally or socially constructed; (4) historical facts are unimportant and irrelevant; and (5) ideas are true only if they benefit the oppressed. Postmodernists generally use Marxist rationale and concepts (e.g., oppression, inequality, revolution, and imperialism) to attack and discredit American culture. Postmodernism brings metaphysics, epistemology, and ethics to an end because these types of studies assume a fixed universal reality. The postmodern subject has no rational way to evaluate a preference in relation to judgments of truth, morality, objectivity, and so on.

Robyn is also a poststructuralist. For the structuralist, an individual is shaped by psychological, sociological, and linguistic structures which he cannot control but which could be discovered by using certain investigation methods. The poststructuralist agrees to a certain extent, but says that there are not definite underpinning structures that can explain the human condition. Unlike structuralists, poststructuralists do not think that culture can be understood through a study of structures. Poststructuralism is closely related to deconstructionism and postmodernism. Poststructuralists hold that the concept of the self as a distinct, separate, coherent entity is a fictional construct. They attack the underlying assumptions of Western culture and maintain that the author of a work is not the primary source of the work's semantic content. The author's intended meaning ranks behind the meaning that the reader perceives. Their goal is to "decenter" the author.

On the first day of the Shadow Scheme Robyn gets lost on her way to the factory. She is unexpectedly drawn into a situation that is unfamiliar to her. The frightened Robyn is offered drugs by a young, black, West Indian drug dealer. She then stops at a gas station to get directions and accidentally runs into Brian Eventhorpe, the Marketing Director at Pringle's, who tells her who he is and then proceeds to lead her to the factory. Eventhorpe has a coarse sense of humor, is usually late for work, and is difficult to locate whenever he is needed. He fancies himself to be sort of a ladies' man.

Everyone at Pringle's expected Robyn to be a man. The workers were surprised to learn that Vic's shadow is a young, attractive female. In turn, Robyn is shocked with what she observes in the factory, including earsplitting machinery, a dirty environment, degrading and distasteful nude pin-ups, unprofessional language, exploited immigrant labor, and so on. She is disturbed by the apparent acceptance of the sexist behavior by the female employees who are few in number. The workforce was largely comprised of Asian and Caribbean immigrant workers. Robyn witnesses apparent racism with white individuals receiving the best jobs. She sees Vic giving the Asian and Caribbean workers the hardest and worst jobs. For Robyn, her first day at Pringle's is a nightmare of noise, pandemonium, and disorientation.

While shadowing Vic at a meeting toward the end of the first day, Robyn learns that an Asian laborer, Danny Ram, was to be fired if he makes a mistake. The managers had already decided to fire him but they are afraid to because he is Asian and that could lead to a strike. They come up with a plan to trick him into making a mistake, thus providing them with the leverage to let him go. The compassionate Robyn feels that this is unfair and voices her opinion. She visits Danny Ram and tells him about the plan to fire him. This motivates the Asian workforce to go on a wildcat strike. By interfering with this human resources problem, Robyn has become a thorn in Vic's side on her very first day.

Also on her first day, Robyn's car is broken down (perhaps it was tampered with). Vic helps by repairing a loosened part on the vehicle's engine. Vic later learns about Robyn's meddling in the Danny Ram situation and he is infuriated. That evening Vic visits Robyn at home and insists that she return to the factory to tell Danny Ram that management actually did not have a plan to fire him. She reluctantly agrees and this ends the strike.

That Sunday, Robyn's brother, Basil, and his girlfriend, Debbie, meet with Robyn and Charles. Both Basil and Debbie are employed at a bank. Robyn does not like Debbie. Basil opines that both Robyn and Charles should consider a career in banking. Charles is tantalized by the amount of money that could be made if one were in the banking field.

After the Danny Ram incident, Vic does not expect to see Robyn again. Much to his surprise, Robyn returns for a second week of the Shadow Scheme and they continue to challenge one another's views and values. That day, Vic and Robyn travel to Foundrax, a competing company, to see if the managers there had offered a lower price to Rawlinsons, one of Pringle's customers. Vic knows that there is some company that is selling at lower prices and he wants to find out which company it is and the reason for such action. The manager at Foundrax denies engaging in any such price under-cutting. On the way back to Pringle's, Vic invites Robyn to have dinner with his family at his home on Sunday. Apparently, Vic had started to, at least subconsciously, develop feelings for Robyn. Perhaps inviting her to have lunch with his family would stop such feelings. In addition, when he observed his secretary and Eventhorpe together he was led to thoughts about Robyn. Later in the novel, Vic finds out that it actually was Foundrax that had dropped its prices for Rawlinsons.

One day at the factory, Robyn has an opportunity to rescue Vic. Marian Russell, one of her students, has a variety of part-time jobs, one of which is "kissograms." Brian Eventhorpe had hired her to kiss Vic while he delivers a speech to the employees. Vic is upset and the crowd is howling. Robyn intervenes and tells Marian to leave immediately.

Robyn learns of an affair between Charles and Basil's girlfriend, Debbie. They had been staying together while Charles was conducting his research. Charles also decides to switch to commercial work by taking a job in banking. Charles, like Basil, has fled to the city.

Throughout the novel, Robyn and Vic challenge each other's perspectives as they are ineluctably drawn into each other's worlds. Their interactions begin as a bitter and argumentative game, but, by the end of the story, they learn to respect and to value portions of each other's positions. When they debate they gain insights and each is forced to reconsider their beliefs. To a certain extent, they develop a mutual respect and understanding of each other, and of the worlds they inhabit. Vic explains industrial reality to Robyn and she explains cultural and literary theory to him. The certainty of their values is gradually weakened as they present intellectual challenges to one another.

In an early exchange in the novel, Vic makes an argument for the "useful" in education whereas Robyn maintains the value of an education focused on ideas and feelings. Vic contends that the only proper criterion to use in evaluating education is the money to be earned as a result of the time and energy being expended. Robyn argues for nice work that is meaningful and rewarding, but not necessarily in terms of money. Vic tells her that men like to work to gain their own self-respect. Robyn says that more money should be spent on creative leisure and work that would be worth doing even if one was paid nothing at all. Robyn feels that people underachieve when they settle for industrial blue collar jobs. Vic defends the worth of these jobs that need to be done if anything of value is to exist.

Robyn and Vic hold conflicting views on capitalism and socialism and they devote much time to debating the proper role of the government. Vic argues for capitalism, innovation, efficiency, cost cutting, and the survival of the fittest. Robyn is dismayed by the corporate culture at Pringle's, which exhibits no concern with laying people off. She also fails to grasp that not everything is free and that her precious universities are due to government taxation and grants. Robyn hails from a privileged background and shuns capitalism and materialism. As an expert on the Victorian industrial novel, Robyn employs deconstructionist analysis to understand factory life.

Vic does not see the value in women's studies and literary studies. He cannot understand how Robyn can call reading "work." He says that reading is the opposite of work. It is what a person does when he comes home from work to relax. Robyn explains that reading is work. Reading is production and what is being produced is meaning. Her idea is that academic work is a type of cultural production.

Robyn teaches Vic to appreciate the symbolic and semiotic dimensions of the world and to uncover romanticism within himself. She even finds that Vic is quick to discern the difference between metaphors and metonymies.

Semiotics, the study of signs, is found in a range of studies including art, anthropology, mass media, literature, and so on. It is frequently employed in the analysis of texts. Scholars such as Robyn believe that semiotics help people not to take "reality" for granted as having a purely objective existence independently of human interpretation. It follows that reality, as a construct, is a system of signs.

Robyn explains to Vic that the essence of metaphors is understanding and experiencing one type of thing in terms of another similar kind of thing. In metaphors, a person substitutes something like the thing meant for the thing itself. Metonymizing, on the other hand, is based on contiguity or closeness. In metonymy a person substitutes some attribute or cause or effect of the thing for the thing itself. Metonymy involves using one signified to stand for another signified which is directly related to it, or closely associated with it, in some way. Examples of metonymy include using the term "press" to stand for journalists and using the term "plastic" to stand for credit card.

By the end of the novel, Robyn and Vic come to respect their different views of work. Robyn becomes more interested in industry, gains insight into the pragmatic ethos, and begins to understand the necessity and practicality of factory production. She also learns that there is something outside the text. Vic falls in love with Robyn and her ideas. By the end of the book, he is reading classic works like *Jane Eyre* and is quoting Tennyson. Vic also takes some steps to make the factory more humane.

Vic asks Robyn to accompany him to a tradeshow in Germany. Vic went there to try to purchase a state of the art core blower that would keep the company competitive for years. With the new machine, Pringle's would be able to significantly cut production costs. They, of course, had reserved separate rooms for the overnight trip.

Unlike Rummidge, Frankfort is beautiful. After World War II, Germany dedicated a lot of money to technology and innovation in order to achieve long run success. This resulted in the prosperous atmosphere experienced by Vic and Robyn. England did not invest in technology, innovation, and infrastructure, and suffered the consequences of not doing so.

Vic and Robyn meet with Dr. Winkler whose company manufactures the machine that Vic wants to purchase. Robyn, who speaks German, is able to discern that Dr. Winkler is planning to sell Vic a machine that has fewer features and capabilities than the one he wants. Robyn thus saves Vic from making a bad deal as Dr. Winkler is trying to trick him. Because of Robyn's help, Vic makes a good business deal. Vic respects Robyn even more after this. Later on in the story, Robyn belatedly realizes that this machine purchase in Frankfort will result in Danny Ram losing his job.

That evening Robyn and Vic have dinner and drinks together and go dancing at a nightclub. They also go swimming and relax in a hot tub. Robyn then initiates a more intimate relationship as she leads him to her room where they come together literally and metaphorically.

Vic is overwhelmed by their one night carnal encounter and says that he loves her. He wants to divorce his wife, leave his life, and start a new one with Robyn. Robyn, who does not believe in love, says no, it was just sex. She wants no such commitment and has no intention of keeping the relationship going. Robyn does not believe in the concept or the reality of love. Ironically, although she is incapable of understanding love, she does express concern for her students as well as for Danny Ram. Vic has a better understanding of love than she does. She also ironically implies that she made a "choice" to be romantic, thus failing to apply her determinist poststructuralist view of life. Robyn believes that, at best, love is a contextual construct. She is convinced that she does not need a man to complete her and that the traditional lifestyle of stay-at-home mom is degrading and is not a real job.

After meeting and learning from Robyn, Vic wants to be a better person and to broaden who he is. He starts reading literature and begins to appreciate the symbolic and semiotic aspects of life. People notice a change in him and his wife, Marge, thinks that she had lost him and that he no longer loves her. Robyn admires Vic and his business skills, but she has no intention of reciprocating his love for her.

Robyn visits her parents for a week at their seaside home to finish writing her book on nineteenth-century women, and to get away from Vic. When she returns, she receives an invitation to a party at the home of Philip Swallow, dean of the literature faculty at Rummidge. At the party she meets Professor Zapp, and old colleague of Swallow, who is intrigued by Robyn and who offers to read her manuscript. Zapp, an influential educator, author, and speaker, reads her book and offers her a permanent teaching position at Euphoria State in California in the United States. Euphoria State is a fictionalized UC-Berkeley. The tenured position would double her current salary. Swallow is pleased with Robyn, but due to financial considerations he may have to let her go at the end of the spring semester. At about the same time that she receives the job offer, Robyn learns that she inherited a great deal of money from her uncle Walter in Australia.

Robyn learns from Philip Swallow that Vic has arranged to participate in a "reverse shadow scheme" in which he will shadow Robyn at the university for eight weeks. Vic attends classes and staff meetings and offers valuable financial advice with respect to the financial situation at the university.

Pringle's is bought out by their competitor, Foundrax, and Vic is let go. At the same time, Vic learns that Eventhorpe had been working secretly to develop his own company when he should have been doing his job at Pringle's. Among the reasons given for firing Vic is that the new owners see as eccentric his spending one day a week at the university shadowing Robyn, as well as his attempts to make the factory environment more humane. When Vic confides to his family and speaks unreservedly with his wife, they offer to help him start a new business of his own. His family's understanding and willingness to aid him provides Vic with a new perspective on his family and his marriage. When Vic loses his job, Marge is not upset. She says that they will get through it and that she would cut back on her spending. Vic has a reconciliation with his wife and their love is rekindled.

Philip Swallow has good news for Robyn. It turns out that the Literature Department can afford an additional permanent position. After much soul searching, Robyn opts to stay at Rummidge rather than to emigrate to America. Vic goes to the university to tell Robyn that he would no longer be able to participate in the reverse shadow scheme because he was no longer employed by Pringle's. He tells her that he wants to start his own business but that he requires financial backing. Confident in Vic and his work ethic, Robyn invests money as start-up capital in Vic's venture to develop a new spectrometer. Having viewed Vic in action in business, she believes in him and his ideas.

At the end of the story, Robyn sees a black gardener, about the same age as a typical college student, cutting grass with a group of students sitting in his way and blind to the fact that he was advancing toward them. They eventually move out of his way but there is no communication between them. Both the students and gardener instinctively and mutually avoid contact. Although they are physically near-at-hand, they inhabit distinct separate worlds.

Nice Work is a story of how people from two different cultural backgrounds and social spheres go from despising one another to understanding and respecting one another's views. By the end of the book each is transformed into a more tolerant, rounded, and thoughtful person. They learned to put their differences aside and to have an open mind about other people. Each of them was better for having known the other. The novel teaches that a person can never know who might have a positive effect on his life, and when this may occur.

Chapter Twenty-Four

Other People's Money

A Tale of Capitalism and Creative Destruction

Jerry Sterner's 1989 play, *Other People's Money*, plays to different groups of people as key players battle for the principles on both sides of a corporate takeover attempt. Both the play, and director Norman Jewison's 1991 film based on the play, present, in dramatized form, both the arguments for and against corporate takeovers.

The story begins with Bill Coles, president, and Andrew "Jorgy" Jorgenson, chairman, of New England Wire and Cable (NEWC) discussing the imminent visit of Lawrence "Larry the Liquidator" Garfinkle (Garfield in the film). Coles is polished and handsome and in his mid-forties. The sixty-eight year old Jorgy's father had built the company, and Jorgy has been the chief executive for thirty-eight years, running the company much like his father had run it. The nervous, skeptical, and concerned Coles warns Jorgy that Garfinkle is a shrewd and cunning takeover artist from New York City, but Jorgy ignores his advice and plays the visit off as unimportant.

The forty-year-old obese Larry targets corporations with undervalued assets and works to acquire a controlling interest in them. The straight-shooting but shrewd Garfinkle goes to NEWC to try to gain approval to buy the company. During the initial meeting, Larry makes known his intentions to take over NEWC. He tells Jorgy and his management team that his computer, Carmen, which specializes in scanning the economy for undervalued stocks, has identified NEWC as an appealing target having no debt, no pending lawsuits, a fully-funded pension plan, valuable assets, and a strong liquidity position. Also identified during the process was an antiquated and obsolete division, the Wire and Cable Division, in desperate and immediate need of reengineering and diversification. The Wire and Cable Division has consis-

249

tently been losing money and its losses have been subsidized by the profits of the other divisions of the company.

Garfinkle, Coles, and Jorgenson discuss the value of NEWC and come up with thirty million dollars of equipment, ten million dollars in land, sixty million dollars in non-Wire and Cable divisions (i.e., plumbing supplies, electrical distribution, and adhesives), and twenty-five million dollars in working capital. Garfinkle rounds the total down to one hundred million dollars and divides by four million shares of common stock to obtain a value of twenty-five dollars per share. Before Larry started buying, the market value of NEWC stock was ten dollars per share. Larry owns just under five percent of NEWC's shares. At five percent he will be required to file statement 13-D with the SEC. Such a filing informs the public of the existence of a significant block of common stock ownership.

Larry leaves NEWC but he is visited shortly thereafter by Coles in his New York office. Coles tells Larry that in two years he will take over when Jorgy retires and that he could grow the company and make the stock worth much more money. Garfinkle says that he will have no part of this waiting business. When Coles returns to NEWC he tells Jorgy that Garfinkle now has eleven percent of the stock and that he intends to take over the company. Coles explains that Garfinkle's goal is to find businesses worth more dead than alive, to gain control, and to liquidate them. He explains that NEWC can do things to protect the company such as changing the by-laws to call for a two-thirds majority rather than fifty-one percent and changing the state of incorporation from Rhode Island to Delaware where it is easier to get changes made. Jorgenson is not worried and points out that he owns twenty-five percent of the stock, the board owns ten percent, and the employee stock ownership plan has five percent. He asks Coles how Garfinkle can gain control and Coles tells him that it would come from the sixty percent left. Jorgy scoffs at this because he has faith in his long-term stockholders.

At a follow-up meeting at NEWC, Larry states that it will be necessary to sell the Wire and Cable Division which has become a victim of obsolescence. Garfinkle explains that liquidating the Wire and Cable Division is necessary to protect the company's three other divisions and to do what is right for the shareholders. He points out that the original business has been losing money for years. The other divisions' profits are offset by these losses. It follows that the Wire and Cable Division should be liquidated and that the proceeds should be redeployed into either the other more profitable divisions or perhaps into new ventures. The infuriated Jorgenson wants nothing to do with such a deal and he sends Garfinkle packing. The paternalistic Jorgy values tradition, community, stability, and predictability and feels that he, his employees, and the community all have too much to lose to permit liquidation of the division. He wants to keep the factory open in order to keep the town alive and its citizens employed. Jorgy cannot believe that Larry lacks a social conscience and Larry is amazed at how nice of a guy Jorgy is.

Bea Sullivan, Jorgy's long-time assistant and lover, has a daughter, Kate, who is an attorney with Morgan Stanley on Wall Street. Bea pleads with her to fly up to NEWC to talk about takeover defenses. Kate resents Jorgy for ruining her parents' marriage as Bea practically moved in with Jorgy after his wife died.

Kate offers a number of good out-of-court options but Jorgy stubbornly turns down each one of them. She first suggests greenmail which is an arrangement whereby the target company buys back the stock at a substantial premium to avoid a takeover. Jorgy says that he does not deal with predators. Kate next suggests hiring private investigators to get some dirt on Garfinkle. Her third recommendation is to find a white knight which is a larger protector company that would buy out NEWC's stock and allow NEWC the freedom to do business any way it wants to. During this discussion, Kate and Jorgy become increasingly impatient and frustrated with one another. Kate continues and offers some more risky options. A shark repellant involves making the company undesirable to an unwanted suitor. This involves selling the most attractive part of the company (i.e., NEWC's non-Wire and Cable Divisions) at a low price. This option gets triggered only if someone not currently on the board (e.g., Garfinkle) amasses thirty percent or more of the stock. The shark's shares will be worth a lot less than he paid for them. Kate's last recommendation is to create a poison pill—a type of shark repellant. Here the board would authorize preferred stock, one share for each share owned by everyone except Garfinkle. These shares would be offered at one dollar per share and NEWC's common share value and earnings per share would be diluted.

Jorgy was resistant to Kate's good suggestions that she made to him thinking he was a rational businessman. Unfortunately, he is stubborn and selfish. He says that he does not want to harm the employees and the town, but he also does not want to lose what he considers to be "his" company. Jorgy was not looking at things from the proper perspective. Both Jorgy and Bea failed to realize that others, including Garfinkle, are also shareholders who have a say in how the company is run. Jorgy is an agent for the stockholders and has a fiduciary duty to maximize shareholders' wealth. He does not have the right to mismanage other people's money in order to indulge his nostalgia for a time gone by. He is spending the shareholders' money, not just his own, in order to keep the Wire and Cable Division operating. The losses of this division keep the company's stock prices and dividends down.

Jorgy is appalled when he hears that it would cost between one and two million dollars for Kate's company to take NEWC on as a client in the attempt to fight Garfinkle. Later, Bea pleads with Kate to take on Garfinkle. Kate decides to do her mother a favor but she was primarily looking out for

herself and her career. She certainly does not have the same loyalty to
NEWC that Jorgy and Bea have. As a Wall Street attorney, she was committed to beating Larry at his own game, thereby advancing her career. Kate
meets with Larry, there is a mutual attraction between them, and a romantic
subplot is added to the story. Kate is bright but also relies on her attractiveness and sexuality in negotiations with Garfinkle. They formulate a standstill
agreement in which they both promise not to acquire any more shares for a
two-week period. Neither party keeps the agreement. Kate uses an outside
brokerage firm to purchase shares to raise the stock price and Larry does his
purchasing through OPM holdings. OPM, of course, stands for "Other People's Money."

Kate arranges for Judge Pollard to grant an injunction preventing Garfinkle from purchasing any more shares. Larry complains that lawyers, through
acts such as this, are destroying capitalism by preventing stock speculators
such as himself from buying stock that they should be permitted to purchase
in a free society. Garfinkle understands that a market for corporate control is
needed for the restructuring that is essential for competition. Assets need to
be used in an economically rational manner.

Kate attempts to engage in greenmail by offering to buy back Garfinkle's
stock at eighteen dollars (and later twenty dollars) per share. Garfinkle has
some high ethical standards and will not take part in activities that he considers to be immoral. He will not accept Kate's greenmail offer explaining that
it is immoral and unfair to the other stockholders. Greenmail is harmful to the
remaining shareholders because money is paid out of the corporation to the
threatening shareholder.

Larry then offers to trade his one million shares for the Wire and Cable
Division. With such a "restructuring," Wire and Cable Division's losses
would disappear and the profits of the other divisions would become apparent. Kate tells Jorgy that when he receives Garfinkle's million shares Jorgy
will have absolute control of the company. Jorgensen refuses this offer, acknowledging that it is about his own pride as well as about the twelve-hundred men who work in the Wire and Cable Division and their families
and their futures. Kate tells him that he deserves to lose the company because
he will not listen to what he should do.

Ultimately, Jorgy and Larry agree to leave it up to the stockholders. They
agree to each run his own slate of directors at the annual meeting. This
involves a proxy contest in which dissatisfied shareholders try to gain a
controlling number of seats on a board of directors by means of a formal
vote. If Garfinkle receives the majority of the votes then he brings everyone
out at twenty dollars per share. If he does not receive the majority of the
votes he will sell his shares back to the company at thirteen dollars per share.

In the meantime Bill Coles, the president of NEWC, had approaches
Jorgy about a golden parachute. Coles was worried about himself and his

career. After twelve years of loyal service to NEWC, he wanted what was coming to him. He knew that he has been very good for the company. He asks Jorgy what will happen to him if they lose. Jorgy says that this is not the right time and fails to give Coles the security he believes he deserves.

Coles saw the handwriting on the wall with Garfinkle knocking on the company's door. He doubts that Jorgenson really understands the situation. Coles, on the other hand, saw that the corporation would not survive in its current manifestation. After Jorgy ignored his pleas, Coles observed that everyone looks out for his own self-interest. Coles approaches Garfinkle and makes a deal giving him the right to vote Coles's 100,000 shares. In return, Coles would receive one million dollars if they make a difference and a half million dollars if they don't make a difference.

Later, Bea Sullivan offers Larry greenmail in the amount of one million dollars from her trust fund. NEWC would also buy back Larry's shares at thirteen dollars per share, which is the average cost of the shares he had purchased. Bea offers this bribe because she is driven by her love for Jorgy. Her offer offends Garfinkle, who says that he makes money for widows and orphans and that he does not take money from them.

At the annual stockholders' meeting, Jorgy and Garfinkle appeal to the stockholders during their proxy fight. Jorgy goes first and makes a heartfelt, impassioned, and unrealistic speech about family, friendships, community responsibility, history, tradition, loyalty to employees, and shareholder loyalty to the company. Jorgenson, a product of a bygone era, talks about how much the company has been through, including a major depression, both World Wars, and the death of one company president. Jorgy ridicules the notion of "maximizing shareholder value" and explains that a business is worth more than its stock price. He says that it is a place where we make our living, meet our friends, and dream our dreams. He has hopes and goals for the Wire and Cable Division that he predicts will stand the test of time and will rejuvenate and make a comeback. Jorgy is in denial and, at best, his approach would only prolong the inevitable.

Garfinkle begins his speech by saying that Jorgenson's tearjerker speech is a prayer—a prayer for the dead. He says that he did not kill the company, rather, the market did. Advances in fiber-optics and other technologies made the Wire and Cable Division antiquated and obsolete. It cannot compete with changing technology and a shrinking market. He tells the stockholders that the business is dead and that they should collect the insurance and invest the money in something with a future. He asks the stockholders if the community and the employees care about them. He explains that they don't care and that, over the last ten years, utilities, the mayor's salary, and the employees' wages have all doubled at the same time that the stock price fell to one-sixth of what it was. Larry states that he is the stockholders' only friend and that they should take the money and invest it elsewhere.

Garfinkle's slate wins by a landslide. Jorgy could not understand how the stockholders could be disloyal, tossing aside tradition and friendship to vote for a stranger who could only offer them more money. He had been confident that his fellow shareholders would support his slate during the proxy fight. Jorgy dies nearly two years later, leaving over thirty million dollars in his estate with Bea as executor. She uses the money to buy the land NEWC used to occupy to set up an employee retraining center which placed about one hundred workers (of the twelve hundred that had worked at the plant) in jobs. Coles moves to Florida to run a mid-sized division of a nationally known food processor. Kate affirms her going against her mother and Jorgy when she leaves Morgan Stanley to work with Larry and shortly thereafter becomes his wife. They have a set of twins.

The film version of *Other People's Money* has a different, tacked-on, stereotypical, happy, Hollywood ending—bad endings do not sell films. The final scene in the movie shows Kate phoning Larry with a solution that comes out of the blue—what could be called a *deus ex machina* solution. Kate has been presented with an offer from a Japanese firm to use the plant to produce automobile airbags from stainless-steel wire cloth. Kate calls Larry with a proposition to sell the plant back to an employee-owned wire and cable company that would manufacture these airbags.

Jorgy's personal pride (hubris) in his company was his fatal flaw. He saw himself as the paternalistic protector of his workers and the community. At best, however, he appears to have merely possessed marginal business competence. He neglects his responsibility to the stockholders, fails to recognize that the Wire and Cable Division is in a shrinking market, and has not kept up with the innovative technology in the industry to which he could have converted. Jorgy did not grow as a manager and he failed to look for ways to make the Wire and Cable Division profitable. He is immutable during the whole story and accepts little advice from anyone. The tradition-oriented Jorgensen did not evolve with the times and ran the company as it had always been run. Ideas basic to capitalism such as market dynamism and creative destruction appear to have no meaning to him. Both capital and employees can be reallocated to more profitable uses.

Jorgensen wants what he thinks would be best for the company, its employees, and the community. He says that he places his workers first, but if he really did care for them he would have upgraded the plant and adjusted to market demands. Although he sounds sympathetic, he failed to do his job well. He could have benefited the employees more if he had kept up to date technologically and manufactured a product that was demanded in the marketplace. Although one can sympathize with the kind and decent Jorgy, who suddenly finds himself having to make difficult decisions, at root he is at fault and could have avoided this situation if he had kept up with the times.

The story can also be viewed as what happens when a traditional corporation such as NEWC is unable and/or unwilling to react to an external threat in the form of a corporate takeover attempt made by a modern organization of the future (Garfinkle Investment Corporation). With no debt, NEWC had an inefficient capital structure. If NEWC had issued a substantial amount of debt to leverage the company, it would not have been as attractive to a takeover artist. NEWC had a lot of cash, many liquid assets, a full-funded pension plan, and a debt to equity ratio of zero. Of course, financial leverage, the degree to which a firm uses borrowed funds, is a two-way street. There can be too little or too much financial leverage. When the debt to equity ratio goes up to a certain number, investor confidence in the company is apt to drop sharply.

Jorgensen could have fought the takeover attempt by implementing one or more of Kate's suggestions but he is too stubborn to do so. Or, even better, he could have recognized that it was the right time to shut down or sell the underperforming division. If Jorgy was really worried about his obligation to the workers, he could have worked things out with Larry. They could have agreed to humanely and effectively use retraining and outplacement services for employees who are laid off due to such strategic rightsizing. The result would not only have been a savings in severance payments, but also good public relations and the maintenance of morale and productivity for the remaining employees in the company's other divisions. It is possible to be sympathetic to the needs of people while, at the same time, recognizing one's obligation to stockholders and the need for creative destruction. Attending to the well-being of one's employees can be compatible with maximizing shareholder value.

Garfinkle is a man of integrity whose moral principles are based on a process or equity theory of justice. He views corporations as voluntary associations and as private property. A corporation is a form of property created by individuals in the exercise of their natural rights. Larry understands that managers have the obligation to use the shareholders' money for specifically authorized shareholder purposes which usually amounts to the maximization of shareholder profits. Managers are employees of the stockholders and have a contractual, and hence moral, responsibility to fulfill the wishes of the shareholders. A manager is an agent of the owners of the corporation and has a fiduciary responsibility to them. When a CEO is not fulfilling this fiduciary responsibility, he is open to be voted out of office by the owner shareholders who take control of the board of directors. From this context, the takeover of NEWC can be seen as a humanitarian act and Larry can be viewed as a hero and not as a villain.

Larry tells Kate that a person should make as much as he can for as long as he can. It is likely that he is referring to much more than money. Garfinkle wants to succeed and flourish by getting as much out of life that he can with respect to his work, lifestyle, love, material well-being, and so on. The story's doughnut metaphor stands for Larry's hunger to obtain, to consume, and to win. Kate, herself, was a challenge for Garfinkle. Despite an awkward and unlikely love affair, they are happy together in the end.

Other People's Money is a fine tale of contrasting opposites. On the one hand, there is a traditional, antiquated, semi-rundown plant in a small town in Rhode Island that is operating in an industry that has seen its better days. On the other hand, there is a New York City investment corporation that utilizes advanced modern technology to identify potential takeover candidates. Most importantly, we have the clash of two men whose worldviews could not be more opposite—the sentimental communitarian, Jorgy, and Larry, the cunning but principled capitalist.

Chapter Twenty-Five

Wall Street: Money Never Sleeps

Wall Street: Money Never Sleeps, a 2010 drama directed by Oliver Stone, is a sequel to the 1987 film, *Wall Street*, with Michael Douglas reprising his role as infamous Wall Street hotshot, Gordon Gekko. The story takes place in New York City during the 2008 financial crisis and housing meltdown. This tale of the financial collapse of 2008 has a plot that intertwines the "reformation" of Gekko and his relationships with his estranged daughter and her boyfriend, and later fiancé, an ambitious young investment banker. Viewing and discussing this film is a great way for students to learn about financial markets as well as about the history and causes of the financial crisis. The first part of this chapter will summarize the plot of the film and the second portion will discuss the background and genesis of the 2008 crisis.

The opening scene takes place in October 2001 when Gekko is being released from prison after serving over fourteen years for insider trading, securities fraud, and other offenses. The film fast forwards seven years to 2008 with Gekko back in the spotlight after the release of his new book, *Is Greed Good?* The author is on television being interviewed about his book. His daughter Winnie (played by Carrie Mulligan) and her boyfriend, Jacob Moore (played by Shia LaBeoeuf), see this interview on television and she walks out. Winnie wants nothing to do with her father. She is unable to forget what her family went through after, and because of, his incarceration, including the death of her brother, Rudy.

Winnie works for a non-profit internet publication called *Frozen Truth* that attempts to bring the truth on a huge variety of topics to the public. Jake is a top proprietary trader with Keller Zabel Investments (KZI) and is the protégé of its executive officer, Louis Zabel (played by Frank Langella). Jake has a passion for green energy and he attempts to raise money for a fusion

257

research project that is a promising source of alternative energy. Unfortunately, Jake has trouble convincing the board to invest in fusion research.

When Jake leaves the apartment he receives a phone call from researcher Dr. Masters, who works with a green energy firm, United Fusion, that desperately needs additional funding. Louis Zabel then summons Jake to his office and confesses that he is confused and that he can no longer understand what is happening in the changing financial markets. The disillusioned Zabel gives Jake a 1.45 million dollar bonus to spend and to keep the economy moving. He uses the money to purchase an engagement ring for Winnie and buys KZI stock with the remaining one million dollars.

One of Jake's co-workers suggests the forthcoming financial disaster when he mentions the growth in home loan defaults and the fact that KZI has billions of dollars of subprime toxic debt on its balance sheet. He tells Jake about the persistent rumor that KZI is being dragged down by holding the mortgage debt in its investment portfolio.

The next day the market reacts drastically with KZI stock falling thirty percent in price in one day. The company-loyal Jake Moore holds on to his shares. Zabel attempts to obtain a bailout and the New York Federal Reserve Board calls together top Wall Street executives to try to find a way to save KZI. The attempt for a bailout is stymied by Bretton James (played by Josh Brolin), the CEO of Churchill Schwartz, a company that Zabel had refused to bail out eight years previously.

Bretton James says that the bailout would be too risky and brings up the notion of "moral hazard." A moral hazard occurs when an individual or an institution does not bear the full responsibility and consequences of its actions. For example, when bailouts are given other banks will be led to take risks because they believe that they will not have to carry the full burden of potential losses. In addition, the head of the U.S. Treasury observes that the bailout of KZI would lead the nation toward socialism.

At the end of the meeting the CEO of Churchill Schwartz insults Zabel by offering to purchase KZI for two dollars per share. It had traded at seventy-nine dollars per share just a few days before. They ultimately settle at a price of three dollars per share. Denied a bailout from the government, KZI has, in effect, fallen victim to a hostile takeover on the part of Churchill Schwartz. This scene resembles the way that JP Morgan Chase bought out the country's fifth largest investment bank, Bear Stearns, for two dollars per share in March of 2008. Bear Stearns stock had sold for 190 dollars per share one year before.

The next day Louis Zabel commits suicide by stepping off of a platform into the path of an oncoming subway train. Later that day the saddened Jake proposes to Winnie and she accepts. The film then depicts Jake attending a lecture by Gordon Gekko in a lecture hall at Fordham University. Gekko is promoting his book and expressing his views on the impending housing crisis. He talks about how the Federal Reserve cut interest rates so that more and more people could buy houses and how banks were willing to lend to high risk creditors. Gekko says that the United States economy is on the verge of collapse as a direct result of leveraged debt and wild speculation. He also spoke of NINJAs which are people with No Income, No Jobs, and No Assets.

After the lecture, Jake tells Gordon that he is going to marry his daughter Winnie. Gekko tells Jake that Winnie will not speak to him. Gekko wants to get back in the good graces of his daughter. The two trade photos of Winnie. Gekko then reveals his compelling theory about the probable reasons for KZI's downfall. He tells Jake that he should search for the person who profited from KZI's demise. Gordon implies that someone started rumors about KZI that led to its collapse and to Zabel's suicide. He has the idea that someone at Churchill Schwartz was behind the rumors because KZI did not want to bail out Churchill Schwartz years earlier. Gekko also believes that Bretton James, the CEO of Churchill Schwartz, is the man responsible for his imprisonment. It appears that the two may have an enemy in common.

Gekko wants to improve his relationship with his daughter and Jake wants to avenge his mentor's death. They agree to help one another. Gordon wants to communicate with, and meet with, Winnie, and Jake wants to obtain information about Bretton James and his firm, Churchill Schwartz. As a result, Jake arranges for Winnie, Gekko, and himself to meet for dinner and drinks. When they meet she becomes upset because she is convinced that her father had not changed at all.

Jake spreads a rumor regarding the nationalization of an African oil rig that Churchill Schwartz owns. As a result, Churchill Schwartz takes a big hit, losing 120 million dollars in one day. Jake is called to a meeting with Bretton James who offers him a job, which he takes.

Jake discovers that a group known as the Locust Fund made a great deal of money by shorting KZI shares as the rumor was spreading. The Locust Fund, an offshore fund in the Caymans, was betting against KZI stock. Short selling occurs when securities are borrowed from a third party and are sold with the intent of buying back identical securities at a later date to return to the lender. The goal of the short-seller is to profit from a decline in the price of the security. Jake and Gordon want to link this account to Bretton James. They discover that he was betting against KZI through the Locust Fund. He was behind the offshore fund and had profited from KZI's decline.

Churchill Schwartz's top salesperson makes a pitch to a group of Chinese investors but they are unimpressed with her projects and ideas. Jake jumps in to explain his idea for investing in fusion research and the Chinese investors appear to be interested in providing funds for that company. At this time the economy is beginning to disintegrate.

Bretton James hosts a fundraiser to which Jake and Winnie are invited to attend. Jake gives Gordon Gekko money so that he will also be able to be there. He wants another chance to reconcile with his daughter. While there, Gekko explains to Jake how Bretton James was responsible for his imprisonment. Jake had thought that it was Bud Fox who had been responsible for this. Gordon explains that Bud did wear a wire to get him on insider trading but that was a small crime compared to his other activities.

During the party Bretton tells Jake that the Chinese investors are very close to putting $100 million in Jake's green energy company. Winnie goes outside to get some air and is followed by her father.

The following day the financial meltdown is in full swing, the economy and Churchill Schwartz are collapsing, and Winnie learns that she is going to have a baby. Soon thereafter, Jake learns from Bretton James that the 100 million dollars will not be going into the green energy project. James had previously given Jake the impression that it was virtually certain that they were going to invest in fusion energy. Jake is angry when he learns that their money is going to be invested in fossil fuels. James is afraid that, if the money was invested in such new technology, then this might reduce the profits that his investments in oil were making.

Jake turns to Gordon for his advice, and he suggests a plan for obtaining the money needed for the fusion project. Gekko had set up an account for Winnie in Switzerland back in the 1980s. It is now worth 100 million dollars. He tells Jake that this money could be used to fund the fusion research project. The only problem is that Winnie could potentially go to jail for tax evasion because she had never claimed the earnings from this account. Jake convinces her to get the money and then to invest it in fusion technology. Jake and Winnie fly to Switzerland where she makes the withdrawal and signs the money over to Jake. Jake then turns the money over to Gekko who "legitimizes" it so that it can be invested in fusion research. Jake tells Winnie what has transpired, that her father has taken the money, and that he has been talking to her father without her knowledge. She breaks off their engagement and tells Jake to leave.

Jake receives a call from Dr. Masters's, research scientist, at the research company, saying that the money had never arrived there. Gekko had tricked Jake, who goes to Gekko's empty apartment. Jake finds Gekko in London where he had started an investment firm with the $100 million. He had used the money to purchase the securities of distressed investment banks, including Churchill Schwartz, before the government does. Jake tells Gekko that Winnie is pregnant and offers him time with his grandson for the return of the money. Gekko declines this offer.

Jake gathers and assembles a packet of information detailing every part of KZI's collapse and who was involved in it. He gives this file of information to Winnie to publish on her website. The story spreads, and Bretton James is exposed and confronted by his board of directors. With James's involvement made public, the board asks him to leave the firm and he is summoned to appear before a Congressional committee.

Jake spots Winnie walking toward her apartment and they talk. Gordon, who has turned the 100 million dollars into 1.1 billion dollars, shows up, apologizes, and tells them that he has deposited 100 million dollars into Jake's green energy interest, United Fusion. Gordon has redeemed himself. The film ends by skipping to one year later with Jake and Winnie celebrating their son's first birthday with Gekko present.

In 2008, a series of bank and insurance company failures set off a financial crisis that severely hampered global credit markets and brought about unprecedented government intervention. The collapse of reckless, parasitic, and corrupt Countrywide Financial was an early trigger in the collapse of the subprime credit bubble. In January of 2008, Bank of America acquired Countrywide in an all-stock deal valued at 4.1 billion dollars. A year later, Bank of America would have to go to the federal government for a bailout largely because of the acquisition of Countrywide's toxic assets.

In March of 2008, Bear Stearns, one of the pioneers of the securitization of mortgages, failed. The company's troubles began when two of its hedge funds, invested in securities backed by subprime mortgages, failed, losing billions of dollars. As a result, investors lost confidence that Bear Stearns would be able to repay their debts. The U.S. government stepped in, injected capital, "lent" money to JP Morgan Chase, and "forced" Bear Stearns to join with JP Morgan Chase. In a way, the government bought Bear Stearns and turned it over to JP Morgan Chase. It is interesting to note that back in the 1990s the government was planning to bail out Long Term Capital Management and that Bear Stearns had refused to help.

On September 7, 2008 it was announced that the U.S. government would take over Fannie Mae and Freddie Mac, government-sponsored entities that brought resources into the housing market by purchasing subprime loans, bundling them with higher quality loans in a process called securitization, and selling shares of the package to Wall Street investors. Congress and the Department of Housing and Urban Development (HUD) wanted these government-sponsored entities to buy these subprime loans and bear the risks associated with possible homeowner defaults. Fannie Mae and Freddie Mac would hold some of these in their own portfolios and would bundle others into mortgage-based securities for sale to investors. With this move, the Secretary of the Treasury effectively took over the majority of the American mortgage market.

The next week Bank of America agreed to purchase Merrill Lynch and American International Group (AIG) was later saved by an eighty-five billion dollar capital injection by the federal government. AIG had numerous credit default swaps (i.e., insurance policies against defaults) and the securities into which the related mortgages had been bundled had tumbled in value. AIG had insured the securitized mortgages thereby permitting the bond rating firms to assign a triple-A rating.

On September 14, Lehman Brothers filed for Chapter 11 bankruptcy protection after failing to find a buyer. Lehman Brothers had borrowed substantial amounts of money to fund its investments in housing-related assets. As a result, its stock plummeted in value and it was losing billions of dollars during 2008. The President of the Federal Reserve Bank of New York called a meeting and the regulators rejected Lehman's request for government involvement with a bailout. The Secretary of the Treasury did not want to encourage a "moral hazard." He was afraid of the probability of risky behavior that occurs when an acting party thinks that the costs of his behavior will be borne, not merely by himself, but by a large number of people. The result was that what was good and worth preserving in Lehman Brothers was bought by other companies.

On September 25, 2008, JP Morgan Chase agreed to buy the good assets of Washington Mutual, the largest American savings and loan, in what was the biggest bank failure in history. During September and October of 2008, the American people learned that more and more of the country's leading financial institutions were insolvent and heading toward collapse. In November of 2008, Fannie Mae and Freddie Mac took some action to help distressed homeowners who could not afford their house payments. Home owners, who were often irresponsible, failed to keep up with their payments and received special consideration from those government-sponsored entities.

A comprehensive bailout package for the financial sector, called the Emergency Economic Stabilization Act of 2008 authorized the Treasury to purchase 700 billion dollars in assets at any one time. The initial purpose of the Troubled Asset Relief Program (TARP) was to take bad assets off the hands of financial institutions. The government wanted to remove the toxic assets from the banks' balance sheets. Later the goal of the bailout package was changed to giving money to banks for shares of bank stock. In time, consumer credit was said to need to be bolstered by the rescue plan. Banks had stopped lending as credit was drying up.

Having noticed that Goldman Sachs was able to profit from the collapse in subprime mortgage bonds by short-selling such securities in 2007, the federal government placed a ban on short-selling. The government official did not understand that short-selling is legitimate and provides information about which firms are sound and unsound. In addition, the FDIC increased the amount of each bank deposit that it would insure from 100,000 dollars to 250,000 dollars.

The government was taking on ownership interests in banks, intimidating banks who did not want to accept TARP money, and putting pressure on banks to lend. Financial institutions that received such money were subject to whatever regulations the government wanted to impose on them. TARP was being used as a means to control the banks. Although the government had urged the banks to make loans, the institutions receiving compulsory injections of government funds were not eager to lend. Instead, they were conservative and careful, as they should have been, given the circumstances.

When the government gives bailouts, businesses are not held to be accountable. Firms should not be kept alive via government bailouts. Government bailouts of the banks, in effect, require the state to become an owner or shareholder of the companies. Such nationalization of the banks is a step toward socialism. In a capitalistic system, if a business is going to fail, then let it.

The financial crisis of 2008 had its roots in the practice of subprime lending. Both residential and commercial properties saw their values increase greatly in a real estate boom that began in the 1990s. Government regulations had encouraged unqualified purchasers to take out mortgages as well as blended the lines between mortgage lenders and traditional investments banks. Real estate loans were spread throughout the financial system in the form of CDOs (Collateralized Debt Obligations), CMOs (Collateralized Mortgage Obligations), and other complex securities in order to disperse risks. When home values failed to increase and home buyers failed to keep up with their payments, banks had to make enormous write-downs and write-offs of their assets. This brought a number of institutions to the brink of insolvency and ruination.

Between 1998 and 2006 home prices increased dramatically. The housing bubble had peaked in 2006 and burst two years later accompanied by a glut of homes, falling prices, a rise in interest rates, lessened demand, and a tightening of credit standards. There are many contributing causes to this crisis.

The explanation begins with the Community Reinvestment Act (CRA) of 1977, a federal law designed to encourage commercial banks and savings associations to help meet the needs of borrowers in all demographic segments of their communities, including low and moderate income communities, especially and initially among preferred minority groups. The CRA opened banks up to discrimination suits if they did not lend to minorities in numbers high enough to satisfy government authorities. Over the years, a number of legislative changes were made to strengthen and broaden the act. The CRA contributed to the 2008 crisis by encouraging banks to make unsafe loans. Many low-income borrowers were lent money by banks so that they could achieve the government's American Dream. In 2007, the Chairman of the Federal Reserve Bank recommended further increasing the participation of Fannie Mae and Freddie Mac in the affordable housing market to help banks meet their CRA obligations by supplying them with more opportunities to securitize CRA-related loans.

The Department of Housing and Urban Development (HUD) was also involved in loosening lending restrictions. In 1996 HUD set a quota that forty-two percent of Fannie Mae or Freddie Mac loans purchased or insured be for families in the low to middle income classification. This quota was expanded to fifty percent in 2000.

All during the housing boom the Federal Reserve kept lowering interest rates by increasing the money supply, pushing them lower than the market would have set them, encouraging excessive leverage, risky behavior, indebtedness, and misdirecting capital into the production of long-term projects in construction and capital goods. This drew resources away from projects related to real consumer demand. The new money and credit was channeled into the housing market where there were lax lending standards, excess home purchases, and speculative behavior on the part of real estate investors who were flipping houses. The Fed encouraged the GSEs, like Fannie Mae and Freddie Mac, to funnel the new money into the housing market and to take on more and riskier loans. The Federal Reserve System itself is practically an arm of the federal government.

The 1999 repeal of provision of the Glass-Steagall Act of 1933 removed the separation between Wall Street investment banks and depository banks. Until then a bank holding company was prohibited from owning other financial companies. The 1999 action removed the separation that previously existed between investment banks which issued securities and commercial banks which held deposits. As a result, Wall Street investment bankers were permitted to gamble depositors' money that was held in commercial banks owned or established by the investment company. The repeal authorized commercial lenders to underwrite and trade instruments such as collateralized debt obligations and mortgage-backed securities.

The government bears much of the blame for the subprime mortgage crisis. Although subprime lending began as a competitive enterprise to tap an underserved market for home financing, the situation devolved as the government's qualifying guidelines kept getting more lenient in order to produce more mortgages. In their efforts to help disadvantaged groups, politicians encouraged financial institutions to take on more risk by extending home mortgages to individuals whose credit was generally not good enough to receive conventional loans. The Clinton administration directed Fannie and Freddie to increase home ownership rates among low-income families.

Fannie Mae and Freddie Mac were instructed to institute programs to buy low-income mortgages and to encourage lenders to issue such mortgages. These GSEs bought up risky subprime loans at an increasing rate in order to meet ever-accelerating government goals. They, along with other financial institutions, took risky loans and bundled them together with higher-quality ones. So-called Collateralized Debt Obligations place cash payments from multiple mortgages (or other debt obligations) into a single pool from which the cash is apportioned to particular securities in a priority order. The use of CDOs enabled financial institutions to obtain investor funds to finance subprime as well as other loans thereby extending and increasing the housing bubble.

Banks sold their mortgages on the secondary market to other financial institutions such as Fannie and Freddie that, in turn, packaged many of them together and marketed them as mortgage-backed securities. Diversification was thought to be the advantage of such an approach. The only problems would be if the entire housing market collapsed at the same time resulting in foreclosures and defaulted mortgages. In such a case the holders of the mortgage-backed securities would be in big trouble.

Fannie Mae and Freddie Mac bought mortgages from banks on the secondary market, held some in their own portfolios, and bundled many into mortgage-backed securities for sale to investors. As a result, the originating bank had more money to use to grant additional loans. In order to share in, and profit from, the mortgage boom, banks, pension funds, brokerage houses, and so on purchased these securitized mortgages. Wall Street investors were quick to buy up these mortgage packages, without worrying, because the GSEs were considered to be government-insured entities. The ratings agencies assigned high ratings to these assets. They did a poor job with respect to assessing risk and rating credit worthiness. The potential to make large profit through trading mortgage-backed securities with artificially high ratings encouraged banks to take a huge amount of risk in granting loans.

To allow them to lend out more money based on the mortgage-based assets they held, financial institutions arranged for insurance companies such as AIG to insure the securitized mortgages. This permitted the financial institutions to receive high ratings and enabled them to lend a great deal more than the value of their mortgage assets. They were also able to get banks worldwide to insure them by buying "credit default swaps." Despite the esoteric name, a credit default swap is simply an insurance policy against default.

A combination of very low interest rates and a loosening of credit underwriting standards brought home borrowers into the market thus fueling unwarranted demand for housing leading to artificially high home prices. With a glut of new and existing homes on the market, real estate prices stop increasing, level off, and begin to fall.

Approximately eighty percent of U.S. mortgages issued to subprime borrowers were adjustable rate mortgages. People were attracted to buy homes by favorable teaser rates that would later be adjusted according to economic indices. Families holding subprime mortgages were hit with huge interest rate increases that they could not afford. There were also many pay-option adjustable rate mortgages that permitted borrowers to pay only a small fraction of the loan interest due each period and none of the principal. The payment deficiency was added to the balance of the mortgage which accrued even more interest. Over time, such a mortgage could grow to exceed the value of the home.

As home prices declined, borrowers with skyrocketing adjustable rate interest and mortgage payments could not refinance to avoid the higher payments associated with rising interest rates, and they began to default and to enter foreclosure. Falling prices resulted in houses worth less than the balance of the mortgage loan, providing a financial incentive to default. With many homes in default, real estate prices plummeted, banks suffered losses, and some subprime lenders filed for bankruptcy.

As housing prices declined, financial institutions that had borrowed and invested heavily in subprime mortgage-backed securities reported major losses. As the underlying mortgages went bad, the mortgage-based securities based on them also went bad. Many banks then called on their insurance companies and holders of their credit default swaps to make good on their obligations to insure the mortgage-based securities. Many of these insurers and holders were unable to make good on their promises to insure these securities. As a result, the assets became toxic driving the portfolios of financial institutions downward. Many companies went bankrupt and banks stopped lending. These failures caused a crisis of confidence that made bankers reluctant to lend money. They cut back lending because they wanted to rein in risky investments. Despite the federal government's bailout and stimulus packages, the banks did not rush to reopen their lending windows.

Conclusion

Business through Literature and Film

Imaginative literature has contributed to the progress of civilization and to the dynamism of society. Fiction empowers individuals' imaginations to transcend the empirical constraints that circumscribe them. Fiction sets people free both as writers and as readers by cultivating their potentials to self-reflect, to devise alternatives to the present, and to freely choose among those options. Literature is a means to study the individual human capacity for imagination and expression. Narrative makes sense out of reality and provides a backdrop from which to view the place of morality in one's life. By reading literature, people are studying the human condition.

The autonomy of imaginative literature mirrors the freedom and independence of the individual human person. Fiction can help people to realize their individuality and their ability to envision, to express, to choose, and to pursue their possibilities for living a flourishing and happy life. The point of reading fiction is to make people reflect about what they believe in and what they want to get out of life. Literature dramatizes how a person in a particular culture and context, given his individual talents and motivations, defines himself, makes choices, and acts. Because literature is, in part, an expression of the culture within which it is produced, it can also supply a tool for examining the social history of that culture. Because literature possesses historical substance, reading fiction from various time periods and places allows one to gain a big-picture explanation of the evolution of civilization.

Reading literature contributes to a richer life. Fiction permits individuals to encounter people who they would never get to meet, travel to places they would never get to go, and to experience situations they would never get to experience. Fiction takes readers beyond their own individual experiences of life. Literature from very different times and places can be a source of pleasure and appreciation here and now. Such works can help a person to shape his general attitude toward life.

Literary texts can be sources of inspiration and character formation and can develop one's capacity to empathize with others. They can provide insights into the subtleties of human nature. They can teach significant truths about the human condition revealing how people think and act. Imaginative fiction presents a variety of fully developed literary characters with a wide range of beliefs, desires, and behaviors. Literature transmits profundity of thought, fullness of emotion, and insight into various characters' value systems. It can be inspiring to see different characters grow and change throughout a fictional work—at times the reader almost feels as though he is growing and changing with them. An individual can take on roles vicariously through reading. Fiction gives the reader the opportunity to know and to follow various characters and to see why they take certain courses or actions. Fiction allows people to observe a wide range of motives, traits, and behaviors. Different perspectives are attained because fiction helps readers see scenarios from various points of view. Stories can enable readers to identify with characters who are quite different from themselves. This can help in understanding the many types of people they encounter in life. Characters in a story can have an impact on the character of the reader. A person's own moral conduct and responses can be affected by the moral imagination of writers. Every fictional work has the potential to prompt a person to make changes in his own life.

Business is the great story of the last several hundred years. Work is an essential and intrinsic part of human existence—a person's identity is frequently defined by the work he performs. Imaginative literature can impart an understanding of the business world and how it works. All of the elements of outstanding fiction are present in every business day including heroism, cowardice, comedy, tragedy, absurdity, romance, genius, stupidity, morality, immorality, catastrophe, emotion, competence, incompetence, independence, teamwork, politics, conflicts, dilemmas, opportunities, threats, decision-making, make or break moments, and so on. Reading fiction dealing with business issues can sensitize and enlighten us to the nature and complexities of the business world.

Literature offers portraits of characters as employers, employees, managers, leaders, consultants, and other professionals and as regular human beings with a variety of drives, desires, and ambitions. Fiction offers superb descriptions of the situations, circumstances, and organizational settings in which workers find themselves. Reading literary texts enables people to observe the issues within large and appropriate contexts—context must be established. The reader is able to encounter descriptions of a variety of successful and unsuccessful, moral and immoral men and women in different work situations. Stories can serve to stimulate the moral imagination, to increase one's understanding of moral dilemmas, and to enhance moral competence. Fiction can heighten a person's ability to relate to complex ethical matters facing the individual and the organization. Literature can strengthen a manager or other employee's ability to resolve specific moral issues. Imaginative literature can be an especially valuable resource for managers attempting to comprehend and to resolve human problems in business. Fiction can help a manager to understand his own needs and the needs of the people whom he manages for things such as individuality, identity, challenges, power and control, responsibility, self-respect and self-esteem, acceptance and recognition, personal integrity, self-fulfillment, and so on.

The use of fiction, including novels, plays, and films, can enrich teaching materials in both educational and business settings. Fiction can be a powerful force to teach, educate, and move students and employees in ways that lectures, case studies, textbooks, articles, and anecdotes cannot. Although cases can be complex, they cannot compare with the multifaceted nature of storytelling. In fiction, we know much more about the characters than in case studies. In addition, readers or viewers can empathize with the characters. Fiction more closely mimics reality and illuminates the full context of a situation. It follows that fiction generates insights that are conceivably different from those emanating from the study of cases. Not only do novels, plays, and films offer an expanded view of businessmen and business relationships, they can also sometimes serve as a way to experience real events that occurred in the past. Studying such works helps people understand what happened in the past so that they can learn to avoid making similar mistakes in the future or, more positively, learn what to do from successful actions taken in prior situations.

Studying fictions of business can provide insight to often inexperienced business students with respect to real-life situations. They can address a multitude of issues and topics and can frequently better transmit a lesson or message than traditional teaching approaches can. Novels, plays, and films have the ability to tell interesting stories and the potential to stick with the reader or viewer longer than lectures, case studies, textbook chapters, etc. Literary passages or scenes are much more engaging and memorable for most students and other audiences. Fiction can be a great supplement to the theories that students encounter in their business curriculum. Studying business fiction helps business students to relate their various business classes, such as management, marketing, organizational behavior, finance, operations management, and so on to real life situations like takeovers, market crashes, layoffs, etc.

Every day business people deal concurrently with multiple issues. Novels, plays, and films are thus realistic because they tend to present several issues together in the context of a story. Fiction can tell a more complete story by dealing with multiple subjects and by demonstrating how issues interact and interrelate. Also, the situations and characters found in fictional works are more realistic than the abstractions found in textbooks and case studies.

Fiction can be used to teach, explicate, and illustrate a wide range of business issues and concepts. Many fictional works address human problems in business such as: managing interpersonal conflict and office politics; using different styles of management; the potential loss of one's individuality as a person tends to become an "organization man"; the stultifying effect of routine in business; the difficulty in balancing work life and home life; hiring and keeping virtuous employees; maintaining one's personal integrity while satisfying the company's demands for loyalty, conformity, and adaptation to the firm's culture; communication problems a business may experience; fundamental moral dilemmas; depersonalization and mechanization of human relationships; and so on. Fictional works tend to describe human behavior and motivations more eloquently, powerfully, and engagingly than texts, articles, or cases typically do. Literary authors and filmmakers are likely to develop and present ideas through individual characters. They depict human insights and interests from the perspective of individuals within an organizational setting. Reading imaginative literature and watching films are excellent ways to develop critical thinking and to learn about values and character.

Many novels, plays, and films are concerned with the actual operations of the business system. Some deal directly with business problems such as government regulation, cost control, new product development, labor relations, environmental pollution, health and safety, plant openings and closings, tactics used and selection of takeover targets, structuring financial transactions, succession planning, strategic planning, the creation of mission statements, the company's role in the community, social responsibility, etc. Assessing fictional situations makes a person more thoughtful, better prepared for situations, and better able to predict the consequences of alternative actions. Fiction can address both matters of morality and practical issues. There are many fine selections in literature and film which prompt readers to wrestle with business situations.

Older novels, plays, and films can supply information on the history of a subject or topic. They can act as historical references for actual past instances and can help students to understand the reasons for successes and failures of the past. Older literature can provide a good history lesson and can help people to understand the development of our various businesses and industries. These stories can be inspiring and motivational and can demonstrate how various organizations and managers were able to overcome obstacles, adapt, and survive. Fictional works are cultural artifacts from different time periods that can be valuable when discussing the history of business. Many fictional works present history in a form that is more interesting than when one just reads history books.

A case can be made that reading the works of playwrights who have taken business persons and a business-oriented culture as their literary subject may be even better than novels for teaching business concepts and for instilling moral values. Plays can more distinctly address the interaction of characters thus enabling the reader to become more involved in their situations. Drama can be a more efficient teaching tool than novels because plays can attend to the same number of business issues in a briefer format. A play's dynamic scenarios more nearly map reality and illuminate a situation's full context. Passages in a play can be used in role playing and readers' theater. This form of active learning can depict a more complete portrait of the business world.

Hollywood films can be effective vehicles to explicate, illustrate, teach, and expand upon business, management, and leadership concepts. Through purposeful viewing a film can become a text or case study. Print media in the form of novels, plays, and case studies are more abstract than films which offer realistic visualizations of abstract ideas. Feature films can breathe life into intellectual concepts. The motion picture is a powerful medium to enhance instruction by illustrating issues and problems. Good movies can be memorable, compelling, and inspiring.

Movies can be used as a catalyst to enliven classroom discussions among business students who do not possess the business experience or frame of reference to comprehend the issues and potential conflicts that occur every day in the business world. Engaging and fun films can be a source of substituted real-world experience for them. In addition, major-release films are more attractive and interesting within a business itself than are traditional training films. It is not surprising that many companies use Hollywood films to educate and train managers. Movies can encourage free-flowing discussions as college students and business employees act as critical evaluators of these cinematic depictions.

Throughout history, business and the businessman have not fared especially well in business fiction. There have been many unflattering depictions of business, businessmen, and capitalism. Many have often attacked business and industry for destroying an old communal order based on equality and have lamented the businessman's preoccupation with material success and the dominance of large dehumanizing organizations in people's lives. A great many novelists, playwrights, and filmmakers have been repelled by business and have criticized the businessman's lack of culture and interest in education. Notably, writers of artistic merit are likely to be hostile and negative toward business ideology.

Fortunately, some fictional works do characterize business and the businessman in a more favorable, more realistic, even heroic image by emphasizing the possibilities of life in a free society, the inherent ethical nature of capitalism and the businessman, the strength and self-sufficiency of the hard-working businessman, and the entrepreneur as wealth creator and promoter of human economic progress. Positive images of business, businessmen, and capitalism do exist but more are needed in order to illustrate the value of free enterprise, innovation, and personal initiative.

Business fiction is a heterogeneous collection of writings and films. Depictions of business and the businessman have changed over time. Literary attitudes in a given time period and part of the world, and for a specific author, are frequently partial, particular to a given social class, and reflective of the author's political convictions. For example, European attitudes toward business have been more negative than the attitudes of Americans who have great faith in progress and who believe in the necessity of material progress. In addition, writers are likely to set their fiction within the professional environment with which they are familiar.

The tradesman has been portrayed in English literature ever since Geoffrey Chaucer's time in the fourteenth century. Chaucer himself was controller of customs and royal business projects for many years. In his *The Canterbury Tales* he paints a positive portrait of a merchant as a worthy and respectable man. During this time a new merchant class with business values was slowly but steadily becoming a factor in a world traditionally controlled by the Church and land owners. In the sixteenth century we find Shakespeare frequently showing respect and honor for the tradesmen. Shakespeare was a fine businessman in his own right possessing knowledge of commerce, contracts, and finance. In addition, the father of the English novel, Daniel Dafoe, started out as a businessman and displayed admiration for the merchant in his works. Beginning with Dafoe, novels have delivered treatments of business and the businessman that are varied, complex, and nuanced resulting in a new literary genre. The businessman was a familiar character in the sixteenth century and the manufacturer became a common figure later.

We will now take a retrospective look at the changing image of business and the businessman in fictional works during various time periods. In doing so, a number of notable works will be mentioned and briefly discussed. This survey will also demonstrate how business and organizations have changed and how the successful ones have been adaptive in order to survive. Through literature, a person can learn about work-life from another person's point of view in a very different time and place.

In the eighteenth century, business was still seen as respectable and virtuous. By the first half of the nineteenth century business and the businessman were beginning to become objects of reprobation. Criticisms were levied at individual businessmen as there were very few American corporations in existence during the first half of that century. Fictions of this era tended to portray salesmen and individual proprietors as uncultured and selfish men who lack scruples. The few corporations that did exist tended to be state-granted monopolies for accomplishing public works. During this period many state officials were bribed by such corporations in order to be granted the required licenses. For example, railroad companies and government officials engaged in unprecedented political and financial corruption.

Two of the best pre-Civil War American works of business fiction are Herman Melville's *Bartleby the Scrivener: A Story of Wall Street* (1853) and *The Confidence Man* (1857). Bartleby is a mysterious clerk and copyist on New York's Wall Street who politely refuses to do work. His employer is a kind and compassionate man. The story is of the relationship between a manager and an uncooperative, inert employee. *Bartleby* can perhaps be viewed as an early ancestor of the recent film, *Office Space*, a satire of helpless employees doing mindless jobs in a bland company. In *The Confidence Man* a master con man or Yankee peddler assumes a variety of forms as he transforms into different characters on a steamboat going from St. Louis to New Orleans. The confidence man is a master of duplicity and deception. The lesson in this novel is that a person is known by what he or she appears to be. The great English author, Charles Dickens, had visited America in 1842 during which he sensed the emerging image of the American businessman as a con man. In his *The Life and Adventures of Martin Chuzzlewit* (1844), he tells of a young Englishman who changes into a confidence man when he travels to America. Of course, the young man is no match for the American con man and he returns defeated and chastised to England. Dickens also authored *A Christmas Carol* (1843), in which he provided an image of a miserly and greedy businessman in the character Ebenezer Scrooge. In addition, his 1848 novel *Dombey and Son* centered around a family-owned shipping business.

In American fiction the revulsion and animus toward business and the businessman were well-developed by the time of the Civil War. Business power had accumulated during the Civil War and expanded throughout the following decades. Following the Civil War, there appeared a variety of novels dealing with success, financial and political corruption and scandals, and economic reforms. The materialistic philosophy and economic system of the Gilded Age promoted a widespread sense of distrust. Many novels after the Civil War disparaged capitalism by emphasizing the contradictions between business sentiments and higher cultural and moral ones.

Horatio Alger is famous for his rags-to-riches glorified stories of small merchants such as *Ragged Dick* (1868), *Strive and Succeed* (1871), and *Paul the Peddler* (1871). Alger's literary optimism was a function of the prevailing beliefs of his times in individualism and laissez-faire economics. Alger emphasized that hard work is the key to success. Alongside the Horatio Alger type of businessman who makes good through his own efforts was the Scrooge-like miser warped by his ruthless struggle for material rewards. The image of the businessmen put forth by the followers of Dickens is one of greed, miserliness, unethical business dealings, and exploitation of, and insensitivity to, the needs of employees. Then after the Civil War in the 1870s there was rampant political and moral corruption inflamed by the national mania for speculation. This corruption was dealt with in several novels.

Mark Twain and John Dudley Warner's *The Gilded Age* (1873) portrays speculation as a national pastime. It is a tale of corrupt Washington politicians conniving with private land and stock speculators who lobby them. The mania for stock and land speculation following the Civil War was intensified by the railroad explosion and financial scandals in Washington during the Grant administration and on Wall Street between 1868 and 1872. The novel recommends moral reform rather than economic reform. Anthony Trollope's *The Way We Live Now* (1873) was also set at the time of the financial madness of the early 1870s and the financial crash of 1873. Trollope's satire of speculation and deception is an indictment of a corrupt society. Trollope's financier protagonist makes a pretense of wealth and respectability and almost succeeds in a manipulative scam of enormous proportions.

There were sweeping transformations in the economy after the Civil War. Industry grew rapidly, cities mushroomed, large groups were dislocated, there was an influx of immigrant foreign workers, labor/industrial conflict grew, economic protests became common, and the leaders of industry became "robber barons" within a short number of years. America was changing from a nation of individual entrepreneurs and small farmers to one of factory workers in routinized jobs. Many of the factory workers were immigrants who felt more at home in America than in Europe because they were free of the class structure of Europe.

The appearance of freewheeling private enterprisers led to regulations such as the Interstate Commerce Act of 1887 and the Sherman Antitrust Act of 1890. By 1890 there were a large number of critics who advocated the replacement of capitalism with socialism. Novelists helped pave the way for the passage of the early antitrust laws. The period between the end of the Civil War and the end of World War I produced hundreds of novels dealing with business, financial speculation, trusts, labor relations, economic crises, and so on. During the 1880s there was a great deal of labor/industrial conflict. There were economic crises including a depression during the 1890s. In addition, by 1900, there was the establishment of the great industrial trusts and the proliferation of mergers. As a result, the railroads and the large manufacturing firms were accused of engaging in ruinous competition.

Success novels, reflecting the belief in Social Darwinism, existed alongside reform and utopian novels that began to appear in the 1880s. The success novels treated corporate empire builders as visionaries, heroes, creators, as well as manipulators. In the success novels acquiring riches proved one's mastery over the environment and his fitness to survive. Utopian novels were numerous in the last decade of the nineteenth century. By then social protest novels were gaining popularity. The discontent and unrest of the 1890s stemmed from the prevailing notion that industries were getting to be too institutionalized and that wealth was becoming too concentrated. The reform novels were intended to explain structural problems beyond the control of any one individual. By 1900, novelists were capitalizing on the widespread distrust of business, especially big business. Their works were keeping pace with the huge transformations in the business world. Since the late 1800s, authors have been quick to criticize monopoly power, employment practices, and income distribution.

William Dean Howells is more realistic and kinder to the businessman than many of his contemporary writers. His novel, *The Rise of Silas Lapham* (1885), is the classic realistic novel of American business and has received a great deal of literary acclaim. Howells did not reduce his hero to caricature and he illustrated the complexities of moral action in the real world. Silas Lapham is depicted as uncultured but he is not shown to be necessarily immoral. He is portrayed as a sympathetic and motivated individual who intended to make something of himself from his early years on. Howells shows that man is a free agent and that the choices in one's life determine his character. By the end of the story, Lapham has come back from financial collapse and is happy running a small version of his former business. How-ells is not as kind to the businessman in his *A Hazard of New Fortunes* (1890). In this novel Jacob Dryfoos represents the dishonest individual in the marketplace. Dryfoos becomes a corrupt speculator on Wall Street. Dryfoos, Howell's version of the contemporary robber baron, fails to repent by the end of the story. He paints a distressing portrait of the newly rich Dryfoos.

In *Looking Backward* (1888) Edward Bellamy describes a new egalitarian American social, political, and economic order in which a technocratic elite manages nationalized industries. This best-selling utopian novel played a large role in shaping public opinion regarding equality. In the novel America has evolved into a cooperative society in which the government owns all of the capital. The people are motivated by pride and each citizen receives the same amount of credit to spend. America has evolved into a command economy made up of one great trust. Another socialist writer, Jack London, penned an interesting, dystopian, futuristic, socialist, and muckraking novel, *The Iron Heel* (1908), twenty years after Bellamy's work. In London's novel there are great divisions between the classes and a powerful oligarchy and dictatorship of monopoly capitalists or plutocrats uses terror to run the country and to deny worker's rights. *The Iron Heel*, focuses on political and social changes. Another important novel written by London is his *Burning Daylight* (1910).

In Mark Twain's *A Connecticut Yankee in King Arthur's Court* (1888), the hero, Hank Morgan, a type of tinkerer or efficiency expert, gets hit over the head at work and awakens to find himself in 6th century medieval England which is suffering from economic problems. The inventor attempts to improve England's economic, communications, and transportation systems.

The resourceful and skilled Morgan wants to free people from ignorance and superstition. He advances the notions of free enterprise and private property. Morgan introduces a new currency in an attempt to promote economic recovery. He also introduces a stock exchange and utilizes knights as traveling salesmen. At one point, the mechanic tries to explain to a group of workers the difference between real wages and nominal wages. He discusses that most people tend to resist changes and he is able to improve life in medieval England in only small ways. The decade of the 1890s then gave us two fine business-related novels: Henry B. Fuller's *The Cliff-Dwellers* (1893) and Robert Herrick's *The Gospel of Freedom* (1898).

Naturalistic writers such as Frank Norris and Theodore Dreiser portrayed the businessman in Darwinian scale, cornering a commodities market, establishing a trust, or through some other grand endeavor. The philosophy of naturalism does not find any distinctive significance in man. Nature is thus indifferent toward men but nevertheless natural laws do provide social benefits. The goal of literary naturalism is to represent in abundant and objective detail that man is a small, finite, and limited being determined by heredity and by social, economic, and psychological factors. In his novels, Norris depicts the naturalism, romance, and adventure of business.

In Frank Norris's novels, economic processes are huge, impersonal forces—the business system is ultimately controlled by natural forces. In his *The Octopus* (1901) independent wheat farmers become pawns at the mercy of the great railroads, politicians, and natural forces beyond their control. In Norris's vision of orderly determinism evil is short-lived. *The Octopus* provides a historical look into a specific struggle between railroad executives and independent wheat farmers in an expanding California. Norris's 1903 novel, *The Pit*, looks at an attempt to corner the wheat market in Chicago. The title refers to the trading room of the Chicago Board of Trade. For his story, the author drew upon a historical speculative grain corner of 1897–1898. In this novel, Norris senses and foresees the possibilities of speculation and Wall Street. In *The Pit* economic laws collide with natural laws. The natural law wins as the speculators and financiers, who attempt to interfere with the natural order of the wheat cycle, are soundly defeated.

Several notable business novels appeared during the first decade of the 1900s. *Calumet K* (1901) by Samuel Merwin and Henry Webster is a Midwestern novel centered around the building of a two million bushel grain elevator. The principal character is Charlie Bannon, a heroic mid-level manager, who has been charged by his company to construct the elevator. The competent hero faces a series of obstacles and complications that threaten the completion of the project. Bannon loves his work and is a great example of the achieving individual. It is no wonder why *Calumet K* was philosopher-novelist Ayn Rand's favorite novel. In contrast, in Robert Herrick's *The*

Memoirs of an American Citizen (1905) tainted money is required for the "success" of the protagonists similar to the case in Norris's *The Pit*.

Upton Sinclair's *The Jungle* (1906) is well-known for bringing about the United States' meat inspection system. This proletarian novel gained meteoric notoriety because of its graphic depiction of terrible slaughterhouse conditions, thus prompting reform of the meat packing industry and the passage of the Food and Drug Act. *The Jungle* is a powerful study of the working conditions in the Chicago stockyards. It describes the exploitation of workers and explains how economically disadvantaged and low-skilled workers have a very small chance to better themselves and to move up the economic ladder. The novel details the corruption, waste, and exploitation of Chicago's "Packingtown." Ernest Bramah's *Secret of the League* (1907) tells the story of the overthrow by businessmen of a left-wing socialist government in England. The weapon of the businessmen in the economic war against socialist government is a mass boycott of coal, a heavily state-subsidized industry.

Theodore Dreiser's trilogy of desire is about the ruthless and manipulative business titan Frank Cowperwood, who believes that he is superior to the moral and legal codes restraining other individuals. Cowperwood has reasoned that the law of civilization is the same as the law of the jungle. The strong feed on the weak and the only choice is to kill or be killed. Like Frank Norris, Dreiser portrays the captains of industry and finance as heroic but manipulative creators and organizers. It is evident that Dreiser admired and sympathized with his nonconformist superman-hero in *The Financier* (1912), *The Titan* (1914), and *The Stoic* (1947). In these novels, Cowperwood shows contempt for conventional notions of morality. Dreiser's best known book in this trilogy, *The Financier*, takes a look back at the financial disasters of the 1870s. The Darwinian Cowperwood seeks satisfaction in wealth, women, and power. He bribes, cheats, and lies to gain these. The man without a conscience rises, falls, and rises again. His motto is "I satisfy myself." He is unrepentant after being found guilty of legally questionable acts. Undeterred, he restores his fortune after being released from prison by taking a bear position in the midst of the great panic of 1873. Throughout his life he uses opportunities presented to him by the limitations and weaknesses of others.

Dreiser does not attack the immorality of the world he describes in his novels. Dreiser understands Cowperwood's faults but he does not pass judgment on him. Like Norris, Dreiser views businessmen as amoral individuals in the era of trusts, monopolies, political corruption, and financial manipulation. Dreiser writes about the unconquerable self-made man who reached his successful position without the benefit of formal education.

Abraham Cahan's *The Rise of David Levinsky* (1917) is a great example of immigrant fiction as well as of business fiction. In the form of a thirty year memoir, it tells the story of the process of adaptation to American life by a Russian Jewish immigrant. Despite his early years of poverty, the protagonist becomes extremely successful financially in the American ready-to-wear clothing industry. He becomes rich in things of the world at the expense of his inner spirit. At the end he realizes that he is no different than he was as a child and that money and power alone cannot make one happy. Unlike many other novelists who explored American business, Cahan paid a great deal of attention to the details of the functioning of business itself.

In the 1920s literary satire rather than outright condemnation of business and the businessman was the preferred vehicle for literary critics of capitalism. Before Sinclair Lewis's *Babbitt* (1922) the businessman had consistently been portrayed as a rugged individualist. *Babbitt* fiercely satirizes the way in which bourgeois culture and standardized mass consumption have affected society. In this novel, Lewis provides a harsher perspective on the businessman than did earlier writers such as Howells. Babbitt gives up his individuality to conform to the values of his community and lives for what others consider to be respectable. Babbitt is a complacent, prosperous, middle-class citizen who is depicted as a helpless victim of social pressure. The author devotes a large section of the novel to describe Babbitt's typical working day. Babbitt dislikes hard work. By the end of the story he realizes and admits that his life is not fulfilling.

Garet Garrett's novel *The Driver* (1922) tells the story of a Wall Street speculator, financier, and entrepreneur, Henry Galt, who acquires control of a failing railroad. When the railroad declares bankruptcy Galt assumes a leadership position in the company and, through his great vision and work ethic, turns it into a spectacular success. The story occurs in the wake of the great panic of 1893. As he succeeds the government conspires with his competitors to regulate and control him. *The Driver* tells how the government cannot get the economy out of recession but, instead, how people like Galt can through investments and productive work.

Certain novels of the 1920s and 1930s look at class differences and class warfare. One of America's best known and most loved novels is F. Scott Fitzgerald's *The Great Gatsby* (1925). It is a story of social stratification and of "old money" versus "new money." The novel centers on an ambitious, self-made man with huge hopes and dreams in an era of excess. Unfortunately, Gatsby could never escape his lowly background. He fails when he encounters the vicious "old rich" world of emptiness, moral decay, and extravagant parties. The best works of the 1920s, such as *The Great Gatsby*, Booth Tarkington's *The Plutocrat* (1927), and Sinclair Lewis's *Babbitt* and *Dodsworth* (1929) were more separated from the everyday actualities of business than novels before them or since them. Lewis's Sam Dodsworth is a noble businessman who has the dream of creating an attractive and practical product. Much later Fitzgerald supplied a portrait of a strong-minded, compassionate head of a major Hollywood movie studio in his unfinished *The Last Tycoon* (1941). The dictatorial tycoon understands his responsibilities to all of his constituencies. He knows what he wants to accomplish and is adept at playing to the strengths, weaknesses, and personalities of others including actors, screenwriters, directors, and others. This movie producer exhibits a command and control management style.

A great deal of the literature of the 1920s and 1930s is of the left. The crash and the Great Depression brought about a new wave of literary social criticism and calls for the federal government to lead the economy. John Dos Passos's *USA* trilogy consisting of *The 42 Parallel* (1930), *1919* (1932), and *The Big Money* (1936) present the story of America from 1910 until 1930. In these works Dos Passos presents a mixture of stories, news items, biographical sketches of important figures, and narrations. He tells the stories of a variety of people. His complex trilogy condemns both capitalism and socialism. In *The Big Money* Dos Passos speaks for the decade of the Depression. In it he continues to interweave fiction, biography, and documentary-style newsreels to witness the pursuit of the American Dream from various vantage points. The author describes two different nations within the United States during the 1920s. This social and political novel contrasts the world of speakeasies, prohibition, and stock speculation with the world of the rebelling working class, the labor movement, labor-management warfare, and immigrants. Much later Dos Passos wrote *Midcentury: A Contemporary Chronicle* (1961) in which he focuses on the damaging nature of labor involvement with racketeering and the Mafia. The author illustrates how union leaders become like monopolistic capitalists when they invest union funds for private gain. He also condemns big corporations and big government. Dos Passos rebuffs the NLRB for its inability to control violence and racketeering in unions.

In *The Grapes of Wrath* (1939) John Steinbeck proposes fundamental questions regarding social justice, land ownership and stewardship, and the proper role of government. This is the story of tenant farmers in Oklahoma driven away by drought, depression, and large companies that wanted to take their land back. They are told that there are "orders from the bank" to force them off the land. Fruit growers in California print flyers asserting the existence of abundant well-paying jobs. This is untrue and when they arrive in California there are so many migrant workers seeking employment that wages are set at extremely low levels. Then, of course, there are the company stores that charge disproportionately high prices compared to the wages received. The necessity of large-scale government intervention during bad economic times appears to be a major lesson in *The Grapes of Wrath* which was later made into a popular motion picture. Business-related films of the 1930s include the anti-capitalism film, *Modern Times* (1936) and the pro-capitalism (1939) film, *Ninotchka*.

The famed poet, William Carlos Williams began a trilogy of business novels about an immigrant family with *White Mule* (1937). The other two novels in the series are *In the Money* (1940) and *The Build-Up* (1952).

During and immediately following World War II the reputation of business improved. Business was applauded for its productivity during the war and for providing jobs for returning servicemen. For example, the 1944 film *An American Romance* celebrates the American Dream by following its immigrant hero from his arrival in America through his progression from miner to steelworker to foreman to automobile entrepreneur. The movie has documentary portions and was used as a propaganda weapon regarding World War II when the hero was shown building airplanes for the war effort. In addition, there is the excellent 1941 film *Citizen Kane* and the fine novels *The Fountainhead* (1943) by Ayn Rand and *Mildred Pierce* (1941) by James M. Cain, both of which were later made into films.

The post-World War II period witnessed a reconsideration of the large corporations as the source of stultifying conformity. A company's demands for loyalty and devotion called for managers to dedicate their lives and efforts first and foremost to the corporation placing one's individuality and family in the background. The fictional image of the middle-level "organization man" was that of an individual having to choose between his personal values and the company's demands. Corporate life was becoming a major challenge for the individual. After World War II the emphasis of literary authors switched from one which includes the entire system of business to one confined to specific segments of that system. Some business sectors such as advertising seem to hardly even receive a fair depiction in fiction. For example, Frederic Wakeman's *The Hucksters* (1946) is a popular satiric exposé of the radio advertising business. It was also made into a movie. The year 1946 also marked the release of the business-themed classic movie, *It's a Wonderful Life*. Samuel Hopkins Adams's business novel *Plunder* was released in 1948.

Arthur Miller's play, *Death of a Salesman* (1949), is the tragic story of a man who wants to believe that he is a success and who is unable to admit failure. Willy Loman is a self-deluded man whose aspirations were much higher than his achievements. The unsuccessful salesman thinks that popularity, personality, and charisma are equal to success. He is not impressive or well-liked and creates fantasies to cover up his failure. *Death of a Salesman* provides a portrait of the coming apart of a man who has chosen the wrong career path and who is now at the end of that path. Several movie versions have been made of this long-running and award-winning play.

In *Point of No Return* (1949) by John P. Marquand, Charles Gray, son of upper-middle-class New England Yankee parents, rises into aristocracy at an elite bank in New York City. Although he has escaped his former small town lifestyle, it still affects him. The successful banker attempts to free himself from a life that seems to be stereotyped and preordained. During a period of time when he is under consideration for a huge promotion, he revisits the town where he was brought up. He struggles to become a vice-president but resents the conformity required. Our sympathetic protagonist gets the promotion but the promotion does not fulfill his life. Gray then understands the superficiality and artificiality of the inter-office rivalry with another manager for the vice-presidency. He also comes to the realization that he would not have done anything differently. When success is thrust upon him he understands that he is part of a system and that he cannot do anything about that. *Point of No Return* thus reflects the doctrine of social determinism. Deterministic philosophy underpins this novel as well as others depicting the "organization man."

In 1951 noted economist Henry Hazlitt released his futuristic novel, *Time Will Run Back*. The novel is set in the year 2100 some 150 years after the victory of socialism over capitalism. A new reluctant leader, who grew up on an island isolated from the workings of the global socialist political state, senses that there is something wrong with the socialist policies. He and his friend engage in Socratic-style discussions and rethink the economic basis of the system. They gradually rediscover the free market and attempt to implement new policies. The clever plot includes an assassination attempt, the founding of a new nation, and a love story. Reading *Time Will Run Back* is a great way to learn about free market economics. The same year saw the release of an English film, *The Man in the White Suit*. This satire tells the story of the invention of a new kind of indestructible fabric that never gets dirty and that lasts forever. Both the mill owners and laborers oppose and fight the new invention. In addition, in 1950 the business-related film, *Born Yesterday*, made its way onto the big screen.

Former businessman turned novelist, Cameron Hawley, truly understands and accurately portrays the world of business. His 1952 novel, *Executive Suite*, attained great success both as a novel and as a film. The story begins with a crisis when the president of a furniture company suddenly and unexpectedly dies before he could develop a succession plan. The company is left in disarray with five vice-presidents competing for the top position. The story details the resulting office politics, machinations, and power struggles. In the end, the vice-president of product research and development is pitted against the vice-president of finance for the position of president. The foreman runs the factory and the latter keeps a close look at the costs. The hands-on factory man makes an impassioned speech explaining that the firm's success depends upon producing quality product. Profit results from doing good work. He wants to give consumers better furniture and the workers more fulfilling jobs. As a result, the controlling shareholders choose him for the position and, in turn, he selects the finance man to be his executive vice-president.

Hawley's 1955 novel, *Cash McCall*, is the story of a justified and benign corporate raider who benefits himself and society by acquiring poorly managed companies and bringing them back to economic health. He is misperceived by many to be a dishonorable tycoon who merely takes over firms, lays off workers, and sells the assets for huge profits. He is actually a man of moral integrity who acquires failing companies, improves them to turn them around, and then sells them to make an earned profit. McCall makes changes to a firm and frequently finds ways to attain synergy with other companies. *Cash McCall* celebrates the power of capitalism and portrays business as an honorable activity. Like *Executive Suite*, *Cash McCall* was made into a successful Hollywood movie. Cameron Hawley went on to write two more novels about the drama of business, *The Lincoln Lords* (1960) and *The Hurricane Years* (1969).

Sloan Wilson's *The Man in the Gray Flannel Suit* (1955) provides a snapshot of life in the United States during the post-World War II era. The novel tells the story of Tom Rath, a returning World War II veteran and educated white collar worker. He longs for a safe, uneventful corporate existence after the chaos of the war. His goal is to balance his fragmented professional and personal lives. Rath values his personal, familial, and social needs more than he values gaining a promotion and moving up the corporate ladder. The sympathetic hero recognizes the costs of success. He understands that a man only has so much time and energy and therefore must choose between work or leisure and job or family. Rath rediscovers his integrity when he faces the choice between being like his mentor, Hopkins, who totally devotes his life and energies to the corporation while destroying his relationships with his wife and daughter or settling for a lesser, more comfortable position with commensurate earnings and status. Work comes first for the dedicated Hopkins but not for Rath, the corporate suburban nine to five man. *The Man in the Gray Flannel Suit* was also made into a popular Hollywood film.

A large number of business novels thematically and/or stylistically similar to *Point of No Return* and *The Man in the Gray Flannel Suit* appeared between the late 1940s and the early 1960s. Many dealt with the submergence of the individual businessman in the culture of the corporation. These works provide a variety of images of middle-level executives as well as CEOs. Some noteworthy novels in this category are: *The Big Wheel* (1949) by John Brooks; *The Power and the Prize* (1954) by Howard Swiggett; *From the Dark Tower* (1957) by Ernst Powell; *Sincerely Willis Wade* (1957) by John P. Marquand; *The Durable Fire* (1957) by Howard Swiggett; *The Empire* (1959) by George DeMare; *Venus in Sparta* (1958) by Louis Auchincloss; *The Big Company Look* (1958) by J. Harry Howells; and *The View from the Fortieth Floor* (1960) by Theodore White. Also worth seeking out is the Rod Serling film *Patterns* (1956) that deals with loyalty and power struggles within a corporation. In *Patterns* a CEO attempts to force out a long-time employee. The film also tells of the disillusionment of a young business executive who has just been hired for a high-level position in the company replacing the older employee.

Not all business fiction of this period concerns the individual working for a large corporation. For example, in Bernard Malamud's *The Assistant* (1957), the small businessman is portrayed as a sympathetic anti-hero. A Jewish businessman has owned his small neighborhood grocery store for more than twenty years. He is a hard-working, trusting, honest, and compassionate man who readily grants credit to the neighborhood's poor. Nevertheless, he is being put out of business by his rival, a store run by a large supermarket chain corporation. In addition, Saul Bellow's *Seize the Day* (1957) tells the story of an out of work salesman who is a failure in a prosperous world. He is a man who lacks entrepreneurial talent. Yielding to the temptations of easy money he tries his hand in the volatile commodity futures market. *Seize the Day* depicts the alienation, isolation, and despair of a low man in a society in which people worship only money. It has been made into a feature film.

Portraying a totally different world is Ayn Rand's monumental *Atlas Shrugged* (1957). This novel depicts businessmen as heroic protagonists whose pursuit of profit is profoundly moral. It tells the story of the last stages of conflict between producers and looters who live by very different moral codes. The heroes are rationally purposeful and the villains are not. The productive men of the mind reject destructive government edicts and the looters' doctrine of altruism, and go on strike by withdrawing from society. By doing so, they illustrate the role of the mind in human existence. The mind is shown to be the fundamental source of wealth and profits. This novel of ideas also has the ability to induce intense emotions. *Atlas Shrugged* is currently being made into a series of three films. The first part was released in the spring of 2011 and the second part was released in the fall of 2012, and the third part will be released in 2014.

Sometimes a Great Notion (1964) by Ken Kesey is the tale of a small, independent, family-owned logging business in Oregon. Henry Stamper is the patriarch of the family and his son, Hank, symbolizes individualism and self-sufficiency. The heroic, hardworking family members are anti-union and against anyone who attempts to tell them what to do. They fight for what they believe in and their family motto is "Never give an inch." Their business is not a union shop so they continue to work when the unions strike the other logging operators in the area. The Stampers have a contract with a big lumber company to provide logs. They pursue a great quest to supply the logs and succeed through their indomitable will despite union violence and sabotage. Like a number of other novels, *Sometimes a Great Nation* has been made into a Hollywood film.

God Bless You Mr. Rosewater or *Pearls before Swine* (1965) by Kurt Vonnegut, Jr. tells the story of egalitarian Eliot Rosewater, the president of a philanthropic foundation set up by his old-wealth family. Motivated by his equal love of everyone he decides to distribute the funds among all of the deserving and non-deserving poor of his county. He tries to love everyone equally merely because they are human. Eliot does not understand that the true nature of love involves discrimination and exception making. Eliot seems to feel guilty for the wealth that he has inherited. His father is a conservative senator who is an elitist and who represents the ethic of capitalism. The senator views the indiscriminate distribution of money and love as devaluing of human beings. The sentimental Eliot wants individual people to be kind and to share. Philanthropy is shown to be an individual and personal choice and action. In general, the novel is against both business and government.

Louis Auchincloss's *The Embezzler* (1966) tells the story of a struggle to succeed in a world dominated by corporate greed. It is a tale of crooked financial practices and the fall of a financier. The novel reflects real Wall Street scandals and still has relevance today. The satiric *Office Politics* by Wilfrid Sheed also appeared in 1966. The novel revolves around the power struggles, disloyalty, and backstabbing that occurs in a publishing house. The chief editor and his two senior editors constantly fight over the magazine's focus and content. When the chief editor suffers a heart attack the others compete for the top position. When the charismatic chief editor returns he restores order because of his effective leadership including the mastery of office politics.

Society, business organizations, and ideas about success and fulfillment were being restructured and transformed during the several decades following World War II. Ideas were changing regarding the American Dream, the good life, social progress, what constituted a good society, the role of government, social responsibility, and so on. During the 1950s, the fragmented world of employees was constrained by corporate culture and hierarchy. By the 1970s, the growing complexity of American society was leading to the loss of all traditional ideals, authorities, morals, and sanctions. These changes are reflected in the fiction of that era.

The film *Save the Tiger* (1973) is the story of a man in a gray flannel suit during the Watergate era. Our businessman is a middle-aged man who grew up during a period that had values but who is now living in a time of decaying values in countercultural Vietnam-era America. He served in World War II and is troubled by horrific memories of combat in Italy. The film highlights the differences between World War II culture and the culture of the 1970s. His garment manufacturing business is failing and heading toward bankruptcy. In order to save his company he considers torching the factory for the insurance money. He suggests his arson and insurance fraud plans to his highly ethical partner who is mortified by the suggestion. Our protagonist thinks of the memories of his youth and his current dubious business practices while choosing what to do. This movie does a fine job exploring the relationship among business, morality, and success.

Joseph Heller's black comedy, *Something Happened* (1974) is the story of the American Dream gone wrong. It takes place in a corporate office where work is routinized and where process has replaced product. Slocum, the "hero," is alienated, unhappy, and beset by constant vague anxieties. The goal of the troubled Slocum is to have no rivals or enemies. He understands the corporate culture and produces (i.e., spins) data to ensure that nobody is unhappy and that the status quo is maintained. He is a proponent of bureaucracy and corporate gospel and understands that getting ahead depends upon one's attitude, style, and appearance. The organization values and rewards style rather than substance. He puts up a façade of niceness in an environment of entropy, irrationality, and immorality. The troubled Slocum loses touch with himself and with reality.

JR (1975) is William Gaddis's easy money novel about a boy who learns about the stock market in a sixth grade class. He becomes a child capitalist and amasses a fortune in paper holdings. He uses a phone booth in his school to create a diversified paper empire beginning with a mail-order shipment of surplus Navy forks. He incorporates, has stockholders, and puts together a team of grown-up marketers, financiers, and administrators. The boy has a thoroughly materialistic value system and mindset. Ultimately, he loses his fortune.

Ben Flesh, the hero of Stanly Elkin's comic 1976 novel, *The Franchiser*, endeavors to help people acquire whatever they need or want. He serves his customers democratically and equally while at the same time pursuing his individual business interests through franchises and within the world of huge corporations. Ben wants to homogenize the country by having the same stores appear all across the country. He wants to obliterate regional destinations. He uses money obtained at low costs to buy a variety of franchises that shape the American landscape in 1970s America, complete with gas shortages and rolling blackouts. Ben's vitality is evident as we observe him relishing existence in a world of possibilities. There are a number of other interesting business novels of the late 1970s including: *Not a Penny More, Not a Penny Less* (1976) by Jeffrey Archer; *The Moneychangers* (1976) by Arthur Hailey; *Rich* (1979) by Graham Masterton; and *Takeover* (1979) by Herb Schmertz and Larry Woods.

Rabbit is Rich (1981) by John Updike in the third novel is a series of four that reveal the life of Harry "Rabbit" Angstrom. The others are *Rabbit Run* (1961), *Rabbit Redux* (1971), and *Rabbit at Rest* (1990). Our endearing but self-absorbed and directionless hero is a former high school basketball star who sold cars and attained "success" through luck by marrying into a family business. The middle-aged Harry now enjoys prosperity as the chief sales representative during the late 1970s at a Toyota agency in a medium-size city in Pennsylvania. The dealership is owned by his wife and his mother-in-law. The novel offers a look back at America in 1979 and into the early 1980s. This snapshot of that period of time includes inflation, gas shortages, the Carter administration, consumerism, the OPEC oil crisis, the Iran hostage situation, and much more. The novel is rich with respect to the issues and problems of the time. Rabbit is now reasonably comfortable, affluent, and his family is firmly in the middle class. American brand car sales are declining because of their low gas mileages. Harry's Toyotas sell because of their high mileage per gallon and their low maintenance costs. He belongs to the Rotary Club and he and his wife enjoy the country club life. Rabbit's son Nelson desires to work as a salesman at the Toyota agency but this would mean dismissing the company's top salesman. Rabbit knows that Nelson lacks competence and maturity and that he possesses a sense of entitlement. Rabbit feels like an economic prisoner when his wife and mother-in-law overrule him and hire Nelson to work at the dealership. The novel does a good job of illustrating problems of an intergenerational family business. There are problems of succession and of accommodating the next generation. Harry is never really happy. He says that people never are because they either want something that they don't have or are fearful of losing what they do have. He thinks that there is always someone out there who wants to get him. Both Rabbit and America are running out of gas. Both have reached middle-age. The novel's theme is entropy as evidenced by the economically vulnerable and spiritually deficient Harry "Rabbit" Angstrom. The novel discusses economic and business issues throughout. For example, it is argued that it is government and those in debt who benefit from inflation. With respect to business, we hear talk about profit margins and pricing of various cars, financing percentages, carrying costs of cars in the lot, what percentage a car salesman makes on new and used cars, and so on.

In David Mamet's 1984 play, *Glengarry Glen Ross*, the reader is able to witness the interactions between real estate salesmen, potential customers, and managers in a small, Chicago office in the early 1980s. This study of human interactions shows four small-time real estate hustlers competing for their very jobs while attempting to revolt and unite against a ruthless, inexperienced, vapid, and heartless company-man boss who answers to his superiors downtown. Anger drives the characters in this bleak world. The premium leads are reserved for closers only. The salesmen try to sell vacation and retirement land to less than financially ideal clients. One desperate and despairing salesman in his fifties, was once a great salesman, but is now struggling to make sales. Two others are shown discussing an opportunity to steal their own company's best leads and then to offer to sell them to a competitor. These representatives of a dying breed will do just about anything to get a sale. They manipulate, scheme, make up stories, improvise, and cheat in order to connive people into buying land. This realistic play was made into a fine motion picture.

Oliver Stone's 1987 film, *Wall Street*, depicts the securities industry as being a rigged game and capitalism as an inherently corrupt zero-sum system controlled by the few at the expense of the many. The film teaches that consistent and atypical success in the stock market depends on asymmetric information. The film is the story of an ambitious young stockholder, Bud Fox, and his involvement with Gordon Gekko, a wealthy unscrupulous corporate raider who buys out firms and liquidates them. The junior stockholder idolizes the investment tycoon who takes him under his wing. Bud gets a glimpse of Gekko's world and comes to realize how ruthless one has to be in order to get ahead. Gekko gives Bud money to manage and asks him to spy and to obtain inside information. Bud is from a working-class family. His father is an honest man who would rather work hard to produce than get rich quickly, illegally, and unethically. Gordon goes too far when he attempts to take over and dismantle the airline where Bud's father works and is a union leader. Bud has a change of heart when he realizes that he has been a pawn in that matter. Bud initiates a plot to make Gekko lose millions of dollars. In addition, Bud is arrested for insider trading and he blows the whistle on Gekko sending both of them to prison.

Francis Ford Coppola's 1988 film, *Tucker: The Man and His Dream*, tells the true but somewhat fictionalized story of Preston Tucker, a charming, persuasive, optimistic, innovative, and visionary maverick who challenged the "Big 3" establishment by creating a utopian automobile. After World War II, Tucker had the dream to design and manufacture a safe, innovative, and revolutionary new vehicle. The exuberant Tucker is portrayed as a Capraesque hero who overcomes obstacles and fights the forces that eventually crush his dream. The film celebrates the American can-do spirit and the entrepreneur as the driving force of capitalism and wealth creation. According to the film, Tucker was the victim of Detroit and Washington, illustrating the need to separate economy and the state. His competitors and their allies in government combine to bring him down.

Nice Work (1988) by David Lodge is set in the Thatcherite mid-1980s in a fictitious city in the English Midlands. It tells the story of the collision of two different worlds, lifestyles, and personalities. An Industry Year Shadow Scheme, a government program intended to foster mutual understanding between university and collegiate communities, has a faculty member shadow a local industrialist for a period of eight weeks. Both of the chosen participants are disinterested in taking part in the project. They have preconceived ideas about each other. The female faculty member is an expert on the nineteenth-century factory novel. She is an ardent feminist devoted to the study of women in the Victorian industrial novel who has never been inside an actual factory. The other person is the practical, hard-working managing director at a casting and engineering firm. They are skeptical and lack appreciation for the other's mode of life. Adversarial at first, the two become understanding of the other's point of view. During their voyage of discovery, they try to make sense of each other's worlds. Their constant and lively debates force both characters to reexamine their assumptions with respect to business, politics, literature, and so much more.

Jerry Sterner's 1989 play, *Other People's Money*, presents two sides of the hostile takeover and subsequent liquidation story line. Corporate raider, Larry "The Liquidator" Garfinkle, wants to take over an outmoded, debt-free wire and cable company that has a lot of cash. His method is to target companies with undervalued assets. Larry plans to sell off the assets of the takeover target firm. The company is worth more if it is liquidated. Larry wants to maximize shareholder wealth by taking the money and investing it in some viable more technologically advanced industry. New England Wire and Cable's aging chairman, Andrew "Jorgy" Jorgenson, is a traditionalist and supporter of community values who doesn't want to see hundreds of people out of work. Jorgy is an idealistic, passionate, and paternal businessman who runs the company based on sentiment and who has pride and faith in his stockholders. The climactic scene is a proxy fight in a shareholders' meeting. It is a battle for control of the board of directors between Larry, who would make the shareholders money, and Jorgy, who would continue business in the dying copper wire industry. They both deliver impassioned speeches, which are masterpieces, explaining the principles underlying their respective positions. The play portrays Larry as a moral, likeable, even heroic person. He wants to make money for the stockholders including retired people who are not rich, while freeing resources to produce things that people want more than copper wire. The play illustrates that an efficient and productive economy has the ability to change and that takeovers are necessary for the efficient operation of a market economy. Unfortunately, some people will be out of work but people are flexible and adaptable to changing conditions. *Other People's Money* was later made into a popular film.

There are a number of other good 1980s novels that fall under the business novel rubric including: *The Power Players* (1980) by Arlo Sederberg; *The Broker* (1981) by Harold Q. Masur; *Money: A Suicide Note* (1984) by Martin Amis; *Confessions of a Taoist on Wall Street* (1984) by David Payne; *Cash* (1986) by Paul-Loup Sulitzer; *Small Business* (1986) by Tom Parker; *Bonfire of the Vanities* (1987) by Tom Wolfe; *The Palace* (1988) by Paul Erdman; *The Real World* (1989) by Charles Knowlton; and *Strong Medicine* (1989) by Arthur Hailey, among others. Three popular 1980s business-related films are *Gung Ho* (1986) about the cultural differences between American workers and Japanese workers, *Tin Men* (1987) concerning aluminum siding salesmen who deceive customers, and *Working Girl* (1988) which deals with the obstacles and frustrations of a woman working hard to get ahead in business.

William H. Morris's 1992 novel, *Motor City* (also known as *Biography of a Buick*) is a tale of media manipulation, dealer pressure, and espionage at General Motors in 1954. This novel offers an optimistic and romantic portrayal of the cultural and social landscape of flourishing and energetic America of the 1950s.

Bombardiers (1995) by Po Bronson tells the story of a dysfunctional San Francisco bond trading office named Atlantic Pacific. This accurate satire of a high-pressure brokerage house was penned by a former insider of the industry. In the brutally competitive environment a new, young bond salesman ignores the house rules. The novel features a variety of fearful and greedy brokers who engage in outrageous deals. The story provides a good primer on the concepts and language of finance.

The hero of Philip Roth's *American Pastoral* (1998) is the owner of a ladies' glove factory in mid-century Newark, New Jersey who sees his life fall apart due to political and social unrest. Radical movements threaten his family and his factory. He is a good and kind employer who treats his craftsman employees well, but he is not perceived that way by outsiders. The owner appreciates human work and initiative and he respects each and every employee who possesses expertise in each manufacturing process. The hero believes that a properly made glove reflects a superior world. It follows that people can flourish through their common efforts to strive for perfection. This is done when each employee contributes to the manufacturing process and to the goals of the company.

Tom Wolfe's *A Man in Full* (1998) is primarily about two characters. One, Charles Croker, is a middle-aged conglomerate king who has a real estate empire. The other man, Conrad Hensley, works in one of Croker's frozen food warehouses and is about to be laid off from his job due to downsizing that the bank has recommended. Croker's real estate business is on the brink of collapse. Both men experience tests of character. Hensley, a man in full, discovers Stoicism and realizes that happiness lies in not permitting oneself to be controlled by external events.

Gain (1999) by Richard Powers is a historical novel about the origins and development of a soap company and how its later years brought the threat of cancer to nearby residents. In *Gain* two stories of different scale are juxtaposed and woven together. The novel describes the rise of Clare, a small soap company, into a multinational corporation over a period of a hundred years or so. From one perspective, it tells the story of enthusiasm, courage, and financial triumph. Not only does it illustrate the benefits of industry, it also shows its dark side. The author offers a good blend of American history, economics, management, marketing, technology, and environmentalism in this work. He also provides a parallel story of a woman real estate agent stricken with ovarian cancer which may have been caused by using Clare products or by living nearby a Clare factory.

Several business-related films appeared during the 1990s. *Mac* (1993) is the story of a hardworking Italian-American carpenter who realizes his dream of becoming a contractor. He is an uncompromising, honest, focused, and hardworking man with extremely high standards. For Mac there are only two ways to do a job "the right way and my way and they're the same." The moral of the story is that each person has a God-given vocation and can contribute to the world by using his talents to the best of his ability. In addition, there is the satiric *Office Space* (1999) and the docudrama *Pirates of Silicon Valley* (1999) that describes the rise of the home computer business through the rivalry between Apple Computer and Microsoft. The following year Hollywood offered us *Boiler Room* and *Erin Brockovich*. *Boiler Room* is the story of a college dropout who takes a position with a small stock brokerage firm where he learns that the company is selling worthless stocks and bonds of non-existent companies. *Erin Brockovich* tells the story of a single-mother legal assistant who goes after a California power company accused of polluting a city's water supply thereby causing serious health problems for the nearby residents.

Max Barry's *Company* (2006), like the comic strip *Dilbert*, is a parody of the corporate mindset. A new hire at the Seattle-based Zephyr Holdings witnesses the wholesale irrationality of company policy. He also realizes that none of the employees have an idea of what the company actually does. As a result, he undertakes a crusade to understand the firm's mission, policies, and so forth. *Then We Came to the End* (2007) by Joshua Ferris is about life in 2001 in a Chicago advertising firm where many layoffs are occurring. All of the copywriters and designers are in constant fear of being fired. Written in the first person plural "we," the novel tells the story of office politics, deadlines, pranks, stress, rumors, arguments, threats, laughter, tears, and much more. Work in this downward-spiraling office is depicted as both boring and vibrant and both as something to be avoided and as essential to people's lives.

Wall Street: Money Never Sleeps is a 2010 sequel to *Wall Street* directed by Oliver Stone. The film revolves around the 2008 financial crisis and is set in New York City. Gordon Gekko has been released from prison and Jake Moore is a young investment banker in love with Gekko's estranged daughter, Winnie. Jake works for Keller Zabel Investments, a firm that collapses because of rumors about sub-prime debt and KZI. KZI is not offered a bailout and Jake goes on a quest to find out who started and benefitted from the rumor. He teams up with the father of his fiancé to find out this information. In turn, Gekko wants Jake to help him to reconcile with Winnie. The movie *Margin Call* (2011) is a thriller involving key players in the earliest stages of the 2008 financial crisis. An analyst discovers that the company is so committed to underwater mortgage-backed securities that the firm's potential loss is enough to bring about the downfall of the company. This information is given to another employee who must decide whether or not these worthless securities should be sold to unsuspecting clients. This film places the viewer in the shoes of company executives who can save their jobs (at least temporarily) by deceiving and swindling investors. The movie makes the point that practically no one knew what was going on in the investment banking industry, not even the majority of the employees.

We have now arrived at our brief analysis of the treatment of business and businessmen in fiction. A large number of works of business fiction have appeared and continue to be published. Some of these are popular works, some have artistic merit, and some have been both well-received by the general population and have also secured a high place in literary canon. Many have treated business and the businessman with derision and hostility while others have held them up for admiration. Many are literary devaluations of business as a way of life, others have generally been more favorable in their treatment of business values and businesspeople, and a few have depicted a career in business as honorable and heroic. The fictional image of business has been varied and has included: (1) overemphasis of the faults and weaknesses of business and the businessman thereby providing a distorted picture; (2) depictions of how business has changed and developed over time; (3) challenges at work; (4) the conflict between personal values and the company's demands; (5) the need for self-analysis and self-management as a first concern in managing a firm; (6) celebration of the opportunity and energy of business life; and (7) positive romantic portraits of businessmen as active creators in free markets.

Business fiction can be an alternative source of insight to the academic observations of social scientists. Fiction permits the unique individuality and richness of variation of its characters. The writer or filmmaker as artist is able to reshape reality in accordance with his own values. Positive business novels such as *Atlas Shrugged, Cash McCall, Executive Suite, Sometimes a Great Notion*, and so on, can serve as a guidepost for a new direction in business fiction.

This author would like to see someone write a novel (or perhaps a series of novels) that creates a fictional world, gathering place, or afterlife of characters that brings together characters from numerous authors of business novels and plays and characters from various business films. Just think how interesting it would be to see the interactions between characters such as Silas Lapham, Frank Cowperwood, David Levinsky, George Babbitt, Jay Gatsby, Tom Rath, Willy Loman, Cash McCall, Hank Stamper, Ben Flesh, Gordon Gekko, Larry Garfinkle, and so on. Are there any aspiring novelists out there who would want to take on this project?

RECOMMENDED READING

Badaracco, Joseph L. *Questions of Character: Illuminating the Heart of Leadership through Literature*. Harvard Business Review, 2006.

Boozer, Jack. *Career Movies: American Business and the Success Mystique*. Austin: University of Texas Press, 2003.

Borus, Daniel H. *Writing Realism: Howells, James, and Norris in the Mass Market*. Chapel Hill: University of North Carolina Press, 1989.

Brandis, R. "The American Writer Views the American Businessman." *Quarterly Review of Economics and Business* 1, no. 3 (1961): 29–38.

Brawer, Robert A. *The Fictions of Business*. New York: John Wiley and Sons, 1998.

———. "10 Great American Business Novels." *American Heritage Magazine* 52, no. 4 (June 2001).

Bumpus, M.A. "Using Motion Pictures to Teach Management." *Journal of Management Education* 28, no. 6 (2005): 792–816.

Cantor, Paul and Stephen Cox. *Literature and the Economics of Liberty*. Auburn, AL: Ludwig von Mises Institute, 2010.

Carroll, Denis. "The Recent Mamet Films: Business Versus Communism." *David Mamet–A Casebook*, edited by Leslie Kane. Garland Publications, Inc., 1992.

Cashill, Jack. "Capitalism's Hidden Heroes: The Literary Establishment Contrives to Ignore the business Giants in the American Novel." *CNN Money* (February 1985).

Chamberlain, John. "The Businessman in Fiction." *Fortune* XXXVIII (November 1948): 134–36, 139, 142, 143, 146, 148.

Clemons, John and Melora Wolff. *Movies to Manage By*. New York: McGraw-Hill, 1999.

Coles, Robert. "Storytellers' Ethics." *Harvard Business Review* (March–April, 1987).

———. "Gatsby at the B School." *New York Times* (October 25, 1987): 2.

———. *The Call of Stories: Teaching and the Moral Imagination*. Boston: Houghton Mifflin, 1989.

Darby, William. *Necessary American Fiction: Popular Literature of the 1950s*. Bowling Green, OH: Bowling Green State University Press, 1987.

Davies, Geoff, and Roger Hancock. "Drama as a Learning Medium." *Management Development Review* 6 (1993).

DeMott, B. "Reading Fiction to the Bottom Line." *Harvard Business Review* 67 (May–June 1989): 128–34.

Dumphy, Steve. "Management Goes to the Movies." *Proceedings of ASBBS* 16, no. 1 (February 2009).

Egger, R. "The Administrative Novel." *American Political Science Review* 53, no. 2 (1959): 448–455.

Erskine, John. "American Business in the American Novel." *The Bookman* LXXIII (July 1931): 449–457.

Formaini, Robert. "Free Markets on Film: Hollywood and Capitalism." *Journal of Private Enterprise* 16 (Spring 2001): 122–29.

Friedsam, H.J. "Bureaucrats as Heroes." *Social Forces* 32, no. 3 (March 1954): 269–74.

Gailey, J.D., and Virsima Schaefer Carroll. "Toward a Collaborative Model for Interdisciplinary Teaching: Business and Literature." *Journal of Education for Business* (September–October 1993).

Garaventa, Eugene. "Drama: A Tool for Teaching Business Ethics." *Business Ethics Quarterly* 8, no. 3 (1998): 535–45.

Guroian, Vigen. "Why Should Businessmen Read Great Literature?" *Religion and Liberty* 12, no. 4 (2002).

Hall, James A. "Management and the Movies." *Journal of Management Research* 3 (Fall 2002): 12–15.

Halsey, Van R. "Fiction and the Businessman: Society Through All It's Literature." *American Quarterly* XI (Fall 1959): 391–402.

Hansen, Drew. "Why Every MBA Schould Read More Literature." *Forbes* (October 2011).

Hapke, Laura. *Labor's Text: The Worker in American Fiction.* New Brunswick, NJ: Rutgers University Press, 2001.

Henderson, George L. *California and the Fictions of Capital.* New York: Oxford University Press, 1999.

Hoivik, Heidi von Weltzien. "Developing Students' Competence for Ethical Reflection While Attending Business School." *Journal of Business Ethics* 88 (2009): 5–9.

James, Harold. "The Literary Financier." *The American Scholar* 60, no. 2 (Spring 1991): 251–57.

Jennings, Kate. "Best Business Books: Business Novels." *Strategy to Business* no. 25 (October 2001).

Jobe, Linda Barnes Gardner. *The Businessmen in the American Novel.* Thesis. Texas Tech University, 1970.

Jones, Howard Mumford. "Literature and the Businessman." *Harvard Business Review* XXXI (January–February 1953): 133–34, 136, 138, 140, 142.

Kavesh, Robert. *Businessmen in Fiction: The Capitalist and Executive in American Novels.* Hanover, NH: Amos Tuck School of Business Administration, 1955.

Keating, Raymond J. "Hollywood's Views of Capitalism." *The Freeman* (March): 92–95.

Kennedy, Ellen J. and Leigh Lawton. "Business Ethics in Fiction." *Journal of Business Ethics* 11 (1992): 187–95.

Lawson, Lewis A. "The Rogue in the Gray Flannel Suit." *College English* 22, no. 4 (January 1961): 249–52.

Leet, Don, and Scott Houser. "Economics Goes to Hollywood: Using Classic Films and Documentaries to Create an Undergraduate Economic Course." *Journal of Economic Education* (Fall 2003): 326–32.

Long, Elizabeth. *The American Dream and the Popular Novel.* Boston: Routledge and Hegan Paul, 1985.

Lynn, Kenneth S. "Authors in Search of the Businessman." *Harvard Business Review* XXXIV (September–October 1956): 116–24.

McAdams, Tony, and Roswitha Koppensteiner. "The Manager Seeking Virtue: Lessons from Literature." *Journal of Business Ethics* 11 (1992).

McGuire, Joseph W. "Bankers, Books, and Businessmen." *Harvard Business Review* 38, no. 4 (July–August 1960): 67–74.

McVeaugh, J. *Tradeful Merchants: The Portrayal of the Capitalist in Literature.* London: Routledge and Kegan Paul, 1981.

Meakin, D. *Man and Work: Literature and Culture in Industrial Society.* New York: Holmes and Meier, 1976.

Miller, Stephen. "The Three Voices of American Literature." Pp. 223–57 in *Capitalism and Equality in America,* edited by Peter L. Berger. Lanham, MD: Hamilton Press, 1987.

O'Rourke, W. (ed). *On the Job: Fiction about Work by Contemporary Writers.* New York: Vintage Books, 1977.

Rajski, Brian. "Corporate Fictions: Cameron Hawley and the Institutions of Postwar Capitalism." *Textual Practice* 25, no. 6 (2011): 1015–1031.

Russell, Norma. *The Novelist and Mammon: Literary Response to the World of Commerce in the Nineteenth Century.* New York: Oxford University Press, 1986.

Sarachek, Bernard. "Images of Corporate Executives in Recent Fiction." *Journal of Business Ethics* 14 (1995): 195–205.

Smith, Henry Nash. "The Search for a Capitalist Hero: Businessmen in American Fiction," in *The Business Establishement,* edited by Earl F. Cheit. New York: Wiley, 1964.

Smith, Howard R. "The American Businessman in the American Novel." *Southern Economic Journal* XXV (January 1959): 265–302.

Smitter, Roger. "Using Feature Films to Integrate Themes and Concepts in the Basic Course." *Speech Communication Association Annual Meeting* (1994): 1–23.

Spindler, Michael. *American Literature and Social Change.* Bloomington: Indiana University Press, 1983.

Stedmond, J.M. "The Business Executive in Fiction." *Dalhousie Review* XLII (Spring 1962): 18–27.

Taylor, D.J. "In Search of Novels about Working Life." *The Independent* (May 2007).

Taylor, Walter Fuller. *The Economic Novel in America*. New York: Octagon, 1964.

Uzzell, Thomas H. "The Novel that Says Something." *The English Journal* 47, no. 5 (May 1958): 255–58.

Van Nostrand, Albert D. "Fiction's Flagging Man of Commerce." *English Journal* XLVIII (January 1959): 1–11.

———. "After Marquand, the Deluge." *The English Journal* XLVIII (February 1959): 55–65.

Ward, R.J. "Business in the American Novel: The Fictional Treatment of the Market Society." *Bulletin of Bibliography* 39 (1982): 195–200.

Ward, Thomas. *The Businessman in American Popular Literature of the 1950s*. Thesis. Muncie, IN: Ball State University, 1990.

Watts, Emily Stipes. *The Businessmen in American Literature*. Athens, GA: The University of Georgia Press, 1982.

Watts, Michael, and Robert F. Smith. "Economics in Literature and Drama." *Journal of Economic Education* 20, no. 3 (Summer 1989): 291–307.

Watts, Michael. "Using Literature and Drama in Undergraduate Economic Courses." In *Teaching Economics to Undergraduates: Alternatives to Chalk and Talk*, edited by W.F. Becker and M. Watts. Cheltenham, UK: Edward Elgar, 1999.

———. "How Economists Use Literature and Drama." *Journal of Economic Education* 33, no. 4 (Fall 2002): 377–86.

Westbrook, Wayne W. *Wall Street in the American Novel*. New York: New York University Press, 1980.

Williams, Oliver F. *The Moral Imagination: How Literature and Films can Stimulate Ethical Reflection in the Business World*. Notre Dame, IN: University of Notre Dame Press, 1997.

Younkins, Edward W. "Cinema and the Capitalist Hero." *The Freeman* (June 1998).

———. "Searching Cinema for a Capitalist Hero." *Le Québécois Libre*, no. 71 (November 11, 2000).

Zayani, Mohamed. *Reading the Symptoms: Frank Norris, Theodore Dreiser, and the Dynamics of Capitalism*. New York: Peter Lang, 1999.

Zimmerman, David A. *Panic! Markets, Crises, and Crowds in American Fiction*. Chapel Hill: University of North Carolina Press, 2006.

———. "Novels of American Business, Industry, and Consumerism." Pp. 409–25 in *Cambridge History of the American Novel*, edited by Leonard Cassuto, Clare Eley, and Benjamin Reiss. Cambridge, UK: Cambridge University Press, 2011.

Appendix A

Novels and Plays about Business

Adams, Samuel Hopkins. *Plunder* (1948)
Albert, Joel. *Crude Policy* (2011)
Alger, Horatio. *Paul the Peddler* (1871)
Alger, Horatio. *Ragged Dick* (1868)
Alger, Horatio. *Strive and Succeed* (1872)
Amis, Martin. *Money: A Suicide Note* (1984)
Andersen, Kurt. *Turn of the Century* (2000)
Apple, Max. *The Propheteers: A Novel* (1987)
Archer, Jeffrey. *Not a Penny More, Not a Penny Less* (1976)
Auchincloss, Louis. *A World of Profit* (1968)
Auchincloss, Louis. *Diary of a Yuppie* (1987)
Auchincloss, Louis. *I Come As A Thief* (1972)
Auchincloss, Louis. *The Embezzler* (1966)
Auchincloss, Louis. *The House of Five Talents* (1960)
Auchincloss, Louis. *Venus in Sparta* (1958)
Barnes, Julian. *England, England* (2000)
Barry, Max. *Company* (2007)
Bellamy, Edward. *Looking Backward* * (1888)
Bellow, Saul. *Seize the Day* (1976)
Bing, Stanley. *Lloyd: What Happened?* (1999)
Bissell, Richard Pike. *7 ½ cents* (1953)
Bourjaily, Vance. *The Man Who Knew Kennedy* (1967)
Boyesen, H.H. *A Daughter of the Philistines* (1883)
Braine, John. *Room at the Top* (1959)
Bramah, Ernest. *The Secret of the League*

Bronson, Po. *Bombardiers* (2003)
Brooks, John. *The Big Wheel* (1949)
Buckley, Christopher. *Thank You for Smoking* (2006)
Bukowski, Charles. *Post Office* (1971)
Bunn, T. Davis. *The Great Divide* (2001)
Burnett, John. *Company Man* (1956)
Cahan, Abraham. *The Rise of David Levinsky* * (1917)
Cain, James M. *Double Indemnity* (1943)
Cain, James M. *Mildred Pierce* (1941)
Caldwell, Erskine. *Tobacco Road* (1932)
Caldwell, Taylor. *Dynasty of Death* (1958)
Chandler, Steve. *The Small Business Millionaire* (2006)
Churchill, Caryl. *Serious Money* (1987)
Clune, Henry W. *By His Own Hand* (1952)
Cohen, Lester. *Coming Home* (1945)
Collett, I.W. and J.W. Greenspan. *Accosting the Golden Spire* (1988)
Colman, Louis. *Lumber* (1931)
Comfort, Will Levington. *Midstream* (1914)
Coupland, Douglas. *Microserfs* (2008)
Cox, Jeff and Dan Paul. *The Cure* (2003)
Cox, Jeff. *Selling the Wheel* (2001)
Crichton, Michael. *Jurassic Park* (1990)
Crumbley, D. Larry. *The Ultimate Rip-Off* (1991)
Crumbley, D. Larry. *Trap Doors and Trojan Horses* (1991)
Cruz, Nilo. *Anna in the Tropics* (2004)
Cuomo, George. *Family Honor* (1983)
Davenport, Marcia. *The Valley of Decision* (1942)
Davis, Clyde Brion. *Thudbury* (1952)
Davis, Rebecca Harding. *Life in the Iron-Mills* (1861)
De Forest, John W. *Honest John Vane* (1875)
Dekker, Thomas. *The Shoemaker's Holiday* (2002)
DeLillo, Don. *Cosmopolis* (2003)
DeLillo, Don. *Players* (1989)
Deloney, Thomas. *Jack of Newbery* (1597)
DeMarco, Tom. *The Deadline* (1997)
DeMare, George. *The Empire* (1957)
Denison, T.S. *An Iron Crown* (1885)
Di Donato, Pietro. *Christ in Concrete* (1939)
Dickens, Charles. *A Christmas Carol* (1843)
Dickens, Charles. *Dombey and Son* (1848)
Dickens, Charles. *Hard Times* (1854)
Dickens, Charles. *Nicholas Nickleby* (1839)
Dickens, Charles. *The Life and Adventures of Martin Chuzzlewit* (1844)

Dixon, Thomas. *The Leopard's Spots* (1902)
Dodge, D. *Death and Taxes* (1941)
Dodge, D. *It Ain't Hay* (1946)
Donnelly, Ignatius. *Caesar's Column* (1890)
Dos Passos, John. *Midcentury: A Contemporary Chronicle* (1961)
Dos Passos, John. *Nineteen Nineteen* (1932)
Dos Passos, John. *The 42nd Parallel* (1930)
Dos Passos, John. *The Big Money* (1936)
Dreiser, Theodore. *An American Tragedy* (1925)
Dreiser, Theodore. *Sister Carrie* (1900)
Dreiser, Theodore. *The Bulwark* (1946)
Dreiser, Theodore. *The Financier* * (1912)
Dreiser, Theodore. *The Stoic* (1947)
Dreiser, Theodore. *The Titan* (1914)
Duncan, Thomas. *Gus the Great* (1947)
Elkin, Stanley. *A Bad Man* (1967)
Elkin, Stanley. *The Franchiser* * (1976)
Ellis, Bret Easton. *American Psycho* (1991)
Emmens, Matthew and Beth Kephart. *Zenobia* (2008)
Erdman, Paul. *The Palace* (1988)
Erdman, Paul. *The Set-Up* (1996)
Erdman, Paul. *Zero Coupon* (1994)
Farrell, James T. *Studs Lonigan* (2004)
Faulkner, William. *The Hamlet* (1940)
Ferris, Joshua. *Then We Came to the End* (2008)
Finder, Joseph. *Company Man* (2006)
Fitzgerald, F. Scott. *The Great Gatsby* * (1925)
Fitzgerald, F. Scott. *The Last Tycoon* (1941)
Flagg, Fannie. *Fried Green Tomatoes at the Whistle Stop Café* (1988)
Fraley, Gregg. *Jack's Notebook* (2008)
Francis, D. *Risk* (2006)
Frederic, Harold. *The Market-Place* (1899)
Fuller, Henry Blake. *The Cliff-Dwellers* (1893)
Gaddis, William. *J R* (1975)
Galsworthy, John. *The Forsyte Saga* (1933)
Garber, Joseph R. *Rascal Money* (1989)
Garrett, Garet. *Cinder Buggy* (1923)
Garrett, Garet. *Satan's Bushel* (1924)
Garrett, Garet. *The Driver* * (1922)
Garrett, Garet. *Wild Wheel* (1952)
Gaskell, Elizabeth. *North and South* (1878)
Giardina, Denise. *Storming Heaven* (1988)
Gold, Michael. *Jews Without Money* (1930)

Goldratt, Eliyahu M. *It's Not Luck* (1994)
Goldratt, Eliyahu M. *The Goal* (1986)
Goode, James. *The Modern Banker* (1896)
Grady, James. *Catch the Wind* (1980)
Greenspan, A.J. *The Burmese Caper* (1990)
Grisham, John. *The Firm* (1991)
Grisham, John. *The Runaway Jury* (1996)
Hailey, Arthur. *Strong Medicine* (1984)
Hailey, Arthur. *The Evening News* (1990)
Hailey, Arthur. *The Moneychangers* (1975)
Hare, David and Howard Brenton. *Pravda* (1985)
Harman, John. *The Bottom Line* (1990)
Harrison, Charles Yale. *Nobody's Fool* (1940)
Harvey, William. *A Tale of Two Nations* (1894)
Hawley, Cameron. *Cash McCall* * (1955)
Hawley, Cameron. *Executive Suite* * (1952)
Hawley, Cameron. *The Hurricane Years* (1968)
Hawley, Cameron. *The Lincoln Lords* (1960)
Hay, John. *The Bread-winners* (1883)
Haydn, Hiram. *The Time is Noon* (1948)
Hazlitt, Henry. *Time Will Run Back* * (1951) (1966)
Heller, Joseph. *Something Happened* (1974)
Hemingway, Ernest. *To Have and Have Not* (1937)
Herrick, Robert. *Memoirs of an American Citizen* (1905)
Herrick, Robert. *The Gospel of Freedom* (1898)
Himes, Chester. *Lonely Crusade* (1947)
Holland, Josiah. *Sevenoaks* (1903)
Hough, Emerson. *The Mississippi Bubble* (1902)
Howells, J. Harvey. *The Big Company Look* (1958)
Howells, William Dean. *A Hazard of New Fortunes* (1889)
Howells, William Dean. *A Traveler from Altruria* (1894)
Howells, William Dean. *The Quality of Mercy* (1892)
Howells, William Dean. *The Rise of Silas Lapham* * (1884)
Huxley, Alex. *Brave New World* (1932)
Hynes, James. *Kings of Infinite Space* (2005)
Isham, Frederic. *Black Friday* (1904)
James, Henry. *The Ambassadors* (1903)
James, Henry. *The American* (1877)
James, Henry. *The Portrait of a Lady* (1881)
Johnson, D.E. *Motor City Shakedown* (2011)
Jonas, Carl. *Jefferson Selleck* (1951)
Kantor, Kinlay. *Glory for Me* (1945)
Keenan, Henry. *The Money-Makers* (1885)

Kennedy, Thomas. *Falling Sideways* (2011)
Kesey, Ken. *Sometimes a Great Notion* * (1964)
Knowles, John. *A Vein of Riches* (1978)
Knowlton, Christopher. *The Real World* (1984)
Krist, Gary. *Extravagance* (2003)
Laing, Frederick. *The Giant's House* (1955)
Lathen, E. *Accounting for Murder* (1970)
Lawson, Thomas. *Friday, the Thirteenth* (1907)
Lefèvre, Edwin. *Reminiscences of a Stockbroker* (2006)
Lencioni, Patrick. *Getting Naked* (2002)
Lewis, Michael. *Moneyball* (2003)
Lewis, Sinclair. *Babbitt* * (1924)
Lewis, Sinclair. *Dodsworth* (1929)
Lewis, Sinclair. *Kingsblood Royal* (1947)
Lewis, Sinclair. *Our Mr. Wrenn* (1914)
Lewis, Sinclair. *The Job* (1917)
Lightman, Alan. *The Diagnosis* (2000)
Lillo, George. *The London Merchant* (1731)
Locke, David. *A Paper City* (1906)
Lodge, David. *Nice Work* * (1988)
London, Jack. *Burning Daylight* (1910)
London, Jack. *The Iron Heel* (1907)
Longstreet, Stephen. *In Our Father's House* (1985)
MacLennan, Hugh. *The Precipice* (1975)
Malamud, Bernard. *The Assistant* (1987)
Mamet, David. *American Buffalo* (1975)
Mamet, David. *Glengarry Glen Ross* * (1984)
Marquand, John P. *B.F. 's Daughter* (1946)
Marquand, John P. *H.M. Pullham, Esquire* (1941)
Marquand, John P. *Point of No Return* * (1949)
Marquand, John P. *Sincerely, Willis Wayde* (1955)
Marquand, John P. *The Late George Apley* (1937)
Marshall, B. *The Bank Audit* (1958)
Marsten, R. *The Spiked Heel* (1956)
Massinger, Phillip. *A New Way to Pay Old Debts* (1810)
Masterton, Graham. *Rich* (1979)
Masur, Harold Q. *The Broker* (1981)
Mazzotta, David. *Business as Usual* (2007)
McCully, Emily Arnold. *The Bobbin Girl* (1996)
McCutcheon, George Barr. *Brewster's Millions* (1902)
Mead, Shepherd. *How to Succeed in Business Without Really Trying* (1961)
Melville, Herman. *Bartleby, The Scrivener* (1853)

Melville, Herman. *The Confidence Man* (1857)
Merwin, Samuel and Henry Kitchell Webster. *Calumet "K"* (1901)
Miller, Arthur. *All My Sons* (1947)
Miller, Arthur. *Death of a Salesman* * (1949)
Miller, Merle. *That Winter* (1967)
Mishima, Yukio. *Runaway Horses* (1973)
Morris, Bill. *Biography of a Buick* (a.k.a. *Motor City*) (1992)
Narea, H.T. *The Fund* (2011)
Newby, P.H. *Barbary Light* (1962)
Norris, Frank. *The Octopus* * (1901)
Norris, Frank. *The Pit* (1903)
O'Hara, John. *Appointment in Samarra* (1934)
Odets, Clifford. *Waiting for Lefty* (1935)
Orwell, George. *The Road to Wigan Pier* (1937)
Othmer, James P. *Holy Water* (2010)
Palahniuk, Chuck. *Fight Club* (1996)
Parker, Tom. *Small Business* (1996)
Payne, David. *Confessions of a Taoist on Wall Street* (1984)
Pearson, William. *This Company of Men* (1963)
Percy, Walker. *The Moviegoer* (1961)
Phelps, Elizabeth Stuart. *The Silent Partner* (1871)
Phillips, David Graham. *The Cost* (1904)
Phillips, David Graham. *The Great God Success* (1901)
Powell, Ernst. *From the Dark Tower* (1957)
Powers, Richard. *Gain* (1998)
Poyer, David. *Thunder on the Mountain* (1999)
Prebble, Lucy. *Enron* (2009)
Prosser, William Harrison. *Nine to Five* (1953)
Rand, Ayn. *Atlas Shrugged* * (1957)
Rand, Ayn. *The Fountainhead* (1943)
Reed, Barry. *The Choice* (1991)
Remarque, Erich Maria. *The Black Obelisk* (1957)
Rice, Elmer. *The Adding Machine* (1923)
Richler, Mordecai. *The Apprenticeship of Duddy Kravitz* (1959)
Ridpath, Michael. *Final Venture* (2000)
Roth, Philip. *American Pastoral* (1997)
Rylee, Robert. *The Ring and the Cross* (1947)
Schisgall, Oscar. *The Big Store* (1959)
Schmertz, Herb and Larry Woods. *Takeover* (1979)
Schoonover, Lawrence. *The Quick Brown Fox* (1953)
Schulberg, Budd. *What Makes Sammy Run* (1941)
Schwartz, Stephen and Nina Faso. *Working* (1977)
Seaver, Edwin. *The Company* (1930)

Sederberg, Arlo. *The Power Players* (1980)

Shakespeare, William. *Merchant of Venice* (1598)

Shaw, George Bernard. *Major Barbara* (1905)

Sheed, Wilfrid. *Office Politics* * (1966)

Simon, Neil. *Prisoner of Second Avenue* (1971)

Sinclair, Upton. *Oil!* (1927)

Sinclair, Upton. *The Jungle* (1906)

Smith, A.C. *The Case of Torches* (1963)

Spears, Tom. *Leverage* (2011)

Stead, Christina. *House of All Nations* (1938)

Steele, James. *Conveyor* (1935)

Steinbeck, John. *In Dubious Battle* (1936)

Steinbeck, John. *The Grapes of Wrath* (1939)

Steinbeck, John. *The Wayward Bus* (1947)

Steinbeck, John. *The Winter of Our Discontent* (1961)

Stephenson, Neal. *Cryptonomicon* (1999)

Sterner, Jerry. *Other People's Money* * (1989)

Stevens, William. *The Peddler* (1967)

Stir, Thomas. *Miller's Bolt* (1997)

Stone, Robert. *Outerbridge Reach* (1992)

Stuart, I. *The Garb of Truth* (1982)

Sulitzer, Paul-Loup. *Cash* (1981)

Swados, Harvey. *On the Line* (1957)

Swierczynski, Duane. *Severance Package* (2008)

Swiggett, Howard. *The Durable Fire* (1957)

Swiggett, Howard. *The Power and the Prize* (1954)

Tarkington, Booth. *The Magnificent Ambersons* (1920)

Tarkington, Booth. *The Plutocrat* (1927)

Teichmann, Howard and George S. Kaufman. *The Solid Gold Cadillac* (1953)

Terrall, *Sand Dollars* (1978)

Toole, John Kennedy. *A Confederacy of Dunces* (1980)

Trollope, Anthony. *The Way We Live Now* (1883)

Twain, Mark and Charles Dudley Warmen. *Gilded Age* (1873)

Twain, Mark. *A Connecticut Yankee in King Arthur's Court* (1891)

Updike, John. *Rabbit at Rest* (1990)

Updike, John. *Rabbit is Rich* (1981)

Updike, John. *Rabbit Redux* (1971)

Updike, John. *Rabbit Run* (1961)

Van Atta, W. *Hatchet Man* (1962)

van Gelder, Robert. *Important People* (1948)

Vidal, Gore. *Empire* (1987)

Vonnegut, Jr., Kurt. *God Bless You, Mr. Rosewater* (1965)

Vonnegut, Norb. *Top Producer* (2009)
Vorse, Mary Heaton. *Strike* (1930)
Wakeman, Frederic. *The Hucksters* (1946)
Walker, Leslie. *The Banker* (1963)
Warner, Charles Dudley. *A Little Journey in the World* (1889)
Weber, Carl. *The Family Business* (2012)
Weidman, Jerome. *I Can Get It for You Wholesale* (1937)
Weidman, Jerome. *I'll Never Go There Anymore* (1941)
Weidman, Jerome. *The Price is Right* (1949)
Weidman, Jerome. *What's In It for Me?* (1938)
Weisberger, Lauren. *The Devil Wears Prada* (2004)
Wells, H.G. *History of Mr. Polly* (1909)
Wells, H.G. *Tono-Bungay* (1908)
West, Nathanael. *The Day of the Locust* (1950)
White, Theodore. *The View from the Fortieth Floor* (1960)
Williams, William Carlos. *In the Money* (1940)
Williams, William Carlos. *The Build-Up* (1952)
Williams, William Carlos. *White Mule* (1937)
Wilson, Sloan. *The Man in the Gray Flannel Suit* * (1955)
Wolfe, Tom. *A Man in Full* (1998)
Wolfe, Tom. *The Bonfire of the Vanities* (1987)
Wouk, Herman. *Aurora Dawn* (1947)
Yates, Richard. *Revolutionary Road* (1961)
Zola, Emile. *The Ladies' Paradise* (1883)

* A chapter is dedicated to this work in this book.

Appendix B

Films about Business

A Civil Action (1988)
A Face in the Crowd (1957)
A Raisin in the Sun (1961)
Ace in the Hole (1954) (aka: *The Big Carnival*)
Adam's Rib (1949)
Agency (1981)
All My Sons (1948)
American Madness (1932)
American Psycho (2005)
An American Romance * (1944)
Apprenticeship of Duddy Kravitz (1974)
Atlas Shrugged I (2011)
Atlas Shrugged II (2012)
Baby Boom (1987)
Barbarians at the Gate (1997)
Barcelona (1994)
Big Night (1996)
Boiler Room (2000)
Bonfire of the Vanities (1990)
Boom Town (1940)
Born Yesterday (1950)
Bright Leaf (1950)
Broadcast News (1986)
Bugsy (1991)
Business as Usual (1993)

Buy and Cell (1987)
Cash McCall * (196)
Chinatown (1974)
Citizen Kane (1941)
Crazy People (1990)
Czech Dream (2007)
Death of a Salesman * (1951) (1966) (1985)
Desk Set (Walter Lang, 1957)
Disclosure (1997)
Do the Right Thing (1989)
Dombey and Son (2006)
Door to Door (2002)
Easy Living (1937)
Ed TV (1999)
Erin Brockovich (2000)
Executive Suite * (1954)
F.I.S.T. (1978)
Fitzcarraldo (1999)
Front Page (1931)
Germinal (1993) (1994)
Giant (1956)
Glengarry Glen Ross * (1992)
Gung Ho (1986)
High and Low (1905)
High Pressure (1932)
His Girl Friday (1940)
House of Strangers (1949)
How to Succeed in Business without Really Trying (David Swift, 1967)
I Can Get It For You Wholesale (1951)
Imitation of Life (1934) (1959)
In Good Company (2004)
Inside Job (2010)
It Happened to Jane (1959)
It Should Happen to You (1954)
It's a Wonderful Life (1946)
Jerry Maguire (1996)
Kidco (1985)
Lost in Translation (2003)
Lucy Gallant (1955)
Mac (1993)
Madison Avenue (1962)
Magic Town (1947)
Major Barbara (1941)

Margin Call (2011)
Matewan (1987)
Meet John Doe (1941)
Mildred Pierce (1945) (2011)
Miracle on 34th Street (1947)
Modern Times (1936)
Moonstruck (1987)
Mr. Deeds Goes to Town (1936)
Mr. Smith Goes to Washington (1939)
Network (1976)
Night Shift (1982)
Nine to Five (1980)
Ninotchka (1939)
North by Northwest (1959)
Nothing in Common (1986)
Office Space (1999)
Oil for the Lamps of China (1935)
One, Two, Three (1961)
Other People's Money * (1991) (1995)
Owning Mahoney (2003)
Patterns (1956)
Pirates of Silicon Valley (1999)
Pittsburgh (1942)
Pleasantville (1998)
Power (1986)
Putney Swope (1969)
Quiz Show (1994)
Rabbit Run (1970)
Repo Man (1984)
Risky Business (1983)
Roger & Me (1989)
Rogue Trader (1999)
Rollover (1981)
Ruthless (1948)
Salt of the Earth (1954)
Save the Tiger (1973)
Seize the Day (1993)
Session 9 (2001)
Shadow Company (2006)
She Hates Me (2004)
Silkwood (1983)
Sometimes a Great Notion * (1971) (aka: *Never Give an Inch*)
Startup.com (2001)

Sweet Smell of Success (1957)
Switching Channels (1988)
Syriana (2006)
Take This Job and Shove It (1981)
The American Ruling Class (2007)
The Apartment (Billy Wilder, 1960)
The Arrangement (1969)
The Bad and the Beautiful (1952)
The Bank (2002)
The Betsy (1978)
The Big Kahuna (2000)
The China Syndrome (1979)
The Devil Wears Prada (2006)
The Efficiency Expert (1992)
The Electric Horseman (1979) (1980)
The Fountainhead (1943)
The Godfather, Part I (1972)
The Godfather, Part II (1974)
The Grapes of Wrath (1940)
The Great Gatsby * (1949) (1974) (2000) (2013)
The Grifters (1991)
The Guv'nor (1935)
The Hucksters (1947)
The Hudsucker Proxy (1994)
The Informant! (2010)
The Insider (1999)
The Last Seduction (1994)
The Late Shift (2005)
The Magnificent Ambersons (1942)
The Man in the Gray Flannel Suit * (1956)
The Man in the White Suit (1951)
The Player (1992)
The Power and the Glory (1933)
The Pursuit of Happyness (2006)
The Revolt of Mamie Stover (1956)
The Secret of My Success (1987)
The Shop around the Corner (1940)
The Social Network (2011)
The Solid Gold Cadillac (1956)
The Story of Alexander Graham Bell (1939)
The Thrill of it All (1963)
The Toast of New York (1937)
The Truman Show (1998)

The Wheeler Dealers (1963)
There Will Be Blood (2008)
Tin Men (1987)
To Each His Own (1946)
Too Big to Fail (2011)
Trading Places (1983)
Tucker: The Man and His Dream * (1988)
Tunes of Glory (1960)
Twelve Angry Men (1957)
Twelve O'Clock High (1944)
Tycoon (1947)
Up in the Air (2009)
Wag the Dog (1997)
Wall Street * (1987)
Wall Street: Money Never Sleeps * (2010)
Waydowntown (2005)
Who's Minding the Store? (1963)
Will Success Spoil Rock Hunter (1957)
Woman of the Year (1942)
Woman's World (1954)
Working Girl (1998)
Written on the Wind (1956)
You Can't Take It With You (1938)
You've Got Mail (1998)

* A chapter is devoted to this film in this book.

Appendix C

The Best Novels and Plays About Business: Results of Survey

My Koch Research Fellows, Jomana Krupinski and Kaitlyn Pytlak and I conducted a survey of 250 Business and Economics professors and 250 English and Literature professors. Colleges and universities were randomly selected and then professors from the relevant departments of these schools were also randomly selected to receive our email survey. They were asked to list and rank from 1 to 10 what they considered to be the best novels and plays about business. We did not attempt to define the word "best" leaving that decision to each respondent. We obtained sixty-nine usable responses from Business and Economics professors and fifty-one from English and Literature professors. A list of fifty choices were given to each respondent and an opportunity was presented to vote for works not on the list. When tabulating the results, ten points were given to a novel or play in a respondent's first position, nine points were assigned to a work in the second position, and so on, down to the tenth listed work which was allotted one point. The table below presents the top twenty-five novels and plays for each group of professors. Interestingly, fifteen works made both the top-twenty-five lists which are in noted bold type.

Business and Economics Professors

1. ***Atlas Shrugged***, Ayn Rand — 457
2. ***The Fountainhead***, Ayn Rand — 297
3. ***The Great Gatsby***, F. Scott Fitzgerald — 216
4. ***Death of a Salesman***, Arthur Miller — 164
5. *Time Will Run Back*, Henry Hazlitt — 145
6. ***The Jungle***, Upton Sinclair — 136
7. ***The Gilded Age***, Mark Twain and Charles Dudley Warner — 95
8. ***Glengarry Glen Ross***, David Mamet — 89
9. ***God Bless You, Mr. Rosewater***, Kurt Vonnegut, Jr. — 57
10. *Other People's Money*, Jerry Sterner — 57
11. ***Bartleby: The Scrivener***, Herman Melville — 55
12. *A Man in Full*, Tom Wolfe — 48
13. ***Babbitt***, Sinclair Lewis — 47
14. *The Man in the Gray Flannel Suit*, Sloan Wilson — 43
15. ***Rabbit is Rich***, John Updike — 41
16. *Major Barbara*, George Bernard Shaw — 39
17. ***Dombey and Son***, Charles Dickens — 33
18. *The Goal*, Eliyahu M. Goldratt — 33
19. *The Driver*, Garet Garrett — 32
20. *Executive Suite*, Cameron Hawley — 32
21. *The Way We Live Now*, Anthony Trollope — 32
22. ***American Pastoral***, Philip Roth — 29

English and Literature Professors

1. ***Death of a Salesman***, Arthur Miller — 282
2. ***Bartleby: The Scrivener***, Herman Melville — 259
3. ***The Great Gatsby***, F. Scott Fitzgerald — 231
4. ***The Jungle***, Upton Sinclair — 143
5. ***Babbitt***, Sinclair Lewis — 126
6. ***Glengarry Glen Ross***, David Mamet — 121
7. *The Rise of Silas Lapham*, William Dean Howells — 98
8. ***American Pastoral***, Philip Roth — 85
9. *The Confidence Man*, Herman Melville — 75
10. ***The Fountainhead***, Ayn Rand — 75
11. *A Hazard of New Fortunes*, William Dean Howells — 66
12. ***The Octopus***, Frank Norris — 65
13. ***Atlas Shrugged***, Ayn Rand — 62
14. *Nice Work*, David Lodge — 62
15. *The Big Money*, John Dos Passos — 59
16. ***The Gilded Age***, Mark Twain and Charles Dudley Warner — 58
17. ***Rabbit is Rich***, John Updike — 55
18. *Seize the Day*, Saul Bellow — 55
19. *Mildred Pierce*, James M. Cain — 54
20. *The Financier*, Theodore Dreiser — 53
21. ***Dombey and Son***, Charles Dickens — 51
22. ***Sometimes a Great Notion***, Ken Kesey — 45

Index

About the Author

Edward W. Younkins is professor of accountancy and director of graduate programs in the Department of Business at Wheeling Jesuit University. He is the founder of the university's undergraduate degree program in political and economic philosophy. He is also the founding director of the university's Master of Business Administration (MBA) and Master of Science in Accountancy (MSA) programs. In addition to earning state and national honors for his performances on the Certified Public Accountant (CPA) and Certified Management Accountant (CMA) exams, respectively, Dr. Younkins also received the Outstanding Educator Award for 1997 from the West Virginia Society of Certified Public Accountants. The author of numerous articles in accounting and business journals, his free-market-oriented articles and reviews have appeared in numerous publications. He is the author of *Capitalism and Commerce: Conceptual Foundations of Free Enterprise* (2002), *Champions of a Free Society: Ideas of Capitalism's Philosophers and Economists* (2008), and *Flourishing and Happiness in a Free Society: Toward a Synthesis of Aristotelianism, Austrian Economics, and Ayn Rand's Objectivism.*

CPSIA information can be obtained at www.ICGtesting.com
Printed in the USA
BVOW07s1119310714

361106BV00002B/4/P

9 781498 500722